DAYTONA

From the Birth of Speed to the Death of the Man in Black

Ed Hinton

WARNER BOOKS

An AOL Time Warner Company

WARNER BOOKS EDITION

Copyright © 2001 by Ed Hinton

Cover design by George Cornell
Cover photo by Allsport

Warner Books, Inc.
1271 Avenue of the Americas
New York, NY 10020

Visit our Web site at www.twbookmark.com.

 An AOL Time Warner Company

Printed in the United States of America

First Printing: November 2002

10 9 8 7 6 5 4 3 2 1

For Snow and Tyler

CONTENTS

AUTHOR'S NOTE

More than forty years of hanging around race tracks, and nearly thirty years of getting paid to write about it, have been a mixed blessing indeed. Mostly the decades have been a merry guilt trip, just like the drivers themselves feel: You mean I get *paid* to do this? But they have also been a struggle. And there has been a recurring nightmare, to this day.

Most of my life has been spent covering this highly specialized sport for general-interest daily newspapers and magazines. In such publications, the writer must strike the delicate balance, time and again, between giving hard-core fans sophisticated substance they can use inside their circles of aficionados, and just plain good storytelling to the vast majority of readers, who know little or nothing about racing.

Having also covered the National Football League, Major League Baseball, the Olympics, and NCAA Division I football a great deal over the years, I feel fairly qualified to opine that properly translating motor racing for general readership is the most difficult sportswriting job there is. Yet I have kept coming back to it, bent on the notion that if the mainstream public could be made to understand motor racing, then it would become a mainstream sport, taking its place alongside baseball, football, and basketball. That is happening at last.

Decades ago, a pioneer NASCAR writer from Atlanta, Bill Robinson, told me that "covering auto racing is as near as a sportswriter ever comes to covering war." You deal literally with life and death, and you yourself, like the war correspondent, are subjected directly to the danger, in the pits and by the guardrails.

For the first couple of decades my jobs were mixtures of motor racing and the stick-and-ball sports—through my first stint at the *Orlando Sentinel,* then the *Atlanta Journal-Constitution,* then two New York–based publications, *The National Sports Daily* and then *Sports Illustrated.* But at every stop, I was always the resident auto racing writer, for whatever degree of coverage the publication's editors deemed warranted. The volume of coverage grew and grew, until, in 1996, *Sports Illustrated* decided to begin publishing special issues about NASCAR, and to run an occasional motorsports column in the weekly magazine. So I became the first *SI* senior writer to concentrate solely on motor racing.

Late in 1999, the editorial board of Tribune Co., with the *Chicago Tribune* as its flagship newspaper, agreed on an experiment: They would hire one specialized writer to cover motor racing for the entire chain. It looked to me like the best motorsports writing opportunity ever offered on this continent—and the only opportunity that could make me leave *Sports Illustrated,* where I'd surely planned to stay until retirement. So I took it, beginning on January 1, 2000. In a matter of months, the job got even better. Tribune Co. acquired the Times-Mirror chain. So now I find myself writing for a dozen newspapers coast-to-coast, from *Newsday* on Long Island in the East, to the *Los Angeles Times* in the West, south as far as the Fort Lauderdale–based *South Florida Sun-Sentinel.* And in this wondrous swirl of audiences there is a sort of homecoming, for Tribune Co. includes the very paper where I began getting away with getting paid for this, the *Orlando Sentinel.*

By this point, some of you may wonder whether I'm the one who wrote the series of stories that appeared nationwide—but most prominently in L.A., Chicago, and Orlando—pointing out the shortcomings of NASCAR safety standards and the danger of racing's most common cause of death, basilar skull fracture, the week before Dale Earnhardt died of precisely such injuries on the last lap of the 2001 Daytona 500. Yes, I'm the guy—either the jerk or the prophet, depending on your point of view—who detonated the national explosion of controversy over how and why Earnhardt died, and whether his death could have been prevented.

I certainly didn't mean to set off such a stir. I had no idea that a man I'd known well since 1979—and who had grown into a grassroots pop-culture figure of Elvis-esque magnitude—would, in the most cataclysmic and internationally visible of all NASCAR tragedies, prove the very point I'd tried to make only days earlier. I deeply wish it hadn't turned out this way.

Millions called him the Intimidator, but others named him the Man in Black, which I dubbed him in print in 1988 because he drove those black cars as if he were wearing them, well tailored…and because, as with Johnny Cash, you could detect a certain sadness beneath the harsh visage.

I would gladly let that series of stories fade into obscurity, in exchange for having Earnhardt back—snapping his surly, smart-ass answers to my questions at press conferences. He would not talk with me one-on-one in the last few years of his life. We had been close—probably closer than a journalist and a sports figure should be—through the first half of his career, his best years, in NASCAR. But as his image snowballed to mythical proportions, he—or rather his handlers, I suspect—became extremely sensitive to stories that dwelled too much on his hardscrabble past. A 1995 story in *Sports Illustrated,* "Attitude for Sale," ended our one-on-one working relationship—temporarily I thought at the time, but forever as it turned out.

I regret that. Earnhardt, wherever you are, your being in

the folk-hero business, and my being in the truth-telling business, ours probably was a friendship doomed from the start. The further each of us progressed through his craft, the more pronounced the conflict of what was required of us.

Still, I'm sorry, Earnhardt, that you died mad at me. I went numb and heartsick when, within ten minutes after you hit the wall, I knew you were dead, that there remained only the grimly traditional hours of waiting before the official announcement came. There had never before been a driver or a figure quite like you. And there will never be another, my old lost friend.

Most of this book was written before Earnhardt died. So in the parts about him—and there are quite a few—I briefly considered going back and softening some of the language, smoothing some of the edges, joining just a little in the posthumous mythmaking.

I decided, No.

Hell no.

That would be a betrayal of the real Earnhardt, who, deep down, was never ashamed of where he came from nor how hard his climb had been. So I have left him as he really was.

The death of Earnhardt is the latest and most relentless recurrence of the nightmare that comes with this job. I have written more driver obituaries than I wish to count. I do recall that the first one was about Tiny Lund and Mark Donohue, in the same column, in the summer of 1975. It hasn't gotten any easier, only harder, because you only knew the men better, down through the decades, before they died.

Through all of this, I think I have developed some idea what sorts of stories will and won't attract general readership to motor racing. That balance of plain storytelling with substantive appeal to aficionados is what I've tried to reach in this book.

Inside the New York publishing industry, there has been a somewhat frantic quest in recent years for "the right

NASCAR book," as editors and agents have so vastly over-simplified it. So far in the stampede, a number of outsiders have stumbled onto the sport, grown fascinated with it, and gushed out giddy accounts of their own fractional enlightenment. Of those versed enough to write about NASCAR from deep inside, over the long term, out to a broad audience, most either died before there was mass demand for such a book—we will never know how beautifully the late Gerald Martin, Joe Whitlock, or George Cunningham could have treated this subject—or have retired from the ineffably draining grind of the tour before it killed them. So part of my motive here is a sense of responsibility as, I suppose, the last damn fool left standing.

I was there when NASCAR was a folksy, simple, fairly obscure world that was ridiculed, when noticed at all, by larger America. I was there when NASCAR stirred as a sleeping titan of inexplicably charismatic appeal to the mainstream, when it flexed and stretched and went to finishing school and headed relentlessly uptown. And I am here upon its arrival with tremendous force among the moguls of Manhattan and Hollywood. (And already, I see the entire realm growing too smitten with itself, too big for its britches, too fast, drivers dying too often, a sport running wide open, over the edge of control.)

My reluctance for several years to enter the New York frenzy for NASCAR-oriented books was largely because I have seen, heard, told, and written far too many stories about motor racing to fit into one volume. Further, it was hard to view NASCAR in a vacuum, coming from all my decades in the pits and garages not only of the NASCAR tracks but of Indy, Le Mans, Monaco, Silverstone, Sebring...Where would I begin? More importantly, where would I finish?

Jim Donovan fixed that. Found a focal point.

Brooklyn-born, Donovan years ago left New York and

set up his literary agency in, of all places, Dallas. From there, unimpaired by the Manhattan tunnel vision that has so stifled the publishing industry, Jim could see the vaster landscape of American reading tastes more clearly and objectively. Yet he was equally free of the NASCAR myopia that infects regional publishing in hotbed cities such as Charlotte.

A. J. Foyt, in one of his classic malapropisms, once said that "Texas just ain't much of a racin' town [*sic*]." And so from the blank page of the flatlands, Jim Donovan, pondering all by himself with an uncluttered mind, had an elegant notion:

Daytona.

Where a complete anatomical study of the rise of NASCAR, compared and contrasted to the other forms of motor racing, is too massive to undertake, Daytona is the carotid artery through which nearly every essential element of motorsport has passed at one time or another. At this singular confluence lies a natural and linear narrative.

Jim didn't know all of this when the concept struck him. But he listened and believed as I told him that a narrative of Daytona must run far deeper and wider than just NASCAR.

The catalyst for this book was, of all people in all places, an Amarillo-born stockbroker in Atlanta named Joe Poirot. We both lived in the Lake Lanier suburbs then, and our sons and wives were friends, and Joe and I became friends. One evening at dinner, Joe mentioned a buddy back in Texas— Jim Donovan—who had an idea for a NASCAR book. Donovan later told me I was on his list of writers to contact about the project, but such was my dysfunctional attachment to New York agents that I might not have listened to some guy from Dallas had not Joe Poirot recommended him.

Rob McMahon at Warner Books was the first New York editor to see the NASCAR tidal wave coming. In his office in the beloved old Time & Life Building, which was then home to both Warner and *Sports Illustrated,* Rob read my "Attitude for Sale" piece about Earnhardt in February of '95 and immediately phoned. I was in Daytona Beach, catching hell about the story, but Rob said cheerfully from Manhattan, "If you and Dale want to do a book together, we at Warner would certainly be interested."

"If Earnhardt ever speaks to me again," I said, "we'll get back to you."

Earnhardt's ire aside, the notion of writing about one NASCAR driver—even arguably the biggest star ever—seemed too narrow. What about Richard Petty? David Pearson? Cale Yarborough? Bobby Allison? And now Jeff Gordon? What about Mario Andretti and A. J. Foyt, the two most versatile racing drivers ever, whose ventures to Daytona had been highly successful? What about NASCAR pioneers, all the way back through Junior Johnson and Fireball Roberts? What about NASCAR's very roots, deep in the moonshine country?

Donovan and McMahon came to understand that we could deliver all of these towering personalities, all at once, plus Daytona's own magnificent pre-NASCAR past, richly populated with the American aristocracy all the way back to the early 1900s.

But much further back than Donovan and McMahon and Poirot, my deepest retrospective gratitude extends to everyone who ever told me a good story at Daytona, or about Daytona.

Even with all the decades of vivid memories, from happy to horrible, I have not been blessed with total recall. My memory sometimes needed refreshing regarding a lot of specific dates and details, and my knowledge of all that transpired at Daytona from the time the first racers arrived in 1903 to the time I showed up in 1974 required some expansion.

Books I found very helpful for reference were Albert R.

Bochroch's *American Automobile Racing* (Viking, 1974)...my buddy Greg Fielden's series of NASCAR history books, including the four-volume *Forty Years of Stock Car Racing,* and *Forty Plus Four, High Speed at Low Tide,* and *Real Racers* (Galfield Press, 1988–98)... Fielden and Peter Golenbock's *Stock Car Racing Encyclopedia* (Macmillan, 1997)...G. N. Georgano's *The Encyclopedia of Motor Sport* (Viking, 1971)...Tom Higgins and Steve Waid's *Junior Johnson: Brave in Life* (David Bull Publishing, 1999)...Bill Libby's *King Richard* (Doubleday, 1977)...William Neely's *Daytona U.S.A.* (AZTEX, 1979)...Dick Punnett's *Racing on the Rim* (Tomoka Press, 1997)...Rich Taylor's *Indy* (St. Martin's, 1991)...and William R. Tuthill's *Speed on Sand* (Ormond Beach Historical Trust, 1969).

Searching through hundreds of my own newspaper and magazine stories from twenty-seven years at Daytona, there were a few occasions when I couldn't find a way to say it a whole lot better now than I did the first time. No single story nor excerpt survives here intact from the originals—they all required some editing, rearranging, and/or updating. Mostly the old phrases and sentences are scattered in fragments, sliced and diced and reassembled in new ways, in a few chapters. But for better or worse, the vast majority of the prose in this book is new.

Excellent editor that Rob McMahon is, I have had no finer, more patient, more meticulous editor for the past eighteen years than my conscripted one, my wife, Snow. And I have no sterner critic than my son, Tyler, who grows more exacting with each of his teen years.

We have settled at last in North Carolina, which is not only the epicenter of all NASCAR activity but the most delightful of cultural paradoxes. We're within easy commuting distance not only of the sprawling, teeming racing complexes of the NASCAR teams gone big-time, but of the intellectual bastions of Duke University and the University of North Carolina at Chapel Hill. There is no fuller, finer milieu for anyone trying to write seriously about motor racing, just at the point in history when mainstream culture is beginning to take motor racing seriously.

Jamestown, N.C.
June 2001

DAYTONA

PREFACE

*T*here is no such place as Daytona. It is not on any map. Oh, there are a few worn-out little towns on the northeast coast of Florida—Daytona Beach and Ormond Beach and Holly Hill and Port Orange—that form a roughly tangible geography for the realm renowned worldwide as Daytona.

And there is of course Daytona International Speedway, with "Daytona USA" painted in huge letters on the white concrete retaining walls in the high-banked turns for the benefit of television cameras. There is even an indoor theme attraction called Daytona USA that is in keeping with life today in that virtually everything is digitally virtual—which is to say that precious little is real. But these are late-sprung commercial beneficiaries of the word. They do not amount to Daytona at all.

Daytona is a place in the human spirit—hearts and minds, soaring aspirations and living nightmares—of all who have triumphed, failed, died, or worse; of all who have hallowed those triumphs and disasters; even of all who have only a vague and distant sense of what has gone on there for nearly a century.

There has not been an official town of Daytona since

1926, when it was absorbed into Daytona Beach by local government consolidation. But even then, "Daytona" already was internationally recognized shorthand for world speed records run on the beach, against the backdrop of the winter frolics of the rich, in the Winter Speed Carnivals of 1903–10. And no sooner had Daytona disappeared as a physical place than Henry Segrave and Malcolm Campbell arrived on the beaches in 1927–28 with their monstrous machines for devouring speed records, to nurture the concept called Daytona. The term has endured as part of the spoken language of racers and vacationers alike, and to this day occasionally some journalist or editor will still place the mistaken dateline "DAYTONA, Fla." on a story.

To Americans and Canadians nowadays, and increasingly to the rest of the world, Daytona mostly means NASCAR— the National Association for Stock Car Auto Racing. Daytona was the birthplace and remains the nerve center of that institution. Daytona is home to NASCAR's showcase race— the Daytona 500 has supplanted even the Indianapolis 500 as North America's premier motorsports event—and to NASCAR's spirit. There on the grounds of Daytona International Speedway stand the bronze statues of NASCAR's founding visionary, Bill France Sr., and his wife, Anne.

To the uninitiated those statues appear larger than life. To the knowing, nothing is larger than the life of Big Bill France, the only American who ever invented, nurtured, and envisioned the fruition of a whole sport, all by himself.

It was as if Dr. Naismith not only nailed the fruit baskets to the wall but founded the National Basketball Association and sketched its marketing schemes right into the billions of dollars a century in advance. It was as if the Harvard-Yale football game of 1869 was organized by a prescient prodigy named Pete Rozelle and he saw instantaneously in his project the Super Bowl as it is today.

Revisionist historians leave us no longer certain who invented baseball, but they do assure us that the game in its first fifty years was often played by thugs and attended by a rabble. And yet it has evolved into the darling diversion of intellectuals and sophisticates, and has been exalted by the literati—George Will, David Halberstam, and the late Willie Morris.

At this moment in history we are seeing NASCAR in the midst of the same sort of demographic transition, albeit on fast-forward—again in keeping with life today—that the older sports leagues underwent. Few Americans alive today are old enough to remember the public perceptions in the 1920s of a league of mercenary ruffians who played on Sundays to blue-collar crowds in a trashy extension of college football. All we see now is the NFL at its most polished stage. But NASCAR's transition from the thugs-and-rabble image to acceptance by the urbane and cerebral is occurring so rapidly that the residual snobs and skeptics who cling to the "redneck" stereotypes are to be forgiven. The old image is still so strong on their retinae, and the new one such a flash, that their perception is distorted. It will clear up soon.

NASCAR is far and away America's fastest-growing sports league, both in attendance and in television ratings, not because the competition is any better than it ever was but because a continent is finally awakening to what a late sportswriter friend of mine often called "the best-kept secret in sports."

And so a great deal of this book has to do with NASCAR—its beginnings, its pioneers, its formative years, and its apparently sudden arrival with tremendous force in the American mainstream.

But fathoming Daytona is a far deeper proposition than just understanding NASCAR and the Daytona 500. Those entities too are but infant heirs to the realm, the mystique. Even Big Bill was a relative newcomer, a pilgrim attracted to Daytona in 1934 by the history already there.

Daytona was internationally synonymous with speed before Bill France was born in 1909; before there was an Indy 500 (1911) or a 24 Heures du Mans (1923); even before the French developed a race important enough to be run for the country's "great prize," or "Grand Prix" (1906). Daytona had a connotation all its own before there were such terms as "hamburger" or "ice-cream cone" (both introduced in 1904) or "zipper" (1905).

It was in March of 1903—the Brothers Wright had yet to fly—that racing began at Daytona, spearheaded by two automotive pioneers, Ransom E. Olds and Alexander Winton; a promoter who was arguably a century ahead of his time, William J. Morgan; and two hotel managers, John Anderson and Joseph P. Price. Their intent was largely technological advancement, exposure for automobile brand names, and the promotion of Florida as a chic place to vacation—which would remain three elements of incentive and appeal at Daytona. But the by-product Morgan shipped to the world would, from then till now, be the emotional commodity shortest in supply and greatest in demand on the world market—daring.

The germinating force and then the blood and marrow of Daytona was, and is, risk-taking—specifically the risk of serious injury or death. It is the world's oldest controversy. It is Tolstoy's theme for the ages: war and peace, two equal but opposite paradoxes. The thrill of the narrow avoidance of injury and death, but the devastation when they are not avoided; the tranquility of peaceful existence, but the banality, the trivial pursuits—the boredom—of peace, day in, day out.

The venerable motor racing commentator Chris Economaki, in his youth, once confirmed face-to-face with the emotionally dying Ernest Hemingway in a Manhattan restaurant that Hemingway had, in his prime, said that there are but three sports: bullfighting, mountain climbing, and automobile racing. And that all the rest are games.

Mountain climbing does not offer much accommodation for spectators, and anyway is too slow and silent and personal for a world now bent on instant gratification. Bullfighting has always been limited to a handful of countries because its peculiar roots in pagan tradition are not widely enough understood to overcome other societies' disdain of the massive spillage of blood and guts of animals for spectator sport.

And so it has befallen motor racing—accommodating to spectators, with the clear-cut object of going as fast as possible without crashing—to be the flash point of all argument about whether risk-taking endeavors are really sports at all, or whether they are in fact the only sports.

This is certain: Motor racing is not a game.

Whatever it is, and all that it is, is embodied to the world in three syllables, Day-TOH-nah, as surely as the microcosm of all music to the world is a four-note phrase, three Gs and an E-flat—ta-ta-ta-TAH!—that opens Beethoven's Symphony no. 5. Isaac Stern has pointed out that music is the only language that needs no translation. It speaks directly, one human mind to another. Only a handful of words, out of all the world's languages, qualify as musical. How did Daytona become one? Why does it resonate, ever clearer? This book is intended as an elaborate answer—not an academic history, but a narrative. Daytona is a lovely story that tells itself.

1

OVERTURE

A. J. Foyt was ready to whip somebody's ass—I mean, even more ready than usual—and the leading candidate appeared to me to be Bill France Jr., the president of NASCAR. This was Foyt in his prime, when he was mean as a rodeo bull and lumbering through life about one tick away from throwing the kind of first punch that was also the last. At this particular moment Foyt was being thrown off the Daytona 500 pole for cheating. So you talk about pissed…

I was standing eight or ten feet away, just out of range of that bridge piling of a right arm of Foyt's (this was before a lot of the muscle in his right forearm was left hanging on a guardrail in Michigan in an Indy car crash). Foyt's left arm was around France's shoulders so that the crook of the elbow was like a vise that hadn't tightened on France's neck—yet. Foyt was pointing his right forefinger in France's face, jabbing, jabbing, so close that I figured one of two things was going to happen any second: Either Foyt was going to poke France right between the eyes with his finger, or he was going to close his fingers into that picnic ham of a fist and nail him between, above, below, and all around the eyes with one pop.

But you know what? Billy France never blinked. Never even gave Foyt what I have come to call, after all these years, the owl-eyed look. When France would get rattled or irate in conversation, he would go wide-eyed. But he wasn't even giving Foyt that little satisfaction.

Anyway, this was just out front of the NASCAR inspection station in the garage area of Daytona International Speedway. Foyt was pulling France slowly along by the shoulders, pointing, talking right in his face, and here they came toward me and then Foyt spotted me and walked France off to my left (his right) and took him around the corner of the inspection station.

I followed.

Foyt turned around and looked at me again, a look that said, You pissant, and he pulled France around yet another corner.

I followed.

Foyt had barely opened his mouth to resume raising hell in France's face when he looked around again and I was there again—You *pissant*.

He let France go and those massive arms flopped down by his sides in exasperation, a gesture that said this goddamn media situation was getting out of hand and racing was going straight to hell if pissant reporters could watch your every move. Stomping back into the inspection station, where media people were not allowed, he pulled down the sliding steel door.

I decided to stick around. I mean, I didn't have any quotes from Foyt for my newspaper story yet, unless you count "Fuck 'em."

Then a passenger car, a big Pontiac Bonneville, came whooshing through the pit gate, through the alleys between the garages, and screeched to a stop with its nose not four feet from the steel door of the inspection station.

Out stepped Billy France's father, Big Bill, who was the

founder and still the czar of NASCAR. At age sixty-six, he remained a genuine, certified, tough old sonofabitch.

He wore a referee's whistle around his neck. He left the car door open and the engine running, as if this wouldn't take long.

As he raised the sliding steel door, somebody in the rapidly gathering gaggle shouted, "Where you going, Bill?"

The old man turned his head slightly and bellowed back, "Wallace told me to make sure these sonsabitches were legal by the time he got here, and I'm gonna do it." George Wallace, the Alabama governor and persistent presidential candidate, was to be the grand marshal of the Daytona 500 that year.

Big Bill went inside and pulled the steel door down behind him.

So began, late in the afternoon of February 8, 1976, the damnedest Daytona 500 week there ever has been.

*Y*ou don't piss on them Pettys and tell 'em it's rainin'," said Joe Littlejohn. This was late in the afternoon of February 15, 1976.

He was addressing Big Bud Moore (no relation whatsoever to Little Bud Moore), who was giving him a ride back to the Boar's Head (the biggest little bar ever in auto racing anywhere) before the race was over.

Big Bud's race car had been driven to death by Buddy Baker as usual—under Baker's maniacal right foot the Ford had barfed its engine in a cloud of shrapnel and burning oil that looked and sounded like an artillery round landing in the middle of the backstretch—and so there was no reason for Big Bud to stay around for the finish.

So they were listening to the finish on the radio and it was down to the final few seconds, and Richard Petty had just done what for years had been deemed impossible. He had retaken the lead from David Pearson *after* Pearson had executed the usually decisive slingshot pass down the backstretch into the third turn. That was tantamount, on the white-flag lap of the Daytona 500, to rising from the dead. Coming out of the fourth and final turn, Petty had the lead with the checkered flag in sight, a thousand feet away.

Big Bud opined in a split second, with a sort of amazed grunt, that Petty had the matter in hand.

"Nossir," said Littlejohn.

Two off-duty South Carolina state troopers were Joe Littlejohn's bodyguards and chauffeurs just about everywhere he went. He had raced on the beach before Big Bill France ever even thought of building Daytona International Speedway. ("Why, hell yes, I won," he would reminisce to striking women a third his age in the Boar's Head. "There wadn't nobody to beat in them days but Bill France.") He had seen Lee Petty start out in stock car racing. He had watched Richard, Lee's son, grow up, become a star, and develop the best rivalry there ever was (and probably ever will be) in NASCAR, with David Pearson.

Littlejohn and Pearson were both from Spartanburg, South Carolina, and Littlejohn's feelings toward Pearson were mixed. Littlejohn was Pearson's benefactor, having helped him put down the paint guns in the auto body shops of Spartanburg and rise out of the hellhole Saturday-night dirt tracks of the Carolinas. Now that Pearson was a star— well, something of an antistar, Petty's chronic nemesis—Littlejohn felt slighted, forgotten, and so he pulled against Pearson a lot of the time, or at least pretended to.

Littlejohn, like everybody I have ever known who has ever been even a halfway decent race driver, had an uncanny ability to see and hear and think in slow motion. And so in the split second after Petty had retaken the lead, Littlejohn saw all over again the final minute of the Firecracker 400 at Daytona in 1974, when Pearson had beaten Petty with what

Pearson's car owner, Glen Wood, called in the immediate aftermath "about the slickest trick I've ever seen in racin'." Petty had been livid at what he deemed a dirty, even deadly move.

And now, in the final few seconds of the damnedest Daytona 500 week there ever has been, Littlejohn reckoned that Petty was pondering payback for the '74 shenanigan.

"You don't piss on them Pettys and tell 'em it's rainin'."

Not unless you were David Pearson.

*T*he shouted whisper, a sort of anguished gasp for help— "Ed!...Ed!"—came on the evening of March 10, 1979, from the shadows in the courtyard of a Holiday Inn in Richmond, Virginia. It was twenty days after The Fight—the oversimplified term that history has attached to the altercation between Cale Yarborough and brothers Bobby and Donnie Allison that occurred moments after the Daytona 500 of 1979 ended.

Where Donnie Allison came from in the dark, I didn't know. What was clear on his face, as he walked toward me, looking about him and over his shoulders for any unwanted eavesdroppers, was despair.

"I don't know what to do," he began, in tones hushed but urgent. "I've never been through anything like this before in my life. I don't know how to handle this."

I had heard about the death threats, even seen one letter, pencil-written in a semiliterate hand on old-fashioned brown tablet paper: "I dont like what you done to ol Cale at Daytona, so you better lookout for a Coke botle through you're winshield or somthing like that when you race at Atlanta."

And I knew that far more daunting hunters were closing in on Donnie—journalists from as far outside the usual NASCAR media circles as *TIME* magazine and the *New York Daily News* were in town. Perhaps not since the Battle of

Cold Harbor, late in the Civil War, had so many national journalists descended upon Richmond, bent on war coverage.

The situation had exploded into The War Down South, or The Feud in NASCAR—or whatever throwback themes were being seized upon by New York editors looking in from outside.

It had begun on national television. For the first time, CBS had televised the Daytona 500 live, flag-to-flag. Most of the nation had been snowed in on race day, and so ratings had soared beyond the expectations of either NASCAR or network officials.

Dueling for the win on the last lap, Cale and Donnie had wrecked each other down the backstretch and into Turn 3. Richard Petty, whose storied successes at Daytona had always been, he said, a matter of "circumstances," benefited this time more than ever. He found himself serendipitously in the lead, shot past the wreckage in Turn 3 with a fiery prodigy named Darrell Waltrip on his bumper, and held off Waltrip at the checkered flag.

All in all, that race should have been to NASCAR what the Baltimore Colts–New York Giants championship game of 1958 was to the NFL—the milestone of a league's transition from blue-collar cult appeal to mainstream national attention.

But just after the race ended, just as CBS was about to cut away from Daytona for the day, came The Fight.

Cale and Donnie, both unhurt, had climbed out of their wrecked cars and were talking, arguing, but not fighting, when Bobby drove up and began the end of his brother's career.

While it is true that Bobby Allison helped his younger brother Donnie into a NASCAR career, it is also true that Bobby spent his entire career against the wind, against the world, and that he sometimes dragged his brother into the teeth of the gales. February 18, 1979 was the worst of those times.

True, Bobby stopped to make sure his brother was all right. But also true, Donnie has always believed, Bobby came looking for Cale Yarborough.

The great tragedy of The Fight was that Donnie, the only innocent party—the only one of the three who didn't land a blow—was the singular victim. Yarborough had already won the race twice previously, and was destined to win it twice more. Bobby had won it once and would win it twice more. The '79 race had been Donnie's best chance. He had never won the Daytona 500. And he never would.

The famous Associated Press photo, which shows Cale and Bobby entangled, with Donnie wielding his helmet from behind Bobby, is what made Donnie look so bad to the public. But it does not tell the whole truth.

That photo is what a snowed-in nation saw that Monday morning, and what catapulted NASCAR and the Daytona 500 into mainstream America's consciousness.

But that was by no means the end of it, nor even the worst of it.

*D*aytona 500 eve, 1981, Boar's Head Lounge. Not a seat to be had at the bar or in the booths, David Allen Coe on the jukebox singing "Jack Daniel's, If You Please," and the Men in Table Cloths (my term for A. J. Foyt's crew, who wore red-and-white-checked shirts that were the trademark of Gilmore-Foyt Racing) keeping order in the joint. The Boar's Head during Daytona 500 week was always as orderly or as disorderly as Foyt's crew decided to make it at any given moment.

Good thing they got along with a new, young, motley crew of North Carolina boys in blue-and-yellow uniforms, or there might be hell to pay in here. The compatibility started with the drivers, for the old Texan had taken a real liking to the young Dale Earnhardt. Four or five of the blue-clad boys were in one of those big horseshoe booths in a corner. Among them, slouched side by side, Earnhardt and I sat.

Earnhardt grinned that tiny mischievous grin of his, sipped his Jack Daniel's and ginger ale—"jeenjale," he pronounced it back then—and looked out across the bar at nobody in particular. (This was when drivers still drank, still partied in public, long before they became fitness fanatics and recluses in their million-dollar motor coaches with a jaded, reclusive, filthy-rich guru named Dale Earnhardt leading their rush to aloof seclusion.)

"Shoulda heard me and Waltrip out there a while ago," Earnhardt said, meaning Happy Hour, the just-concluded final hour of practice before the race.

I turned and looked at him and didn't say anything. Didn't need to. No driver has ever been under Earnhardt's skin more than Waltrip was in those days. Waltrip in his prime was every bit as ruthless as Earnhardt, and twice as slick about it. He got away with anything and everything. He got Earnhardt's goat. Totally. (This was long before the nickname the Intimidator was even thought of, and Earnhardt at the time was, if anything, the Intimidated.) But conversely, Earnhardt was beginning to get to Waltrip. You could sense Waltrip "hearing footsteps," as they say in football. He sensed Earnhardt as a force, coming hard, coming wild. A hurricane on the horizon of the peak of Waltrip's career. So I just waited for Earnhardt to continue talking. I knew he was going to— had to.

"We're sitting there on the pit road waiting to go out to practice. Waltrip's in his car right beside me. He hollers over—he says, 'Hey Earnhardt! Can you *see* out that window net of yours?' " Waltrip's implication was clear: When Earnhardt slammed against whatever came alongside him on the track—the wall, other cars, whatever—was he aware of the particular object he was slamming at any given moment, or was he just slamming blindly, indiscriminately?

"I said, 'I don't need to *see* you coming up beside me. I can *feel* you.'

"He said, 'You wanna go practice drafting together?'

"I said, 'O.K.'

"He said, 'You're not gonna hit me in the ass, are you?'

"I said, 'Nah. This is just practice.' "

Earnhardt smirked.

To and from our booth there paraded an array of racing people, stopping to chitchat. To some of them I related the just-told anecdote, and Earnhardt sat there smirking, satisfied with himself and the story I was spreading.

"So," I said after a while. "How you gonna run tomorrow?"

"WFO," he said. (This was long before that expression became so well-known around NASCAR that you could just about use it for a book title.)

"WFO?"

"Wide fuckin' open," he said. "Only way I know."

"So who's gonna win?"

"Me," he said. "I ain't got enough sense to lose."

I laughed out loud and Earnhardt's face clouded up. Now he was pissed, but I thought he was just, you know, momentarily pissed.

So I said pretty loud to some people sitting at the bar, "Hey, you know what Earnhardt just said? I asked him who was gonna win tomorrow and he said, 'Me—I ain't got enough sense to lose.' "

So then half the bar erupted with laughter, and from Earnhardt I got an elbow in the ribs that was more than a nudge. I turned and looked at him, and he was seriously, unequivocally pissed. (Actually, hurt—embarrassed—I realize all these years later.)

"Why don't you *shut up*," he said.

"Aw, c'mon, Earnhardt."

"*Shut up,* Hinton!"

He was seething, staring straight down the barrel of his Jack Daniel's and jeenjale. Some of Foyt's boys came by and we got into a conversation and before I knew it Earnhardt was gone.

This was how it always would be with Earnhardt. He would tell you what was on his mind, and then be proud for you to tell some of it, and furious if you told other parts of it.

*B*obby Allison sat there beaming but saying little, letting his son Davey chirp on and on about what Davey called this day, Valentine's Day, 1988—"the happiest day of my life." If you'd walked into that press conference at that moment as an outsider, you would have thought surely the son had won the Daytona 500 and had asked his father to join him in the celebration and the doting dad was just sitting there soaking it all in while his son described the emotion of the moment.

It didn't work that way with Bobby and Davey. Never had.

Davey Allison and Kyle Petty had grown up playing together on weekends at the race tracks—even while their fathers were at war with each other, in one of NASCAR's nastiest feuds, during the boys' elementary school years. But when the pair told their fathers they wanted to be racers, their paths separated drastically.

Richard Petty placed, on the silver spoon already in Kyle's mouth, the finest race cars Petty Enterprises could build. And Kyle embarked on a career as a chronic disappointment. Bobby Allison looked at his son and shrugged and said, "There's the shop. There's all the tools. Go to work." And left him there. And Davey channeled his adolescent resentment of the old man into by-god determination to show him, and set about acquiring and piecing together junk and making it tick and then hum and then roar, up from the quarter-mile and half-mile bullrings of Alabama, up through the minor leagues of stock car racing. By 1987 he not only had made it to the Winston Cup Series but had won there as a rookie, right on the Allisons' home track, Talladega.

By the final few laps of the 1988 Daytona 500 it was clear that Davey Allison was the best young driver in NASCAR. The race was down to a duel—between him and his father. Surely to God, I thought, the old man is going to cut the kid some slack at last. But no, hell no, exiting the fourth turn on the final lap the old man floored the throttle and left the kid.

But the most endearing quality of sons is that they love their fathers unconditionally, and so, "This is," said Davey, "the happiest day of my life. It's better than if I had won myself…He's always been my hero."

Again and again as the sun went down Davey would say it—"He's always been my hero"—while Bobby sat there beaming.

Four months and five days later, on June 19, 1988, at Pocono Raceway in Pennsylvania, Bobby Allison would be critically injured—God, what an inadequate expression for what happened to him—in a wreck sickening to behold. Time after time, driving by the wreck slowly behind the pace car, under the caution flag, Davey would pass by his nearly dead father, struggling with the decision of whether to pull out of the race or not. Davey would stay in, finish fifth, and all the while his car owner, Robert Yates, could hear between the lines of Davey's radio conversations with his pit crew. "You could almost hear him thinking, struggling," Yates would say. "It was as if he was debating with himself, saying to himself, 'I love my daddy. My daddy loved this sport. I love this sport. This sport has taken my daddy. I hate this sport. My daddy taught me to love this sport. I love this sport.' "

And that night at the hospital, a neurosurgeon "called me

over into a corner," Davey would say later. "He said, 'Son, tonight you're going to have to make yourself be the man of this family. Because if your daddy lives through the night, he'll probably never be able to do anything again.'

"It took the breath out of me," Davey said. "It took my legs out from under me. I fell straight down onto the floor."

From those weeks that summer when Bobby hovered near death until the day Davey died, July 13, 1993, the refrain from Davey came countless times: "He's always been my hero."

*F*ebruary 16, 1992. Daytona 500 morning, Richard Petty's last one, dawning cloudy, misting rain.

Already in the garage area there was a funereal vigil, a ring of people encircling the latest car to wear the fabled number, 43, all of them silent, all heads bowed to one unwitting degree or another, their hands clasped in front of them. Impromptu as it was, it was so like a graveside ceremony, and the big Pontiac was as the coffin of something.

When Richard Petty was gone, there would come no more like him to this earth. He would remain in NASCAR as a team owner, but "the Richard Petty y'all know will be dead," his son, Kyle, had said that morning.

Thirty-four seasons down, one to go, and the home stretch of Richard Petty's career—he had chosen to call it not his farewell tour but his "Fan Appreciation Tour"—was beginning, entirely appropriately, with the Daytona 500. He and the race had made each other famous. He had won it seven times, more than anyone else, and as many as the second and third drivers on the list combined (Cale Yarborough four times, Bobby Allison three).

He was fifty-four years old and partly deaf—the engines had sung to him too long—and so he would not hear the crowds roaring their farewells, nor had he heard the snide remarks of younger drivers in recent years that he was long over the hill.

"Sometimes," the King had said, "it's a blessing to be hard of hearing."

Over the years he had been injured literally from head to foot, concussions to broken toes, with myriad multiple fractures in between. In 1980 he hid from NASCAR officials the fact that his neck was broken, and drove on, knowing that even the slightest bump from another car could kill him. "You do what you have to do," he said then. But the public had ravaged him as much as the cars had. His most telling surgery came in 1978, when forty percent of his ulcer-riddled stomach was removed, likely the price of being too nice to too many people for too long.

And now on his last Daytona 500 morning, he emerged from the toilet of the first million-dollar motor coach in NASCAR.

"The greatest luxury of this bus," he said, "is the bathroom. I can go whenever I like. Out in the garage area, it takes half an hour to get from my race car to the rest room, and half an hour to get back."

This was due to the mobs of autograph seekers, even in such a highly restricted area. And so it had gone, all these years. Everywhere. Mobs. And from amidst them always you could spot that huge, pearly grin and the ever-working right hand. Signing, signing, ever signing... Smiling, smiling, ever smiling...

Petty glanced out the huge windshield of the coach, at a crowd that had already gathered near the gate in the high fence around the motor home compound.

"Soon be time," he said, "to go out there among 'em." He grinned again—although there was a little pain in it—at the prospect.

"Look at that," he said. "There's probably more people in

that garage area right now than there were people in the grandstands when we started runnin' here in '59."

Yet you sensed a sort of death knell for NASCAR's folk appeal when the King was gone, and this was why: There was but one other visitor in the coach, a woman, a friend of Petty's wife, Lynda, and she had been telling about the scene that had developed at the gate a little while earlier. She said that when Dale Earnhardt tried to walk through that gate, the crowd went into a frenzy and began holding out various objects, mostly caps and posters, for him to sign, and that he growled to them that he wasn't coming through there if they were going to stick all that stuff in his face, and he turned around and got into a rental car and had someone drive him into the garage by another route, to avoid the autograph seekers.

Earnhardt was the Man now, the Intimidator, the man whose merchandise and memorabilia all of race-watching America was buying (whether he would sign it or not), for an estimated gross of more than $50 million a year. One man. One image. One season. Fifty million dollars.

And so I asked the King, "Will Earnhardt be the next Richard Petty?"

He gestured at my tape recorder.

"Turn that thing off," he said.

He looked at me hard and pursed his lips in that mannerism that always let you know he was about to be profoundly candid, and he said simply:

"No."

And out the door of the coach, right through the gate and into the throng walked the King, signing, smiling—never flinching at the risk of being trampled by the five hundred or so people who wanted to get even closer to him than the rest.

Maybe fifty yards across the garage, a busted-up old man was hobbling along, alone, peering at the milling throng, which now included a flock of minicams and microphones, moving with Petty.

"He's handled y'all well," the old man said, meaning the media. "Because, I'm gonna tell you now, y'all can be a pain in the ass."

The old man limped along on legs that were an orthopedic surgeon's jigsaw puzzle, put together from bits and pieces found at a wreck scene where he told the emergency physicians, when the morphine didn't help him, "Just find a goddamn hammer and knock me in the head!" This old cuss too was about to embark on his last Daytona 500, and mainly he was just goddamn glad almost nobody was pestering him about it. He had always preferred to do his suffering in solitude.

He glanced once more at the swarm surrounding Petty.

He shook his head.

"I always kinda looked up to him," he said.

Those words were towering, monumental, from this particular old man, name of A. J. Foyt.

After this day, after the essence of Richard Petty was dead, he would return to Daytona physically—"He'll be standing there in the pits," said Kyle, "but you'll know he'd give everything he had, all two hundred wins, all seven championships, if he could go just one more time.

"Guys like Daddy and A.J., guys who have done this for so long, they look at quitting as a terminal illness."

*T*hursday, February 11, 1993. The kid looked ridiculous with that little black peach-fuzz mustache—it was as if he drew it on with a Magic Marker, playing grown-up.

But he was standing there in Victory Lane, clearly smitten with the striking model—"Miss Winston" these women were called after they were hired out of the agency in Greensboro, North Carolina, to present trophies and smile for cameras, mainly to gain "brand exposure" for the series sponsor.

And he was winking at her.

And it would look so ludicrous coming from this almost pubescent-looking kid, if the twenty-three-year-old model weren't…well…

Winking back.

Her name was Brooke Sealey. His name was Jeff Gordon. She was fresh out of the agency. He had just become the youngest driver ever to win a race at Daytona International Speedway.

And here they were winking at each other in Victory Lane, moments after the first of the traditional twin 125-mile qualifying races that determine most of the starting order for the Daytona 500.

Thus began a romance, very secretive—Winston models and Winston Cup drivers are forbidden from dating each other by unwritten rule. It's just tacit policy on the part of both NASCAR and Winston, to keep racing from looking, well, too racy to the public. The wild exploits of the flamboyant driver Tim Richmond, who died of AIDS in 1989 after surreptitiously dating some Winston models and reportedly transmitting the disease to one, cemented the rule.

So the secrecy, as this 1993 season progressed, would make the kid a master of slipping unnoticed in and out of hotels.

The inner circles of NASCAR would gossip. The model never seemed to have any dates, and neither did the kid. Nobody would add it up. The hard-bitten Earnhardt would saunter up to Gordon in midseason and ask flat-out if the kid was gay.

But here in Victory Lane at Daytona, here was what was so scary about the kid: He looked like he had about as much business trading winks with Brooke Sealey as Macaulay Culkin would have trading winks with Kim Basinger. But he had just driven that car like the macho men of yore who would plant huge, lingering kisses on the mouths of models in Victory Lane—Fireball Roberts and Joe Weatherly and

Curtis Turner. No. He had driven better. Smoother. Quicker. Ballsier. He had just shown up at this storied 2.5-mile tri-oval for the first time, and had driven it as if he had been driving it for twenty years. He had a gift for sniffing the draft that usually took a decade to learn. He had a superb feel for every bump and rise and dip in every stretch and turn of the pavement.

Earnhardt went out and won his 125-miler as usual, the second one of the day, and in his press conference was asked to name his top competitors for Sunday's race, and he clicked off the usual suspects, Davey Allison and Ernie Irvan and Geoff Bodine, and in just a fleeting afterthought he remembered that some kid had won the first 125-miler, and added, "and, uh, the Gordon boy."

Gordon boy my ass.

Watching just that one 125-miler, you couldn't say that Jeff Gordon was the best there was—maybe the best there'd ever been.

But you damn sure couldn't say he wasn't.

2

MONTAGE

Daytona 500 morning. Just before dawn. Already the garage area is a frenzy of crewmen in the dark and mist. The cars sit halfway out of their stalls to dissipate exhaust and noise, each one a monstrous patient in intensive care, tubes and wires running out of it, back to computer monitors and electronic oil warmers. The engines are barely awake with the slow, meticulous beginnings of the final tunings, beginning to mutter, but muttering is a relative term here. Each idling engine sounds like eight sawed-off shotguns firing in machine-gun staccato. Mufflerless, with short exhaust pipes that end just beneath the numbers on the sides, forty-three cars join in an anarchistic chorus of noise that is almost the full volume of the synchronized explosions in the cylinders.

The mountainous streets of Monaco are mystical to walk on a Grand Prix morning as the five-million-dollar engines shriek at being awakened by the tuners and are massaged into soprano screams that are more piercing than any siren and resound down the granite canyons and off the facades of palaces and villas and grand hotels and the casino. And all is elegance.

The forests of northwestern France teem with milling legions that are like great armies gathered in the hours before the afternoon start of Vingt-Quatre Heures du Mans. In the warm winds of summer solstice the flags fly for as far as you can see—Rising Suns and Union Jacks, the red cross of Austria and the white cross of Switzerland, the globo of Brazil and the earth-sun-and-forest colors of Germany...on and on...And from somewhere in the distance come the somber opening strains of "Deutschland Über Alles" (Germany is "Allemagne" in French, and therefore first alphabetically in the playing of the national anthems of all drivers competing). And later there is the enormous cheer evoked by "God Save the Queen," for the British love the 24 Hours of Le Mans perhaps even more than the French themselves. And finally the rousing "La Marseillaise," and then the abrupt command that is shrieked with emphasis on the second syllable: *"Moteurs!"* Which is to say, simply, "Engines!"

And the Indianapolis 500, God rest its once-titanic soul. Back before the race was disemboweled of its magic and its meaning by a silly split of factions in Indy car racing—the pullout of Championship Auto Racing Teams (CART), which had been the backbone of each year's field for the 500, in outrage after the Speedway's formation of its own Indy Racing League (IRL)—there was perhaps no more electric moment in all of motor racing, or indeed in all of sports, than when 400,000 voices erupted at the last strains of a cornball song that once a year became resounding, haunting, hair-raising: "...How...I...long...for...my...In...di...aaa...nahhh...home."

Still there is nothing—nothing—quite like a Daytona 500 morning.

Come.

Somewhere down the line, one engine tuner, having

checked his on-site barometer and thermometer and humidity gauges for the final time—there are no better meteorologists for local weather than NASCAR's "engine men," as the specialists are called—jets the airflow in his carburetor just so, and with his timing strobe light sees the perfect rhythm he wants to see, and reaches up for the throttle arm on the carburetor, pushes it with his thumb, and the muttering becomes the sudden sum of scream and roar and explosion: *UM-OW!...UM-OW!*

Down the way there comes an answer: *UM-OW! UUUUMM-OW!*

Then another. Louder. Longer. *UM-OW! UUUUUUUM-MMM-OW!*

And all is sound—an ear-splitting symphony that would startle even Beethoven in his deafness, for he could feel the trembling of the air and earth.

And if you know this place you know it is time to put your earplugs in, that or prepare to put your fingers in your ears at the critical notes of song, or this one morning could damage your hearing permanently. All who have worked in these garages suffer some hearing loss—it is only a matter of degree.

Now the songs grow dangerous: *UUUUUUUMMMMMM-OW!*

This is the engine tuners' version of the pregame stretching of a football team, exercising the engine first to 5,000 rpm—the limit beyond which a passenger car's engine might blow. But these engines are all hand-built to microscopic tolerances in rooms pristine enough for neurosurgery, with parts made of ultra-strong alloys and finished by robotic machines whose movements are orchestrated by mainframe computers. So now, if the horrific song is pure enough for the tuner's ear, it's on up to 6,000 rpm, and 7,000, and 8,000...

Soon into the first revving of the first engines, the several thousand seagulls that have been foraging in the infield and about the sprawling grounds of the speedway flee back toward the ocean, their horrified squawking drowned out by the iron screams.

And the sun comes up on sound and fury signifying everything to seven hundred uniformed crewmen, some of whom still are sprung from the Carolinas, but amidst the din of engines there are shouts in Jersey accents, Brooklynese, New England "aahs" in "these caahs," the rolling, lilting nasalities of W'skaaansin, the burly southern/midwestern blends of Iowa, the unaccented dialect of California. NASCAR is southern-born, but is no longer southern-only. New York and California birthed more current Winston Cup drivers than did North Carolina, and it has been estimated that more than 200,000 weekend racers nationwide aspire to fill the fifty existing Winston Cup rides. Project those figures to include crewmen, and there may be five million mechanics, fabricators, and formally trained engineers with ambitions of breaking into the two thousand jobs available with Winston Cup teams. Still, the most critical labor shortage in America is in these garages, for people who *want* to do this work are one matter; people who *can* do it are quite another.

Throughout the garage area, even the smell of new rubber—thousands of tires being mounted and measured and pressure-gauged—is stifled like all other smells on Daytona 500 morning by exhaust.

The frantic revving puts out clouds of exhaust like mustard gas's deadly billow across battlefields in 1917. Carbon monoxide poisoning, like hearing loss, is taken as an occupational hazard. And yet the exhaust feels stifling in a worthwhile way, as when you breathe it thickly in the streets of London or Tokyo. It is the breath of vibrance and vitality, part of the action.

And now the chassis specialists set to their work, their air wrenches ripping off lug nuts for the final stripdowns and inspections of the cars, *B-r-r-r-r-t! B-r-r-t-B-r-r-r-r-t!* like

M-16s firing on full automatic. Now the checklists are taped to the cars, four or five white legal-size sheets to each car, each list containing hundreds of items, from brake fluid levels to rear-spoiler angle to driver safety harness couplings.

It is at about this point of the morning that walking through the garages becomes no effort at all, feels like floating, through a swirl of colors, and on every face there is a story.

Here comes Richard Childress, the only filthy-rich man you'll ever see who deserves every cent. Twenty years ago he would ride through stifling nights in Mexico and Arizona and California in a beat-up Chevrolet C-300 truck hauling a shit-box race car on a trailer whose brakes were iffy. He was an "independent" (the euphemism for almost sponsorless) driver in those days, plowing every dollar he made back into his team, speaking of his dream to get out of that car someday and put a younger, better driver in it, and attract major sponsorship, and win races and championships. The younger driver he hired was one Dale Earnhardt, who was such a chronic crasher, and so hard on engines, that fellow car owner Big Bud Moore warned upon releasing Earnhardt to Childress: "Boy, he'll break you."

But when he leaves Daytona this evening, Childress will fly off to his ranch in Montana on his private jet.

Indeed, at this day's end, the taxiways of Daytona Beach International Airport, just behind the speedway's back-stretch, will be jammed with jets, for nearly everybody who is anybody in NASCAR nowadays owns at least a Lear, and often something bigger. (Was it not just the other day that these guys would leave here exhausted, sprawled in the sleeping compartments of their trucks?)

And there comes Darrell Waltrip, who stayed too long because he loved it so and couldn't let go—what a pity. A whole new generation of fans have no idea just how good he was. All they saw was a senior statesman puttering around the track, getting lapped and laughed at, when and if he even made the field. He was on his way to becoming the best there'd ever been—more talented, and smoother by far, than even Earnhardt—until his bad crash in the Daytona 500 of 1983, and after that his style changed and he decided that "I want to win as many races as I can, going as slow as I can." And that was not the way to be remembered for his early greatness.

Here limps Bobby Allison, broke and almost broken but not bowed. His two sons dead of the passions he gave them for racing and flying. Maybe the most independent-minded man on earth, the summary of all a man can bear, the man among all of NASCAR's men. Of Allison, Waltrip once said it best: "He's the only man in racing I can walk up to and just start crying." But Bobby does not cry nor even brood, and on this as all Daytona 500 mornings he is smiling; he is as deeply in love with the milieu as ever.

And Dave Marcis, God love him, one sinewy, perpetually moving mass of indefatigable human spirit, always working, always eating—"And don't come back," he has been told at many an all-you-can-eat place along the highways of the NASCAR tour—and forever skinny, forever rationalizing, "If you work, you gotta eat." For him, "last of a breed" is far too weak an expression. Time was when there were dozens like him filling out Daytona race fields, the independent drivers, the James Hyltons, the D. K. Ulrichs, the Frank Warrens—the saddletramp cowboys of NASCAR. But that was when NASCAR was still struggling, when only a handful of teams were well financed. And now every team but Marcis's runs on multimillion-dollar budgets, anywhere from $5 million to $35 million a year. And yet, in this era when several big-buck teams fail to qualify and are sent home from each race, Marcis—not at all changed from when he ventured down from Wisconsin thirty-five years ago, living on bologna sandwiches and sleeping in the cab of his truck—

managed to make the field for the Daytona 500 every year, someway, somehow, until 2000. After thirty-two straight Daytona 500 starts, a record even the big names couldn't match, the tidal wave of money grew too strong for even "ol' Dave" to swim against. Still he comes back, trying again. And still he carries himself with something of a swagger in those old wing-tip shoes in which he still drives, while every one of his peers pushes the pedals in custom-made driving shoes suitable for spacemen.

Richard Petty, anywhere he walks in the garages, remains the eye of a hurricane of worshippers, and still he smiles and signs, smiles and signs, smiles and signs. But a light has gone out in him as surely as his son, Kyle, predicted that it would when the King retired as a driver. Richard Petty the icon is one thing; Richard Petty the driver who would walk these alleys on these mornings when there was a chance—no, a probability—that he would win, now *that* man used to tower over all of this.

Uh-oh! Move out of the way or be trampled by that on-rushing drove of people all in a wad, a swirl, whence protrude half a dozen microphone booms, and a dozen minicam operators backpedaling hurriedly to capture the scene, and this can only mean that Jeff Gordon is walking. That's all it takes to gather such a storm—just Jeff Gordon walking, maybe merely from his luxury motor coach to his garage stall.

Far across the garage area stands the man who conceals a broken heart so well, John Bickford, the stepfather who *made* Jeff Gordon, trained him to race from the age of four, sacrificed and slaved and pleaded and plotted to move the kid up through the ranks. And now he stands passed-by. All but forgotten in the deluge.

The morning's tide begins to ebb from the garages, out toward the pits, out to the war zone, for the pits are always enormously reminiscent of some great 19th-century battle, with the ebb and flow of men and equipment to and from the front. But now the men and supplies are being moved only forward—carts stacked with tires, carts of tools, carts hauling the ponderous eleven-gallon "dump cans" for gasoline. And you can always tell the commandos from the regulars, for the Guys Who Go Over the Wall, as they are called so reverently in the inner circles of NASCAR, wear fire-retardant uniforms and Nomex underwear and hoods, to do the terribly dangerous, terribly thankless jobs. Soon they will sprint over the wall with the coordination of a football offensive line firing off the ball, swarm the pitted car, and after ten seconds of slamming movements, each of which could sever a hand, each to the tune of the quick bursts of the airguns against the wheels, the car will not so much roar away as disappear. Evaporate before your eyes.

And now in the pre-race moments, as yet another grating country singer warbles and trills through another god-awful version of "The Star-Spangled Banner," the only sopranos in NASCAR break into a ghostly echo that resonates to the far retaining walls, the airguns at their final oiling, testing, *WheeeeeeeeOW! WheeOW! WheeeeeeeeeeeeeeeeeOW!*

There is nothing like a morning deep inside Daytona, before "Gentlemen, start your engines" signifies simply another five hundred miles to faces that have come a million miles each, between nobody and somebody.

3

THE BEGINNING

*T*he Ormond Hotel stood forlorn and ghostly in the years when you couldn't go in there. It faced the Halifax River, with its back to the sea. The remains of the largest wooden structure on earth were condemned, fenced off, boarded up.

Miles of deserted corridors, hundreds of empty rooms, peeling facades, rotting gazebos and verandas and promenades—all were silent with forgotten stories of the grandeur that was, in the springtime of American ingenuity and industry.

As the Ormond stood deserted in the late 1980s and early '90s, the February throngs would rush past on the Ormond Bridge, commuting from the beach hotels on the peninsula, across the river to the giant-come-lately Daytona International Speedway that lies inland. They were oblivious to the old hotel's forgotten significance:

Here, high speed was born. Here, the concept known worldwide as Daytona was germinated.

The Ormond was demolished in 1992, to make way for luxury high-rise condominiums. That was the final atrocity of neglect of America's most important monument to the dawn of international motor racing.

In the year the Ormond was built, 1875, there were two unincorporated settlements by the Halifax. The hotel's immediate environs were called New Britain, settled in 1874 by a group from Connecticut. To the south lay a hamlet founded by an Ohioan, Mathias Day, in 1870.

There actually came to be a town called Daytona, named for Day (perhaps with a nod at the Ohio city of Dayton) when it was incorporated in 1876. Just up the coast, New Britain was incorporated and renamed Ormond in 1880.

But first had come the area's first grand hotel, named for a British sea captain, James Ormond, who had been enticed away from the Bahamas in 1815 by a Spanish land grant along the Halifax.

Daytona would be absorbed into Daytona Beach in the consolidation of 1926. The town of Ormond would be renamed Ormond Beach in 1949. But before the names all passed into lore, the towns of Daytona and Ormond, and the Hotel Ormond—as it was originally dubbed in that grander, French-style syntax—would all become universally understood terms in the international racing vocabulary.

Bought and enlarged by railroad tycoon Henry Flagler, the Hotel Ormond reopened on New Year's Day, 1888, as a winter palace to robber barons. The town of Ormond was then somewhat like Palm Beach is now. John D. Rockefeller built his winter home, the Casements, near the hotel. Then came Vanderbilts and Goulds. South Florida, with its even more tropical climate, was so inaccessible that the rich tended to stop in the first towns they found reasonably warm in winter. From the Georgia playgrounds of Augusta and Savannah they ventured farther south as the railroads lengthened, to Jacksonville, St. Augustine, and on to Ormond and Daytona.

They had seen no beach in all the world quite like the one that lay but a stroll across the peninsula from the Hotel Ormond. The beach was (and is) five hundred feet wide at low tide, paved with hard-packed trillions of quartz granules brought by the rains and rivers of the ages down from the granite mountains of Georgia and the Carolinas, and ran straight and flat for twenty-three miles, south from Ormond, past Daytona, until it was breached by Ponce Inlet.

This beach was wonderful for walking, and yet too vast to limit one's movement to walking. The Ormond's well-heeled guests bicycled there, then attached sails to their bicycles for greater ease over the long distances. Informally, they began to race their bicycles and sailcycles and horse-drawn buggies and carriages, and then their motorized cycles, and then, at the dawn of the 20th century, their horseless carriages.

In the hotel's salons and bars and dining rooms there was much discussion of the era's rage, the automobile.

Out on the beach, it occurred to the automobilists: Here. Yes. Of course. This had to be the safest place on earth to try it. The sand was as smooth as any pavement of the time, far smoother than the rutted dirt roads that were the only routes through America's countryside. There was no system of paved highways then. Interstates? It would be another fifty years before President Dwight D. Eisenhower would even propose such a system. The best emerging "race tracks" were old fairgrounds horse tracks, mostly one-mile and half-mile ovals, dirt or clay or worse, too treacherous and confining for running even primitive cars as fast as they were capable of going. Here by the Atlantic lay a natural race course, its width and length amounting to all the forgiving distance in the world, it seemed, for speed. It was entirely safe even if brakes failed, and there were the natural buffers of surf on one side, soft dunes on the other. Here. Yes. Of course.

Who first had the notion? Local legend says it was Ransom Eli Olds, father of the Oldsmobile, with quick con-currence from Alexander Winton, a fellow—and rival—automotive industrialist of the time. Olds and Winton clearly played early and profound roles on the beach, but they were more likely followers than initiators. Local historian Dick Punnett points to campaigns in the northern press by two lesser-known winter residents of the Hotel Ormond, C. W. Birchwood and J. F. Hathaway, who suggested that their fellow automobilists come down and try the beach. Likely there were other proponents, lost to history.

But certainly the ones who executed the notion, the three men who did the most, the earliest, to make beach racing a reality, were the managers of the Hotel Ormond, John Anderson and Joseph P. Price, and veteran New York sports promoter William J. Morgan.

So in several minds was sown, gradually in 1902–3, the concept that here, automobiles could be driven to the limits of their engineering, faster than anyone had yet imagined, free from impediments of terrain or construction.

Men had already been racing automobiles sporadically for several years, beginning in 1894, but on streets and roads meant for carriages, at speeds hardly impressive to hackney drivers. The one fairly impressive exception was the world land speed record—in fact, simply the world speed record at the time—which in 1902 was barely 78 miles per hour, set by Maurice Augieres at Dourdan, France.

Here, speed would be redefined, drastically upward to uncharted velocities that, some physicians of the time feared, might do severe and permanent damage to the eyes, heart, and brain of any human.

Here would commence the Winter Speed Carnival, the direct ancestor of modern-day Daytona Speedweeks.

*O*rganized racing began on the beach no later than March 26, 1903, with Olds and Winton as the most prominent figures of the event. Winton actually drove, but Olds didn't—he placed one of his engineers, H. T. Thomas, at the wheel.

For most of the 20th century, a lovely story persisted that Olds and Winton, on their own initiative after a conversation at the Hotel Ormond, drove in an informal contest on the beach in the late winter or early spring of 1902, racing to a draw at 57 miles per hour. Though the tale was always questioned by some automobile historians due to lack of documentation, it proliferated in several books.

Then, in 1997, enter Dick Punnett, an Ormond Beach resident with a little-known, sparingly published—but extremely well-researched—book about the first eight years at Daytona, titled *Racing on the Rim*. Punnett makes a strong, if not airtight, case that the '02 story is pure myth, created over generations by domino-effect embellishment.

What really matters, and is certain, is that racers and racing enthusiasts filled the suites and bars and parlors of the Hotel Ormond, well before their ilk gathered on the roads between the town of Le Mans and the village of Mulsanne in western France for the first Grand Prix race in 1906...even before the storied Vanderbilt Cup road races began on Long Island in 1904 (their founder, William K. Vanderbilt Jr., initiated them after his participation at Ormond-Daytona earlier that year)...before industrialist Carl Fisher conceived and built, out of farmland and woods northwest of Indianapolis, a 2.5-mile rectangular track in 1909...before Fisher decided to conduct the world's first 500-mile race in 1911...before cars were durable enough, and had powerful enough headlights, to race for *vingt-quatre heures,* twenty-four hours, at Le Mans in 1926...

Well in advance of all those milestone gatherings, the Hotel Ormond's registry contained a wealth of signatures unmatched in all of motor racing. After Olds and Winton came Henry Ford, Louis Chevrolet, Glenn Curtiss, Vincenzo Lancia, Barney Oldfield...and then there was the enigmatic, arrogantly scrawled signature so synonymous with tempest in the sport of the time: simply, "Hemery."

Four years before a Chicago engineer named Ray Harroun drove to victory in the first Indianapolis 500, he fielded a car at Ormond-Daytona in 1907.

And so of all the history of all the world's great motor racing places, Daytona's is the longest-running and the richest. That's what matters.

*W*illiam J. Morgan, the first race promoter at Ormond-Daytona, was a Welshman. The Welsh tradition of musical language, which would give rise to the poet Dylan Thomas and the actor Richard Burton, ran deep in the almost songlike Welsh tongue itself and translated into a mesmerizing dialect of English.

Lovely speech was at the core of Morgan's being. And that may have been what kept the initially troubled Winter Speed Carnival alive from 1903 until it could blossom in '04, and begin to grow toward what the motor racing world now calls Daytona.

Morgan apparently was born sometime during the American Civil War, in South Wales, though precisely where—Pontypridd, perhaps, or Pen-y-bont (hear the music?) or Casnewydd, or Caerdydd (Cardiff in English)—is not clear.

He migrated first to Canada, then to the United States, as a competitive bicyclist, turning professional in the 1880s. The first essential trait for any sports promoter is a gift of gab—to this day, one must be better than merely a salesman; he must be eloquent, selling subtly—and so Morgan was a natural at promoting bicycle races. He learned from the best showmen of his day, including one William Frederick Cody, "Buffalo Bill," with whose Wild West show Morgan paired his cyclists for an exhibition in London that delighted the British royal family.

All the while, Morgan was also working as a journalist. By modern American standards, working as a promoter and a publicist, and as a journalist at the same time, would be considered a major conflict of interest. But things then were not what they are now. Further, Morgan was British by birth, and to this day, there are Brits and Europeans who think little of having commercial involvement with sporting interests that they cover.

When, in the winter of '02–'03, Morgan got word that automobilists were roaming the beach and that locals were interested in staging races, he headed to Florida by train, on the expense account of *The Automobile Magazine*. Its editors were actually willing to put up money to help stage a racing meet. (Remember, this was only five years after newspaper tycoon William Randolph Hearst was suspected of having his agents blow up the U.S. battleship *Maine* in Havana Harbor, so that the Hearst papers would have something new to cover—the Spanish-American War.)

Morgan met with—more accurately, was eagerly met by—the Hotel Ormond's managers, John Anderson and J. P. Price. Just as the barons of modern-day Las Vegas are always interested in promoting sports events that fill their hotels and casinos, so Anderson and Price happily offered to help birth beach racing with money and complimentary rooms for the racers.

A Winter Speed Carnival would commence in March. Morgan returned north to recruit competitors, but while he was gone, two local automobile clubs went at loggerheads for dominion over the event, and one of them publicly canceled the meet. Nationwide, potential competitors didn't know what to think.

By the last week in March, when the meet began, only two real racing cars were brought—and they were in vastly different categories of competition. All the rest were production cars, mainly Oldsmobiles, with a Stevens-Duryea here and a Stanley Steamer there. The Hotel Ormond was packed, but not with the world-class racers that Morgan, Anderson, and Price meant to attract. The real star of the show was Winton's "Bullet," which had a chance to break the world speed record. The Bullet was in the "over 2,000-pound" class, the best of an era when heavier meant faster, odd as that might seem to modern-day racing enthusiasts. Olds also brought a thoroughbred racer of sorts, but it was in the much slower "under 1,000-pound" class.

Except for a few minor events, the racing wasn't head-to-head, nor was turning involved. It was in the form of straight-line speed trials, one by one.

The show essentially was a flop. Winton ran only 68.966 mph, or nearly 10 mph slower than the world record over the measured mile. Thomas, in Olds's apparently hastily assembled racer, got up to 54.381 mph, an American record for its class (ho-hum). The only world records set were for motorcycles, by Oscar Hedstrom, 57.357 mph over one kilometer and 56.962 mph over the mile.

What was Morgan to do in the aftermath?

"The crowd must always leave believing it saw a much better race than it actually saw," legendary track announcer Chris Economaki would say decades later. It was the first commandment of post-race promotion of the next event. Economaki had learned it as a youth in New Jersey in the 1930s, working for dirt-track promoters. Even then, it had been passed down for decades.

Where did the adage originate?

Probably with William J. Morgan, in 1903. Clearly he practiced it, even if he'd synthesized it from 19th-century managers of Wild West shows, boxing, bicycle racing, circuses.

Any estimates of spectator attendance numbers would almost certainly have been inflated by Morgan. Likely there was but a smattering of the well-to-do. But Morgan accomplished something far more important. He got print reporters (the only media people in those days) to leave believing they had seen a much better event than they actually saw. And it didn't hurt, of course, that Morgan the promoter was himself one of the reporters, who could see it any way he chose.

After a disappointed Winton criticized the beach course, Morgan deftly hyped Olds's car, which was a stripped-down—rather, probably not completely built—little machine whose appearance was that of a primitive rail dragster. The flimsy seat was far to the rear of an assembly that looked like two four-foot rockets (the fuel tanks), mounted parallel and pointed forward on either side of the little 15-horsepower engine, with a boxy radiator on the front.

Winton's Bullet was a substantial piece of machinery, but today's racers in their own jargon likely would have viewed Olds's spindly contraption as "a shitbox."

But listen to the Welshman Morgan's dispatch from Florida back to New York regarding the Olds, as cited by Punnett from *The Automobile Magazine:* "The new vehicle was a piratical looking 15 hp affair, which was at once christened the Pirate since it was such a 'long, low, black, rakish looking craft' to use the words of a dime novel."

Who christened the Pirate? It probably was Morgan himself.

Other reporters, no doubt regaled with electric language by Morgan as they stood on the sands, marveled in print at what Olds had wrought. Winton had already named the Bullet himself. And from the Pirate, legend sprouted.

During the meet, Morgan had staged an exhibition handicap race between the two grossly unequal cars, in which Winton in the Bullet let Thomas in the Pirate get a huge head start, so that they crossed the finish line almost abreast. There, probably, lay the beginnings of the stories of an '02 encounter in which Olds and Winton, in the Pirate and the Bullet, raced to a draw. But because Winton manufactured his first car in 1896 and Olds was marketing passenger cars in 1901, it is possible that they raced informally on the beach in '02, but in cars other than the Pirate and the Bullet—though almost certainly not at 57 mph.

Remember, in March of 1903, Orville and Wilbur Wright's

"aeroplane," the *Flyer I,* was still but an earthbound prototype that would not take successful flight for another eight months, on December 17, at Kitty Hawk, North Carolina.

So in the spring of 1903, the Bullet and the Pirate, as sung by Morgan, were made to sound like the two most marvelous machines in America, if not on earth.

*W*illiam Kissam Vanderbilt Jr., "Willie K.," was a thoroughbred of the sporting life. His father was the first in the Cornelius Vanderbilt lineage to become bored with the family business empire. William K. Sr. had taken to financing the Metropolitan Opera, and to sailing, skippering *Defender* to U.S. retention of the America's Cup in 1895. Willie K.'s brother, Harold, would win the Cup three times, and invent the game of contract bridge.

Willie K.'s thrill threshold was higher. Motor cars and speed—*that* was the ticket to exhilaration. At the age of seventeen, in Paris in 1895, he had been smitten with an exhibition of cars about to embark on a race from Versailles to Bordeaux, and had promptly made a 3,000-franc contribution to the purse. Back home, while he studied at Harvard, his passion for motoring grew.

By the spring of 1903, Willie K. was twenty-five years old and just settling into his perfunctory position in one branch of the family empire, the New York Central Railroad. Reading about the new Speed Carnival in Florida, he decided that next time he would participate. He ordered, from Germany, a monstrous machine named by its designer, Gottlieb Daimler, after the daughter of a financial partner. The girl, and the car, were called Mercedes.

Berna Eli "Barney" Oldfield, only a few months older than Willie K., was a commoner from Wauseon, Ohio. That same spring, Oldfield was making a name for himself as a daredevil, driving for Henry Ford's embryonic racing venture. Twice that spring at exhibitions in the Midwest, Oldfield beat Winton's Bullet. If Winton, by now forty-three years old, couldn't beat Oldfield, there was only one thing to do: hire him, and take him to the second Winter Speed Carnival in Florida.

Willie K. Vanderbilt and his entourage were just the sort of guests the Hotel Ormond's management had been looking for. Barney Oldfield would use the servants' entrance. But the beach was a level playing field.

*H*aving made a remarkable recovery from the previous year, Morgan had a full-fledged Carnival to offer in January of 1904. Before the main show even started, early arrivals Charles Schmidt in a streamlined Packard "Gray Wolf" and Otto Nestman in a rail-like Stevens-Duryea "Spider" had set new American lightweight records. Cleveland industrialist Walter Baker was on the way with a car that introduced a new concept, aerodynamics—his aptly named "Torpedo Kid."

And on January 12, a fortnight before the Carnival began, Morgan got the windfall of his life: not only a new world record to shoot at, but one set by an American and therefore the talk of the nation. On the ice of Lake St. Claire in Michigan, Henry Ford, driving his "999" racer himself, averaged 91.37 mph.

Enter Willie K. and Barney.

Willie K. couldn't even wait for the official opening of the event. A day early, on January 27, he asked officials if he could have a go. Vanderbilts were not denied much in those days; Morgan let him rip. Willie K. rumbled onto the beach and loosed all 90 horsepower of the Mercedes. He averaged 92.308 mph, eclipsing Ford's world speed record. And that was just a warmup.

Winton had brought a 90-horsepower, over-2,000-

pounder as well, "Bullet II." In it sat the Scottish-born industrialist's secret weapon: Oldfield.

The second Carnival had drawn so many cars that there were plenty for head-to-head competition in each class. On the second day of the meet, Vanderbilt won his heat, and Oldfield won his. They were in the same class technologically, but not socially.

And so the final came down to the small-town American common man versus the enormously wealthy New York sportsman and socialite.

Barney blew past Willie K. and won by as much as a hundred yards at the finish line, according to some accounts.

Barney Oldfield was in at least two ways the Dale Earnhardt of his day. First, he had—if you'll pardon our contemporary garage-area French—"a set of balls on him that wouldn't fit in a fifty-five gallon drum." Second, because the equipment didn't belong to him, he had no qualms about driving it to, and then past, its limits. The final results of the 1904 Winter Speed Carnival give few indications of what a force Oldfield really was. On the third day of the meet, Oldfield blew the engine in the Winton Bullet II. Winton had not brought sufficient spare parts, let alone spare engines—the rules of the time may not have allowed it—and so the car was finished in that year's competition.

Some in Vanderbilt's entourage got their backs up that their darling boy would not get a chance to redeem himself against the Ohio bumpkin. They claimed Oldfield and Winton had taken a dive to avoid a retributive thrashing from Willie K. later in the meet.

Willie K. blithely ignored all this, knowing that one little loss on the beach was nothing compared to the world speed record he owned, and that he would go unchallenged for further records in runs of from five to fifty miles each. In February, he returned to New York and set about organizing the first of the Vanderbilt Cup races over the roads of Long Island that so many racing enthusiasts, even today, erroneously assume to be the first major motorsports events held in the United States.

Among all classes of cars, a stunning eleven world records and four American marks were broken at Ormond-Daytona in January and February of 1904.

Gasoline Alley," reads the sign above the main entrance to the massive garage area at Indianapolis Motor Speedway. The modern buildings are the third version, in the same spot, of what was widely believed to be the original Gasoline Alley.

But the original Gasoline Alley lay just off Granada Avenue in Ormond, Florida, and ran between a garage—built by Hotel Ormond owner Henry Flagler in 1904 for the 1905 Winter Speed Carnival—and a dormitory for mechanics. Like the hotel, the Ormond Garage is gone now, destroyed by fire in 1976.

But in and around it in January of 1905 worked virtually everybody who was anybody in the developing American automobile industry, including Henry Ford himself. The president of the burgeoning Ford Motor Company spearheaded the American manufacturers' assault on the world racing prominence that the Daimler family of Germany had virtually been handed, gratis, by Vanderbilt's jaunts of the previous winter.

Willie K. was back with a new Mercedes, but nothing like the twin-engine monster H. L. Bowden had devised. An odd rule, by today's understanding of technology, upset the world record quest. Bowden's Mercedes thundered down the beach at 109.756 mph, but his record was declared unofficial because the car was found to be *over* the weight limit (which is unspecified in historical accounts). Arthur MacDonald took the official world record home to Britain, 104.651 mph in a Napier.

Ford, perhaps infected by the machinery-torturing driving

style of his former protégé Oldfield, blew the engine in his "666" racer and withdrew from the meet. Willie K., warned by his physicians that he had developed a heart condition—which they thought was likely caused by his speed obsession—was hardly a factor, and saw most of his records fall. Barney Oldfield never had a chance—America's first professional racing driver had opted for money over competitiveness, hiring out to drive an underpowered, 60-horsepower Peerless.

The Carnival of '05 was the greatest single assemblage of prominent motor racing figures in the world to that point. And yet they were all overshadowed, tragically, by one more wealthy sportsman. As Frank Croker, the twenty-seven-year-old son of wealthy New York political boss Richard Croker, charged down the course, a motorcyclist on the beach veered suddenly into his path. Croker's evasive swerve sent the Simplex rolling into the surf. He and his riding mechanic, Frenchman Alexander Raoul, became the first men ever killed racing at Daytona.

The singular place name Daytona, rather than Ormond-Daytona, is appropriate from here forward. For the '05 meet, one more building had been added—a clubhouse constructed by the hosting Florida East Coast Automobile Association, at the southern end of the course. Henceforth, thousands of stories, down through the decades, would begin with the dateline "DAYTONA BEACH, Fla. "

*W*ith Croker's death, the pioneering gentlemen drivers had seen and stomached enough. They finally understood that motor racing is not a game. By 1906 they were all following the precedent Winton had set in '04: They brought hirelings. Professional racing drivers. Front-wheel-drive proponent J. Walter Christie brought Switzerland's Louis Chevrolet. Fiat sent Italy's Vincenzo Lancia. Oldfield was America's best. But none of these was the best in the world. That distinction belonged to a man who was but a surname on the Hotel Ormond's register:

Hemery.

Controversy still swirls about the Frenchman, even regarding his given name. Most automobile historians call him Victor, others Auguste.

Hemery.

That's what matters.

Pronounced, Ah-meh-ree.

If Barney Oldfield was the Dale Earnhardt of his day, Hemery was the Michael Schumacher of his, with a lot of A. J. Foyt and Ayrton Senna stirred into the cauldron. Hemery was, apparently, the embodiment, the root, the essence of all arrogance, bluster, tempest, talent, and self-certainty in a thoroughbred professional driver.

Hemery is viewed by historical consensus—and almost certainly by his contemporaries—as an asshole. But so have the just-mentioned modern-day drivers been perceived, at least at one time or another—though in truth they simply suffered no fools nor foolishness. Laser focus, inherently, can have no tolerance.

On the warpath—temporarily banned from racing in his native France, fresh off a major flap with the Italian automobile club and another set-to at a Vanderbilt Cup event in New York—Hemery marched into the main entrance of the Ormond and scrawled his name, which in his mind ought to have been sufficient notice for all but the imbecilic, as the lead driver for the four-car French Darracq team. He was the current owner of the world speed record with a run in France at 109.65 mph before he was banished.

The question of overweight cars arose for the second straight year at Daytona—nowadays, even floor-sweepers on racing teams know that the heavier the mass, the more energy required to bring it to a high velocity—and that's what set off Hemery's foul temper. The notion that heavier was better likely had arisen for two reasons. One, understanding of aerodynamic downforce was virtually nil in those days, and so the only way to gain it was with brute weight. Second, on the hard-packed sand, many early drivers experienced tire slip at high speeds. More weight meant better traction.

Anyway, one of the Darracqs was declared overweight. Hemery withdrew all four, in protest of what he considered official absurdity. Not only might he have sensed what we know today—that lighter is better, assuming you can keep the car on the ground—but he realized that the officials had misinterpreted their own regulations. Officials later reread the rules, and with some minor adjustments the Darracq in question was declared legal. Hemery returned to race, but only briefly—and with the most storied tantrum in the first decade of beach racing.

At the starting line, Hemery in the 200-horsepower V-8 Darracq pulled alongside the low-slung, rear-engined Stanley Steamer—the design a forerunner of modern Formula One cars—driven by mild-mannered American Fred Marriott. The third car in the heat was a Fiat driven by H. W. Fletcher.

What happened next is a matter of interpretation. Hemery and Fletcher left Marriott at the starting line. Some witnesses wrote it off merely as a false start, and maintained Hemery was thrown out of the meet for unsportsmanlike conduct because he refused to engage in a restart. Others believed the reason Marriott's Steamer was left behind was that Hemery had intentionally pulled up in front of it, and, with an enormous blast of fiery exhaust from the powerful Darracq engine, tried to set the cedar-and-canvas body of the sleek little Steamer afire. The latter version, outrageous as it may seem, has some support in circumstantial evidence—manufacturers and advocates of gasoline-powered cars certainly had no love for the quiet, efficient, and marvelously fast little Steamers produced by the Stanley twins, Francis and Freelan.

Hemery was disqualified by officials, fired by his team,

and replaced on the spot by Louis Chevrolet. The Swiss-American, who would later sell his name to General Motors as a label for the popular line of passenger cars, teamed with Victor Demogeot to give Darracq three record runs in the Carnival.

Marriott, his Steamer undamaged by Hemery's outburst of temper and exhaust, went on to a new world speed record, 127.660 mph. Steaming too, though, were the ill-willed proponents of the gasoline engine. They weren't done with Marriott and the Stanley twins.

*F*red Marriott's crash occurred at somewhere between 150 and 197 mph, and the Stanley Steamer either barrel-rolled or became airborne before rolling into the surf, depending on which accounts you believe. But in 1907, with Fred Marriott wearing no seat belt and no head protection other than his hair and mustache and a pair of goggles, a barrel roll at 150 mph—which would have been another world record—qualified quite adequately as a horrific crash.

Incredibly, Marriott survived and recovered. He was found lying amidst part of the wreckage in the surf. One of his eyes had been jerked completely out of its socket. But a local doctor in the crowd put it back in, intact, with a spoon.

Gasoline proponents despised the steamers so much, for what they considered an unfair advantage in acceleration, that there was a dearth of gas-powered cars—something of a boycott—at the '07 Speed Carnival. Automotive reporters of the time joined in the disdain of the steamers. The writers were fairly conservative, and they likely had been wined, dined, and indoctrinated by the bigger, richer, gasoline-car companies.

After Marriott's crash, the gasoline-heads spread stories that the boiler had exploded, even causing damage to buildings in Ormond. Total falsehoods. Roundly, the steamers were written off as unsafe. To bring back the pouting gasoline-engine teams, rules were changed in their favor for the 1908 Winter Speed Carnival.

Francis E. Stanley, the techno-wizard of the twins, ceased racing after Marriott's crash. The brothers continued to sell production steamers until the 1920s, but without the developmental theater of racing, the cars died out entirely.

Gasoline engines ascended to dominance worldwide, and the rest is petroleum-addicted, ozone-damaged history. It cannot be said with certainty that quiet, efficient, simple-to-maintain steam cars, were they prevalent in the gridlocks of all the great cities of today, would have made the world any better. But it is fair to assume that they couldn't have made it any worse.

After the war over the steamers, all was ebb for the Speed Carnival. To preclude steamers and other nonconformist power sources—and to try to follow international trends—Morgan turned to distance-racing in 1908. Most races were 100 miles or more. Still, only nine cars competed. Interest in the beach eroded, and turned back toward Europe, where Hemery won the longest race in the world up to that time, from Paris to Moscow. The other craze that was sweeping the globe was the "aeroplane," and so Morgan hyped major air races on the beach in 1909. But only one plane showed, and it didn't fly.

Oldfield, by now a master showman, resuscitated the Winter Carnival in 1910 with a world record 131.723 mph in a "Lightning Benz," whose name Oldfield had Americanized from its actual German name, "Blitzen Benz." (This was not a Mercedes. Not until 1926 would the companies of Gottlieb Daimler and Karl Benz merge to form Daimler-Benz and produce Mercedes-Benz automobiles.) Oldfield chomped his trademark cigar and proclaimed, "A speed of 131 miles an hour is as near to the limit of speed as humanity will ever travel."

So ended William J. Morgan's lovely production. It had run for eight years, longer than most of the shows staged near his offices, at 1777 Broadway, New York. Oldfield's proclamation of a speed superlative was short-lived, for in 1911 another driver, Bob Burman, in the same car (its Blitzen moniker restored) ran almost exactly 10 mph faster, 141.732. But Burman's run was effectively a barnstorming stop at the beach. The Winter Speed Carnival was finished.

Up north, a short train ride out of Indianapolis as it existed then, Carl Fisher completed his revolutionary 2.5-mile rectangular track in 1909, christened it Indianapolis Motor Speedway, and began staging 100-mile races.

While Oldfield gave the Carnival its last gasps, Fisher was contemplating an entirely different type of race—not as outrageously long as Paris-Moscow, and yet a combination of distance and sustained high speed that would test automotive engineering to the fullest.

As Burman made his anticlimactic run in April of 1911, Russia was emerging from a winter of socialist uprisings, and the government stabilized under its kindly, inept czar, Nicholas II. That same spring, Kaiser Wilhelm II of Germany—who had telegraphed Oldfield congratulating him on his record run in 1910 in a German car—visited his cousin, King George V, in England, and the two assured the world that there would be perpetual peace between their nations. Britain's White Star Line commissioned construction of the world's grandest passenger ship, a veritable Hotel Ormond of the seas. It would be faster than any others designated RMS, or Royal Mail Ships. It would be christened *Titanic*. Not for nearly a year after Burman's run would *Titanic* embark on its maiden voyage, bound for New York.

And in Indianapolis, Carl Fisher had settled on the distance his new race would cover. Based on the earlier 100-

mile races, Fisher and his planners projected that a winning race car would average about 70 mph in a longer event. The distance should be determined by the number of daylight hours for racing, and for crowd ingress and egress. The track was out in the countryside. Passenger cars in those days had poor headlights. And many spectators still would come by horse-drawn vehicles. Spectators should be given enough daylight before and after the race to drive to the Speedway from their homes in surrounding areas, and then return home for dinner. At the very least, Fisher needed to clear his grounds of the crowd during daylight hours.

In the month of May, with days growing longer, Fisher figured his race could last for seven hours. Seven hours times 70 mph equals 490 miles. *Voilà!* Fisher would stage the world's first 490-mile race. His publicists suggested he round off the number to have a nicer ring. Could the race go ten more miles, to make it 500?

Indy would overshadow Daytona for decades to come. But on May 30, 1911, even as Ray Harroun averaged a blistering 74.602 mph to win the first "500-Mile Race," a toddler was just learning to talk in a middle-class household in Washington, D.C. He would grow into a way with words and an eye for promotion that even the Welshman Morgan would have admired. Born on September 26, 1909, the child was bestowed with a third given name, after a family of oil barons to whom he was not related. "Getty" was placed by his father as a talisman on the boy, to remind him always of his destiny of great accomplishments. His full name was William Henry Getty France.

4

SIR HENRY, SIR MALCOLM, AND THE PRODIGY

*M*ajor Henry O'Neal de Hane Segrave was a graduate of Eton and Sandhurst, a Royal Air Force veteran of the Great War, and winner of the French Grand Prix in 1923—for which he at least introduced, if he did not invent, the crash helmet.

Captain Malcolm Campbell was an adventurer of the first order, a London businessman, a millionaire many times over (not in mere dollars but in pounds sterling) from the diamond trade, real estate, and insurance. He lived on a suburban estate at Povey Cross, Surrey, where a dozen ferocious Alsatian dogs patrolled grounds that included a nine-hole golf course Campbell had designed himself.

The rivalry between Segrave and Campbell was enormous and bitter.

Frank Lockhart was raised an impoverished prodigy by a widowed mother in Los Angeles. Even with subsistence formal education, he was so brilliant at higher mathematics and engineering that he was accepted at Cal Tech—but he couldn't afford to go. The only rookie ever to win the Indianapolis 500, he was probably the best Indy car driver of all time. He would not live long enough to prove it.

The three of them, in the late 1920s, made the long, flat stretch of sand between Ormond and Ponce Inlet what old-timers still call it today: "The World's Most Famous Beach."

In March of 1927, radio was just emerging as a mass medium, Babe Ruth was still in spring training for what would be his sixty-home-run season, and Charles A. Lindbergh was in the planning stages of his nonstop solo flight from New York to Paris.

And so the world's hottest sporting and technological rivalry of the moment was between Segrave and Campbell. They never raced head-to-head, nor even in the same place at the same time. Each just read the headlines the other made. Their enormously expensive game of one-upsmanship in land speed records had begun on the Pendine Sands of Wales in 1924 and continued onto the beach at Southport, England. But when a third rival, Parry Thomas, was killed at Pendine early in 1927, the two surviving rivals began to look elsewhere. Britain's beaches were too confining for the rapidly advancing technology of power and aerodynamics.

Campbell began to focus on a dry lake bed in South Africa, and designed and built a 900-horsepower behemoth especially for that course, where he reckoned he could become the first man ever to travel at 200 miles per hour and thereby deliver the coup de grace in the rivalry with Segrave.

Meanwhile, Segrave set about such an elaborate maneuver of stealth, high technology, and daring that, when he sprang the immense scheme on Campbell and the world, he may well have won the admiration of a budding part-time writer in London—the nineteen-year-old Ian Fleming. Allowing for the technology of the day, Segrave's incredible covert raid on a speed milestone, and on Campbell's pride, was truly a job fit for James Bond.

Segrave had never seen the beach at Daytona. He had only read about it, and had heard a little from those who had raced there. Speed trials had resumed in 1919 with record runs by the charismatic driver Ralph De Palma, but Daytona really hadn't reemerged on the world map until Sig Haugdahl became the first man to hit 180 mph in 1922.

Secretly, with clandestine financial and technological support from the Sunbeam Motor Car Company Ltd. of Wolverhampton, England, Segrave prepared "Mystery S," a 1,000-horsepower monster tailored for a course he'd never laid eyes on. Fore and aft of the cockpit were V-12 aircraft engines of more than 1,300 cubic inches each. The car's aerodynamics were tested in a wind tunnel. Segrave's inner circle of engineers calculated that Mystery S was capable of 212 miles per hour on the beach beyond the Atlantic.

He quietly boarded an ocean liner in early March, with Mystery S crated and hidden in the hold. Not even the city fathers of Daytona Beach had any idea he was coming. Word finally leaked when he arrived at Jacksonville. As he began the ninety-mile drive south by passenger car, Daytona officials hurriedly checked hotel reservation lists. By the time Segrave arrived at his beachfront hotel, an ad hoc committee of dignitaries and reporters was there to meet him in the lobby.

There, he admitted the purpose of his visit: He intended to become the first man ever to travel at 200 miles per hour.

Over the ensuing week, the motor racing world came to him—and back to Daytona. Officials qualified to certify the record, and journalists to chronicle it, poured in.

By then, motor racing's world governing body, the Federation Internationale de l'Automobile in Paris, recognized only speed records that were run in two stages, in opposite directions, so that assists or impediments by wind would be negated. As virtually the entire population of the town poured onto the beach to watch—this was the first real crowd of commonfolk there—Segrave first whoosh-thundered north, against the wind, from Daytona toward Ormond. He stopped for a tire check, turned, headed south, even faster, and officials certified the average speed: 203.79 miles per hour.

He had beaten Campbell to 200.

But the game between Segrave and Campbell was not volatile; it was chesslike. Calmly, deliberately, determinedly, Campbell designed and built a new Bluebird, which he would take to Daytona in 1928.

*F*rank Lockhart had come off the dirt tracks of Southern California with nothing but his uncanny intellect, lightning eye-hand coordination, and enormous will. At age twenty-three, he drifted to Indianapolis in 1926 to watch the 500, and to hang around Gasoline Alley on the off chance of securing a ride. The dominant cars there at the time were designed and built by the automotive genius Harry Miller, whose tiny 90-cubic-inch engines were producing 300 horsepower. They had dethroned even the storied Duesenbergs, the powerful racers fielded by the company whose luxury road cars were the most desirable of the era, affordable only to tycoons and Hollywood stars. One of the eleven Miller drivers who had qualified at Indy that year, Peter Kreis, took ill and chose Lockhart as his replacement. With little practice, Lockhart started twentieth in a twenty-eight-car field. To the crowd's amazement—and to Harry Miller's—the unknown kid from California shot up through the field, took the lead after 150 miles, and went on to win a race that was shortened by rain to 400 miles. He was Indy's youngest, and most resounding, winner to that point.

But the marriage of the geniuses Lockhart and Miller was fitful. They squabbled over Lockhart's insistence on his own innovations to improve Miller's engines. Miller utilized superchargers to enhance combustion with compressed air. Lockhart invented an intercooler system to make the superchargers more reliable. Miller snubbed the upstart's idea, but the rest of the racing world soon welcomed the innovation. Lockhart bought a Miller, fitted it with his intercooler, and was running away with the 1927 race when a connecting rod broke in the motor—a failure unrelated to the intercooler—after 300 miles.

Still, his lap-leader bonuses, plus eighteenth-place money, added up to $11,000 for Lockhart. He had an idea what to do with it. But he needed much more money for his plan, which was to barge in on the speed-record dueling of the Englishmen Campbell and Segrave. He went to the Stutz company of Indianapolis, manufacturers of the high-performance road cars called Bearcats. His meteoric reputation as a driver and as a visionary if self-trained engineer got him additional funding from Stutz that was estimated as high as $50,000.

But Stutz was merely his sponsor. The engineering was all Lockhart, and it was so exotic that he blew his budget before he even got to Daytona.

When Malcolm Campbell arrived in Florida in February 1928 with his new Bluebird, fitted with a monstrous, 1,464-cubic-inch Napier aircraft engine, he was thinking only of beating Segrave's record. He hadn't counted on, but was immediately impressed with, the sleek, all-white Stutz Black Hawk Special, with each wheel shrouded individually by bodywork, and a tiny 182-cubic-inch engine in an unheard-of configuration—a V-16. Campbell immediately wanted to meet the marvelous engineer who'd wrought such a thing. He was introduced to the shy, boyish-looking Lockhart.

By now the cars were going so fast at Daytona that the beach surface had to be taken into account daily. Ripples in the sand, created by wave action, could be deadly. By February 19, Campbell had grown weary of waiting for nature to give him an ideal course, and set out on the rough sand anyway. His ride was harrowing, but he bounced and swerved to a record average of 206.96 mph.

Lockhart had to await Mother Ocean's pleasure. His car, far lighter than Campbell's, was much more sensitive to sand ripples. But his funds were waning fast. On February 22, in dense fog but with a reasonably smooth beach, he decided to go.

Down the beach, with the ultra-siren scream of sixteen cylinders through the thick mist at 225 miles an hour, Lockhart's Black Hawk came. Most witnesses thought it must have hit a ripple or a soft spot in the sand a millisecond before it began to flip end over end into the sea. Spectators rushed into the surf and found Lockhart still in the car, incredibly alive with only bruises and lacerations.

The car appeared irreparable, but Lockhart, still fearless and irrepressible, headed back to Indianapolis to rebuild the Black Hawk, working round the clock.

On April 25, the beautiful white Black Hawk was towed back onto the beach at dawn. The brilliant Lockhart was out of money. He had one more chance. Into the wind he went, up the beach, at nearly 200. A return, with the wind, surely would give him a world record average. But at the Ormond end, he decided not to change tires, as Campbell had advised him that he must after each run. Whether due to lack of money or to youthful impatience, the decision was fateful.

Witnesses believed that Lockhart was traveling faster than any man ever had when the banshee wail of the V-16 was interrupted by one shotgun-like blast—the explosion of the right rear tire. The Black Hawk shot sideways and barrel-rolled for a thousand feet, flinging Lockhart out onto the beach, dead.

*M*ajor Sir Henry O'Neal de Hane Segrave died one-up on Campbell—knighted first, by King George V, for becoming the first man to hold both land and water speed records. In 1929 he regained the land speed record with a run of 231.36 mph at Daytona, then went home to claim the water speed record later that year. Then on June 13, 1930, Segrave's speedboat, *Miss England,* hit a floating log at 86 knots, or 99 mph, on Lake Windermere in England, a moment after he'd improved on his water speed record. The boat disintegrated, and Segrave was killed.

Campbell would not rest. He would thrash Segrave in his grave. Time and again. That Segrave was dead hardly mattered—the Great Depression likely would have finished his efforts anyway. Segrave had always relied on corporate sponsorship. Campbell would have none of that. His private fortune remained intact, depression be damned.

In 1931, Campbell's latest Bluebird blistered the beach at 245.73 mph, and he at last would kneel and feel the flat of the sword of George V touch either shoulder. Knighthood. Arise, Sir Malcolm. His service to king and country in 1932 was 253.97 mph at Daytona.

By the time Campbell returned in 1933, the irony of his expensive adventures in depression-ridden Daytona Beach was not lost on the great journalist Henry McLemore, who would live to chronicle the advent of NASCAR for the United Press, later United Press International. McLemore learned in February of 1933 that Campbell was spending $100,000 of his own money to improve on his own world speed record at Daytona—this while local businesses were barely surviving, and previously affluent American men were streaming into Florida to pick citrus or shuck oysters for fifty cents a day.

Wrote McLemore from Daytona to the world, not so much in loathing as in wonder for the time, "Sir Malcolm has no backers, does not make his runs as an advertising stunt for any firm. When the mighty Bluebird roars down the beach it roars solely for the honor of Sir Malcolm and the Union Jack."

For king, country, and colors—but mainly for Campbell—Sir Malcolm ran a mile of sand at 272.108.

By 1935, Campbell and Daytona were wearing thin on each other. He had to steer out of a broadslide at 275 mph. Then he clocked a one-mile leg at 330, but to make it official, he had to make a return run.

He nearly lost control again at over 300. He barely recovered.

Enough.

Ab Jenkins, then mayor of Salt Lake City, had made it a point to visit Daytona regularly, befriend Sir Malcolm, and advise him of an even less confining place to run, in the Utah desert.

It was called the Bonneville Salt Flats.

After his harrowing experiences in 1935, Campbell finally decided he would take Jenkins up on the invitation.

The World's Most Famous Beach, it surely seemed, would now be left to the surf, sandpipers, gulls, and strolling tourists. The lovely speed trials were no more.

On the beach, watching Campbell's scary slides in '35, was a wide-eyed spectator not quite twenty-six years old, who would have been but a face in the crowd if not for his height—six feet five inches.

It was the full-grown William Henry Getty France.

5

BILL AND ANNIE
AND THE OUTLAWS

*T*he most important romance in the history of Daytona—
indeed, in the history of American motor racing—
lasted sixty-two years and then was immortalized in bronze.
It began at a charity dance in Washington, D.C., in 1930.

Anne Bledsoe was a nurse from Nathan's Creek, North
Carolina, who had moved to Washington to work. Bill
France, at six feet five, was a commanding presence in any
room. He was a native city boy, preoccupied with venturing
out to the Maryland suburbs to race, and to support his passion he worked as a bank teller, mechanic, messenger, whatever. He had begun by sneaking his father's Model T out to
Laurel, to one of the board tracks typical across America at
the time. (Big Bill France would chuckle often, for the rest of
his life, recalling how bewildered his father was that the tires
kept wearing out so fast.) Then he and a friend had built, of
wood and canvas and an old Ford engine, a racer of sorts that
Bill drove on the dirt track at Pikesville.

Bill was a dreamer with an urge to drift. Anne, though de-
lightfully sweet and personable, was a pragmatist. She would
follow Bill's dreams, but would keep them orderly and real-

istic. (There is a reason the bronze statue of Big Bill outside Daytona International Speedway today does not stand alone, but has an arm draped around the shoulders of "Annie B.," as she would come to be known, a term of endearment to most, but intimidation to some. Annie B. suffered no fools nor foolishness.)

*A*s Bill courted Anne in Washington, a sixteen-year-old runaway from the moonshine country of north Georgia arrived on the streets of Atlanta, alone, looking for some way to survive the gathering depression. He would start by running moonshine. He would build an empire in bonded whiskey, slot machines, jukeboxes, and vending machines. His name was Raymond Parks. (Not long before the turn of the 21st century, when he was well into his eighties but still looking sixty, he would be asked how he made the money to run the first great stock car racing team. He would chuckle deeply without smiling, and say, "Any way I could get it.")

*B*ill and Anne were married on June 23, 1931. Bill managed a gas station near the Potomac and, with Anne's indulgence, campaigned his little open-wheel, canvas-bodied car on the area's dirt tracks.

Two factors in racing bothered him enormously.

One was the dishonesty of race promoters. One night at Pikesville, the public-address system heralded the start of a race that would pay the enormous sum of five hundred dollars to win. France in his little homemade car finished third. He received ten dollars. He went to the promoter to argue about the huge dropoff in pay between first and third. The promoter told him the five-hundred-dollar talk had just been hype for the crowd, and that the winner had actually received only fifty dollars.

France's other beef was that motor racing was a rich man's sport, beyond the common man either as competitor (you couldn't expect to win unless you could buy a Miller or a Duesenberg for up to $20,000) or spectator (who in the grandstands could identify with these exotic, terribly expensive cars that they could never own?).

Bill France dreamed that if he ever got control of a race track, he would (a) run it on the up-and-up, and (b) make racing reachable for the commonfolk.

Herbert Hoover's Washington was a less than pleasant place as the nation's population grew desperate under his passive economic policies. World War I veterans set up a shantytown and became the "Bonus Army," demanding early payment of cash bonuses for their military service, until Army Chief of Staff Douglas MacArthur sent in regular troops to destroy the camps and throw the veterans out of town. In 1933, Franklin D. Roosevelt's radical—for the time—new government began gradually to turn the economy around, but hard times had set in for years to come.

At least, Bill France figured in the fall of 1934, it was not necessary to freeze to death while working as a mechanic. In November, with twenty-five dollars in his pocket, towing a small house trailer behind a Hupmobile, Bill, Anne, and their toddler son William Clifton—"Billy"—headed south, bound, they thought, for Miami.

*T*hey passed through the Carolinas and Georgia on U.S. Highway 1, bypassing the Blue Ridge mountain country altogether, far to the east of the Whiskey Trail. That storied road, which was officially designated as Georgia State Highway 9, ran from the mountain town of Dahlonega south to Atlanta. Along it at night roamed the greatest driver Bill France would ever see.

Not yet fifteen years old, still too young to get a driver's license, Lloyd Seay was already an accomplished "tripper," or moonshine runner. In the code language of bootleggers, a run was called a "trip." Just south of the hotbed hamlet of Dawsonville, the central loading point for the outlaw distillers, the Whiskey Trail was "hot with law—ever' night," a retired tripper would recall in the 1990s. "Sometimes Lloyd would swing out west and come down to Atlanta from Marietta. Sometimes he'd swing east and come down from Gainesville. Most nights he came right down the gut. They never caught him. Never. Oh, he had to jump off [tripper jargon for abandoning] a car one night, down behind the Fox Theatre in Atlanta. But he run off. They didn't get him."

Seay never bothered to drive with both hands. The right was sufficient, gripping the steering wheel at the bottom so that he could swing it all the way around in one motion. The left arm he casually propped in the driver's-side window.

Seay, the fourteen-year-old maestro, was already mentoring his thirteen-year-old cousin, Roy Hall. Across the Blue Ridge, in North Carolina, the moonshine-running legend-to-be, Robert Glenn "Junior" Johnson, was a three-year-old, playing on crates of fruit jars filled with liquor.

Ninety miles south of Jacksonville on U.S. 1, Bill France felt a kind of compulsion. He knew that just to the east lay the World's Most Famous Beach. Automobile repair was his trade, but automobile racing was his passion. All that history. All those titans of speed. He couldn't help himself. He told Anne he was going to turn left, onto Granada Avenue, toward the beach. She humored his dreaming, as usual.

Across the Ormond Bridge the Hupmobile puttered, past the old Hotel Ormond on the left, across the peninsula to the sea. Without realizing it, William H. G. France drove onto the beach at precisely the spot where William J. Morgan had first walked onto the sand with hotelmen John Anderson and

J. P. Price in 1903. France turned right and drove south on the beach, past the spot where Frank Lockhart had died, gliding down at 10 miles an hour over the sand that Segrave had traversed at 200.

Here. Yes. Of course. Bill France would drift no farther.

Down through the years and even now, the legend would persist that France's car broke down and he had no choice but to stop in Daytona Beach. "Hell, I was a mechanic," he would tell a young sportswriter decades later, in a plush office. "If my car had broken down, I would have fixed it."

He got a job in the service department of the local Cadillac dealership, and Anne found a house they could rent for $13.50 a month. Off duty, in the evenings, he would drive the beach, feel out the sand for traction, try to feel it as Winton and Oldfield and Hemery and Segrave and Campbell had felt it. Indeed, Sir Malcolm was to return in '35 for another record attempt. Bill France meant to see that.

When Sir Malcolm left, Daytona seemed finished. If he wouldn't race there, then who else could afford to? The depression only seemed to worsen with the years. The city struggled to conceive of some sort of beach race that would salve its devastated economy. Sig Haugdahl, the record setter of 1922, had settled in Daytona and opened a garage. City fathers asked the most prominent racer in town for advice. Haugdahl came up with an idea for a road race, along a new course that would include a stretch of beach and a length of the peninsula highway, U.S. A1A. It would be for the type of automobiles anyone could buy from the showroom.

France of course would enter the race as a driver, in a '35 Ford with a newly introduced production engine, the V-8. But more and more, he found himself involved with Haugdahl in planning the race.

France just had this feeling, this really strong hunch, that common people, who wouldn't turn out to see custom-built race cars, would be much more interested in seeing a race among the very same type of cars they could buy, and work on, themselves. They could relate. They could identify.

The race, 250 miles, was scheduled for February of 1936, and would be managed by the city. It was mismanaged. The city lost $22,000, a devastating sum at the depths of the depression. Even with a large field of the relatively cheap cars, and national press coverage, the scheme to jump-start the local economy had backfired. The city would have no more of it.

*B*y 1936, Raymond Parks had built enough of a bankroll to get out of the moonshine business. He entered more legitimate enterprises—one exception being the very fine slot machines he would place in various private clubs throughout Atlanta.

Central to Atlanta's netherworld was Red Vogt's garage, where ordinary cars off the showroom floor were modified, transformed into the fastest whiskey-running cars in America. Mechanic Red Vogt, the first maestro of high performance, plied the moonshine trade from both ends—he also souped up cars for law enforcement. (The trippers had more cash to pay for his innovations than did the government people entrusted with taxpayers' money. So guess which side got Vogt's best stuff?)

It was an interesting crowd that hung out at Red Vogt's place. Raymond Parks stopped by often (although, he would maintain years later, not to purchase any whiskey-hauling hardware, mind you). The place was usually crawling with trippers from up in the mountains. And cops. And federal agents. Red's place was sort of neutral ground, sort of the Switzerland of moonshine running and moonshine chasing.

* * *

*F*rance and Haugdahl convinced the Elks Club to stage the race in 1937. It wasn't as big a financial disaster as '36, but it was enough to send the Elks back to the humbler but more reliable bingo and chicken supper fund-raisers.

By 1938, France was out of civic-minded locals. Haugdahl had gone back to running his garage. A big-time race promoter from Pennsylvania, Ralph Hankinson, had moved to Orange City Beach, down the coast. Maybe he'd help France. The call was long-distance from a Daytona Beach phone booth. The toll was a quarter. France didn't have a quarter. He called collect. Hankinson wouldn't accept the charges.

France decided to promote the race himself. He made a local call to restaurant owner Charlie Reese.

"We promoted the 1938 races ourselves," Big Bill would say decades later. "On race day, Charlie sold tickets and I was one of the competitors." They charged fifty cents per spectator and made two hundred dollars.

They scheduled a second race that year, for Labor Day. They doubled the admission price to a dollar, got just as big a crowd—about 5,000—and made $2,200.

A living could be made in the race promotion business— but it could be a headache. After local bar owner Smokey Purser won the race, he kept right on driving, away from the course. France was by now fanatical about his "strictly stock" concept, and he reckoned Purser had something on that Ford that wasn't stock. France gathered a sort of ad hoc posse and began scouring the town for Purser and the cheater Ford. They found him at a local garage, hurrying to replace the cylinder heads. He'd used "Denver heads," made especially for high-altitude performance out West, and clearly an unfair advantage in the far denser air of Daytona.

They disqualified Purser, and then realized they were in even deeper trouble. The second-place finisher had been Bill

France. If the promoter of the race, who'd also driven and finished second, disqualified the winner and claimed the winner's purse, there would be an outcry. France did credit himself with the win, but the winner's share of the purse went to Lloyd Moody, who'd actually finished third.

Quietly, without advertising it to the public, Bill France backed off his "strictly stock" notion. The main point was that everything should *look* stock. Modifications such as Purser's would be allowed in 1939.

France was a bona fide frontrunner in the first race of '39, dueling with a rakish rooster of a man named Joe Littlejohn from Spartanburg, South Carolina, until France's pit crew shorted him on gasoline and the cocky Littlejohn flipped his car, leaving the victory to Sam Rice in a brand new, strictly stock (looking) '39 Mercury.

*B*y 1939 Raymond Parks had not only survived the depression, he had prospered in it. Around Red Vogt's garage, he ran into a Dawsonville whiskey tripper named Roy Hall. One thing led to another, and Hall introduced Parks to his cousin, Lloyd Seay. So they stood around talking, kicking tires, propping their feet on fenders, and the subject of racing came up.

Word was that Lakewood Speedway down in south Atlanta was going to try something new. Lakewood was at the time considered the Indy of the South—it was only a one-mile dirt track, but, located in the region's most prosperous city, it was a regular stop each summer for the "Big Cars," as Indy cars were then called, as they toured out of Indianapolis after the 500.

But this year, Lakewood was going to host a "stock car" race. Stock. Yeah. Sure. Everybody knew what "stock" meant in Georgia. Red Vogt had been building the best "stock" cars anywhere, for years. He just *adjusted* them a little, that was all. A special carburetor here, a set of high-swirl cylinder heads there—who would know the difference?

And they'd been racing in dark pastures and fields for several years. The moonshine kingpins would hang around Red's place bragging about who owned the fastest cars and employed the best trippers, and one thing would lead to another, and the bets would be laid, and off they'd go to some pasture in the wee hours to settle the arguments.

The way Hall and Seay saw it, "stock car racing" was just polite parlor talk for liquor-car racing. And, Godamighty knew, if you'd had to outrun "revenuers" (federal agents) at 120 miles an hour in a '39 Ford coupe with "a load on"—180 gallons of moonshine aboard—down the serpentine Whiskey Trail, you could handle any race track. As Junior Johnson would describe the thrill of whiskey tripping over organized racing decades later, "It was a race to win or go to prison—and that got a lot more exciting than beating some other race driver ever would."

Now if some of these dandies from around town wanted to show up at Lakewood with "stock" cars, that was their business. Hall and Seay reckoned that with their experience, plus a few, uh, mechanical adjustments from Red, they would have the Lakewood situation in hand. But of course these adjustments cost money. A lot of money.

Just how much money Raymond Parks spent on the first great stock car racing team was unknown even to him. "I have no idea," he once said. "No records were kept. We paid for everything in cash."

Lakewood Speedway's promoters knew exactly what they were doing. They were bringing in the wild bootleggers and whiskey trippers from the Blue Ridge highlands, undercover. So that the preachers of the city wouldn't rail against the outlaws, Lakewood called them "stock car racers."

Lakewood held two stock car races in 1939. Seay won one, Hall the other. "We sho' '*nuf* got the fever then," Parks would recall of the year he turned twenty-five. Seay was nineteen. Hall was eighteen.

*B*ill France's beach-road course promotions were going all right. He was making a living. He didn't know exactly how, and didn't really care. He wasn't one for numbers and book-keeping. That was Anne's forte. Bill had the dreams. Anne managed them.

But France's races hadn't found their character, their charisma, their taste-of-sin appeal. They were not the stuff of folklore.

Not yet.

First must come the outlaws to the beach.

6

WHAT MIGHT HAVE BEEN

When Big Bill France was old and rich and famous and ineffably powerful, after he had made Lee and Richard Petty famous, and Fireball Roberts, and Little Joe Weatherly, and Curtis Turner and Junior Johnson and David Pearson and Fred Lorenzen and Cale Yarborough and Bobby Allison and Darrell Waltrip, he was asked to name the best he'd ever seen. He did not hesitate. "Fella from up in Georgia," he said. "He would come through the North Turn of the old beach course on only his right-side wheels, with both left-side wheels up in the air, so that the car always looked as if it was going to turn over. I've never seen anything like that, before or since. Fella by the name of Lloyd Seay."

The north Georgia mountains are rife with Seays. In Dawson County they still pronounce it "See." In neighboring Forsyth County, the Seays who want none of the bootlegging legacy pronounce it "Say."

From a photograph encased in glass, set in a weathered tombstone in the often overgrown town cemetery of Dawsonville, Lloyd Seay smiles, forever young, forever at the brink of greatness.

The picture, as clear and fresh as if it had been placed there yesterday, is embedded in a bas-relief of a 1939 Ford coupe on the stone. Beneath the image of the car is the image of a trophy, inscribed, "Winner, National Stock Car Championship, Sept. 1, 1941." And just to the right is the date of his death: "Sept. 2, 1941."

In those years when Bill France was only formulating the idea of organizing stock car racing at a national level, record-keeping was poor. But in Seay's obituary, the *Atlanta Journal* reckoned that "he had driven in about 30 races, winning well over half of them."

He didn't die in a race car. He was shot through the heart with a .32 Smith & Wesson revolver whipped out of the bib overalls of Woodrow Anderson in a bootleggers' quarrel. At the seasoned, savvy, jaded age of twenty-one, "Lloyd was dead when he hit the ground," according to the last living witness to his murder, Clint Chastain. "I was in the house. I saw Woodrow, Lloyd, and Jim [Lloyd's brother] all talking out there at the well. First thing I knowed, Woodrow just shot the hell out of both of 'em."

Roy Hall never was right after that, as they say in the South. Trying to burn out the sorrow, he went on a wild rampage, did prison time, suffered a bad head injury soon after his release, sat and stared at the passing of half a century, and died in a nursing home in 1991.

How devastated was the fledgling sport of stock car racing?

No one will ever know.

Probably terribly.

Had Lloyd Seay lived, and Roy Hall lived even halfway right, NASCAR might have been far bigger, far earlier. The thing about Seay and Hall and even team owner Parks was that they didn't look at all like the stereotypes of Appalachian mountain boys. They were all dashing, and drop-dead handsome. Put them in the newsreels, and they might have been idols before Frank Sinatra, Elvis, or the Beatles.

Parks brought an entirely new concept to rough-and-tumble liquor-car racing: Class. He was repulsed by the battered, junky-looking machinery he saw at the dirt tracks. He issued a standing order to Red Vogt: All of his cars were to be immaculate—every dent and nick repaired, and a fresh, gleaming paint job, after every race.

I heard Lloyd say he could take a '39 Ford coupe and climb a pine tree," Clint Chastain would recall. "I wouldn't doubt it."

Highway 9, wider now and more smoothly paved than when the trippers ran it, is still a series of switchback curves over and around rolling foothills. The road is particularly precarious over the nineteen miles immediately south of Dawsonville, down to the town of Cumming. That was the stretch that was "hot with law," according to the retired tripper. Now, even in a modern German road car with computerized brakes, high-tech suspension, and high-performance tires, anything over 75 mph on that road is enough to take one's breath away. If you've ever driven that stretch, then the idea of Lloyd Seay heading south at 130 or 140 mph in a souped-up but primitive '39 Ford, with 180 gallons aboard and the law in hot pursuit, is almost impossible to comprehend.

Down through the decades, retired federal, state, and local lawmen would embellish their own memories, claiming to have caught Seay. But none of them dared lie so outrageously as to claim they'd run Seay down—they claimed to have shot out his tires. That never happened either, as Clint Chastain would recollect: "They never got close enough to Lloyd to shoot out his tires."

One legend told and retold in Atlanta even today is that one night, Seay was speeding north from downtown, bound for Dawsonville to pick up a load, when he was stopped by the state police—for speeding only, since there was no liquor on board. Seay supposedly handed the trooper two ten-dollar bills, and the officer said that was too much, that the fine was only ten dollars. Seay supposedly said the second ten was in advance for later—"I'm gonna be in an awful big hurry when I come back through here headed in the other direction."

Cute story. But here's the way the law and Lloyd Seay usually dealt with each other, according to Clint Chastain, who was there:

"One night I was riding back from Atlanta with Lloyd in that maroon '41 Ford convertible of his [Seay's personal car at the time of his death]," Chastain would remember. "He was running about 120 miles an hour, and we met the state patrol coming the other way. They didn't even turn around to try to come after us. They knowed there wasn't no use. They knowed who it was."

*W*hat Bill France the promoter wanted most on the beach in 1940 was Raymond Parks's kind of class—Parks would even lend his new '40 Cadillac, his personal car and the snazziest machine in Daytona Beach that March, to France to use for show as the "pace car."

What Bill France the driver wanted most was a piece of Roy Hall. France had found himself in several duels with Hall around the South in the summer and fall of '39, and had lost every one. Hall was coming to France's home turf— rather, home sand. "If I can't beat him here," France told the local papers, "I never will."

He couldn't. And he wouldn't.

Parks obliged France by entering Hall, but not Seay. Hall was plenty. Hall blew into town not only as France the driver's challenge, but as France the promoter's dream—the rakish, fearless outlaw. Hall would have to return to Georgia to face several federal and local moonshine-running charges, and his driver's license had been suspended.

Hall won a sand-slinging duel, not with France, but with Joe Littlejohn. Sportswriters present were not only amazed at Hall's driving, but at the clockwork quickness of his pit crew—it was as if they'd been synchronized with intensive pre-race training. (There again, Raymond Parks was half a century ahead of his time.) The feisty Littlejohn held on for second place, Bob "Cannonball" Baker was third, and France fourth.

The drop-dead-handsome Hall lit a cigarette and basked in the attention of the media. He would not be able to return to Daytona for the other two races of 1940—a Georgia state prison cell awaited his occupancy on a moonshining charge. Reporters asked if he would be back in '41.

"Sure," he said. "If I'm still alive."

And there it was.

The mystique, the charisma, the taste of sin for Everyman.

Bill France had his magic. Daytona had a whole new meaning.

*H*all survived a little prison time and a lot of outlaw lifestyle, and returned in '41, and won, of course. Seay came with him and dominated most of the race, but he was just learning traction on the sand, and on the thirty-ninth lap as he came through the North Turn with the car turned up high on its right-side wheels, driving with his right hand while his left arm lay in the driver's-side window, he finally miscalculated. The car barrel-rolled off the course. He returned, flipped again, came back again, still finished seventh.

"The Racing Team," as they called themselves, coining a term in stock car racing, was formed. That spring and summer of '41, Parks and Seay and Hall traveled the country, "wide open, all the time," Parks would recall—as fast as

Parks's brand-new '41 Cadillac would carry them from town to town, state to state, with either Seay or Hall chauffeuring, right foot always to the floor, with Parks so confident in his drivers that he nearly always dozed at 100 miles an hour–plus on the two-lane highways. It was left entirely to Vogt to make the race cars themselves immaculate and fast, and get them to the tracks on time.

In Lloyd Seay's time, just about everybody in north Georgia was at least distantly related to just about everybody else. For example, Parks on one side of his family was a distant cousin of Seay; on the other side of his family he was a distant cousin of Hall; Seay and Hall were cousins to each other, but not in the same way they were cousins with Parks. And so it went in the isolated society of the southern highlands.

Another of Seay's cousins, in another way, was Woodrow Anderson. In 1941, at the age of twenty-nine, Anderson was already a big-time moonshine distiller with a police record. Seay, as Anderson's ace tripper, got a percentage of the action—but also had to pay a share of the cost of the ingredients. Anderson watched those costs closely. That summer, while Seay was away racing, Anderson convinced himself that Seay hadn't paid his rightful part of the price of a load of sugar, the final ingredient added to corn or rye mash before distilling.

On August 24, at Daytona, Seay set out on the most meteoric winning streak stock car racing had ever known. He won three major races in nine days. And then he was gone.

He began with a spectacular win on the beach. Rain had prevented any time trials, so drivers drew for starting positions. Seay drew the fifteenth spot. But he had the beach course figured out by now, had that breathtaking style, of roaring through the North Turn with the Ford turned up high on its right wheels, down pat. He flashed past fourteen cars to lead the very first lap. As Seay pulled away, Hall literally drove his car to death, and retired it with a broken frame. Seay led every one of the fifty laps.

Then, up the coastline Parks's Cadillac flew, taking the trio to High Point, North Carolina, for the next race, on August 31. Seay won easily. The Caddy hurtled back toward Georgia through that night—their normal cruising speed was 120, whether they were in a hurry or not. This time they had to go. The next day was Labor Day, time for the climactic National Stock Car Championship race at Atlanta's Lakewood Speedway.

On a farm just north of Dawsonville, Woodrow Anderson, with pencil and paper, calculated and recalculated what he reckoned Lloyd owed him.

For reasons no one—not even Parks—would remember to this day, Seay changed the number on his Ford from his usual 7 to the more ominous 13 for the race at Lakewood on Labor Day. Soon after the green flag dropped, he found himself in a four-way dogfight for the lead that included another moonshiner, Bob Flock. But Number 13 broke away and went on to dominate and win.

Nine days. Three wins. No one had ever seen the likes of Lloyd Seay, and he was the toast of Atlanta. Then, in that maroon convertible of his, he headed north toward home, wide open, at 120 miles an hour, with its six forward-mounted lights (two spotlights and two huge fog lamps in addition to the two headlights) burning down the Georgia darkness.

*E*arly the next morning he was awakened in his bed at home by Woodrow Anderson, shaking him. Then Anderson rousted Lloyd's brother Garnett, known as Jim. Anderson demanded that they "go settle up." He meant the money he thought Seay owed him for a load of sugar, several tons, recently purchased for the moonshine operation.

"They were arguing over a nickel a bag," according to the late George Elliott, father of modern-day NASCAR driver Bill Elliott, and a lifelong Dawsonville resident who knew Lloyd Seay.

How many bags at a nickel a bag? That takes some calculation.

"A fair-sized still would run off about 250 gallons of whiskey a day," according to an anonymous former bootlegger in Dawson County. "You got ten gallons of whiskey for every hundred-pound bag of sugar." So such a still would consume 2,500 pounds of sugar a day, or 17,500 pounds a week.

If the dispute involved a week's worth of sugar, 175 bags, at five cents a bag, then the fight was over $8.75—an especially paltry sum, considering that a week's liquor production, 1,750 gallons at the going price of eighty-five cents a gallon, would have grossed nearly $1,500. And it is likely that Seay had at least $225, his half of the previous day's winnings at Lakewood, in his pocket.

All of this at a time when the average Georgia workingman earned about forty cents an hour.

Woodrow demanded that they all go see "Aunt Monnie" Anderson, a relative they all trusted, to let her do the figuring. But on the way, he decided to stop at the home of his father, Grover Anderson—ostensibly so that he could fill his car's radiator from the well.

"Lloyd was the coolest feller you ever seen," Clint Chastain would recall, "at ever' damn thing he ever went at." So cool that Chastain didn't even know there was trouble until he heard the gunshots.

Jim Seay was shot first, in the neck, but survived. Lloyd, shot in the chest, died instantly, and Chastain "was scared heartless. I stayed in the house, by God. I stayed out of their argument. Didn't have nothin' to say in it. The law was there in a little while. They even took me and locked me up at first, as an eyewitness."

Woodrow Anderson would later claim that the Seays attacked him, and that he had to run into the house to get his father's .32 Smith & Wesson revolver. Jim Seay would testify that Anderson was the attacker, and that he had pulled the gun from his bib overalls.

A jury would later agree with the Seay side of the story, supported by Chastain, and sentence Woodrow Anderson to life in prison.

*E*ven as Lloyd Seay fell, the Japanese naval genius Isoroku Yamamoto was planning the catastrophic bombing of Pearl Harbor. It would happen in just over three months. And America's entry into World War II would shut down stock car racing in its infancy.

Parks quietly commissioned Seay's magnificent tombstone, then went off to enlist. With the First Army, he would spend the most awful winter of his life in a foxhole in a relentless blizzard somewhere in Belgium, and then learn later that the whole ordeal had been called the Battle of the Bulge.

Bill France realized that racing at Daytona was a hopeless proposition when food containers and other refuse bearing labels in German began washing up on the beach. Clearly, U-boats were lurking just offshore, and their captains would be delighted to surface and shell any large crowds of American civilians. France spent the war as a foreman at the Daytona Beach Boat Works, which was involved in the locally relevant endeavor of building submarine chasers.

Roy Hall rode out the war in the Georgia mountains, running 'shine, which was in more demand than ever, what with the military installations of Georgia and South Carolina becoming packed with enlisted men who wanted whiskey but could hardly afford the bonded stuff.

* * *

*R*aymond Parks came home to even more opportunity than he'd found during the depression, and immediately began buying prime Atlanta property to build liquor stores—maybe he'd just take another crack at his sporting passion. With the end of the war, France immediately set about planning the revival of his beloved stock car racing.

In October of 1945, barely two months after the atomic bombing of Hiroshima, France went to Charlotte, North Carolina, to promote a "national championship race" on the half-mile dirt track in Charlotte's fairgrounds. *Charlotte Observer* sports editor Wilton Garrison told France that from the looks of the field—Roy Hall of Georgia was about the most exotic name in it—the race could hardly be rated "national championship" caliber.

The days of hucksterism and empty hype were over. France needed to come up with a system for a real national championship. He asked the American Automobile Association, the longtime sanctioning organization for the Indianapolis 500, for help. The AAA snubbed him and what it treated as his redneck jalopy sport.

Again, France would do it himself. For 1946, he created the "National Championship Series." And for a fleeting few days in June, at Daytona, Roy Hall would be his star again.

But Roy was acting crazy—or, at least, crazier than usual—when he tore into town in the predawn hours, three days before the race. You know those "doughnut" tire marks that drivers of the 1990s liked to leave on their way to Victory Lane? Roy Hall was cutting doughnuts in downtown Daytona Beach, just for the hell of it, at four in the A.M. on June 27, 1946, and was promptly taken to jail for it, charged with reckless driving.

"It was almost," historian Greg Fielden would write, "like he wanted to get caught this time."

The war was over and people acted happy all around, but

Lloyd Seay was dead and Roy Hall was adrift, an early manifestation of the "Beat Generation" that the writer Jack Kerouac would soon spawn and describe. Before Kerouac took a trip *On the Road* with the wild Neal Cassady, and turned him into the fictional character Dean Moriarty, Roy Hall rolled into Daytona looking and acting *beat,* numb to authority, casually defiant. It was the same syndrome Kerouac would notice in young men on the streets of post–World War II America—they already felt whipped, done, finished, wild with hopelessness. Beat.

Hall got out of jail in time to win Bill France's race—led it start to finish—at Daytona on June 30, 1946.

And then Roy Hall went on the road. Turned out he'd been involved in a bank robbery in Jefferson, Georgia, the previous January. Details are few and murky—Hall's exploits were barely noted even at the time. But next up the road, in August, in Greensboro, North Carolina, a gun battle with police just happened to break out at the hotel where he was staying, and he was hauled in, charged with aiding the escape of a criminal—which could have been one of any number of Roy's acquaintances, considering how good-hearted he was when it came to friends in need. Because the Georgia authorities wanted Hall more than even the North Carolina authorities did, he was extradited and did three more years in the Georgia state pen, for the Jefferson bank robbery.

Hall would return to racing immediately after his release from prison in 1949, but that September, at High Point, North Carolina, his car would flip end over end, crushing the roof in on him, leaving him with severe head injuries and ending his career—as a racer and a hell-raiser—at age twenty-eight.

And so Bill France, still laying the foundation of a unified league for stock car racing, was without his charismatic cornerstones, Hall and Seay. There were other outlaws. But none with quite the dash and swagger.

7

SEIZING
THE DREAM

*I*t is said that at the moment Napoleon Bonaparte was about to be crowned emperor of France, he snatched the crown from the hands of an archbishop and placed it upon his own head. No less swiftly but far more subtly did Big Bill France assume, for himself and for his heirs for generations to come, absolute power over an entire sport and its future.

When he took control, on Sunday afternoon, December 14, 1947, it was almost sleight of hand. He began with a speech to twenty-five men assembled around some tables pushed end-to-end in the Ebony Bar of the Streamline Hotel in Daytona Beach.

Whenever Big Bill made a speech, he would somehow sing his words, in a sort of Gregorian chant, musical in such a soothing way that it was boring until you thought about it later. In pre-race ceremonies for Daytona 500s in the 1970s he would croon through his list of distinguished guests, "The hon'rable am-BAS-sador from EC-uador..." And you wouldn't care in the least at the moment. But somehow his words had a way of lingering in the back of your mind, so that hours or days or weeks later it would dawn on you just how important such-and-such a Saudi sheik was, to, say, keeping motor racing well-supplied with gasoline while the sport was under fire during petroleum shortages.

And so he must have seemed innocuous enough to the assembled kingpins of the far-flung realms of early stock car racing as they sipped their highballs, played with their packs of Camels and Luckies, and drummed their fingers on the tables, half-listening to France drone on and on.

And yet the power of purpose in his words resonates to this day, in a speech whose text survives in several history books.

He complained that "an average man in a fast automobile can still win races." He chose, as an example, a fair-to-middlin' driver in an expensive Indy car who'd been able to run away from "a boy in a cheap Ford" back on the board track at Laurel, Maryland. Triumph of wallet over talent must cease, he maintained, if automobile racing were to capture the fancy of Everyman as competitor, and Everyman as fan. The race cars themselves must be affordable and therefore simple, so that the person, not the machinery, would stand out. And of course, the closer to showroom variety, "stock," the car was, the more the fans could relate.

"We don't know how big stock car racing can be—I doubt if anybody here knows that," he said. "But I do know that if stock car racing is handled properly, it can go the way Big Car [Indy car] racing has gone…And if you have an event where you can publicize talent, then there is much better cooperation from the newspapers."

Having seen how classy Raymond Parks could make stock cars look, France addressed image. "Even if you take a new Cadillac and pull the fenders off and let it get real dirty, it would still be a jalopy to most people," he told the kingpins. One of the first rules of the organization that was beginning to take shape that afternoon in '47 would begin, "All cars must be brightly painted…"

These men present at the Streamline must all unify, under uniform rules, nationwide, with a bona fide national championship points system. The reasons why they must were articulated by Big Bill in a mantra that his son, Bill France Jr., would repeat often, almost verbatim, as the sport boomed through the 1990s and the second czar in the France dynasty further consolidated power by gobbling up ownership of most of America's best race tracks: "Nothing stands still in the world. Things get better or worse, bigger or smaller."

Throughout December 15 and 16, eight other stock car racing kingpins would arrive in Daytona Beach. By the time the meetings broke up on December 17, the total attendance had been thirty-four men. But through the decades since, if you counted all those who *claimed* to have been there, the number would have been in the hundreds.

France was in control, largely by a path that would not be articulated until Peter Uberroth became czar of the 1984 Los Angeles Olympics: "Authority is fifteen percent given and eighty-five percent taken." So the other kingpins gave France the floor, and he took total control.

France knew what he was going to do before he ever walked through the door of the Ebony Bar. He and right-hand man Bill Tuthill had studied all previous racing associations in the United States, and had determined that democracy didn't work. Ruling boards were also bound to fail. There were too many complexities about automobile racing, and therefore there was too much fertile ground for dissent.

This had to be an absolute monarchy. But it had to be achieved with a legerdemain unprecedented in sports. All the assembled kingpins had their own interests, wanted their cuts of the action. As the meetings progressed, one of them demanded a constitution for the organization, a set of bylaws. He was deftly put off—told it would be handled later, that there were more pressing issues. Other troublemakers were shuffled off to committees, to bicker over mundane issues, out of the way.

But none of the superfluous conversations mattered. France's attorney, Louis Ossinsky, was working on incorporating the new organization as a private company—privately owned, of course, by William Henry Getty France. (His heirs remain today the private owners of the corporation.)

So France stood before the barons of stock car racing as their czar, even as they sipped their highballs and smoked and half-listened to him.

Thirty years later, in the 1970s, when the Indianapolis 500 had become a virtually annual can of worms of technological and political disputes, Indy car people would go to Big Bill France for advice. He told them they had too much bureaucracy. "I can hold my board meetings," he said, "in a phone booth." In other words, wherever there was room for that six-foot-five, 220-pound man to stand and ponder a situation, a firm and final decision would be forthcoming.

As the Streamline meetings rolled on, France's proposals for unity and uniformity were roundly agreed to in principle, with the—hrrrmph—details to be worked out later.

They wanted to name the organization before the meetings ended. France had already made himself head of the "National Championship Stock Car Circuit." But NCSCC sounded clunky. The idea of another name France had been using, the Stock Car Auto Racing Society, came up. But SCARS seemed a repulsive acronym in a sport in which drivers could get hurt or killed. Someone proposed "National Stock Car Racing Association," NSCRA, which was indeed the most accurate, but somebody else warned that a group thus named, with NSCRA pronounced "Nescra," was already running races in Georgia.

It was Red Vogt, Raymond Parks's crack mechanic who'd prepared cars for Roy Hall and Lloyd Seay, who suggested the name National Association for Stock Car Auto Racing, and the acronym NASCAR.

Anne Bledsoe France did not attend the meetings. A literally smoke-filled room where men drank hard whiskey and made their points in hard language was no place for a lady. Besides, there was much to do in the background, where Anne remained. How would this new organization work, day to day, and how would it be financed? Where would the money come from, and where would it go? How would the drivers be provided with accident insurance, a cornerstone of Big Bill's plan? Who would receive the hospital bills, and who would pay them promptly? All of that was Anne's little-known but absolutely crucial department.

"While Dad was climbing high to reach his far-out goals," Bill France Jr. would say decades later, "Mom held the ladder."

And sold the tickets. And kept account of the money, dollar by dollar. After one NASCAR beach race in the formative years, journalist Chris Economaki stopped by the Frances' modest bungalow near the Halifax River late on a Sunday evening. "Bill answered the door, but didn't invite me in," Economaki would recall. "That was very unusual—he was always very friendly and hospitable. On this evening he was very nice, but he stood in the doorway with the door opened only a couple of feet. I got a glimpse inside. There were stacks of money—cash—everywhere on the floor. And in the middle of all that money sat Annie B., counting."

Sports Illustrated would eventually refer to her as "NASCAR's eagle-eyed bookkeeper."

Or, as a tough NASCAR insider in the 1970s would put it, "Make no mistake. That sweet little lady knows where every goddamn dollar in this organization is, where it came from, and where it's going."

"Dad certainly had visions and dreams," Bill France Jr. would say. "Mom was his reality."

France's goal of gleaming, new-model, "strictly stock" cars would have to be put on hold. From 1943 through '45, Detroit's retooled assembly lines had been rolling out jeeps, heavy military trucks, tanks, and airplanes. No new cars. When Detroit did start turning out cars again in '46, the manufacturers were so far behind demand that it would take years to catch up. If France had started NASCAR with new cars, he (a) would have faced severely limited fields of competitors, and (b) would have taken it on the chin from the media for wrecking and wearing out cars that were in such short supply to the public.

So once again he turned to the cars whose lineage was in liquor running, by now called "modifieds."

He could of course count on Raymond Parks. With Lloyd Seay dead and Roy Hall back in the slam, Parks turned to another Georgia moonshining family, this one from Atlanta, the Flocks—Bob, the eldest, and Fonty, the middle brother. (Tim, the youngest, would come along later and become the real star of the family.)

And Parks hired an Army Air Corps veteran with a mangled left leg, suffered when his bomber was shot down, that required a specially extended clutch pedal for him to drive at all: the red-headed Robert N. Byron Jr.

Born in Alabama but raised in Colorado, Red Byron had aspired to race in the Indianapolis 500. After spending more than two years in military hospitals while doctors saved his left leg, Byron returned to Alabama and began running stock car races, listing his hometown as Anniston. The little town where he actually lived, to the west of Anniston, was so obscure in those days that nobody outside the state would have any idea of where he was talking about—Talladega.

Parks's cars had won all five beach races at Daytona in 1946 and '47—one by Roy Hall, two by Bob Flock, and two by Red Byron. And Fonty Flock had won the "National Championship" of '47, such as it was.

France just couldn't wait until attorney Louis Ossinski got all the legal matters nailed down. On February 15, 1948, six days before NASCAR was incorporated, France held the first NASCAR race—on the beach at Daytona, of course.

Red Byron won it for Parks. They would go on to win the inaugural season points championship, though with a "modified" car.

When at last there were enough new cars available to get the "Strictly Stock" class rolling—the class would evolve into first the Grand National division and then into the Winston Cup Series—Parks responded with the premier team.

The first Strictly Stock race was held at Charlotte Speedway, a three-fourths-mile dirt oval in the fairgrounds, on June 19, 1949. It was won by one Jim Roper, who would never catch on as a NASCAR regular, in a locally owned Lincoln. But the second race, on July 10 at Daytona, was won by Byron in a Parks Oldsmobile—and he went on to win the 1949 Strictly Stock season championship.

And so, except for the Charlotte race, Raymond Parks and Red Byron swept NASCAR's formative milestones—its first race ever, and its first two season championships.

But North Carolina drivers, especially, were taking to France's fledgling tour as regulars—among them Elzie Wylie "Buck" Baker out of Charlotte, and Lee Petty out of the hamlet of Level Cross, near Greensboro. Though still in the modified ranks, a young, still-active whiskey runner named Robert Glenn Johnson Jr., called "Junior," was beginning to make a name for himself—on both road and track.

Moonshine running was still the primary feeder system for NASCAR. Lee Petty and his family would always deny any association with the liquor trade. But the late Wendell

Scott, NASCAR's first—and still only regular—black driver, who himself had been a whiskey tripper, would say that "I heard Lee Petty had a car with two transmissions in it," long before Petty began racing—and of course, two transmissions would have been illegal in the Strictly Stock class anyway. The late Bob Welborn, another tripper turned racer, would get a sort of incredulous look on his face when he would hear people say that the Pettys had never dealt in liquor. "All I know is, I used to take fifty gallons a week to Lee's house," Welborn would say, and shake his head. "I don't know— maybe he drank it."

NASCAR would take one star out of baseball. Glenn Roberts, a pitcher out of Daytona Beach, was turning down college scholarships and minor league contracts in order to pursue a racing career. He was still on short tracks in modified cars, but he would be a regular in NASCAR soon, still carrying the nickname he'd gotten as a pitcher: "Fireball."

*I*n 1950, the ever image-conscious France decided to add some class by renaming the Strictly Stock division. Borrowing a classy-sounding name from horse racing in the British Isles, he rechristened his elite division "Grand National." (This is not to be confused with the current Busch Grand National Series, which was so named after the original Grand National division was renamed the Winston Cup division in 1986.) The excuse at the time, and the one historians usually buy, was that "Strictly Stock" didn't have enough pizzazz, sounds too much like a garage mechanics' term, and was just too technically oriented for mass appeal to fans.

While all of that was true, France surely realized by then that "strictly stock" was turning out to be more and more of a technologically impossible dream. Showroom cars had to be made stronger in order to race safely. And since most of the contestants had moonshining backgrounds, modifying cars for greater speed was second nature to them. If the rules wouldn't allow modifications, they'd just do it anyway and see if they could get away with it. Disqualifications for cheated-up cars were common, and even so, subtle tricks were getting harder and harder for France's technical inspectors to police.

And so the term "Grand National" allowed France gradually to back off the strictly stock notion. While the outer appearance of the cars remained "stock," the concealed components would evolve into pure racing equipment until, by the 1970s, Grand National cars would not be stock at all, and "stock car racing" essentially would be a term connoting race cars with full bodies on them. By the 1990s, Winston Cup cars would evolve into such thoroughbred racers—not even the bodywork on Chevrolet "Monte Carlos" and Ford "Tauruses" was remotely like that of the street models—that NASCAR publicists would drop the term "stock cars" altogether.

But midway through the 1950 season, the cars and even the drivers became back-burner issues. Suddenly the crux of NASCAR's future lay in the distance of the races, and in the type of tracks they would be run on.

8

LEAVING THE BEACH

*I*ndianapolis Motor Speedway, with its 500-mile race, was of course the ever-present paragon in the back of Bill France's mind. But the acute catalyst for NASCAR and Daytona, in 1950, was bulldozed out of cotton and peanut fields by another big dreamer, outside the obscure hamlet of Darlington, South Carolina.

Harold Brasington moved faster than Bill France—perhaps precipitously; perhaps that's why the homespun visionary would eventually lose every racing facility he ever built. After Brasington attended the 1948 Indy 500, he came home obsessed: "I thought, Why not combine the concepts of this enormous, two-and-a-half-mile paved speedway that was relatively flat, and our high-banked, but short, dirt tracks back home?" he would say in the 1970s.

Brasington immediately set to work, without architects or engineers—just with his eyes and hands, and what earth-moving equipment and construction workers he could muster. They scraped up mountains of dirt here—yeah, that looked pretty good—and more mountains there—that should be sufficient banking for Turns 3 and 4, shouldn't it? Brasington didn't even own all the land at the construction site. Indeed, the reason storied Darlington Raceway remains a true egg shape today, with one set of turns much sharper than the others, is that "the fellow who owned some of the land told me, 'Don't you dare disturb my minnow pond,'" Brasington would say. "And so we had to tighten up the turns on that end in order to miss his minnow pond and leave it intact, outside the track."

What Brasington had, by the time the bulldozers stopped in the summer of 1950, was a high-banked, paved—and warped—1.3-mile oval so revolutionary that it would be more than twenty years before a term for it would even be coined: superspeedway.

What Brasington also had, that summer, was Bill France in a quandary. France wasn't at all sure stock cars could endure 500 miles of racing—and if none finished such a race, it would be a public relations disaster. So Brasington, bent on a 500-miler to complete his dream, at first got sanctioning from the midwestern-based Central States Racing Association, for a race Brasington scheduled for Labor Day, 1950. France let the matter slide at first. But then Atlanta promoter Sam Nunis announced that *he* would stage a 500-mile race, on Lakewood Speedway's one-mile oval.

The 500-mile mania had France's back to the wall. He could either be swept away by the moment, or he could seize it.

First he had to pick a side: bizarre Darlington, far out in the farmlands, ninety miles from even the medium-size town of Columbia, South Carolina; or good old mainstay Lakewood with its solid fan base in Atlanta. Lakewood in late 1949 had drawn more than 33,000 fans to a Strictly Stock race—far and away the biggest crowd of that season on the tour.

All right: If France was going to catch this 500-mile wave, he would ride it at its crest. He rolled the dice on Darlington.

The upstart rival league from the Midwest was having trouble drawing a full field of competitors for Brasington's race. France informed Brasington and the CSRA that he could damn sure fill their field—if they would give NASCAR equal billing as the co-sanctioning body.

By Labor Day weekend, a field of seventy-five cars had qualified for the first Southern 500 stock car race. Spectator traffic was gridlocked, in the infield and outside the track. Attendance was only about 25,000, but access was only by country roads, and upon arrival, passenger cars were parked every which way—Brasington hadn't asked France to lend his expertise at parking cars, learned from years on the beach. Nobody could get out of the infield. Food and water ran out. France would often tell the story that upon his arrival in the infield, "I was confronted by a man with a crisis. He said he couldn't get his family out of the infield, and that his wife was in dire need of a breast pump. I just said, 'Man, can't *you* help her?' and moved on."

As for the racers, few knew what to make of such a track. Lee Petty, showing the first signs of a wariness of big tracks that would haunt him for the rest of his career, had reinforced the roof of his Plymouth—in case of rollover at high speed—with some pipe, and called it a "roll bar." His rivals guffawed, and allowed as how that was just about the most sissified device they'd ever seen in a race car.

"None of us knew what it would take to go 500 miles," pioneer NASCAR driver and two-time season champion Buck Baker would recall. "A lot of us rigged containers of something to drink. One guy took beer. After only a few laps of racing on that banking, with the car jerking and pitching around violently, that beer foamed up. The car had so much foam pouring out of it that it looked like a washing machine was overflowing inside it. I decided to take a jug of tomato juice—figured it would keep me hydrated and give me a little energy. Well, then I wrecked. The tomato juice spilled all over me, and I was slumped over in the seat. When the emergency crew got there, one of them looked inside and hollered to the others, 'There ain't no helpin' this 'un! Po' sumbitch has done got his head cut off!' "

The only driver present who had an inkling what it would take for a stock car to go 500 miles and win was Johnny Mantz, an Indy car veteran from Long Beach, California. France and one of his officials, race flagman Alvin Hawkins, had bought a new Plymouth to use as a NASCAR staff car— to run errands in. Mantz talked them into letting him drive it in the race. One look at the Darlington banking told Mantz that standard passenger-car tires would wear out with maddening rapidity. To go 500 miles at Indy, special tires made of an extra-hard rubber compound were used. No such tires existed for stock cars, so Mantz recommended truck tires.

Mantz also introduced a whole new race strategy to NASCAR. All the moonshine boys still had a lot of hotdog in them, and were bent on giving the crowd a show. They would run hard, challenge one another for the lead, early in the race. Sprints of showmanship would be foolish in a 500-miler, Mantz knew. The way to win was to keep a steady pace—one that probably wouldn't even be noticed in the early going—all afternoon.

Almost immediately, the NASCAR regulars began to eat up tires, and had to drop into the pits for replacements. Their problem was chronic. In Red Byron's pits, things grew so frantic that the usually unflappable Raymond Parks himself peeled off his coat and tie and began helping change tires on the team's brand-new Cadillac.

While the hares alternately showboated on the track and limped into the pits for new tires, tortoise Mantz, running always at about 75 miles per hour, took the lead on the fiftieth lap. No sooner would Byron in the Caddy or Fireball Roberts in a big Olds 88 roar past Mantz in the little six-cylinder Plymouth, trying to unlap themselves, than another tire would blow on one of the big cars. Mantz led the rest of the way and won.

Being the winning car owner, and having outcalculated everybody else, amounted to little consolation for France. He'd had the future of his sport shoved right in his face—500-milers on big, banked, paved tracks.

Worse, almost instantaneously, the entire focus of stock car racing enthusiasts had been shifted away from Daytona Beach, to Darlington. The hard-packed sand that had held its own since 1903 was suddenly obsolete.

*E*ven as Fireball Roberts and Tim Flock became stars on the beach in the early 1950s—Roberts with his charisma and flat-out driving style, and Flock with his showmanship, including a monkey named Jocko Flocko who rode on the driver's shoulder during a few races—France realized what must be done.

By 1953 he told government officials of Daytona Beach that the cars were now simply going too fast for the beach-and-road course. Further, the beach was becoming quite a resort on its own. Hotels and houses were going up everywhere, and those who preferred to stroll or lie in the sun weren't necessarily race fans. There were complaints about the noise, the commotion, the crowds.

Daytona's days were numbered as a world focal point of racing—unless a giant, paved oval could be built.

First, it must lie inland, on the western fringes of the town, where there was plenty of sparsely populated land. Second, the construction effort must be organized, and coordinated with the state of Florida. The project would be so enormous that both local and state government approval and assistance would be vital.

On October 17, 1955, the Daytona Beach City Commission approved a long-term lease of 377 acres of city property, located near the airport east of town, to a cooperative of France and local government officials called the Daytona Beach Racing and Recreational Facility District.

*P*ersonalities were blossoming everywhere on France's Grand National tour. Tim Flock, winner of the 1952 championship in a Hudson Hornet—always billed as "The Fabulous Hudson Hornet"—switched in '55 to the richest, most powerful NASCAR team yet—a fleet of Chryslers fielded by the flamboyant outboard boat motor magnate Carl Kiekhaefer. Raymond Parks had suddenly tired of racing and quit altogether in 1951, but Kiekhaefer more than replaced Parks's pizzazz, usually showing up at races with so many cars that they were brought in on one of those new-car transporters of the type you still see plying the interstates laden with passenger Chevrolets or Toyotas.

Star driver Flock won another championship in '55 and Kiekhaefer dominated the season—except for one round-faced, moonshining, Blue Ridge–born thorn in Kiekhaefer's side: Junior Johnson.

Still an active tripper, Johnson had enough money to put together a little racing team of his own and move up to the Grand National circuit. He thought he'd take a crack at it, just to see what he could do—truth was, racing bored him, compared with tripping. Where Kiekhaefer and others always brought plenty of backup cars for their stars, Johnson campaigned in a single '55 Chevrolet, crewed by a few of his friends from "around home," which was Ingle Hollow in Wilkes County, North Carolina. This was still prime moonshine country. The local boys knew more about making cars go fast than anybody—even more, Junior Johnson would maintain later, than Detroit's best engineers.

In a six-week stretch of May and June of '55, Johnson won five races. After the first win, at Hickory, North Carolina, Kiekhaefer pissed off Junior something fierce by throwing a hissy, demanding an inspection of the '55 Chevy, claiming nobody could have beaten the fleet of mighty Kiekhaefer Chryslers legally. So in the remaining four victories, Junior just by-god lapped the entire field, including the Kiekhaefer armada.

And Johnson brought the bootlegger style of driving back into NASCAR—indeed turned it up several notches. He ran wide open, all the time. Winning was the only thing—otherwise he'd just as soon crash, or blow the engine.

"I whipped their butts," Johnson would recall nearly half a century later, still cherishing '55 as the happiest season of his life. "That was before I went off."

Went off, that is, to the federal prison at Chillicothe, Ohio. In 1956, federal agents finally bit into Bill France's cadre of trippers turned racing stars.

Junior Johnson never got caught running liquor on the road. Never.

He had ranged the Southeast in a variety of vehicles. The old Georgia 'shiners recall the night that Junior backed an eighteen-wheeler up to the barn of Ben Chastain. The feds had come down hard in North Carolina, pretty well dried up the stills, and Junior—as he often did during such periods of temporary shortages—went to other sources. Most of the north Georgia distillers were by then taking their wares to Ben Chastain's for central distribution. One night in the '50s, Junior just showed up with that eighteen-wheeler, bought every drop that was stored in the barns, and casually drove back to North Carolina at the legal speed limit.

One of the great myths about whiskey trippers is that they drove wide open, all the time. That would have been foolish. They never wanted to attract attention to themselves for mere speeding. But when lawmen came after them, when they had to go, they went like hell.

After you've driven a '49 Ford that has been modified to pack a supercharged 454-cubic-inch Cadillac engine, with 120 to 180 gallons of 'shine on board, well, no "race car" built to Bill France's stock regulations was going to get you very excited.

But after '55, Junior realized that this racing business was a good way to make a living without risking prison. So for the 1956 season, he agreed to drive for Ford Motor Company's factory-entered NASCAR team. Ford's fancy-pants engineers of course couldn't come up with anything nearly as fast as Junior and his local boys had, so as he waited winless through thirteen races for the team to get its act together, he continued running liquor.

Still the revenuers couldn't catch him. But they wanted him in the worst way. His father, Robert Glenn Johnson Sr., was what would be called today a habitual offender—one of the biggest and most often-raided distillers in all of the Blue Ridge foothills. Junior's brothers, L.P. and Fred, were hellacious trippers, but Junior was the ballsiest of the lot. Indeed, he'd gotten his start racing at age sixteen because L.P. wanted to enter his liquor car in an outlaw race at North Wilkesboro Speedway, and L.P. asked Junior to drive because "he figured I had a little more nerve than the rest of 'em," Junior would recall.

That midsummer night in '56, the feds who crept into the woods were simply after a Johnson—any Johnson. They had located Robert Glenn Johnson Sr.'s still, but it wasn't operating—"cooking." So they began a stakeout.

Moonshiners always started the fires under their stills in darkness, so that the smoke would be lost against the night sky. Then, as the sun came up, the fire burned down so that the smoke was wispy and white, blending with the clouds as revenuers rode the country roads, scanning the treetops with binoculars, looking for smoke.

In the wee hours of a Monday morning, Glenn Johnson asked his son to go on down and fire the still. Then Junior could leave as the fire burned down, and his father and brothers would tend it later in the day.

The feds at first didn't know which Johnson it was when they detected a figure coming down through the dark woods. Glenn? L.P.? Fred? No…wait…Godamightydamn, it was Junior! They got ready.

When Junior spotted them he flung a shovelful of coal in the first agent's face and took off running. He almost made it. But in the pitch-blackness, he ran into a barbed-wire fence, entangled himself, and the agents tackled him.

When word reached Daytona Beach, Bill France scrambled to fight the setback. He tried to intervene—sent a telegram to the federal judge, promising a high-paying, legal job for Johnson as a race driver, if only he were put on probation. But the judge had the prize Johnson of them all, and wasn't about to let him go.

France's brightest budding star, the one who'd captured the imagination of the public faster than any other driver, was gone. France had little idea that this one little prison sentence amounted to a public relations investment that would pay off enormously later on.

France continued to wheel and deal on every front, at every turn, seizing the moment wherever he could find it. After a grisly epidemic of auto racing deaths in Europe and the United States in 1955, a movement began in the U.S. Senate to ban motor racing altogether in this country. Formula One world champion Alberto Ascari had been killed at Monza; two-time Indy 500 winner Billy Vukovich had been killed at the Brickyard; worst of all, Pierre Levegh's Mercedes had flown into the grandstands at Le Mans, killing him and more than eighty spectators instantly.

France immediately began his own political maneuverings to combat the ban, but serendipity turned him toward a whole new opportunity: international recognition, and therefore another echelon of respectability, for NASCAR.

Under all the political pressure, the American Automobile Association, AAA, the longtime sanctioning body for the Indianapolis 500 and other major events, ceased its association with racing, beginning with the 1956 season. Indy quickly formed a puppet sanctioning body of its own, the United States Auto Club (USAC). But Indy made a crucial error of omission. Its officials had never bothered much with international politics—they pretty much sat and waited for the world to come to them. The AAA had always been American racing's member organization in the Federation Internationale de l'Automobile, the Paris-based world governing body of motor racing. With the AAA gone, there was a void. France rushed to fill it. From 1956 through '58, he spearheaded organization of the Automobile Competition Committee of the United States as the new American member of the FIA—with NASCAR, of course, as the cornerstone of ACCUS.

Henceforth, around the planet but especially in the eyes of Europe, the most important American in international motor racing would not be Indianapolis Motor Speedway owner Tony Hulman, nor any of his lieutenants, but Monsieur Bill France. As his first driver-ambassador to the world from NASCAR, France in June of 1958 took Fireball Roberts to drive a Ferrari in the 24 Hours of Le Mans.

Back home, as Big Bill and Fireball sported with the French, the grassroots racers of NASCAR hadn't a clue what good all this international diplomacy could possibly do. But here's what it meant: If and when he ever got his dream speedway built at Daytona, then a 500-mile race in February, when the rest of the world's racing was shut down for winter, could easily be made an "FIA-clear date." That meant it would be the only race in the world on that day officially recognized by the FIA, and that the Paris body would never schedule another race against it, anywhere on the planet. Also, the race would be open to any driver, from any country, who held an FIA license. And regular NASCAR drivers, as holders of FIA licenses, would be internationally recognized on their own.

And so, a 500-mile race at Daytona would, from its very first running, be one of the most prestigious races in the world.

*T*he *Indianapolis Star,* typically chauvinistic with regard to the inimitability of the storied old Brickyard, had smugly editorialized about this man France's "Pipe Dream Speedway" in Florida. It wasn't the first time France had been snubbed in Indiana. On a goodwill visit to the Indy 500 in the early 1950s, France had been summarily escorted from the pits and ejected. A long-running story is that upon being thrown out, France bellowed, "I'll own this place some day!" but neither he, relatives, nor associates ever admitted he said that. He did love to say late in his life that after the Indy insult, "Annie and I left and went back to Florida and built our own track."

One thing was certain in his mind: His track would be better by far than that flat, archaic, over-hallowed rectangle Carl Fisher had scraped out of the farmland in 1909. France's track would be the same circumference as Indy, 2.5 miles. But it would be high-banked—31 degrees, so that the heavy stock cars could be as fast as the little thoroughbred racers at Indy. Unlike Brasington's Darlington Raceway, France's track would be carefully engineered for uniformity all the way around. To give more fans a better view of the start-finish line—from more high-priced seats, of course—France would put a dogleg in the front stretch. Surrounding seats would then be angled to face directly toward the line—and the kink in the track would give drivers an extra bit of challenge.

All this, if only he could get it built. In the mid-'50s, the Indianapolis papers seemed justified in their printed smirking. France kept saying year after year that the beach races were the last—that his new speedway was at the brink of reality. But initial financial backing had fallen through—Milwaukee Braves franchise owner Lou Perini had withdrawn support for the speedway, fearing the projected crowds couldn't be handled by Daytona Beach's essentially small-town infrastructure.

But indefatigably France pressed on. He and Annie B. scraped together what loans they could secure, and construction began. Even Big Bill and Bill Jr., who was growing into a role as his father's right-hand man, personally operated earth-moving equipment.

By 1958, the initial layout of the track was in place. But the projected price of complete fulfillment of France's dream was now $2.9 million. He wasn't even close. Sadly he began contingency plans to make the 2.5-mile speedway, with its revolutionary "tri-oval" design, a flat track, perhaps not even as fast as Indy.

Then began a chain reaction of unlikely events, triggered by the unlikeliest of saviors for Bill France's highly capitalistic vision: Cuban revolutionary Fidel Castro.

*L*ike a lot of other men who loved auto racing, Bill France also loved airplanes. He was a licensed pilot, and by 1958 owned his own private plane. Beleaguered as he was with the speedway project, he took a break that spring and flew up to Eglin Air Force Base in the Florida panhandle, to watch an air show. There, he met one Clint Murchison Jr., scion of an oil-rich family in Texas. Murchison had sporting interests of his own—indeed, he was putting together a new National Football League franchise to be called the Dallas Cowboys. He was fascinated with France's plan for a speedway. Indeed, he asked France to keep him informed on the project. Murchison owned a huge construction company, and perhaps could be of help.

At the air show, Murchison got word that there was big trouble on a major construction project of his in Cuba. It seemed the rebels led by Castro were threatening to shoot all of Murchison's construction workers if they didn't quit work. Well, Cuban dictator Fulgencio Batista couldn't have this pest Castro shutting down major construction projects—it would give the rebels too much credibility with the Cuban populace. So Batista ordered his soldiers to shoot Murchison's men if they *did* stop the project.

Murchison figured he could straighten out this mess if he could just get down there in a hurry. But how? If he could just get to Miami, he could get to Havana quickly from there. But here he sat, on the opposite end of the state of Florida.

Well, Bill France had his plane. He'd be glad to fly Murchison down to Miami. France dropped Murchison off and headed back to his own problems, while Murchison waded into the trouble in Cuba.

A few weeks later, France wondered how his new pal had fared down there. He phoned Murchison, who was back in Dallas. Yes, he'd gotten the equipment out, and—well, some of that equipment was being shipped back through Florida anyway. Murchison would just have one of his top lieutenants, Howard Sluyter, stop off in Daytona Beach to have a look. Maybe he could return France's favor.

Sluyter found France discouraged, ready to call off the moving of millions of cubic yards of dirt for the high banking that was crucial to the dream speedway, and settle for a 2.5-mile flat road.

"Don't stop, Bill," Sluyter said. He gave France a personal check for $20,000. Then he and Murchison helped France arrange a $500,000 loan. Now things were clicking again. Others pitched in: Harry Moir of Pure Oil (now Unocal), Harley Earl of General Motors, even big-band leader Paul Whiteman.

In came the earthmovers. Up went the banking. On went the pavement.

Bill France had himself the damnedest speedway in the world. *Sports Illustrated,* in its February 16, 1959, issue, heralded the imminent grand opening, for that year's Speedweek, with a five-page article. Wrote Kenneth Rudeen, "This impressive racing plant is called Daytona International Speedway. It is the greatest achievement of a rumpled, 49-year-old, deceptively casual giant of a man named William Henry Getty France. Many other hands were involved in it, to be sure, but it was Bill France who dreamed the dream and bulldozed it through."

9

MAIDEN VOYAGE IN EERIE AIR

*W*e came out of the tunnel under the fourth turn, into the infield, and suddenly it was like being on the surface of the moon. It was mostly barren—still a construction site. And 'w-a-a-y in the distance, you could see that high banking of the first and second turns…It looked like it must have been 30 miles down there to the banking."

Those were the impressions of a twenty-one-year-old driver named Richard Petty as he and his father, Lee, entered Daytona International Speedway for the first time, in February of 1959.

"There wasn't a man there who wasn't scared to death of the place," Lee Petty would admit later.

Marshall Teague was dead before all the preliminary appraisals of the place were even in. Teague was a Daytona Beach resident, a local hero, a master of the old beach-road course, and a sometime Indy car driver.

France had scheduled an Indy car race for that April. But, keen to show right away that his track was the fastest in the world—not only faster than Indy, but faster even than the 2.64-mile oval with parabolic banking that existed at Monza,

Italy, at the time—France invited Indy car teams down for test runs in February. The world record on a closed course was 177.038 mph, set by Tony Bettenhausen Sr. at Monza the previous June.

On February 8, Teague went out in Chapman Root's specially reconfigured Indy car, with covered wheels and a canopy over the cockpit. Actually, in its aerodynamic concepts, Root's car wasn't far off the design Frank Lockhart had brought to the beach thirty-one years earlier, except for the roof. On his first run, Teague averaged 171.82 mph, less than 6 mph off the record at Monza—and he was "just playing around," he said afterward. Jim Rathmann went out in another Indy car, was visited terribly by the ancient banshee from over on the beach—high wind—and averaged 170.06. But the Monza record seemed sure to fall later in the week.

But on February 11, a new kind of ill wind—aerodynamic uncertainty—emerged. Teague's car lifted, floated, flipped five times, scattered as it went, ejected Teague—seat, safety belts, and all—and killed him. Indy car activity at Daytona was called off until that April, when George Amick would win the pole at 176.887 (right to the brink of the Monza record), and then be killed instantly during the race in a crash at about 190 on the backstretch.

Nevermore would Indy cars race at Daytona.

*L*ee Petty was an excellent driver, but not a great driver. Mostly he was dogged. What he was great at was protesting the results of races after they were over. To this day he remains the most dogged protester of race results in the history of NASCAR.

In the mid-1950s, at Macon, Georgia, the toughest man ever to promote a stock car race, the late Nineva E. "Alf" Knight—he once fought off a crowd of sixty, solo, with a pine knot, to quell a fan riot—became so exasperated with the bickering of Buck Baker, Lee Petty, and others over the payoff after a race that he turned a strongbox of cash upside down, emptied it onto the floor of his makeshift office, and bellowed, "All right, goddammit! Ever' man for hisself! You sonsabitches just fight over it! That's what you want, ain't it?" And after some initial diving, punching, clawing, kicking, gouging, and scratching for the cash, it dawned upon all the boys that what they wanted most was to argue. So they got up and asked Alf if they couldn't just continue with their little debate over who finished where and who deserved what. But Alf just walked away. Which was one of the few times Lee Petty was ever outdone in a protest.

The most ruthless protest Lee Petty ever filed was at Lakewood Speedway in Atlanta in 1960, after a pearly-grinning youth took the checkered flag and the crowd and attending media went wild over the first NASCAR win by this charismatic kid. Here came Lee Petty stomping up to the officials to spoil it all. Lee demanded that the scoring sheets be checked; said such an audit would prove that he had won, not that grinning young'un over there—yes that one, name of Richard Petty. Lee's protest was upheld. And his own son's first victory was taken away.

But the greatest protest Lee Petty ever filed—and the most monumental thing he ever did as a driver—was on the afternoon of February 22, 1959.

It came immediately after the finish of the first Daytona 500.

William J. Morgan and Barney Oldfield in their primes, in all their glory, couldn't have milked that finish for every drop it was worth, nationwide, worldwide, the way Big Bill France and Lee Petty milked it.

You could say that all the first Daytona 500 really amounted to was a bunch of backwoods dirt-track drivers so scared and so cautious—and having more room to roam and to err while running flat-out than they'd ever known—that there wasn't a single wreck or caution flag. Or you could say they all drove flawlessly and brilliantly and fearlessly.

There were thirty-three lead changes, far more than the Indy 500 had ever seen, and so Daytona seemed more competitive than the Brickyard. But a lot of the passes were made by drivers who didn't know how or why they were passing—suddenly some terrific and inexplicable force would suck one car past another. Fireball Roberts started forty-sixth but shot into the lead after only twenty-two laps, forever sealing his garage-area nickname, "Balls"—but was his nerve really what swept him to the lead so quickly before his car broke down? Why were Lee Petty and Johnny Beauchamp able to exchange the lead so often, virtually at the will of one to pass the other? Something strange was going on out there. Something in the air—literally and eerily.

The race that had already been set up as the most important in the world that winter—by designation of the Federation Internationale de l'Automobile in Paris—had the closest, most controversial finish to that point in the history of motor racing.

On the final lap, Lee Petty's Oldsmobile and Johnny Beauchamp's Thunderbird came side by side out of the fourth turn, down the homestretch, nose-to-nose. "Little Joe" Weatherly's Chevrolet was actually one lap down, but Weatherly made it three abreast at the finish line. And that may have been what threw everything into sweet chaos.

Weatherly's car flashed past the flagstand a glint ahead of the two that were gunning for the win. If Little Joe's car didn't obstruct the view of Bill France and flagman Johnny Bruner as they stood on the flagstand, it at least was a millisecond's worth of distraction for them.

France and Bruner called Beauchamp the winner by two feet. Petty drove into Victory Lane, proclaiming himself the winner by two feet.

No one will ever know, really.

But that was the moment when Bill France and Lee Petty transformed automobile racing's national image from that of an engineering exercise into entertainment. That was the moment at which NASCAR began to stalk every other form of motor racing for the heart and mind of Everyman.

This was sport by Hollywood script. All it needed was exposure. France seized the moment. Amid the hubbub, he announced he would immediately begin to search for the first photo-finish equipment in the history of automobile racing. Then he let Lee Petty do what he did best—simmer and stew for three days, protesting, talking to the media—while France put out an all-points appeal on the wire services for any photos or film footage that might help in the decision. Film and photos poured in for days.

On Wednesday, February 25, at 6 P.M.—just in time to make the first-edition deadlines of virtually every major morning newspaper in the Eastern time zone—Lee Arnold Petty of Level Cross, North Carolina, was declared the winner of the first Daytona 500 NASCAR-FIA Grand National stock car race.

Supposedly some movie newsreel footage, rushed from New York to Daytona Beach in response to France's plea, cinched the verdict. In absence of photo-finish equipment, no film, no camera angle, could have provided absolute proof.

Beauchamp was a "foreigner" from Harlan, Iowa, who had run only four NASCAR races previously, to Lee Petty's 337. Petty had already won two NASCAR Grand National season championships, was the defending champion from 1958, and would go on from Daytona to win a third title in '59. NASCAR was getting its most consistent and concentrated media exposure, by far, in North Carolina and Virginia. Minor league baseball, long the passion of the region, was just then dying out, and sportswriters had already leapt on the subject of Lee Petty and his personable and photogenic son, Richard.

A press-box poll of print-media writers taken by *Daytona Beach News-Journal* sports editor Bernard "Benny" Kahn, soon after the race, went unanimously in favor of Petty. But the writers knew they would have more, and better, material to write about Petty than about Beauchamp.

Joe Weatherly said he thought Petty clearly had won—but Weatherly clearly was prejudiced. At the finish, he admittedly had been trying to help Petty, a NASCAR regular like himself, against the outsider.

Lee Petty won the first Daytona 500, and that is final—and, probably, correct. But it all coincidentally worked out nicely for the Pettys, Bill France, NASCAR, and Daytona.

Richard Petty, by the way, finished fifty-seventh in a field of fifty-nine in the first Daytona 500. His dad had dumped him into a leftover '57 Olds convertible. He had no chance at all, and no preconceptions whatsoever. "Not knowing anything was a blessing," he would say later. The veterans had all their experience from dirt tracks and Darlington, but at Daytona, "my guess was as good as theirs." He was free to feel the turbulent air as it pulled and pushed his car.

Richard Petty and Daytona International Speedway were rookies together. After a few thousand miles, each would owe much notoriety to the other.

"I came along at the right time for Daytona, and Daytona came along at the right time for me," he would recall more than forty years later. "We grew up together."

But in 1959, after only one running, the Daytona 500 was already the second most prestigious automobile race in America. And coming fast.

10

TEMPESTS

*R*eleased from prison in 1958, Junior Johnson was arrested again later that year on more moonshining charges, along with the rest of his family, except for his father—who was already in Atlanta Federal Prison. Junior and his mother, Lora Bell, surrendered voluntarily the day after his brothers, Fred and L.P., were arrested. Junior's brothers went to prison, and his mother got off with a fine and a suspended sentence.

But Junior beat the rap entirely. His alibi was that he'd been driving in NASCAR races in the spring and summer of '58. He had of course been running liquor all the while, but the feds couldn't prove it this time—not with the parade of Bill France lieutenants and associates to the witness stand to corroborate his story.

Prison had changed Johnson. He was quieter, more introspective, had learned to swallow his temper. He wasn't as quick to "crawl a man"—Junior's term for wading into a foe and whipping his ass. Those ice-blue eyes were in constant surveillance of all around him, taking everything in, processing, ever calculating, in silence. When he did speak, his words resonated. When, for example, a young senator from Massachusetts named John F. Kennedy was elected president of the United States in 1960, Junior Johnson softly noted a personal irony: "His daddy was a bootlegger, and he went to the White House. My daddy was a bootlegger, and both of us went to federal prison."

So it had gone for all of Robert Glenn Johnson Jr.'s life, in—and roaring out of—the hardscrabble hills of Wilkes County, North Carolina. As in the mountains of north Georgia, the Wilkes farmland was poor except that it would support a little corn. Moonshining was considered an honest trade, and the locals would have gladly made liquor legally if federal taxes hadn't been too high to make it profitable. The "southern highlanders," as sociologists called them, had been distilling whiskey for generations, some all the way back to their ancestry in Scotland and Ireland. They saw nothing wrong with it. If the government had a problem with it, that was the government's problem. But it did amount to an occupational hazard for the workingfolk. Federal agents had been raiding Robert Glenn Johnson Sr.'s operations since 1935, when Junior was four years old.

Junior Johnson could not vote, could not get a passport, could not own a firearm. (That would not change until 1985, when he received a full pardon from President Ronald Reagan.)

What he could do was drive. Balls-out. Wide fucking open, all the time. Junior Johnson drove that way, before those terms were terms.

By the late 1950s, the moonshine road cars whose ancestry lay back in Red Vogt's garage in Atlanta had been refined to such a state that no "race cars" anywhere—except perhaps at Indianapolis—were as fast. Johnson had already driven two-lane country highways faster than he would ever drive any race track. (In the 1980s, as a team owner, he would say, "I never drove at Daytona as fast as I'd driven Highway 421 coming out of Wilkesboro. Course, when I was racin', we weren't runnin' but 180-something on the backstretch at Daytona." He would recall nights coming out of Wilkes County with a load on and the law in hot pursuit, "so fast that the road looked maybe two feet wide up ahead, so fast that with no seat belts, you hung on to the steering wheel to keep from flying out of the car when you went around a curve.")

There wasn't a race track on the planet that could scare Junior Johnson—not even Bill France's 2.5-mile, 31-degree-banked monster at Daytona.

During practice and qualifying for the second Daytona 500, in 1960, all that bothered Junior was that his Chevrolet, fielded by Ray Fox, wasn't fast enough. Pontiac's factory team had brought a fleet of cars that seemed sure to dominate.

But those eerie invisible tempests in the air, which had scared the bejesus out of a lot of drivers the year before, became a point of fascination for Johnson. He experimented, waiting for the faster cars to come by him in practice, then tucking the nose of the Chevrolet right up on the rear bumpers of the Pontiacs. He discovered he could latch on to them and stay with them—like giant magnets, they were towing his car along. He calculated what was happening: The big, heavy stock cars must be knocking huge holes in the air, creating a semi-vacuum behind them. Then the air would rush back together, reconcentrating itself. As long as he stayed in that little pocket, he could ride with any car he chose. In their conversations, Johnson and Fox began to refer to this effect as "the draft."

Fireball Roberts and Miami driver Bobby Johns were the stars of the Pontiac team. When the race started, Johnson locked on. Roberts, as usual, drove so hard that his engine blew after only fifty-one laps, barely a quarter of the race. In a horrific turnabout from the caution-free inaugural Daytona 500, the speedway was a wrecking yard this time. Thirty-two laps were run under caution. That allowed Johnson to shadow the Pontiacs into and out of the pits, and the draft kept him with them under green-flag conditions.

Then, with nine laps to go, the mysteries of the air surprised even Johnson. He was drafting Johns so tightly, creating even more of a vacuum behind Johns's car, that the suction blew the rear window right out of Johns's mighty Pontiac, sending it swerving. Johnson steered past the spinning Johns, and the inferior Chevrolet with the extraordinary man aboard cruised to victory.

As winner of the Daytona 500, Johnson began to draw general public attention, and so did the injustices he had suffered in his life. The moonshiner as hero began to move out of the mountain culture and into mainstream American lore.

And by discovering and harnessing "the draft," Johnson made Daytona unique among all the race tracks in the world, in a way not even Bill France had anticipated. From now on, because the draft was the great equalizer of slower cars with faster ones, competition would be much closer at Daytona than anywhere else. From February 14, 1960, forward, the Daytona 500 would be, if not the biggest American automobile race, the best.

*T*im Flock died of cancer, without medical insurance, without pension, at the age of seventy-four, in 1998, just days after Darrell Waltrip drove carrying Flock's traditional car number, 300, at Darlington, and took up a collection from other racers so that Flock's widow, Frances, wouldn't lose the family home.

Tim Flock died exactly the way he hadn't wanted to—without anything he'd fought for back in 1961.

Flock had been the winningest driver ever on Daytona's beach-road course—two victories in Grand National, one in convertibles, one in modified. All told he had won thirty-nine Grand National races and two championships.

Then, in his twelfth season, 1961, he crossed Big Bill France.

And he was gone. Banned for life. Caught in a cross fire between Big Bill and Jimmy Hoffa.

"No known Teamster can compete in a NASCAR race, and I'll enforce that with a pistol," quoth Big Bill in August of '61.

It all started over the mad rush to build superspeedways that had been detonated by France's opening of Daytona International in '59. In '60, Atlanta International Raceway (now Atlanta Motor Speedway), and Charlotte (now Lowe's) Motor Speedway opened.

The driving force at Charlotte was Curtis Turner, another ex–whiskey tripper who'd made it big in the timber business and was one of France's most flamboyant drivers. Turner now saw the big-money potential in track ownership. But he and his right-hand man, Bruton Smith, ran out of money for the project when construction crews hit a half-million cubic yards of solid granite during excavations for the speedway, and costs skyrocketed far past his budget.

Turner played pretty rough himself—at one point sending in men with shotguns to forcibly remove equipment that had been left by one contractor to block further construction until he got his money. Turner's armed men moved into the infield, hot-wired the bulldozers and earthmovers, and drove them out of the way.

On June 19, 1960, Turner hosted the first World 600, three weeks behind schedule. But in June of '61, he was ousted as president in an uprising of stockholders and his board of directors. To regain control of Charlotte Motor Speedway, Turner needed a big loan, fast, and banks wouldn't touch a project that was already deeply in trouble.

The pension-fund operation of the Teamsters Union was in the business of granting high-risk, high-interest loans.

Turner could get a loan of nearly a million dollars in return for a little favor: unionize the NASCAR drivers.

Turner began organizing the Federation of Professional Athletes, which he described as "a union of its own, affiliated with the Brotherhood of Teamsters, Chauffeurs, Warehousemen and Helpers of America."

In his opening manifesto, Turner made several demands that, at face value, seem justified and valid in retrospect. He wanted, for drivers, a larger share of gate receipts, retirement pensions, health insurance, better accident and life insurance, improved safety conditions, set procedures for complaints, and a scholarship fund for the children of fatally injured union members.

Turner also wanted pari-mutuel wagering on automobile races.

Hoffa wasn't directly involved—one of his lieutenants in Chicago, Harold Gibbons, was handling the deal. But Hoffa did have ambitions of organizing all professional athletes in the United States, under the Teamsters.

One whiff of Hoffa, and gambling, sent France through the ceiling, and thus the initial "with a pistol" outburst. After he cooled down a little, he issued a massive statement in response to Turner's demands.

France's statement began: "A recent newspaper story suggests that I might be some rootin', tootin', hootin', shootin' cuss, waving a pistol and itching to shoot up anyone who might disagree with me. Honest, I'm nothing like that." But now, notice how he didn't really back off: "But I am an American who believes in our Constitution and our laws, and that the bearing of arms to repel invasion is part of our great American heritage."

Interesting word, "invasion." There were rumblings of strikes, boycotts, pickets, and court injunctions against the staging of races.

France headed for Winston-Salem, North Carolina, where

Turner had set up union headquarters and where, on the night of August 9, 1961, a Grand National race was scheduled. He gathered the drivers together and warned that "before I have this union stuffed down my throat," he would "plow up" Daytona International Speedway and "plant corn in the infield." Turner hooted that France's long list of investors and creditors might have something to say about that.

To close the meeting, France summarily suspended the three ringleaders of the union movement: Turner, Tim Flock, and Fireball Roberts. And oh, by the way, those suspensions were "for life."

Roberts was the crucial figure—the brightest star involved in the movement, with his charismatic personality, his widely recognized nickname (the nearest to a household word that NASCAR could claim at the time) and his win, wreck, or blow driving style that was so akin to Junior Johnson's.

On August 11, France's right-hand wheeler-dealer and pressure man, Pat Purcell, got Fireball Roberts to take a little ride with him. They drove almost a third of the way across North Carolina, from Winston-Salem to Asheville, talking. Pat Purcell had come out of the circus and carnival industry. He was the first man in NASCAR to carry a briefcase. "What he carried in there all the time was three bottles of scotch, for powwow purposes," an old-timer would recall. In NASCAR's first year, 1948, Purcell had gone to Virginia to a meeting of dirt-track owners and invited them very cordially to join NASCAR. Casually he mentioned that if any of them chose not to join, "We'll put you out of business," according to Martinsville Speedway founder H. Clay Earles.

There is no record of the conversation between Purcell and Roberts on that little ride they took on August 11, 1961, and both men are long dead. There is a record of what Roberts said when the ride was over: "I'm withdrawing my support from the union and resigning from the Federation of Professional Athletes."

France promptly reinstated Roberts. Flock and Turner remained banned for life—they would appeal their suspensions in court, but would lose. Meanwhile, Ed Otto, then a NASCAR vice president—and the slickest auto racing promoter the states of New York and New Jersey would ever know—sent out an appeal to the drivers. Otto had, ten years earlier, helped fight off a New York State labor judgment against a track in Freeport, Long Island, over the deaths of two midget-car drivers. The state had originally held the two dead drivers to be de facto "employees" of the race promoter, and ordered their families compensated accordingly. Otto and others had gotten the decision reversed, the judgment being that the dead drivers were in fact "contestants" and "independent contractors."

To this day, "contestants" and "independent contractors" are bedrock operative terms in NASCAR.

Roberts's bailout was soon followed by that of Ned Jarrett, the points leader that August and the eventual winner of the '61 season championship. One by one, the drivers came back, and signed loyalty pledges.

The union was busted. Turner and Flock would not capitulate. They remained banned.

After all the union strife of '61, it was barely remembered that the third running of the Daytona 500 had gone caution-free, won by Marvin Panch after Fireball Roberts dominated the race, only to blow another engine with only thirteen laps to go. He'd been leading Panch by nearly a lap.

It had been a devastating week for Petty Enterprises. In Thursday's qualifying races, both Lee and Richard's Plymouths, the only cars they'd built for the season, were destroyed when they flew completely out of the ballpark—crashed through the guardrail and over the banking, out into the parking lots— Richard's in the first qualifier, Lee's in the second. For months afterward, the organization would hang by financial threads.

Worse, Lee was badly injured in a horrific crash with Johnny Beauchamp—yes, those were the same duelists from the '59 finish. They tangled in Turn 3, and before they reached Turn 4, both cars went over the high banking and plummeted about four stories to the ground.

It effectively ended the careers of both Beauchamp and the elder Petty. Beauchamp, who received head injuries, would never run another NASCAR race. Petty, who suffered massive internal injuries and multiple fractures, would return to run half a dozen short-track races from '62 through '64, but never again would he take on a high-banked superspeedway. He would leave all that to his oldest boy—to Richard.

Roberts had won the inaugural Firecracker 250 (later to evolve into the Firecracker 400 and then the Pepsi 400), and was destined to win that relative sprint race twice more, but had driven his equipment to death in the 500-milers. At last, for the 1962 Daytona 500, Roberts's car owner, the mechanical genius Henry "Smokey" Yunick—a self-educated engineer and racing innovator—put a Pontiac under Fireball that he couldn't ride into the ground.

Fireball Roberts despised this newfangled notion of "the draft." In his mind, men were supposed to win races on the sheer size of their *cojones* and the might of their cars, not by hitching aerodynamic rides with their betters.

And so, for most of the afternoon of February 18, 1962, it pissed off the great Fireball, "Balls" among his peers, to no end that this kid Richard Petty in an underpowered Plymouth kept clinging, clinging, clinging to the mighty Pontiac by utilizing the draft.

Where the wily Junior Johnson had hardly been noticed in his drafting trickery in '60 until the race was all over, Richard Petty made it obvious in '62—*so* obvious, in fact, that to this day, many historians give him, not Johnson, credit for discovering the draft at Daytona.

It is a retrospective wonder that Roberts didn't blow yet

another engine near the end of the race, because in the final fifty laps he was so annoyed with Petty's leeching that he urged the big Pontiac even harder, and drove away from the kid out of sheer loathing, to win by twenty-seven seconds.

If the myth that Richard Petty first implemented the draft grew out of the '62 race, a far more romantic myth, probably instigated by speedway publicists, came from the '63 race. That legend abides as fact in the mind of virtually every NASCAR expert, even today.

DeWayne "Tiny" Lund was a gentle (most of the time) behemoth of a man. He stood six feet six, and weighed close to three hundred pounds. (He probably wouldn't even fit into one of today's Winston Cup cars; his size might have contributed to his death in a race at Talladega in 1975—his enormous chest was crushed.) A lot of people will tell you Tiny weighed only about 250—"Hell, 250 only accounted for an arm and a leg of Tiny," as driver Buddy Baker, Buck's son, once put it. Buddy Baker, himself six-four, 220, should know a giant when he saw one. Once in a short-track race, Buddy and Tiny locked horns. "After it was over, I got out of my car and immediately saw Tiny stomping across the pits, toward me," Baker would recall. "You talk about a scary sight. Here he came, and he looked furious. Those big old feet of his were just about making the earth tremble. I just stood there for a moment, frozen, watching him come. Then I noticed an axle lying on the ground nearby. I thought about grabbing it to defend myself—then I thought, Nah, he'd just take it away from me. When Tiny got to me, he grabbed me and picked me up under one arm and he gave me a buzz [rubbing Baker's scalp tortuously with his huge knuckles], laughing the whole time."

The legend, part true, part myth, is this: The unknown Tiny Lund arrived at Daytona International Speedway in February of 1963, not only without a ride for the race, but broke—supposedly with only eighteen cents in his pocket. He was watching as Marvin Panch, testing a Maserati sports car, crashed and the car flipped over and caught fire. Panch was too badly injured to drive in the Daytona 500, and, while lying in the hospital, supposedly persuaded his team owners, the Wood Brothers (who later would send Cale Yarborough, A. J. Foyt, and David Pearson to Daytona 500 wins), to give his unknown savior a chance—to put Lund in the powerful Ford that had been designated for Panch. Lund then went on to a storybook victory in the '63 Daytona 500.

When Tiny Lund arrived at Daytona in February of 1963, he was not nearly the poor unknown that he still is made out to be in the abiding myth. He had driven in more than one hundred Grand National races, beginning in 1955. Though he hadn't yet won a major race, he was highly respected by his fellow drivers, and by car owners.

Lund did arrive without a ride for the Daytona 500. He was indeed watching when Panch crashed the Maserati. And he did rush to help rescue Panch. But so did four other men.

Lund did get into the Wood Brothers' car, take the lead over a handsome, flashy Chicagoan named Fred Lorenzen with eight laps to go, and drive away from the "Golden Boy" at the finish to win the Daytona 500.

But it was not the grateful Panch who made the decision. "Glen and Leonard Wood made that decision," Glen Wood, eldest of the brothers—and the boss of the team—would say many years later. "We made it because Tiny Lund was the best driver available."

And so Lund might just as easily have been sitting at his fish camp near Cross, South Carolina, and simply gotten a phone call from Glen Wood asking him to hurry down to Daytona to substitute for Panch.

But it made for a lovely story that Panch had pleaded with the Woods as they stood at his bedside. So Daytona's publicists nurtured it, and reporters dispatched it to the nation.

* * *

Johnny Rutherford had won the pole for the 1963 Daytona 500 at 165.183 mph. Paul Goldsmith won the pole for the 1964 Daytona 500 at 174.910. That was too big a leap. Something was up. More blatantly, young Richard Petty, in a Plymouth both years, upped his qualifying speed nearly 20 miles an hour, from 154.785 in '63 to 174.418 in '64. Goldsmith and Petty were in Plymouths. The top Ford drivers—Fred Lorenzen, Fireball Roberts, and a young Indy car regular sent in by Ford Motor Company, A. J. Foyt—couldn't even crack into the 170s.

Competition, if you could call it that, was beginning to look very lopsided. Operative here was the greatest mechanical villain Bill France had faced yet. It would go down in NASCAR lore by a single, short, bittersweet name:

Hemi.

Secretly, Chrysler Corporation had developed, for its Dodge and Plymouth teams, an engine that featured "hemispherical" cylinder heads which, when fitted on top of the engine blocks, made for greatly enhanced combustion, not so much during acceleration as at top-end speeds—perfect for Daytona. The hemi raised the bar by about 100 horsepower, to 500, in a single leap.

Richard Petty, who previously had been a personable kid with "potential," suddenly fulfilled it—in 1964 he dominated the Daytona 500 like no one else ever had, leading all but sixteen laps, never trailing after the fifty-second of the two hundred laps. And he lapped the entire field. He finished a full lap plus nine seconds over second-place Jimmy Pardue, who was also driving a Plymouth. Goldsmith completed a Plymouth sweep of the first three positions.

Now France had a problem. Ford had not only sent Foyt and Dan Gurney to bolster its Daytona effort, but Ford's Mercury division had fielded another flock of Indy car stars—Parnelli Jones, Johnny Rutherford, Jim McElreath, and Dave MacDonald. Petty in the Plymouth had made all that Ford effort look futile.

This enormous Chrysler advantage couldn't be allowed to continue. It would run everybody else out of racing. The hemi had to go. France just had to figure out how.

But he had worse worries. A lot worse. The stars were beginning to fall. Already that January, in the opening race at Riverside, California, Little Joe Weatherly—the clowning, lovable pudge of a tough guy from Norfolk, Virginia—had been killed. Little Joe wasn't wearing shoulder belts—didn't like them. He wore only a lap belt, for quick exodus from his car, just in case of his worst-case scenario.

Little Joe died due to impact, not due to his worst fear.

Which was fire…

Junior Johnson and Fireball Roberts probably became fast friends because they spent so much time in pits and garage areas looking over their wrecked or blown equipment long before races were over, while less ferocious drivers kept on running.

Junior and Fireball were both balls-out, all the time. Win, wreck, or blow. Nothing in between.

In 1963 at Atlanta, a young chemical engineer named Leo Mehl drew his first assignment as a racing-tire engineer for Goodyear. Mehl would later become Goodyear's director of worldwide racing, and then in the 1990s the executive director of the Indy Racing League. But at this point he was apprenticed to Goodyear's senior NASCAR engineer, Jim Earley. Mehl got an astounding initiation.

Goodyear and Firestone, competing intensely to make the fastest—so necessarily the softest, and therefore the most fragile—tires, were having durability problems at Atlanta. There was a danger of tires blowing soon after the race started. Young Mehl, eager to do the right thing, suggested there should be mandatory pit stops early in the race to check tire wear.

Earley didn't seem worried, but Mehl was. He consulted one of the top car owners, Big Bud Moore, about how to handle the situation.

"He said, 'We'll all change tires after Junior hits the wall,' " Mehl would recall. "He didn't seem very concerned.

"I went back to Jim Earley. I said, 'Jim? They'll stop—won't they? They won't just crash—will they?'

"Jim said, 'Junior might.'

"That's how they handled it. They knew Junior was going to lead the race, that he wasn't going to stop, that he was going to go faster, wear tires faster, hit the wall, and then everybody else would know when to change tires.

"Sure enough, Junior took off from the pole in his white Chevrolet, made it about forty-five miles, wore through the right front tire, blew it, hit the wall, and everybody else came in and changed tires."

*F*ireball and Junior were balls-out entering the seventh lap of the World 600 at Charlotte on May 24, 1964. Junior's car wiggled exiting Turn 2 and tangled with Ned Jarrett's car. Fireball roared up to the entanglement and spun backward trying to avoid it.

Fireball's Ford hit a gate in the retaining wall. The fuel tank ruptured and exploded. Suddenly a cloud of fire rose over the backstretch of Charlotte Motor Speedway. Johnson's car skidded far down the backstretch, clear of the fire.

Jarrett got out of his car and rushed to Fireball's aid. Roberts was conscious and trying to escape the flames. Jarrett helped him out of the car. Roberts did say, "My God, Ned, I'm on fire," Jarrett would recall—but Roberts wasn't particularly panicked. Together, Roberts and Jarrett began tearing away pieces of Roberts's burning uniform—which wasn't fire-retardant; just a uniform for show. Jarrett would recall burning his hands on the numerous pocket zippers that had been sewn into Roberts's uniform mainly for decoration.

Johnson, who'd had a long run back up the track toward the fire cloud, arrived in time to see Fireball standing against the guardrail, his body covered with second- and third-degree burns. Johnson took blame for beginning the multicar crash that left his friend in critical condition.

For more than a month Fireball would lie in a Charlotte hospital. At times he would rally, almost miraculously. One old story has it that a nurse in the corridor outside his room once heard him singing to the top of his lungs—indeed, Fireball did have a favorite song with a theme and title he deemed perfect for himself: Faron Young's "Hello, Walls." Supposedly the nurse advised him to stop singing, and when he wouldn't, she summoned a doctor, who said, "If you don't settle down and behave yourself, you're gonna die." And Fireball supposedly replied, "If I'd ever worried about that, I wouldn't be here in the first place."

Fireball Roberts died on July 2, 1964. Richard Petty's twenty-seventh birthday. They brought his body back to his native Daytona Beach on the eve of the Firecracker 400, the race he'd won on the previous two Fourth of Julys in a row. They buried him in a plot that lies within a mile of the third turn of Daytona International Speedway. And to this day, when the cars are racing or practicing, you can stand and face his tombstone and the roar coming over your shoulder is so intense that you have the urge to move, to get out of the way, lest the cars run right down the thousand-yard backstretch and right over this plot—then suddenly they bank off into the third turn and are gone, like F-16 fighter pilots in ceremonial salute to some head of state.

It was raining when they put Fireball in the ground, so that no one was sure if there were tears on Junior Johnson's face.

* * *

*A*t last, even Junior Johnson's nerve found its limits. By the summer of '64 he and Ford's meteoric Fred Lorenzen both were pleading for a bridling of race speeds. Ford Motor Company—by then the most active manufacturer in the world in motor racing, on all major fronts—had engineered an answer to Chrysler's hemi engine, and things were getting out of hand. In October, another Wilkes County–born driver, Jimmy Pardue, was killed during a tire test at Charlotte. Rising star Billy Wade of Houston went on a tear of four straight wins in '64, then was killed during a tire test at Daytona in January of '65.

Effective with the '65 season, Bill France banned both the hemi and Ford's high-swirl combustion chambers. Now the man who'd stared down the Teamsters must face Detroit. Ford, which saw the advertising value of winning as just as important, if not more so, than technological advancement, agreed to the changes. Chrysler decided to boycott the '65 NASCAR season altogether.

And so young Richard Petty, reigning champion of both the Daytona 500 and the '64 NASCAR Grand National season, was forced to forfeit his defense of both titles. He would join in Chrysler's boycott.

France held firm. In 1965 the Daytona 500's deck was stacked with twenty-six Fords or Mercurys in a field of forty-three. A few privately owned Dodges and Plymouths showed up, but the almighty factory team, led by Petty, was absent. Fred Lorenzen led a parade of Fords and Mercurys that finished in the first thirteen positions, then sat in the pits, in the rain, after only 330 miles, until the race was called due to darkness.

It had been a dismal day for France. And the season unfolded as merely a matter of which of the Ford drivers would win on a given Sunday—Junior Johnson, Ned Jarrett, Fred Lorenzen, Marvin Panch, or Dick Hutcherson.

Despairing promoters of other tracks met and demanded that France reinstate Curtis Turner and Tim Flock, for the sake of restoring some pizzazz. France capitulated. Turner would return to race sporadically, but the magic was gone from his name—at one race, he crashed with a young driver named Bobby Isaac, and as they climbed out of their cars, Turner growled, "You just wrecked me because I'm a big name!" To which Isaac replied, "Man, I've never seen you before in my life! I have no idea who you are!"

Tim Flock would not return. After the strife of '61, his heart just wasn't in it anymore.

By midseason of '65 it had dawned on Chrysler Corporation that it was the big loser in the boycott. Ford was getting all the brand exposure. Petty had gone drag racing in a Plymouth Barracuda with disastrous results—at Dallas, Georgia, a transmission failure had sent the vehicle out of control, into a crowd of spectators, and an eight-year-old boy had been killed. (Petty, ever the fatalist, publicly made himself get over what he considered a pure accident. But because he always internalized so much emotion anyway, only he could know how long or how deeply the tragedy rode with him.)

On July 25, 1965, the boycott broke. The Dodge and Plymouth factory teams came back, first to the Volunteer 500 at Bristol, Tennessee. It was too late for Chrysler to salvage much of the season. For Ford, Jarrett won the Grand National championship, and Johnson the most races, thirteen. Through the remnants of the season, Petty won but four races.

But Petty was back. In '66, he became the first two-time winner of the Daytona 500. When the race was stopped due to rain after 198 of the scheduled 200 laps, Petty's Plymouth was a full lap ahead of upstart Cale Yarborough's Ford.

Bill France's house was back in order. The iron of his will and his hand had prevailed. Again.

11

CI SONO MOLTE CORSE IN AMERICA!

*O*n July 16, 1955, the Italian ocean liner *Conte Biancamano* had steamed into New York Harbor. Upon sighting the Statue of Liberty, a family of five had begun singing, but the teenage twin boys' hearts hadn't been in it. Amidst the singing they had muttered to each other, *"No corse in America...No corse in America..."*

No racing in America. Back in the refugee camp in Italy they had read a little about the Indianapolis 500, but it seemed to be the only race in America. Europe was teeming with racing. The twins' passionate dreams of it had gotten them through the escape from Communist partisans in their native Istria, an ethnic Italian peninsula that would become part of Yugoslavia and is now part of Croatia. Their idolization of the great Formula One driver Alberto Ascari, learned from old racing magazines, had gotten them through seven years in a refugee camp at Lucca, Italy, near Florence. The twins at age thirteen had left the camp on weekends, claiming to be going to "Boy Scout camp," to race little Formula Junior cars provided by kindly benefactors who'd understood their passion. Had their father had any knowledge of this, he likely would have walloped the daylights out of both boys. Here he was unable to find work, and his boys were dreaming their lives away about an endeavor that produced nothing, other than the risk of injury or death. "Crazy kids!" he would say whenever he found them reading their tattered racing magazines.

Then their mother had informed them that she had an uncle who had migrated to a town called Nazareth in a place called Pennsylvania, in America. He had written to her, inviting her to bring her family to live in America. She and their father had decided this was best. *Immaginano, bambini! America!*

No corse in America.

By 1956 they had settled in, and their father had gone to work at Bethlehem Steel. The twins were sixteen and had gotten jobs at a gas station. It was from that gas station, with glorious news, that one of them ran home one afternoon and bounded upstairs, shouting to his brother, who was lying down with a headache.

"Eh, Aldo! Nazareth ha un pista per le corse!"

Nazareth had a race track. They rushed out to see it. What they found was a strange sort of *pista* indeed. It was oval-shaped, and its surface was dirt—nothing like the paved, serpentine road courses of Europe. The good news was that here, instead of the expensive thoroughbred cars of Europe, the racing was done with inexpensive machinery—huge American cars modified for racing. They were called "stock cars."

Learning that, Mario Andretti maintains to this day, "was probably the happiest moment of my life. Instead of looking at racing as something that was way down the road for us, this was something we could begin working on right away!"

It took Aldo and Mario three years to raise enough money and build a car, learning every component as they went. By 1959 they had become U.S. citizens, and they had one race car between them—a '48 Hudson Hornet. They took turns driving. Together they went on a tear, winning nine races in a row between them.

Their father, Alvise Andretti, called "Gigi," was too proud to admit he didn't understand enough English to know what his co-workers at the steel mill were saying when they met him at the time clock on Monday mornings. He thought the men were just complimenting the job his twins were doing at the gas station, and would respond, "Yeah, yeah, good boys! Good boys!"

Their mother, Rina, knew. But she dared not tell Gigi, who despised the whole notion of motor racing. Surreptitiously the twins ventured to another track, at Hatfield, Pennsylvania, bent on winning the richest purse they'd ever heard of—the winner would be paid $1,500. Aldo was probably the better driver of the twins, and was even more fearless than Mario. So Aldo would drive in the big event.

Aldo crashed. Bad. The Hudson Hornet flipped end over end, forever separating the life paths of the twins. Aldo went into a coma.

"When I got to the hospital, hell, they'd given him his last rites," Mario would recall.

Gigi had to be informed, and summarily gave the nineteen-year-old Mario a licking. For more than two weeks Aldo lay unconscious. The doctors told the family to talk to him, to try to get his attention somewhere deep in his coma.

"When he was lying there," Mario would remember, "you know what the hell I was whispering to him? I was whispering, 'I'm building a new car.' That's the only thing I knew to say to him that, somewhere in his subconscious, would excite him."

Aldo would awaken, be able to lead a normal life, and would continue to love racing. But he would never drive in big-time races. His reflexes would never again be as quick as Mario's.

And so Mario would drive not only for himself but for his brother, in every type of car, everywhere he went. It turned out that *Ci sono molte corse in America*—there was much racing in America—and Mario was bent on doing it all— enough racing, in enough variety, for a dozen men. That is how much it would take to fulfill the dreams of both Andretti twins.

By the 1960s, on the United States Auto Club sprint car tour, Mario was getting Christmas cards in July. That was an old, black-humor gesture of enormous admiration from his peers. The connotation was, they'd better send the greetings in the middle of racing season, because the way he drove, he probably wouldn't live till Christmas.

*T*he big, tough, grassroots southerners of NASCAR reck- oned the five-foot-six Eye-talian was a cute little fellow, all right, when he arrived to drive a factory-entered Ford in the 1967 Daytona 500. But he'd come out of those prissy—if deadly—open-wheel sprint and Indy cars.

What did he know about stock car racing?

One helluva lot more than they ever imagined.

Indy cars went fast, didn't run very close to each other— there was too much danger of one set of open wheels "climb- ing" the other and sending a car flipping skyward. What did this Andretti know of banging fenders, slamming each other around?

Had he the balls for this?

They would soon find, in their own vernacular, that "You couldn't fit 'em into a boxcar."

He had driven, very briefly, in the Daytona 500 the previ- ous year, in a so-so car, but crashed early—after only thirty- one laps, before the regulars had time or reason to notice him. But now here he was in a factory car prepared by Ford's top team of the time, Holman-Moody. They began to pay attention.

They half-snickered, half-groused at the driving style he displayed in practice—coming off the straightaways, he would dive the car to the bottom of the banking through the turns. What was this about? Why, that little fellow was liable to bust his ass big-time, darting around like that.

When he dropped down on the banking like that, the effect was to rev the engine even higher—give it maximum power through the turns. Where the NASCAR regulars believed in making their turns as wide as possible, running right up by the outside retaining wall and letting the 31-degree banking slow them to sane speed by natural centrifugal force, Mario Andretti was going balls-out, right down at the bottom of the race track. No other driver would get near him on the track, for fear of being caught up in what they felt was Mario's inevitable disaster.

He was not quite twenty-seven years old. And he was twenty years ahead of his time. Not until the 1990s would the consensus of drivers accept "the bottom of the race track" as "the quickest way around" Daytona.

Mario blew their doors off—including his Holman-Moody teammate, defending Daytona 500 champion Fred Lorenzen. The race finished under caution, robbing Andretti of a win by the huge margin he deserved. Just before Richard Petty's engine blew, causing an oil slick on the track and therefore the final caution flag, Andretti had built a whopping twenty-two-second lead over Lorenzen, who theoretically was in identical equipment to Andretti's, and had vastly more experience at Daytona.

Before Mario Andretti became the most famous racing driver in the history of the planet...before he won the Indianapolis 500... before he teamed with the late Pedro Rodriguez of Mexico to give Ferrari its most popular endurance-racing duo ever...before he won the World

Driving Championship when Formula One was the deadliest and most glamorous sport in the world (Emerson Fittipaldi in those days rated an F1 driver's chances of surviving any given season at one in seven)…

…Before any of that, Mario Andretti won the Daytona 500…he was, first, a stock car driver. And in one part of his heart, he still is.

12

Yar-BURROW, Yar-BRO

No tougher kid has ever grown up around Timmonsville, South Carolina—or anywhere else—than William Caleb Yarborough. "Cale."

As a boy he was bitten by a rattlesnake, felt sick for a while, sloughed it off, and a few days later found the snake under a bush, dead.

"I reckon after that snake bit me, he just crawled off and died," he would recall, quite seriously.

Another day he was standing by an open window in his mother's house, savoring the sight of a violent thunderstorm flying across the farmland.

"I saw lightning hit out in the field, and the bolt sort of bounced, and suddenly there was this blinding ball of fire that looked like it was heading straight for me...

"I woke up lying on the floor, and the room was full of smoke. The lightning had hit me right square in the chest."

No problem.

Before skydiving was fashionable, Cale took a plunge out of an airplane. Sure was pretty up there, until he noticed that his parachute hadn't opened.

Down he plummeted, calmly fiddling with the ripcord, trying to untangle it, until, with about two hundred feet between him and the ground, he felt and heard the comforting WHUMP of the chute opening.

"It probably helped that I hit in some tall, thick, soft weeds," he would recall, matter-of-factly.

Cars? He loved to drive them as fast as they would go. That was about it. All he really understood was the steering wheel and the gas pedal—other than that, he'd have been hard-pressed to fix a flat tire. (His mechanical savvy never would grow much, unless you count his eventual comprehension of the purpose of a brake pedal. At the pinnacle of his NASCAR career, driving for a car owner named Junior Johnson, Cale rarely could tell the crew specifically what was wrong with the car. Once, at Riverside, Cale complained that the car was just "uncomfortable"—after which the grizzled Johnson turned and remarked to a small audience in the pits, "Hell, if I'da wanted the boy to be comfortable, I'da built him a Rolls-Royce.")

He came up hard through the Carolina hellhole dirt tracks, beating and banging with the likes of Ralph Earnhardt (who often brought into the pits a gangly son named Dale). Cale was a fireplug high school football fullback—was, as football coaches like to say of players who pack more punch than their size indicates, "wound tight as a golf ball." But at his height it would have been tough to take on major-college linebackers, and so off he went on a small-college scholarship—for a few days. "Then Friday night came and it was time to go racing, so I came home. Didn't go back."

The first time Cale Yarborough showed up at Daytona, in 1962, it was in a Ford that wasn't even close to factory-backed, and he finished dead last, and he and his bride, Betty Jo, started home to South Carolina and when they got to the drawbridge at Jacksonville they discovered they didn't have enough money between them to pay the toll. So the guy in the tollbooth ended up loaning these kids, who claimed they'd just come from the Daytona 500, the thirty-five cents to keep moving toward Georgia.

LeeRoy Yarbrough was not related to Cale Yarborough. Look again at the spellings of the surnames: Cale Yarbor-ough—"Yar-BURROW," as ABC's Keith Jackson used to emphasize on televison—and LeeRoy "Yar-BRO."

Soon after LeeRoy (or what was left of him) tried to kill his mother and was locked up in a psychiatric cell—this was in 1980—the family lawyer explained: "The reason the fam-ily name is spelled 'Yarbrough'—without the first 'o'—is that LeeRoy's daddy didn't know how to spell his own last name."

Neither, apparently, were Lonnie and Minnie Yarbrough dead-solid perfect on the given name in filling out the birth certificate, if their intent was "LeRoy." They apparently spelled 'em like they heard 'em. And so if "LeRoy Yarbor-ough" came out sounding like "LeeRoy Yarbrough"—which it did on the southern periphery of the Okefenokee Swamp, where the child was born, in 1938—then that would be the name etched in the granite of the tombstone of stock car rac-ing's most enigmatic tragic figure.

LeeRoy was no more enigmatic than Lloyd Seay, but was mysterious in a vastly different way. LeeRoy was far more tragic, in that his dying took so long and was so hard. There is no evidence that Lloyd Seay had many, if any, inner demons—LeeRoy had enough to sell out the grandstands of Daytona International Speedway.

LeeRoy was a midnight brawler, a night cruiser in a street dragster. Then he was harnessed into the dirt tracks of Jack-sonville and thence up the coast through Georgia and the Carolinas, where he got a reputation as the only s.o.b. tough enough to take on the titanic Tiny Lund fist-to-fist in the pits.

LeeRoy and Tiny were not exactly enemies—they were more friends who often didn't see eye to eye and didn't take time to talk things out. Another star of the Carolina short tracks of the time, Little Bud Moore, would recall the night LeeRoy, who owned a private plane, invited Lund and Moore to fly with him from one short-track race to the next.

"Well, LeeRoy and Tiny started fighting before the race," Little Bud would remember, "and they fought some more after the race. Then we took off. We got up in the air and LeeRoy and Tiny started fighting all over again. I thought they were gonna tear the sides out of that thing. It's a wonder we didn't crash, with them two boys fightin' like that."

*B*y the 1968 Daytona 500, Yarborough and Yarbrough had big-time rides in Mercurys—Cale with the Wood Brothers, and LeeRoy with Junior Johnson, who'd quit driving in 1966 to become a full-time car owner. (Despite the death of Fireball Roberts and the escalating speeds, Johnson would maintain decades later that he retired as a driver mainly because "I just got tired of it.")

Glen and Leonard Wood had hit on their combination of chassis setup, engine, and aerodynamics better than Junior and his crew had. So Cale had a stronger car than LeeRoy, but God knew who had the stronger will. LeeRoy would hang in on sheer tenacity and nerve, and the duel would go on so long that ABC's announcing crew would have to explain to the audience time and again that Yarborough and Yarbrough weren't brothers, weren't even related.

As the laps waned, LeeRoy led, but Cale began to close fast after he broke free of traffic and there was only air and asphalt between their two cars. Cale ran up behind LeeRoy with five laps to go, and it was Yarborough will versus Yarbrough will until, with three laps left, Leonard Wood's superior engine and the turbulent drafts of Daytona broke the deadlock.

Drivers had discovered that the draft, in addition to creating a semi-vacuum directly behind the lead car, sent a huge wash of air out from the front car at an angle, very much like the wake of a boat on water. You could pull out to pass and if you caught this wash of air just right, it would "slingshot" the second car past the first.

And so Cale beat LeeRoy with a slingshot. LeeRoy, the baddest boy in the field, was helpless. He would file that little experience away in that haunted head of his.

*B*y 1969 Junior Johnson held a royal flush. All that remained was to lay down the cards, beginning with the Daytona 500. His Fords were the strongest cars by far in NASCAR—and he just happened to have the only driver with balls enough to run as fast as those cars would go: LeeRoy Yarbrough. Never again would Junior be so completely satisfied with a driver. He would win six Winston Cups, three with Cale Yarborough and three with Darrell Waltrip, in the 1970s and 1980s. But all the while, Junior would mutter about this gnawing urge. "I want me a driver I can slap up 'side the helmet and say, 'Lissen, boy: You go out there and you hold that thing wide open until you crash or I tell you to quit. You understand me?' "

What he always wanted was another LeeRoy Yarbrough.

Charlie Glotzbach, "Chargin' Cholly," had a monstrous Dodge under him, prepared by Cotton Owens, for the Daytona 500. With nineteen laps to go, as LeeRoy pitted, Glotzbach had an eleven-second lead.

But here came LeeRoy, and by the beginning of the final lap, Glotzbach could look in his mirror and see that it was all over, that he had lost. "There is no known defense against the slingshot," Glotzbach would say afterward, as LeeRoy drove into Victory Lane.

Amidst the celebration, LeeRoy yelped, "I'm going crazy!" It was taken as a term of jubilation. Nobody took it as literally as they should have.

But in the weeks ahead, it would come to be said that LeeRoy was no longer a driver—LeeRoy had become a missile pilot.

He flew through the Rebel 400 at Darlington—win; World 600 at Charlotte—win; back to Daytona for the Firecracker 400—win; Dixie 500 at Atlanta—win…and a romp through the Southern 500 at Darlington on Labor Day made it official: LeeRoy Yarbrough was the first man ever to win NASCAR's "Triple Crown"—the Daytona 500, World 600, and Southern 500 in the same year.

*A*nd then, as suddenly as LeeRoy had come, he was gone. Finished.

Even at the pinnacle, "I think," Cale Yarborough would muse more than a decade later, "LeeRoy was drinking a lot more, even then, than any of us realized."

Peers remembered bizarre violence. There was, for example, the afternoon LeeRoy returned from the track to his motel at Darlington, seething for no clear reason, looking for his wife, Gloria.

"LeeRoy went into that room and he snatched that woman out of the bed by the hair of her head," Little Bud Moore would remember. "He dragged that woman out of the room and down the breezeway, still by the hair of the head, kicking her in the ass as he dragged her along."

LeeRoy had a bad crash during a test session for Junior Johnson in April of 1970. From there, rumors began that he might be abusing painkillers along with the booze. There were times, relatives would remember, that he would buy several pints of whiskey, row a boat out to the middle of a lake near Jacksonville, and just sit there all day, silent, staring, drinking.

Both LeeRoy and Cale ventured into Indy cars in the early 1970s. Cale realized his mistake, and came back to NASCAR with his best years, by far, still ahead. But LeeRoy could not leave behind the effects of another bad crash, this time at Indianapolis, in 1971. Years later, neurological examinations would show evidence of "several brain lesions," according to his lawyer.

*F*or years the stories and rumors came out of Jacksonville. Maybe LeeRoy had gotten into a fight over a couple of quarts of beer...maybe he'd been picked up on such-and-such a charge...sad, but fairly mundane stuff for a man wandering the streets aimlessly...

LeeRoy was staying at his mother's house on the morning of Thursday, February 13, 1980. It was the day of the twin 125-mile qualifying races at Daytona that would determine much of the starting order for that Sunday's Daytona 500. And here sat LeeRoy in Jacksonville, destitute, his ebbing mind playing tricks on him.

"I was standing in front of a mirror, brushing my hair," Minnie Yarbrough, then eighty years old, would say a few days later. "LeeRoy came up behind me and put his hands on my shoulders. I thought he was going to give me a hug.

"Then LeeRoy said, 'Mama, I hate to do this. Mama, I've got to kill you.'"

She thought for an instant he was joking, but when she felt his hands on her throat and saw his eyes in the mirror, she knew he meant it. She struggled. She kicked.

One of LeeRoy's teenage nephews heard the commotion and came in. The kid couldn't get LeeRoy off of her. Looking around, desperate, the boy saw a quart jar full of preserves sitting on the kitchen table. He grabbed it and came down hard on LeeRoy's head, shattering the jar and knocking LeeRoy cold.

The police came and took LeeRoy away to a psychiatric cell. He was judged incompetent to stand trial. When I got to Jacksonville, the Yarbrough family lawyer, who'd been taking care of their problems for many years, showed me stacks of medical reports that were inconclusive about LeeRoy—several "lesions on the brain" had been noted, but their origins had not been determined.

The crashes were what did it, Little Bud Moore reckoned. "You know," he said, "LeeRoy hit that wall awful hard in Texas [at old Texas World Speedway near College Station], and he hit that wall awful hard at Indianapolis. I'm telling you, sometimes you can hit that wall so hard that at first you don't know which life you're in—this one or the next one. I believe you can hit that wall so hard it turns your brain around inside your head." (Not for another decade would trauma specialists and neurosurgeons attending injured race drivers explain that horrific "G-spikes" associated with hard crashes into concrete retaining walls can indeed cause the human brain to move inside the skull, even if the skull itself is not injured.)

Only Junior Johnson knows—and he won't talk about it—how many hundreds of thousands of dollars he spent on LeeRoy, beginning in 1980, taking him to the best psychiatrists and hospitals available. It was hopeless. LeeRoy died of a seizure in a mental hospital in 1984.

13

THE KING

*T*o realize beyond doubt that Richard Petty was NASCAR's greatest man of the people, ever—and that he will not, cannot, ever be replaced—we must fast-forward for a while to the point in his career when he was washed up. Far over the hill. Just hanging on as a driver.

April 8, 1989, was a Saturday. It rained hard all day at the high-banked half-mile hellhole in the mountains of eastern Tennessee, Bristol International Raceway (now more rationally known as Bristol Motor Speedway). Richard Petty hadn't qualified in the first round on Friday, and now the second round was being washed out completely. He hadn't enough season points to get a provisional start (this was before NASCAR instituted provisional berths for former Winston Cup champions).

Richard Petty would not race in the next day's Valleydale 500. That would make two out of three races for which he had failed to qualify. The Richmond event, two weeks earlier, was the first time he'd missed a Winston Cup race since 1971—and back then, he and several other stars simply hadn't shown up for a race at Macon, Georgia, because the promoter had refused to guarantee appearance money, which was and is customary in NASCAR. Richard Petty's career was dotted with absences from races due to "circumstances," as he put it, such as the Chrysler boycott of 1965. Illness didn't stop him—in 1978 he drove when doctors told him he shouldn't, and then at season's end surgeons removed forty percent of his ulcer-ravaged stomach. Injuries didn't stop him—he had driven hurt, literally from head to foot at one time or another.

But Richard Petty was not used to missing races due to failure to qualify.

I looked around me in the media center and said generally, to no one in particular, "Wonder where the King is."

"Who knows? Who cares?" some writer said, without looking up from his computer screen.

Yeah, who cared. NASCAR's all-time winningest driver with 200 victories...at the time its only seven-time champion (Dale Earnhardt at this point had won only three)...the only seven-time Daytona 500 winner there ever had been, or, it appeared at the time, ever would be...winner in 1967 of a record 27 of 48 races...winner in 1975 of a "modern-era" record 13 of 30 races after the old, unwieldy schedule was reduced in 1972 (Jeff Gordon would not tie the 13-win total until 1998, and even then on a 34-race schedule)...the singular figure who had brought NASCAR out of the boondocks and up through ABC's *Wide World of Sports*...the man whose name was known by Americans who didn't even know the term "NASCAR."

Who cared. I headed out into the darkening deluge.

It took a while. Then through the fog and rain, sitting directly behind the backstretch pit area, I saw a Pontiac station wagon. To be allowed into the tiny infield at Bristol, this car had to be one of the "loaners," or courtesy cars, that the Detroit manufacturers let their NASCAR drivers use. Petty drove Pontiacs. Maybe...

Sure enough, there he sat, alone, on the passenger side of the front seat. All that was visible was the cowboy hat with the band of rattlesnake skin and pheasant feathers. The hat was tilted down—his head was bowed—so that it covered the face.

I tapped at the passenger's-side window. He looked up slowly. The sunglasses were off. The face was as weary as I had ever seen it. Especially the eyes. An electric motor zzzzzzed and the window lowered four or five inches. He just looked at me. No expression.

"Look, I know this is a tough time—"

"Then why're you fuckin' with me?" he said.

He knew why. Nobody in NASCAR—hell, in all of sports—has ever understood the role of the media better than Richard Petty. He made a circling motion with that giant right forefinger, around toward the driver's seat.

"Git in," he said.

He put the sunglasses back on, and his head dropped again and the hat covered his face. Nothing was said for a while—probably several minutes. There are times when sportswriters do better without asking anything. Once I'd sat with Bear Bryant like that as he stared out his office window for a long time and finally he'd said, "I can't coach 'em anymore." And two weeks later he quit, and two months after that he was dead.

There was no point in asking Richard Petty about being forgotten. We'd already been through the times on the far backsides of garage areas at tracks where he'd been banished far from the stalls of the frontrunners of the day and he would say, with a wry smile, "This is where they put you when they don't need you anymore."

Finally he said, "Drive over to the inspection station."

The keys were in the ignition. He wanted to go and ask if qualifying had been officially scrubbed, so he could go home. I started driving, slowly—the Bristol infield was a maze of trailers and toolboxes and stacks of tires that could hardly be negotiated on a motor scooter, let alone in a big station wagon. And for three or four minutes, Richard Petty was the worst backseat driver I had ever encountered—"Hell, just turn in here…Why don't you just back in there?…Damn, Ed, you can turn it around right here…" Maybe he could. I couldn't. I didn't argue—it was all part of his bleak mood. The inspection station was deserted. He would have to wait for official word. We drove back to the original spot behind the pits, with him bitching about my driving all the way.

The radio was on. Only faintly. Very faintly, even to me. And Richard Petty was partly deaf. But Richard Petty hears what he wants to hear. The news came on. Pete Rose's gambling activities were a major news story that spring.

"Pete's in a lot of trouble," Petty said. Over the decades he'd gotten to know, or had at least met, many stars from various sports—mostly as part of promotional appearances he'd made for network television.

As the story about Rose concluded, Petty stared out through the fogged windshield, at nothing.

"A compulsive gambler can't quit," he said of Rose. "Can't quit when he's winning, can't quit when he's losing…sort of like me."

He tried to smile. It was faint and fleeting. His head dropped again.

Then there came a tapping at his window. He raised his head slowly. Outside in the downpour stood three little boys, maybe ten or eleven years old. One of them held a felt-tip pen that was dripping black fluid in the rain. Another held some soggy pieces of paper.

And Richard Petty was transformed.

He summoned that famous, pearly grin of his. He lowered the window completely.

"How 'bout it, boys?" he said with all the cheer in the world in his voice.

They were all dumbstruck for a moment as they stared face-to-face with that legendary visage. Finally one of them blurted, "Can we have your autograph?"

He glanced at the soggy paper and the dripping felt-tip and, in a swift motion that did not indicate rejection of their useless materials at all, gestured for me to hand him my reporter's notebook and my ballpoint pen. By reflex I handed them over, as I had many times, for many years, when fans would approach him without any pen or paper at all.

He turned to a blank sheet, and across it swirled and flourished that magnificent signature that is like no other in all of sports—he'd learned it at a penmanship school decades earlier, so that he could give the fans something far more fulfilling than an ordinary autograph.

He tore off that first sheet and held it in his left hand.

Across a second sheet the signature flew again. He tore it off.

The boys' eyes grew wider with every second. The grin didn't let up.

He signed the third sheet as carefully as the first. When he was done, he fanned the three sheets like three playing cards, so that all three boys could snatch their individual sheets at the same time. By now he had transmitted to them that sense of familiarity—no, of bond—with the King that untold tens of thousands had felt over the decades as they walked away from him.

"Where'd you qualify?" one of the boys blurted.

"Yeah! Where'd you qualify?" another joined in.

He looked at them through the sunglasses. He turned up the intensity of the grin about three notches.

"Well," he said, "we're workin' on it."

"O.K.—thanks!"

"Yeah, thanks!"

"Yeah, *thanks!*"

And they were gone. Happy as could be. Giddy.

Richard Petty's weathered right hand covered his eyes again, sunglasses and all, and he slumped deeply into the passenger's-side seat again, and his head dropped so that his chin was on his chest again, and the enormous cowboy hat covered his face again.

He sighed. It was the longest sigh I have ever heard.

A couple of hours later it stopped raining. Too late. Qualifying had been canceled. Bristol's public relations staff reminded the press corps on the media center public-address system that Petty had failed to qualify for the second of the last three races. A dozen or so of them trudged dutifully out to find the King—maybe they could use this as an item in their "notebook" columns for the next day.

He was out of the station wagon, grinning, waiting for them, and they surrounded him, and it doesn't matter much what he said at that point—just that there was no bitterness in it, and that he'd come back again and try to do better next race.

There was a very young and unduly arrogant driver at the time named Ben Hess. He too had failed to make the field for the Valleydale 500. He was destined not to make it in Winston Cup racing, but you couldn't have told him that then. Anyway, Ben Hess marched right into the middle of the gaggle surrounding Richard Petty, broke up the conversation, and looked around at each of the assembled reporters.

"I just want all of you to know," said Ben Hess, "that more than one good car will miss this race."

None of the reporters asked him a question, or even said anything. We all just sort of looked at him in amazement.

Richard Petty broke the silence.

"Tell you what," he said, looking at Ben Hess in the gathering darkness through his sunglasses. "If this is the biggest disappointment you ever have in this sport, you're gonna be in good shape."

He clapped Ben Hess on the shoulders and grinned as he said it. That big, doubly intense grin he had given the three little boys.

*I*t had started on the dirt tracks in the late '50s. Before Richard Petty ever won a race, writers were writing about him and, most importantly, fans were flocking to him. Petty and the common people mixed as naturally to form something vital as two molecules of hydrogen bond with a molecule of oxygen to make water.

"It just happened," he would say. "The Good Lord just does these things, and I don't know why, and the people don't know why."

Back then, "We didn't have sponsors. We didn't have nobody to please. We didn't have nobody to tell us when to do right. We just done it. To begin with, it was an honor—and has been ever since—for a cat from Level Cross to go down to South Carolina or up to New York and somebody wants his *autograph*. It was a big deal. Big honor. Once you got doing it, you didn't mind doing it. You seen how it pleased the people."

The beginnings of his winning were a gift from his father. Lee Petty was the first of the natural-born businessmen in NASCAR, and negotiated the best factory deals for the best equipment and placed his son in cars that were head and shoulders above the rest. Chrysler's hemi engine took Richard Petty to his first Daytona 500 win in '64, and factory-backed Plymouths had taken him to the twenty-seven wins in '67.

But Richard Petty's *demeanor* as a winner, and then as the biggest winner of them all—that was the phenomenon that made him infinitely more than a star performer, that made him a folk hero.

And so when, in 1971, the Detroit manufacturers stopped supporting NASCAR teams—at least officially—and outside corporate sponsorship had to be found to pay the enormous expenses of racing, Richard Petty was the first to get a major sponsor. It wasn't that he was fan- and media-friendly because STP was his sponsor. It was that STP sponsored him because he was fan- and media-friendly.

*I*f there was a peak of Petty's career, it was from 1971 to 1974. In that span he won three of four Daytona 500s (only A. J. Foyt would intervene in Petty's onslaught, winning the 500 in '72) and three of four Winston Cups (interrupted by Benny Parsons's dark-horse championship in '73).

Entering the '70s, Petty was the only two-time winner of the Daytona 500, in '64 and '66. But after a fourth straight Daytona loss in 1970, he would roar to his permanent place atop the lore of Daytona, and of NASCAR.

A blown engine took Petty out of the 1970 Daytona 500 after only seven laps, but the day wasn't all bad. A protégé, Pete Hamilton of Dedham, Massachusetts, carried on in a Petty Enterprises team car, a Plymouth Superbird, and held off a late charge by David Pearson to win. It was the fourth Daytona 500 win for the Petty team overall, coupled with Richard's two and Lee's victory in the inaugural race of 1959.

Then in 1971, Richard led Petty Enterprises' most dominant day ever at Daytona, winning by a ten-second margin over his teammate, Buddy Baker. The only driver who finished even in the same lap with the one-two punch of Petty Dodges was the bull-like intruder from Indy car racing, Foyt.

"If Foyt had run with us regular," Petty would say decades later, when both were nearing retirement, "then nobody might have ever heard of Richard Petty." Then he would ponder, and grin. "Then again, nobody might have ever heard of A. J. Foyt."

What might have been a magnificent duel between Petty and Foyt in the '72 Daytona 500 was cut short when a valve broke in the engine of Petty's Plymouth while he was leading on the eighty-first lap. Previously, he and Foyt had exchanged the lead nine times. Foyt was never challenged after Lap 81, and in Victory Lane he admitted the second half of the race hadn't been much fun after Petty fell out.

Petty's '73 win at Daytona was closer than the records indicate. He finished a whopping two laps ahead of second-place Bobby Isaac. But Petty was able to cruise only for the final six laps, after he'd forced a blistering duel with old friend Buddy Baker, which left the engine blown in Baker's Dodge. With twelve laps to go, Petty pitted for a "splash-and-go" gas stop, with no tire changes, that took only eight seconds, compared to Baker's ten-second stop a lap later. When the stops were done, Petty had a four-second lead, and Baker, in trying to cut the deficit, overtaxed his car.

Petty's most-cited ingredient for winning, "circumstances," ebbed and flowed for him in the '74 Daytona 500. Late in the race, circumstances first went against him—a tire was cut on his Dodge with nineteen laps to go. Because the flat occurred in Turn 4, he was able to duck into the pits. But when he emerged with fresh tires he was more than half a lap behind leader Donnie Allison. Then, as so often in the career of the King, circumstances turned for him—Allison ran over debris, shredded a tire, and spun with eleven laps left, leaving Petty to cruise to the win.

"I was leading the race and blew a tire, but I got into the pits and got mine changed," Petty would recall many years later. "Then Donnie was leading the race and blew a tire, and he wasn't as lucky as I was. He blew his tire past the pit road; I blew mine before I got there. So that was a luck situation.

In some of the other Daytona 500s, we'd just driven off and left 'em."

That fifth win alone would have left Richard Petty, to this day, the all-time leader in Daytona 500 victories. There would be two more.

But first there would be a five-year drought at Daytona, during which an old rivalry would boil over. By 1974 Richard Petty was the unchallenged charismatic leader of NASCAR drivers. But not necessarily the best. Since 1963 he'd found himself in fairly regular one-two finishes, one way or the other, at various tracks on the tour, with a media-shy driver who was far less comfortable in the limelight than Petty, but even more comfortable in a race car. Lately, season championships had begun to bore the bashful rival, who had won three of those in the '60s.

In 1973, entering only eighteen selected races, this other guy had won eleven—a winning percentage of sixty-one percent, better even than Petty's fifty-six percent in 1967.

And now in '74, Petty's rivalry was about to billow—with David Pearson.

14

THE FOX

Somebody once asked David Pearson what he'd be doing if he weren't a race driver. "Probably painting cars," he said, meaning in an auto body shop. "That's what I was doing before."

And then somebody asked him if he read all the newspaper and magazine stories about him, which at this point were coming at the rate of dozens per week. Barely discernibly, Pearson's head tilted to one side, in the mannerism of a bird suddenly going on alert, sensing something. When Pearson got your drift, his head always flicked to one side.

"No," he said. "But I look at all the pictures."

Pearson's wit was like a razor-sharp rapier that slices all the way down a man's torso before he even realizes he's been cut.

His counterpunch to the subtly demeaning question duly absorbed and acknowledged, Pearson grew serious.

"I've always been kind of a shy person," he said. "Kind of uneducated."

He was an elementary school dropout who was dumb like a fox with an eighty-gigabyte chip implanted in his head and programmed to capacity with all the savvy he'd ever need to survive and prosper.

In the Carolinas there was a generic term for any village, or cluster of company housing, that had sprung up around a textile mill. "Mill Hill," all were called, and genteel southerners condescendingly referred to the inhabitants as "lint heads," because of the lint and fabric dust that covered their hair as they got off from the long, godawful shifts in the de facto sweatshops that went ununionized for decades after such despicable labor practices had been outlawed in the North. Their fate was as often "brown lung" disease as "black lung" was that of coal miners.

David Pearson never saw any point in denying that "I was a boy from Mill Hill," this one in Spartanburg, South Carolina.

As poor white kids looked for a way out of the Mill Hills of David Pearson's youth, it damn sure wasn't basketball (the kids couldn't stay in school long enough; they had to go to work before they reached puberty) or football (few were well enough nourished to grow to suitable size). Some, like Shoeless Joe Jackson, had made it through baseball in earlier decades. But by Pearson's time the strong minor league franchises had dried up in the Carolinas, and baseball had waned in the social fabric.

But for every few Mill Hills there was a dirt track. And that's where you headed on your way out. Pearson painted passenger cars by day and worked on race cars by night, and he was as nearly a natural driver as any, ever, anywhere. And after he'd won a few dozen races a year on dirt, and struggled into NASCAR with what money he could scrounge in 1960, an old racer turned real estate operator, an old rival of Big Bill France on the beach at Daytona, named Joe Littlejohn, thought Pearson deserved a real chance. And so Littlejohn and some other Spartanburg businessmen went in 1961 to team owner Ray Fox and convinced him to put Pearson in his car for the

World 600 that May. With that, his first real opportunity, Pearson won.

He stormed up through the ranks with three season championships, in '66 (fifteen wins in Cotton Owens's Dodges), '68 and '69 (sixteen and eleven wins, respectively, in Holman-Moody Fords). Wily on the track and prematurely gray, he was dubbed the Silver Fox.

Since '63 a recurrent quinella had been emerging. More and more races, it seemed, and then was confirmed by NASCAR statisticians, were being won by David Pearson, with Richard Petty second—or by Richard Petty, with David Pearson second. Over a sixteen-year period between '63 and '77, the Petty-Pearson quinella would come in an incredible sixty-three times.

But in the mid-'70s, only in the inner circles of NASCAR was "Petty-Pearson" spoken as one word. Everywhere else it was just "Petty."

Nowhere in sports has there been a more marked difference between a winner with pizzazz (Petty) and a winner, period (Pearson).

David Pearson could be the most outgoing, friendly, witty man in the world—if he knew you well. But if he didn't—and that applied to the overwhelming majority of media people—well, then…"I was bashful," he would remember, somewhat ruefully, in retirement. "I would hide from the media, and Richard would talk to them. I once saw him ask a TV reporter if he wanted an interview. I would never have done such a thing! And…well…it hurt me in the long run. Richard did it the right way."

Once during pole qualifying for the Daytona 500, Pearson suddenly slowed the red-and-white Wood Brothers Mercury drastically on the backstretch, drove into the garage, parked, and climbed out. A bunch of us ran up to him and asked, "Why did you stop?"

"Hell, I can't run in the rain," he said, and walked away.

The situation was this: It was cloudy over most of the track, and in the garage area, but not raining. Daytona International Speedway being such a vast expanse, a light shower was falling in the third turn, but went unnoticed to everyone inside the track but Pearson, who drove into it. On his second lap, coming down the thousand-yard backstretch, Pearson with his uncanny eyesight had seen that the shower was worsening far ahead, and backed off the throttle lest his slick tires slide on the damp pavement.

Pearson was often baffled that others didn't exercise the enormous degree of common sense he displayed. His reasoning was that if it was cloudy and misty, and was common knowledge that it could be raining in one corner of the speedway and dry everywhere else, any fool should have known he had backed off because he'd spotted a shower. Anybody who couldn't see that didn't deserve an explanation. And so he didn't bother.

Here's how Richard Petty probably would have handled the same situation:

"Well, the car was running real good on that first lap until I got into Three over there. There was a little shower—really more of a heavy mist, I guess you'd say—and as I came through Three, I noticed that the car wiggled, I mean j-u-u-s-t a little bit. Just enough to get my attention, if you know what I mean. So I came on around and the rest of the track was still dry, and I got another good run down the backstretch, but I was watching real close for the shower in Three, and it looked to me like the drops were falling a little harder, and so I thought, Whoa, no sense tearing up a car that's working this good. I'll just bring 'er in and wait'll they dry the track. It's kind of a shame, in a way. We might have had a lap good enough to win a pole, and I don't know if conditions are going to be this good again today. It was nice and cloudy and the track was cool and had plenty of grip where it wasn't raining. Once the sun comes out and makes the asphalt sort of liquefy and get slippery, I just don't think the track will be this good again. But hey, what can you say? It's just circumstances. We'll go back and try again. Anything else, boys?"

All that, where David Pearson figured, "Hell, I can't run in the rain" was enough explanation.

*D*avid Pearson was the only race driver of any renown who couldn't tell you what the inside of an ambulance looked like. He never rode in one. Not once in his entire career. Where Petty was injured practically all over through the years, Pearson was never hurt—"I've never had a broken bone nor anything," Pearson would say from time to time, even while he was still racing. And he wouldn't even bother to knock on wood—strange, for a man who seemed so superstitious otherwise.

You'd hear stories...One guy swore he was riding in a passenger car with Pearson down a country highway when Pearson, with that magnificent eyesight, spotted a black cat crossing the road maybe four hundred yards ahead—the passenger didn't even see it—and turned around in the middle of the road and drove several miles out of his way just to avoid taking the path the black cat had crossed. The late Tom Tucker of the *Atlanta Journal* got along famously with Pearson and once was kidding him about all his superstitions, and Pearson was denying, denying, denying that he was superstitious at all. "But David," Tucker finally asked, "What about the black cats?" Pearson's head cocked to one side. "Now that's *different*," he said. "Them bitches is *bad*."

But when David Pearson got into a race car he was one great mass of pure, cold logic. Early in his career some sports scientists were measuring NASCAR drivers' heart rates, and they found that the more intense the situation, the more Pearson's pulse actually slowed.

He believes to this day that going uninjured through a

twenty-six-year career was a matter of luck. Likely it was more a matter of rapid calculation at enormous speed while always remaining completely calm.

Pearson had an uncanny ability, at any given millisecond, to put himself in the optimal position. Even when it was impossible to avoid crashing, he usually managed to avoid crashing as badly as another driver might have.

He always made it look so very easy, because to him, it was. You could stand inside treacherous old Turn 4 at Darlington and watch practice for five minutes and see the difference in Pearson and all the rest. The others would exit the turn flailing at their steering wheels, fighting for control. Pearson would come out of the turn with his steering wheel barely moving at all, so precisely did he position himself through one of the toughest corners in NASCAR. Nearly all drivers wore open-face helmets in those days, and if you looked closely, you could see Pearson chewing his gum, oh so slowly, as he rocketed out of that corner. And when he would win the pole or a race at Darlington, invariably he would be met with questions about the treachery and difficulty of the warped old oval, and invariably he would reply, "Why do y'all keep talking about this race track? Hell, there ain't nothing wrong with this race track. It's just another race track."

Every one of them, including Daytona International Speedway, was just another race track to Pearson. They were all easy, all a matter of common sense, and because he never was injured, there was nothing to fear. To Pearson, there was nothing gallant or ballsy or romantic about what he did. There was, really, nothing to it. And so Pearson's brilliance was in fact at the root of his image problem—he never could bring himself to make it sound hard or risky or frightful to the public, because to him, it just wasn't.

And yet, "Time and again," Bobby Allison would recall when their careers were over, "a race would be over with, and my fenders would be rattling and my tires would be smoking and my brake pedal would be going to the floor, and Richard Petty and I would be sitting there with scratch marks all over our cars, and David Pearson would be sitting over there in Victory Lane with a pretty girl."

It was not that Pearson always let the competition wear each other out and then scavenged victory. To win 105 races, second only to Petty's career total—when in a lot of years his equipment was inferior to Petty's—Pearson had to take a lot of chances. But when he took them, he had calculated the risks, anticipated his opponent's reaction, even planned his escape routes if one thing or another went wrong.

Who was the best driver ever in NASCAR?

"Pearson," Petty would say, without hesitation, after their careers were over. "Pearson could beat you on a short track, he could beat you on a superspeedway, he could beat you on a road course, he could beat you on a dirt track. It didn't hurt as bad to lose to Pearson as it did to lose to some of the others, because I knew how good he was."

Petty would maintain that it didn't bother him that of their sixty-three one-two finishes, Pearson had won thirty-three to Petty's thirty: "When you lose to somebody better than you are, you don't mind it."

But at 12:53 P.M. on July 4, 1974, when the checkered flag fell on the Firecracker 400 at Daytona, Petty minded very much indeed.

And from that moment, the merely exciting would no longer qualify a Daytona finish as memorable. Henceforth, it must be electrifying.

The bar was not just raised; it was launched. Before that day, Daytona had slipped briefly into doldrums, with wide margins of victory and boring finishes where superior equipment prevailed. A. J. Foyt had won the '72 Daytona 500 by a margin of more than a lap. Petty had won the '73 Daytona 500 by more than two laps, and the '74 race by forty-seven seconds, nearly a lap.

The Firecracker 400 in those days started at 10 A.M. Big Bill France had several motives for starting so early, but they all had to do with Daytona's midsummer weather. Thunderstorms blow in almost invariably in the afternoons, starting around 3 P.M., drenching the speedway if only for short periods. And Daytona in July is so stifling hot that the beaches and swimming pools are the primary thought of anyone there from lunchtime on. By finishing the race early he avoided rain delays, and gave fans plenty of beach time afterward.

From the moment the green flag dropped that morning, the race was a kaleidoscope of lead changes on the high banking, and relentless charges of three cars abreast down the backstretch. Foyt and Donnie Allison, teammates for the new DiGard Racing team, shot their Chevrolet Lagunas to the front, and mingled there with Bobby Allison's oddball AMC Matador, and Buddy Baker's Ford. It was such a scramble in the draft through late morning that even an upstart kid named Darrell Waltrip, driving his own Chevrolet with a modest sponsorship from his father-in-law, led three laps.

Petty and Pearson each led from time to time, but neither showed his full hand as the wildness wore on. Everybody else was shooting craps. The King and the Fox were playing chess, focused only on each other as the circus swirled around them at 180 miles an hour. Then, with fourteen laps to go, Pearson took the lead and Petty tucked in behind him.

And then it was time. Flagman John Bruner Jr. pulled the white flag from the rack on his stand and held it furled against its staff, as Pearson exited Turn 4 leading, with Petty on his rear bumper.

How long does it take to unfurl a white flag to signal one

lap remaining in a race? Maybe three-quarters of a second? Release it from its staff and the wind catches it and whoosh you wave it.

That's how long it took David Pearson to do all the calculating he would need. The decision was made between two lazy motions of his jaw on his chewing gum. He must not get to the backstretch on that final lap with Richard Petty behind him. If he did, then he would be a sitting duck for a slingshot move by Petty. Pearson must put Petty in front of him, and he must do it in the next second or so. He could slow down, but Petty would slow right behind him. There was no way to get Petty to go around him to begin the final lap. Unless...

Just past the flagstand, Pearson didn't just slow down. He lifted his foot completely off the accelerator pedal. In the pits, even Pearson's team owner, Glen Wood, thought the engine had blown in the Mercury.

Petty had no choice. He whipped his steering wheel to the right and darted to the outside, lest he ram Pearson from behind at top speed and wreck them both. There were about 70,000 spectators and 125 media people present. And as the red-and-blue STP Dodge, Number 43, whipped past the red-and-white Purolator Mercury, Number 21, going into Turn 1, everyone at Daytona International Speedway—from every fan to every reporter to every crew chief, tire changer, and jackman along the pit road—thought that David Pearson's engine had blown, and that Richard Petty had won the Firecracker 400.

Petty himself reckoned the same for a few more seconds, until, on the backstretch, he saw in his mirror the unlikeliest of apparitions:

Pearson's Mercury.

No sooner had Pearson let the Dodge pass him than he'd floored the throttle of the Mercury again, but the shenanigan had allowed Petty about a three-hundred-yard margin. Utilizing his slightly more powerful engine, and aligning the

Mercury in the tail end of the Dodge's draft, Pearson shot right back up on Petty's bumper.

Checkmate.

Pearson ran out of room on the backstretch to execute a textbook slingshot, but what he did have, as the two cars came through Turns 3 and 4, was overwhelming momentum. Normally there's not enough room to mount a slingshot charge between Turn 4 and the finish line, but Pearson already had such a run on Petty that he needed only a slight wash of air from Petty's car to get alongside. It was at about that moment that Richard Petty started seething, with full realization of what had happened. He crowded Pearson low on the track, but Pearson kept coming, and won by a car length at the line.

Seething turned to steaming when Petty drove into the garage and climbed out of his car in time to hear Glen Wood saying on the track public-address system, "That trick David pulled on Richard out there just now was about the slickest trick I've ever seen in racin'."

*T*hen as now in NASCAR, the winning driver's press conference was held in the press box. It's for the winner only—no other drivers are invited. But in those days Richard Petty went damn well where he pleased, when he pleased.

After the Victory Lane ceremonies, Pearson was ushered up to the press box. He perched himself on one of the long desktops, pushed his Purolator cap back on his head, took a microphone, and began answering questions, admitting up front that he'd meant for Petty to think the Mercury's engine had blown. He was perhaps ten minutes into the mass interview when Petty walked in—no pearly grin this time, mind you; his mouth was pursed tightly around a cigar.

The rows of press box seats were tiered, so that Petty walked to the bottom left corner of the room. Pearson sat at the highest point, in the center, so that he looked back and down over his right shoulder at Petty.

Petty pointed, cigar between the fingers of his right hand, up at Pearson.

"I just wanted to say I was surprised," he began, and Pearson cocked his head, in that birdlike gesture of sensing something awry. The flick of the head said he got Petty's drift, all right, as in, Here he goes again, bullshittin' the press, courting them again, couldn't beat me on the race track so here he comes forcing a duel where he knows he's got me beat, debating for the media.

"I was surprised and I'm disappointed," Petty said, "because David usually drives a safer, *saner* race. I could have hit him and wrecked us both at 180 miles an hour."

Pearson popped his head back like a welterweight avoiding a straight right hand. He countered that he'd picked a safe place for the move—"Where I did it, it wasn't a risky move." He had backed off after the dogleg in the front stretch, and pulled to the inside so that Petty had room to pass on a straight. And Pearson had enough confidence in his archrival to know that Petty would avoid a collision.

Petty was partly right in that there had long been an unwritten law of trust among drivers drafting together, their bumpers less than a foot apart, at Daytona. To run that closely you had to trust the man in front of you not to do anything foolish—and Petty's rain of verbiage implied strongly that Pearson had violated that trust.

But there was a higher unwritten law—that on the last lap, gunning for the win, you did what you had to do, short of wrecking the opponent.

Petty won the debate, of course, in the media. The quintessential example was a United Press International story designated for afternoon newspapers of July 5, 1974. David Pearson had won a major race at NASCAR's showcase speedway with, arguably, the wiliest move in the history of NASCAR to that point. And yet the story began:

"DAYTONA BEACH, Fla. (UPI)—Richard Petty was steaming."

And *that* was the microcosm of the way the Petty-Pearson rivalry was, and always would be, perceived by the public. It was whatever Richard Petty said it was. David Pearson saw no point in spoon-feeding what, to him, should be obvious to any damn fool—that he was better.

As Pearson saw it, what he'd done at Daytona was by no means dangerous. He'd known precisely what Petty would do, and had given Petty room to do it. And so it was a calculation. A shenanigan of common sense.

"Shenanigan" comes from the Irish Gaelic expression *sionnachuighim.* It means, "I play the fox."

*T*hat was David Pearson's third consecutive victory in the third straight Pearson-Petty one-two finish in the Firecracker 400, though the first two hadn't been nearly as electrifying to see, nor as notorious in aftermath. Pearson, like Fireball Roberts before him and Dale Earnhardt after him, mastered and virtually owned every square foot of the asphalt of Daytona International Speedway—except on the third Sunday of February.

Even after what seemed in July of 1974 to be the crescendo of the rivalry, the most conspicuous and important of facts remained: Richard Petty had won the Daytona 500 five times, David Pearson none.

16

CHARITY AS PAYBACK

*B*enny Parsons took one bite of ham and eggs, felt as if he would throw up, and stopped trying to eat. He had slept little for the past several nights. It was Daytona 500 morning, February 16, 1975. He had driven in this race before, but never with a chance to win it.

Top teams usually brought seven or eight engines per car to Daytona in February. For time trials they'd use an engine built for high performance but short life, sort of like a drag-racing engine—indeed, some of the engine builders literally used drag-racing parts for "qualifying engines." Then there was an engine for the 125-mile qualifying races, and a backup, and a practice engine and a backup, and the designated "race motor" and several backups for that.

Benny Parsons had come to Daytona with one engine. And it had failed in his 125-miler on Thursday, leaving him to start a lousy thirty-second of forty-three cars in the 500. His only engine man, a then-unsung wizard named Waddell Wilson, had worked around the clock to rebuild that one motor.

If the engine held together, it would be a rocket, at least in

Parsons's frame of reference. He had come up hard through the ranks of stock car racing, through the minor league Automobile Racing Club of America (ARCA), and it was still hard for him in NASCAR. He drove for the wealthy but—hrrrmph—frugal L. G. DeWitt, who owned a trucking company and partial interests in North Carolina Speedway at Rockingham, and Atlanta International Raceway, but wasn't at all interested in spending on a race team to match, say, Petty Enterprises or the Wood Brothers.

Benny Parsons was a former cabdriver from Detroit. Well, sort of from Detroit. He had grown up dividing his time between his grandmother's home in North Carolina and his parents' home in Michigan. Benny's blessing and his curse was that he was just a good, humble, considerate man. On the race track, he was often shoved around by more ruthless drivers—he was just too nice a guy for his own good. But there was no one who didn't like Benny Parsons. In 1973 he had won the Winston Cup championship on the strength of a massive outpouring of charity in the final race of the season. On the 13th lap at Rockingham, Parsons had been caught up in a wreck that ripped the entire right side off his Chevrolet, and it had appeared that he would lose the season points championship to Petty—until, without a word, crewmen from several other teams swarmed Parsons's wrecked car, and, with parts cannibalized from other cars, patched it together enough that he could limp around the track, finish the race, and win the championship. Such was the consensus of feeling for the man among his peers.

That Daytona 500 week in '75, Richard Petty had said a strange thing to Parsons: "If not me, why not you?" If Petty couldn't manage a sixth Daytona 500 win, why couldn't Parsons get his first one?

There were of course plenty of reasons, and the biggest one was David Pearson, who would start the Daytona 500 on the front row. Donnie Allison was on the pole, but it was a virtual given that his hot-but-fragile engine, built by the enigmatic Mario Rossi, wouldn't last.

As Benny Parsons pushed away his plate of ham and eggs, it was as sure as the sun rising over the beach that the race would be decided, one way or another, between Richard Petty and David Pearson. Parsons understood this, and yet somehow his gut was so tight with the potential of winning that he was functioning solely on adrenaline. It was a mixed, confusing feeling—but one that was right on the money.

*P*etty, starting fourth, shot quickly out front, atypically showing his hand early—his Dodge was so superior to the rest of the field that there was no point in hiding it. But after only seventy-seven laps, the engine began belching steam and water—a cylinder head had cracked. From there, all afternoon, Petty still had the strongest car on the track—when it was on the track, and not in the pits with Dale Inman and the crew refilling the radiator. This repeated exercise eventually put Petty eight laps behind the leaders.

With ten laps left, David Pearson appeared to have a lock on his first Daytona 500 win. He was ten seconds ahead of the second-place driver, Benny Parsons.

That's when Richard Petty roared out of the pits after a final gulp of water in the radiator. He was up to full speed by Turn 2, and down the backstretch he looked in his mirror, saw Parsons coming, and waved for him to fall in behind and follow.

Suddenly it was obvious. Petty was *towing* Parsons, by allowing him to draft the powerful Dodge, right up to within shooting range of Pearson.

"If not me, why not you?"

Every lap was more electric than the one before. Petty was bringing Parsons up on Pearson at the rate of a little more than one second per lap—meaning that by the white flag, there should be a duel.

Now if it came down to the Silver Fox versus too-nice Benny Parsons, there might be no contest. But no one was sure what Waddell Wilson's engine had left for a one-lap, all-or-nothing showdown. And how would Richard Petty figure in the final fray?

Pearson didn't want to find out. He had nothing to prove. He picked up the pace—he would win it going away if he could.

On the backstretch, Pearson ran up on the lapped cars of Richie Panch and Cale Yarborough. Panch, the struggling son of Marvin Panch, hadn't enough experience to deal cleanly with a leader trying to fly past him, gunning for the win. And Cale Yarborough was—well—Cale Yarborough, who didn't believe in giving any other driver so much as an inch, at any time, anywhere, no matter what. So Panch couldn't, and Yarborough wouldn't, let Pearson pass cleanly.

There was no more time for Pearson to exercise his storied patience. There were three laps left, and here came that damned 43 car right up in his mirror, pulling Parsons. Pearson had to go. Now.

Exiting Turn 2, Pearson slipped the Mercury slightly to the inside of Yarborough's Chevrolet. But entering the backstretch, Yarborough drifted low too—"You don't just let anyone go by you, no matter where you are in a race," he would say afterward. The two cars touched. And then all was dust and tire smoke as the white Mercury spun and slid, perhaps halfway down the thousand-yard backstretch, before it came to a stop. Pearson's day was done.

In the Victory Lane ceremony, Benny Parsons thanked the Good Lord and Richard Petty. Petty claimed that "it wasn't done to beat David." He called it "just something you do in racing."

Of Parsons, Petty said, "He's had a hard time, and he's a good guy. All I wanted to do was give him a chance."

That Daytona 500 would change Parsons's life considerably more than the Winston Cup championship had. In '73 he'd won only one race—still a record for fewest wins in a championship season. Prior to that he'd won only one other NASCAR event, a 100-miler at South Boston, Virginia, in 1971. So the '75 Daytona 500 was only the third win of his career. But it would catapult him into better rides that would take him to eighteen more major victories in his career.

All thanks to five minutes of electrifying charity from Richard Petty. But as the King basked in his humanitarian role, the bottom line remained intact:

Richard Petty five Daytona 500 wins. David Pearson none.

17

THE BULL

A. J. Foyt should have been dead since 1965. If not for Parnelli Jones he would have been.

"Don't hurry. He's dead," said the first doctor to peer into the upside-down stock car at the motionless body on that Sunday afternoon in '65 at Riverside, California.

Like he was about most things, Foyt's feelings were sometimes contradictory about NASCAR. He was first and foremost an Indy car driver; he loved the precision of the little open-wheel cars, and by comparison stock cars were big and crude—"A stock car is just a big ol' turd," he would tell one of his engine tuners. "Hell, *you* could drive one." And yet he had this attraction to NASCAR—couldn't stay away from it. Mostly he loved being around the NASCAR drivers. They were his kind of people. From Indy car races to the dirt sprint car tracks across America, Foyt was notorious for bullying other drivers. "But you never seen him try that down here, did you?" Richard Petty once pointed out. "You know why? Cause he knowed he'd get his ass kicked." NASCAR officials were another matter. It was as if Foyt relished run-ins with them.

He and Parnelli Jones and Dan Gurney always managed to show up at Riverside for the NASCAR road race. "I never would go near them," Kyle Petty, Richard's son, would recall of his boyhood around the Riverside garages. "They just looked mean, Foyt and Parnelli and Gurney, looked like they might just take a kid like me and turn you upside down and dip you in a barrel of grease or something."

"One time at Riverside," Foyt would recall, "NASCAR had this real badass technical inspector who kept messing with Parnelli. Parnelli finally said, 'Show me where my car's illegal.' The inspector stuck his head under the hood, and Parnelli slammed the hood down on his head. Wham! Of course they threw him out. But we didn't care if they threw us out. See, we were there to run a race, and if they didn't like us, piss on 'em."

Then on that Sunday afternoon in '65, Foyt lost the brakes in his Ford and was trying to fall in behind Junior Johnson, the driver he trusted most, when suddenly he felt the Ford flipping and then he was unconscious.

When the emergency crew got to him he was hanging upside down in the car. Parnelli got there within seconds. After the first doc said Foyt was dead, Parnelli heard a faint gagging sound from the body and said, "Well, wait a minute."

Parnelli crawled into the car and with his fingers began digging the mud and sand from Foyt's mouth and throat so that he could breathe again. Otherwise, old racers might have reminisced all these years about the late, potentially great A. J. Foyt and what he might have accomplished. Foyt had won the Indy 500 only twice at that point, and had not yet won the 24 Hours of Le Mans (1967) nor the Daytona 500 (1972). And so had he died that day, he never would have been renowned as the most versatile racing driver in the world.

Broken back, crushed sternum, bad concussion, but all the toughest sonofabitch ever to drive a race car needed was that one gift of breath from Parnelli and here he would come again, kicking ass, raising hell, winning races.

And now, late on the afternoon of February 8, 1976, pole qualifying day for the Daytona 500, here he stomped again, proclaiming:

"Fuck 'em."

He was walking with his car owner, Hoss Ellington.

"But A.J.," Ellington said.

"Fuck 'em. Let's go home."

"But A.J., I've got sponsors—"

"Let's load up."

Foyt, driver of the Number 28 Hoss Ellington Chevrolet, and a fiery upstart named Darrell Waltrip, driver of the Number 88 DiGard Chevrolet, were acting like victims—sort of a Who, me, Officer? posture—after qualifying on the front row, Foyt on the pole and Waltrip outside, only to have their cars fail technical inspection.

Nitrous oxide, "laughing gas," was one of the oldest tricks in the book of NASCAR cheating. Smokey Yunick, the wily pioneer NASCAR mechanic who'd sent Fireball Roberts to stardom, had discovered it in a dentist's chair in the 1950s. Recovering from his laughing-gas high, Smokey asked the dentist, "What is that stuff?" The dentist told him it was essentially a high concentration of oxygen. Oxygen, Smokey knew, was the key to combustion. This stuff could enhance combustion enormously. "In fact," Smokey would recall, "I ran it on my cars for years before they declared it illegal. My drivers never knew what it was. They just knew that to start the second lap of qualifying, they should push this button or flip this switch or pull this string, and hold on. They were going to get a burst of power like a rocket booster."

And so A. J. Foyt was on somewhat credible ground when he maintained he had no knowledge of what was under the hood of Hoss Ellington's car. But even if he flipped no switch, even if the nitrous oxide were set to go off automatically, he should have known. And Waltrip should have known. Hell, Bill Gazaway, NASCAR's chief technical inspector, reckoned what was up just by looking at their lap times.

Both Foyt and Waltrip tipped their hands to Gazaway in that both drivers' second laps in time trials were more than 2 miles per hour faster than their first laps. Waltrip ran 184.173, then 186.617. Foyt ran 185.259, then 187.477. Those increases, in Gazaway's mind, were too dramatic to be a mere matter of tires warming up, or of drivers finding more precise lines through the corners. Nitrous oxide was the likely culprit, because its effects only lasted for short bursts. Typical concealment, say, in a fire-extinguisher bottle, would shoot into the carburetor only enough laughing gas for one fast lap, not two. Not that Foyt and Waltrip were the only two. As it turned out, hell, there was enough laughing gas in the garages of Daytona International Speedway that day to get half the grandstands giddy. Some teams were using it because they knew other teams were using it—it was just one of those little escalations of weaponry that occur at Daytona from time to time. But Foyt as the pole winner, and Waltrip as the second-fastest qualifier, were the ones under the most scrutiny. The two front-row spots are the only ones for the Daytona 500 that are set in pole day. The rest are determined by a combination of finishing orders in the two 125-mile qualifying races on Thursday before 500 day, and individual time trials run intermittently during the week.

Gazaway called 'em in, and he tore 'em down.

And after that, there was hell to pay.

"Fuck 'em."

Foyt decided he would just withdraw from the race. Could the Daytona 500 do without him, the great A. J. Foyt? He stomped off toward Ellington's hauler truck, and Ellington followed, pleading, trying to reason.

Inside the NASCAR station, the inspectors were tracing lines of metal tubing that terminated in the carburetors, but whose sources were mysterious. The lines were run every which way, meandering even down around the engine blocks, so that it was extremely difficult to find their source ends, where, the inspectors suspected, lay nitrous oxide containers.

They were cutting and drilling, performing such radical metallic surgery on the cars that Waltrip finally gave up, threw up his hands, and told them just not to tear his car up any further.

Foyt stomped back into the inspection station, and the next time he came out, it was with Billy France under his massive right arm. Adamant as he was, Foyt was talking barely above a whisper, and Foyt when angry has a surprisingly high voice and tends to mumble anyway.

Media bystanders suspected, however, that Foyt was threatening to sue NASCAR and/or the speedway if terms such as "cheating" were used. Foyt had his image, as he saw it, to think about. And it is possible that he did not know what was inside Ellington's car, if only because he didn't want to know.

Lawyers were called in to supervise the drafting of a press release which, late that night, would say that Foyt's and Waltrip's qualifying times had been "disallowed" for "use of fuel pressure assists which are not allowed."

Fred Seeley, a Jacksonville sportswriter, got an incredulous look on his face as France sat there among lawyers reading the statement at a press conference, and he blurted out: "Hell, Billy, why don't you just say they were cheatin' and be done with it?" All he got in return was that owl-eyed look of Billy France's. Big Bill France had in 1972 turned over the presidency of NASCAR to his eldest son. William Clifton France was not in fact a "Junior" to William Henry Getty

France, but in years to come he was widely referred to, even by his staff, as Bill France Jr. In those days he was mostly called Billy, and few around stock car racing were sure he was capable of filling the shoes of his iron-willed, iron-handed father in such a pressure-cooker job, even if it was a dictatorship. Besides, everybody knew that when things got tough, really tough, the old man had a way of appearing out of the woodwork.

So it had gone that afternoon. Within minutes after the big Pontiac Bonneville came flying into the garage area and Big Bill got out with a whistle around his neck and left the car door open and the engine running as if this wouldn't take long at all, the matter was settled, in granite. All that remained was the drafting of the press releases to appease the seething Foyt.

After hollering back over his shoulder at bystanders that Wallace had said to make sure these sonsabitches were legal and that he aimed to do it, Big Bill walked into the inspection station and pulled that heavy sliding steel door down behind him.

Within maybe five minutes—six or seven at most—he came walking out, and he had *his* right arm draped around *Foyt's* shoulders, sort of the way Foyt had had Billy around the shoulders earlier, and Foyt's head was bowed and his eyes were downcast and he was muttering, "Yessir... yessir...yessir..."

Only three men who ever lived could quell the rages in A. J. Foyt: the late Anthony Joseph Foyt Sr., "Tony," his father; the late Anton "Tony" Hulman, longtime owner of Indianapolis Motor Speedway; and the late Big Bill France. It's doubtful that Foyt ever so much listened to them as he simply obeyed their authority.

For the next twenty-three years, every time I would ask Foyt what Big Bill had said to him that day in that inspection station, he would evade the question. Usually he would just say, "Well, you know, I always had a lot of respect for Mister France…"

Then on Labor Day weekend, 1999, Foyt came to Darlington to announce that he would field a full-time NASCAR team in 2000—not of course as a driver anymore, but as an owner. After his press conference, we went over to his motor coach to talk—and as usual, wound up rehashing some old times.

At one point, I said, "You remember Daytona in '76—"

Foyt bristled all over again, almost instantaneously. "That's when they throwed me off the pole—said I was *cheatin'.*"

"And remember how you had Billy France around the neck and I thought you were going to—"

"Damn!" Foyt huffed, and looked around him. Several prim-and-proper executives and PR people from the financial conglomerate that would sponsor his new NASCAR team were in the motor coach. He wanted to make a good impression. He squirmed at mention of his rowdiness of yore. "Don't give these people— Hey, folks, we're talkin' about something that happened twenty-five years ago. Don't get the wrong idea."

"But anyway, you had Billy—"

"Shhhhh!"

"Well, then, just exactly what did Big Bill say to you inside that inspection station that day?"

Foyt smiled. His voice went soft. There are times when A. J. Foyt's voice can plummet into depths of humility that are touching.

"He walked in and he looked at me. He said, 'A.J., are you illegal?'

"I said, 'Nossir. They are.' And I pointed at Darrell's car.

"He said, 'A.J., I think you're illegal.'

"I said, 'Nossir.'

"He said, 'A.J., I still think you're disqualified.'

"I said, 'Yessir.' "

Foyt stopped.

"And that was it?" I asked. "That was all?"

"Yes."

"But why did you just accept that, so quickly?"

Foyt looked at me incredulously. "Why, because he was a *good man!*"

"A good man? That was all?"

"That was enough. That was plenty."

*B*ill Gazaway was the kind of guy who clearly relished kicking ass and taking names, and he wasn't finished that day at Daytona. The third-fastest qualifier was Dave Marcis in Harry Hyde's Dodge. Gazaway disqualified Marcis for having too large a sheet-metal shield to block off his radiator. It was a gimmick that served two purposes: One, it created enough aerodynamic downforce on the front of the car to make the steering "loose." That is, the car oversteered and the rear end slid around to the right through the turns. The loose condition is dangerous because the car can slide right out of control and crash. But looser is faster, because it gets you through the turns quicker. Two, the blocking off of the radiator caused the engine to heat inordinately fast—also a bad thing under race conditions, but it maximized performance on short, banzai qualifying runs.

Marcis quietly admitted he and Hyde had blocked more of the radiator than was allowed in the rules. Hyde, on the other hand, was raising more hell than a televangelist caught soliciting a hooker. His car was legal as could be, he swore, and "I don't know why Billy France did this to me," he howled.

But you had to know Harry Hyde. In fact, you do know Harry Hyde if you saw the film *Days of Thunder.* That movie on the whole was lousy, except for Robert Duval's performance. When Robert Duval played a supposedly fictional crew chief named Harry Hogge, Robert Duval *was* Harry Hyde. The late Harry Hyde made a life's work of preaching, to anybody who would listen, just how stupid other crew chiefs were when it came to qualifying. He would rave on about how important it was to wax the car before qualifying, and how important it was to take a pocketknife and shave the sidewalls of the tires of all those tiny rubber tips, about the thickness of needles, that are left on by the molds when the tires are made. All of this was supposed to make the car slicker, aerodynamically. And all of this was, of course, quintessential Harry Hyde bullshit, his verbal legerdemain— watch this hand over here, boys, so you won't see what I'm really doing with the other hand.

Gazaway also nailed ninth-fastest qualifier Bruce Hill for using nitrous oxide, but few noticed amidst the other hoopla.

All in all, it was the biggest cheating bust in the history of Daytona to that point. And it remains the most famous, to this day.

By the attrition of disqualification, the pole was inherited by an erstwhile bean farmer from Keokuk, Iowa, named Ramo Stott. Most of his racing experience had come on two stock car circuits that were weaklings compared to mighty NASCAR—the United States Auto Club and Automobile Racing Club of America tours. Stott had managed his fourth-place qualifying run in a Chevrolet that was as legal as a car could be at the time. Not that the crew chief, Dick Hutcherson, didn't have the savvy to stretch the rules to the limit. It was just that the car owner was a Maryland dairy farmer with a weathered face and an honest heart, Norris Reed. He was new to NASCAR, in it solely for the sport, and had given Hutcherson and Stott strict orders before qualifying started: No cheating. None.

After starting on the pole, Stott would have no impact on the Daytona 500 itself—except that he would nearly wreck on the first lap, under heavy pressure from Waltrip and Marcis, who started on the second row after they each won their 125-mile qualifying races on Thursday (presumably with legal cars this time). Stott would struggle along until a blown engine on the 113th lap forced him out of the 500.

After that race, Norris Reed would never have any more impact on NASCAR as a team owner. He was a sportsman who limited the amount he would spend on racing. He could hardly compete with the hardballing businessmen who owned and fielded teams in full quest for race wins and season championships by whatever means necessary.

But Reed had brought a fresh breeze of a notion to NASCAR, one that resounded: No cheating.

Until then, cheating had been a way of life for NASCAR crew chiefs. Like running liquor, you just did it out of necessity and took your chances on getting caught. They cheated anywhere and everywhere on the cars. To conceal an oversize fuel cell—the more gas you could carry over the twenty-two-gallon limit, the fewer pit stops you had to make—they would place a beach ball inside the cell and then inflate it. NASCAR inspectors measured fuel cells by filling them up. With the beach ball inflated, the trick tank would hold only twenty-two gallons. After inspection, you simply deflated the beach ball, and there was your extra gallon or so per pit stop—often enough to make the difference in a race. For less wind resistance, even the pioneer crew chiefs wanted their cars lower to the ground than the rules allowed. So they would extend the shock absorbers and drill through them with thin metal bits. Then they would leave the bits in the shocks to hold them open, and make the car sit higher. Once the race started, normal bumps in the track surface at high speed would cause the drill bits to break off, and that would drop the front end a few inches lower, and you had an aerodynamically superior car. Dropping buckshot was the most common occurrence. To meet weight minimums, they would conceal bags of lead buckshot in the cars. Then when the race started, the driver would release the buckshot, to lighten the car, while the pellets scattered everywhere and the evidence of cheating therefore vanished.

Oh, cheating didn't stop in '76. It's still done occasionally, but the methods are so high-tech they're no fun to talk about anymore. They involve illegal exotic metals (for high performance of, say, brakes, with reduced weight), or highly sophisticated moving panels inside intake manifolds (to defeat the purpose of restrictor plates by sucking more air into the combustion process). Few simple tricks remain. (Although, if NASCAR officials were to watch closely today, they would notice that one particularly huge crewman, on one particularly famous team, has a peculiar habit as he helps push the car across the scales. He has a way of looking like he's standing straight up when in fact he is applying considerable downward pressure on the rear bumper with one knee. He can add maybe fifty pounds of weight to the car as it sits on the scales.)

But after the uproar over Foyt, Waltrip et al., cheating became a less romantic, more unsavory thing to do. Sponsors now often stipulate that a contract is null and void if a team is caught cheating. They just don't want the embarrassment.

18

MILL HILL ZEN

Richard Petty never slept right. Never ate right. Image doesn't sleep. Image doesn't eat. Image walks and talks and grins and signs, grins and signs, grins and signs. Image gives the man inside it just enough time, occasionally, as Petty would tell a younger driver many years later, to "go out behind the building to cuss and throw up."

And so Richard Petty arrived at Daytona in February of 1976 fresh off twelve days of intravenous feeding in his favorite hospital in Greensboro, North Carolina. The ulcers were acting up something godawful.

His physicians told him not to race.

Yeah. Right.

"He don't care if he's dying," said his wife, Lynda, "if there's a race to run…"

His one concession was to guzzle Maalox straight out of the bottle in the pits and garages at Daytona, all day, every day. Where A. J. Foyt's diet in those days consisted mainly of chili and cheeseburgers and iced tea, even for breakfast— you could stick your veggies up your ass—Richard Petty's diet was mainly over-the-counter headache powders by the handful, and Maalox by the case.

David Pearson blew into town acting like he didn't give a shit.

As usual.

Just another Daytona.

Just have to see what happens.

Pearson would show up and climb into the car and go out, run a few laps, drive back into the garage, climb out, tell the Wood Brothers what adjustments needed to be made to the car, and disappear again.

Not only did David Pearson never have an ulcer. He probably never even had heartburn.

Pearson had an uncanny ability to set the swirl around him into serene slow motion. Perhaps it could have qualified as a sort of Zen—tranquility, fearlessness, spontaneity—sprung from Mill Hill, whence the only way to go was up and so there was no sense worrying about anything. Maybe it really was a matter of just not giving a shit—although you always got the impression that David Pearson knew and thought a lot more than he was saying.

Whatever it was, it would even the Daytona 500 score with Richard Petty in a single afternoon. Going into the '76 race, no one had even considered the idea that Pearson could erase such an overwhelming score, Petty five, Pearson none—could even it in the public's perspective of history—in a matter of seconds.

A. J. Foyt and Darrell Waltrip had requalified—Waltrip had even won his 125-mile qualifying race on Thursday—but they were in Chevrolets. The Chevy engines of the time worked well enough on short and intermediate-size tracks.

But, pushed to the limit at Daytona, they were fragile. Their valves and valve springs failed often. So Foyt's and Waltrip's prospects of being around for the end of the race were iffy.

The most durable engine of the time was Ford Motor Company's "351 Cleveland," so called because the blocks were cast at a Ford-owned foundry in Cleveland, Ohio. NASCAR's displacement maximum had dropped in 1974 from 427 to 351 cubic inches (actually 358 in full-performance trim), and the Ford teams, especially the Wood Brothers, had come up with a bulletproof combination for high-stress Daytona, well ahead of Chevrolet. Petty Enterprises had the singularly durable Dodge engine. Maurice Petty, Richard's brother and the team's engine guru, always surgically assembled his power plants with durability as the priority over top-end speed.

And so almost mathematical logic stated that this race would be settled among the Ford-powered entries—Bobby Allison in Roger Penske's new, frontline effort with Mercury; Buddy Baker in Big Bud Moore's Ford Torino; David Pearson in the Wood Brothers' Mercury—and Richard Petty in the Dodge Charger.

But Buddy Baker's driving style was the antithesis of his father's. Where Buck Baker had won many a race by cooling it until the frontrunning hotdogs broke or crashed and then cruising to victory, Buddy Baker loved to lead every lap he could. He was a pure charger—as if, growing up, he'd been influenced more by watching Junior Johnson than his own father. And so in the middle of the backstretch on the eighty-third lap of that Daytona 500, Baker provided the frontstretch grandstands with a clear demonstration that light travels faster than sound. There erupted beneath Big Bud Moore's Ford Torino an enormous flash and then a cloud of light, and one or two seconds later the noise of the explosion rattled the windows of the press box.

Waltrip's Chevy expired predictably after eighty-seven

laps, replete as it was with engine builder Mario Rossi's hot but fragile drag-racing parts. Penske's fire-engine red Mercury caught some hotdog wrappers in its grille and began to overheat, and expired after 123 laps, and so Allison was gone.

Foyt, who was always far better at nurturing a car than his image implied—all his sound and fury were outside the car, and inside he was a precision driver who almost never made a mistake—lasted 143 laps, even leading intermittently, before the Ellington Chevrolet engine died.

Defending race champion Benny Parsons was still around for the final fifty laps, but this time Petty had business of his own to attend, and so Parsons was able to lead a few late laps only in the immediate aftermath of pit stops by the duelists:

Petty and Pearson.

Up to this point, they had finished one-two an astounding fifty-seven times in thirteen years. This, it was clear as the laps waned, would be the fifty-eighth.

With thirteen laps to go, and no more pit stops left, Petty took the lead from Pearson. This was odd. This was precisely the time when Petty should have been refusing to pass Pearson, and setting up for the slingshot on the last lap.

Petty would say afterward that he'd observed that Pearson's car was faster than his down the straightaways, but wasn't handling as well through the turns. So, rather than setting up for the slingshot, Petty decided to go out front, run as hard as he could through the corners, and force Pearson to run equally hard to keep up. That, Petty hoped, would heat up Pearson's tires, make the Mercury slide around, and allow Petty to get away clean.

It didn't happen. Pearson kept the Mercury tucked right on the Dodge's bumper, shadowing Petty's every move.

As they took the white flag, no observer would have been surprised if Petty had tried something, anything, to drop back into second place. But he kept the lead.

Now it all appeared mathematical. Pearson had Petty set up for a classic slingshot. He pulled out from behind Petty halfway down the backstretch, and took the lead entering Turn 3.

And that, 125,000 spectators thought, was that.

What happened next was next to impossible, in all our frames of reference at the time. The slingshot could not be counterpunched on the same lap. The driver who shot from second to first, with less than half the final lap to go, simply had too much momentum to be re-passed in the final set of turns.

And so at the moment Pearson and Petty came flying into Turn 4, watching them created a sensation of having a hallucination. The thunder from the grandstands—it was more of a massive "awwwwwwwwwwww" of bewilderment than a cheer—indicated that everybody else in the place was as stunned.

It was an apparition. It was as in a dream.

The red-and-blue Dodge dropped low on the track and Petty retook the lead.

Petty would say later that Pearson's car had slid high on the race track, giving him an opportunity to dive underneath. But that wasn't apparent—not live, nor in numerous replays of the videotape, in real time, slow motion, or freeze frame. Pearson's groove of choice at Daytona was the high one, and through Turns 3 and 4, that Mercury held that line precisely. Indeed it wiggled only once, when Pearson appeared to drop down by one-third of a lane, probably in an attempt to crowd Petty and stifle the pass. But Pearson was never the type to wreck someone else intentionally, and so when he dropped down and Petty kept coming, Pearson let him go.

Exiting Turn 4, Petty led. It was Daytona's own version of rising from the dead. The new score was in his grasp: Petty six, Pearson none.

"You don't piss on them Pettys," Joe Littlejohn was saying as he listened on the radio, riding with Big Bud Moore out on Highway 92, behind the main grandstands, "and tell 'em it's rainin'."

Then the Dodge made yet another spectral move. Rather than merely taking the lead, it shot in a diagonal path right across the front of the Mercury. Pearson had nowhere to go. His car was pinched between the right rear of Petty's car, and the outside retaining wall.

Was this Petty's split-second attempt at revenge for Pearson's faked blown engine in '74? He would always deny that.

The right rear of Petty's car touched the left front of Pearson's. Petty would maintain that "he slid into me," and freeze-framing the tape does show that Pearson's car for a split second appeared to turn hard left—but only *after* it was initially brushed by Petty's car. But then the Mercury was knocked hard right, head-on into the wall, and the Dodge for a moment appeared to be getting away free. Petty six, Pearson none.

But at that moment...*Tranquility:* Pearson's dry-ice calm remained intact, even as he headed into the wall. *Fearlessness:* Even at the moment of hard impact, David Pearson, never injured and so with no sense of dread, maintained total concentration. *Spontaneity:* As the Mercury's hood and front fenders were crushed, Pearson rammed in his clutch pedal, focused solely on keeping the engine running at all costs, knowing there was still a chance, knowing that Petty simply could not come through such an impact without going over the edge of control himself.

Pehaps thirty yards down the track, Petty's car fishtailed and turned into the outside wall. He corrected with the steering wheel, but "I overcorrected," he would say. Had Petty merely been able to keep the Dodge pointed just somewhat forward, momentum would have carried him under the checkered flag.

Pearson's car careened off the wall and shot, backward,

down through the infield grass and onto the pit road. As it slid, Pearson was talking on the radio to the Wood Brothers crew in the pits, asking, "Where's he at?" meaning Petty.

Joe Frasson, in a slower car, drove down onto the pit road to avoid the Petty-Pearson wreck, and managed to get to the pit road entrance at the same instant as Pearson. BAM! Pearson's car bounced off Frasson's.

Again from Pearson on the radio as he felt the shock of the second collision: "Where's he at?"

Glen and Leonard Wood hadn't even time to blurt anything in response. That's how fast everything was happening. But all was in slow motion to Pearson.

Tranquility, fearlessness, spontaneity.

When Richard Petty hit the wall, he did not ram his clutch pedal in. As the Dodge spun into the infield grass, coming to rest twenty yards short of the start-finish line, the engine died. Petty was still a hundred yards ahead of Pearson. He sat there frantically trying to restart the engine. But the fan had been driven back into the radiator, and the engine wouldn't start.

Pearson's car was terribly crippled but the engine was still running. And so he drove along the infield grass, calmly turning hard right to avoid the Petty wreckage, and puttered under the checkered flag at "about ten miles an hour," he would reckon later. Some believe it was more like 20 mph. On the old videotapes it looked more like 30 or 40 mph. But when you've been running nearly 200 mph, you're immune to the sensation of speed, and so it must have felt agonizingly slow to Pearson.

His exact speed, though, really didn't matter. Clearly it was, and remains, the slowest that any Daytona 500 winner has ever taken the checkered flag.

On the grass just past the line, Pearson let the Mercury die. As he calmly unfastened his safety harness, the car was suddenly swarmed by blue-shirted Petty crewmen, in fighting mode—whenever there's a crash, the knee-jerk reaction of crewmen is always that it was the other guy's fault, not their driver's. But then some of the crewmen rushed over to see whether Petty was all right, and he told them immediately, "If you're going to blame somebody, blame me."

Petty would admit fault in the crash: "There wasn't enough room to make the move I made."

Said Pearson, "He had me beat until we wrecked."

*I*t would be David Pearson's only Daytona 500 victory. Petty would go on to two more, in 1979 and 1981, for a total of seven.

"But the race I'll be remembered most for, and the one I'll remember most myself," Petty would say long after both careers were over, "was one I lost."

The score was even.

Nossirree. You don't piss on them Pettys and tell 'em it's rainin'.

Not unless you're David Pearson, the greatest NASCAR driver there had ever been.

*A*nother event in 1976, completely unnoticed by the NASCAR community, would be the seed of enormous impact on the sport in the distant future. A child, four years old, almost five, would get his first race car.

In faraway Vallejo, California, in the San Francisco Bay area, a young sprint car aficionado named John Bickford had married a divorcee, Carol Gordon, who had two children, a boy and a girl.

John was bent on being a real father to the kids, but he made an extraordinary effort with the boy, focusing on bona fide, high-quality father-son time. John was not a stick-and-ball kind of guy, and besides, the boy was small for his age.

John's all-consuming passion was racing. And so he got the boy started at age four in bicycle motocross, or "BMX," an enormously popular sport for West Coast kids. But that made Carol nervous.

"We saw older kids get hurt, hauled away in ambulances," Bickford would recall. "We saw broken ribs, broken arms, broken legs. My feeling was that if you get three hundred kids on a course, racing, you're going to see more broken bones—that's just life. But Carol said to me, 'We are stopping BMX.'

"And so she thought I was nuts when I brought home cars."

They were quarter-midgets. It was springtime, 1976.

"I wasn't yet five," Bickford's stepson would recall. "I remember John coming home and saying, 'Look out the window. I've got a surprise for you.' I was so thrilled. But I didn't even know what a quarter-midget was. It was just something that looked like fun. He'd brought home two cars. The other one was for my sister, Kimberly, who was four years older than me. She never even sat in hers. Never once did she get into it. I loved mine. John and I started going out to the local fairgrounds and laying out our own race tracks. By the time I was five, we were actually competing with other cars on race tracks."

That summer, John Bickford knew these little cars had given him and the boy more than just a bond. He was looking at a prodigy.

The child's name was Jeffrey Michael Gordon.

19

WITH THE BREEZE AND AGAINST THE WIND

Winning the 1977 and 1978 Daytona 500s had entirely different meanings to the respective victors, Cale Yarborough and Bobby Allison. For Yarborough, the '77 win was the pinnacle of the peak of his career. For Allison, the '78 victory was deliverance from the abyss.

In the shadow of the Pearson-Petty heart-stopper of '76, Yarborough had gone on to win that year's Winston Cup season championship, which was not yet a very big deal. Yarborough would make it the big deal it is today by winning it again in '77 and '78, becoming the first driver ever to win the NASCAR championship three years running.

And Yarborough in those years was the most celebrated NASCAR driver for an entirely different reason. A month before the '77 Daytona 500, his good buddy Jimmy Carter had been inaugurated as president of the United States. Yarborough's very vocal support of Carter had won the candidate untold thousands of NASCAR fans' votes, while the staunch Republican Richard Petty refused to support the biggest

NASCAR fan ever to run for the presidency. And yet Petty wasn't a tub-thumper for Republican incumbent Gerald R. Ford, either. David Pearson had remained largely apolitical. Yarborough was so closely associated with Carter by the general public that a new comedy show on NBC, *Saturday Night Live,* would mention them together in skits.

Yarborough hadn't won the Daytona 500 since 1968, for the Wood Brothers. And his current car owner, Junior Johnson, hadn't won it since LeeRoy Yarbrough guided the missile in 1969.

But this time would have been a cakewalk for Cale even if the blizzard hadn't occurred.

It was the oddest weather phenomenon ever during a Daytona 500. High winds set in from the northwest, off toward Gainesville. The aberrant winds came straight through the back of the open grandstands that faced southeast, caught tens of thousands of hotdog and hamburger wrappers just right, and sent the paper swirling onto the track. It looked like a snowstorm of mutant flakes, huge and greasy. When they caught in the grilles of the race cars they stuck. Radiators boiled over. Engines overheated. Engines failed. Richard Petty's. David Pearson's. Bobby Allison's.

Didn't matter. Junior Johnson built the mightiest engines of the time, had cured the Chevy durability problems with better metallurgy, and Chevrolet had introduced an aerodynamically slick Laguna, meant solely for Daytona and Talladega, where it knifed through the air at high speeds. Everywhere else, where aerodynamics weren't as important as handling, Cale and Junior would utilize the boxier, but better-balanced, Monte Carlo.

Benny Parsons clung to Cale's draft until it was time for Yarborough to show the pat hand and drive away at the finish. Nobody behind Parsons was even in the same lap.

* * *

*N*o established star in NASCAR has ever put himself in the position of standing more alone against greater odds than Bobby Allison in 1977.

Allison and Roger Penske had had a falling out at the end of '76. It was the culmination of friction through three years. Had they gotten along, Bobby Allison might today be ranked alongside, or above, A. J. Foyt and Mario Andretti in versatility. Allison was that good in all sorts of race cars, and Penske over the years fielded all sorts of race cars—Formula One, NASCAR, Can-Am, Indy...

But Allison couldn't get along with Penske much better than he'd gotten along with Junior Johnson in their brief but brilliant season together in 1972, when Allison won a dozen races while he and Johnson weren't even speaking—this due to disagreement over the sort of chassis they should be running—until finally, as he and Johnson stood staring at each other one day in August at Johnson's shop, Allison told a third party, crew chief Herb Nab, "Tell Junior to kiss my ass."

And that was that.

(The type of chassis Allison wanted to use, which allowed the car to settle more surefootedly through turns, would be introduced by Johnson a decade later at Daytona. That was a prototype of the ones used by every NASCAR team today. Bobby Allison as usual had been twenty years ahead of his time—that's how brilliant a self-taught engineer he was.)

Twenty years after that divorce, Junior Johnson would say that "If we'd been able to keep Bobby Allison, we would have won two hundred races and Richard Petty wouldn't have."

Oh, well. Just another of a dozen stories of what might have been for Bobby Allison, who spent his career against the wind.

Allison had won the final NASCAR race of '74, at Ontario, California, in Penske's Matador. But during the post-race teardown to determine whether the car was legal, NASCAR inspector Dick Beaty—later to replace Bill Gazaway as NASCAR's top enforcer—had caught Allison coming out of the inspection station with a part wrapped in "shop rags," or work cloths. "I stopped him and took it from his hands," Beaty would recall. "I unwrapped it. It was a camshaft. It was warm. I suspected he had switched the camshafts for inspection. Then I reached down and felt the cam that was in the engine. It was cold. So I knew it couldn't have just been through a race. If he had just heated the replacement cam, with a blowtorch or something, he would have gotten away with the switch." Beaty examined the warm part, and found it to be an illegal "roller cam." Allison was allowed to keep the victory, but was fined $9,100—big money in those days—for cheating. To him it was all part of the game. You did what you had to do, and if sometimes you got caught, so be it. Watching others over the years in the garages, "We had seen some very nice setups with the roller cams—it was nothing new," Allison would recall. But for the image-conscious Penske, the cheating incident was an enormous embarrassment. From then on, "Roger would no longer allow us to massage the engines," Allison would recall.

In other words, no more cheating.

So for Roger Penske, Bobby Allison was driving in handcuffs.

Then in '75, Penske took Allison to Indianapolis and put him in a car made of spare parts but given a fancy paint job and passed off as an equal car to that of Penske's lead Indy driver of the time, Tom Sneva. Bobby Allison didn't go to Indy to glad-hand sponsors, bow to the crowd during driver introductions, and then race only nominally. Bobby and his brother Donnie were both capable Indy car drivers—Donnie had driven one of A. J. Foyt's spare cars to a fourth-place finish and rookie of the year honors at Indy in 1970—due to

their vast experience in open-wheel modified and supermod-
ified cars on the weekend bullrings of Alabama, Tennessee,
Mississippi, and Florida in the '60s.

Indeed, some of Bobby Allison's most brilliant walks into
the wind had been in open-wheel cars. "I seldom used a car
as a weapon," he once said. (Note "seldom" as the operative
adverb.) "The first time was in modified cars. Huntsville, Alabama, 1962. A high-dollar, four-driver team had come out
of Nashville. Malcolm Brady. Charlie Stoffel. Jack Marlin
and his brother, Coo Coo Marlin [father of modern-day Winston Cup driver Sterling Marlin]." In meticulous detail,
thirty-five years after the fact, Allison recounted how the
Marlins and Stoffel had pestered him in the early races of that
evening, and how Brady had wrecked him in the race immediately preceding the feature event. Officials wouldn't wait
for Allison to fix his car, and started the feature without him.
But he continued to work feverishly on the car, even after the
feature had started. "About the fifteenth lap of the feature
[halfway], I rolled off the pit road. As soon as I got onto the
track I saw Charlie Stoffel, and I stuck him into the fence
right there. And I looked, and here came Jack Marlin, and I
stuck him into the fence *right there.* I had to go around another car to get to Coo Coo Marlin, but when I found him, I
stuck him into the fence *over there.* And then. Well. There
was a picture I kept on my office wall for a long time. It
showed me and Malcolm Brady tearing down the guardrail
and the signs behind it in the third turn at Huntsville, and you
could see my hands like *this* [he moved his hands as if turning a steering wheel hard to the right].

"All four of 'em," he said, and sighed with a sort of ec-
stasy of remembrance. "I stuck all four of 'em, right then and
there. And then I drove into the pits, and I climbed out, and I
said, 'O.K., boys, what do you want to do next?'

"And I never had any more trouble out of any of 'em."

And that story is the quintessence of Bobby Allison. And

it was in open-wheel cars, the deadliest kind there ever has been.

So Roger Penske should never have expected Bobby Allison to cruise around in the Indy 500 just for show, just to entertain a few VIPs from the corporate sponsor, a brand of motor oil called CAM2.

But he put Bobby Allison in a shiny shitbox that blew its engine and shamed the man with the most towering pride and the most independent mind in motor racing.

Bobby Allison never raced in the Indy 500 again. Which is a pity. God knows how many times he should have won it.

But by 1976 the sorest point between Allison and Penske was what Allison should be doing with his spare time. Allison loved racing on small-time short tracks as a diversion—"It is," he said, "my golf game"—and piloted his own airplane all over Podunk America to do so, amidweek, between NASCAR races.

He suffered multiple injuries, more painful than serious, driving for Penske at Rockingham in the spring of 1976—the fire-engine red Mercury flipping end over end down the backstretch. But that was the occupational hazard of Winston Cup racing.

Then that summer, in an outlaw race on a bullring at Elko, Minnesota, Bobby Allison hit the end of a gap in a concrete retaining wall head-on, and suffered fractured bones from his face to his feet. This was not O.K. with Roger Penske.

"He didn't mind my standing in front of some discount store, selling a can of oil," Allison would say, "but he didn't want me racing on short tracks."

To exacerbate matters, Allison and Penske went winless in NASCAR in '76—largely because Penske wouldn't cheat, but also because for the second half of the season, Allison was so busted-up from head to foot that he often had to be lifted, physically, in and out of the car.

At the end of that '76 season he quit Roger Penske—said

he was forming his own team. Bobby Allison had gone out on his own before, every time he'd fallen out with a car owner, from John Holman to Junior Johnson—but this was a masterpiece of pissing into the wind. He chose, for 1977, to run an AMC Matador. It was the only one in NASCAR.

In the Daytona 500 Cale Yarborough cakewalked to win in '77, the Allison Matador blew its engine, and it didn't do much better the rest of the season.

In midsummer 1977, Allison fired both of his engine builders and for a while did all the work himself—meaning eighteen-hour days at the minimum, and sometimes twenty-four. Allison in those days could, and often did, go for days on end without sleep.

Alone. Absolutely alone, he was doing the work of an entire shop crew, getting ready to go compete with Cale Yarborough and Richard Petty and David Pearson, who rarely even bothered to visit the sprawling engine departments of their teams' racing shops. He could not beat them. No way. But he wouldn't quit. He worked virtually around the clock for the entire year in 1977.

And so when Bobby Allison arrived at Daytona in 1978, newly hired by Big Bud Moore to drive Fords, he was in the abyss. At least now he could sleep at night, while Moore's staff did all the work. But Allison was forty years old, winless in his last sixty-seven NASCAR races, and had never won the Daytona 500 in eighteen years of trying. Only Bobby Allison could have believed that his glory days at Daytona were just beginning.

Allison came roaring out of the depths, winning the Daytona 500 in Moore's Thunderbird by pressing the race's hardest charger, Buddy Baker, so hard that the engine in Baker's Oldsmobile blew with eleven laps to go. The second-place finisher was Cale Yarborough, more than half a lap behind.

20

EARNHARDT

There was an electric sort of feeling of—what?—*arrival* from the outset of Daytona 500 week of 1979. CBS producers, directors, and technicians were all over the place. In recent years, ABC Sports had been airing more and more of the Daytona 500 live, but never "flag-to-flag"—start to finish. ABC still treated NASCAR as an offbeat sport, suitable mainly for *Wide World of Sports,* which also aired such endeavors as arm wrestling and curling. But CBS, upon buying the rights to the race, intended to treat it very seriously indeed. CBS would carry the race live, flag-to-flag. And so every crewman stepped livelier; every driver smiled broader; tangibly, you could feel NASCAR going big-time.

The network's brightest producer, Bob Fishman, and director, Mike Pearl, had hit the ground running off the plane from New York. They were setting up some innovative experiments—such as placing cameras at low angles on the retaining walls. They knew they might lose some expensive cameras to shrapnel from crashing cars. But it was worth it, they calculated, in that the low angles would eliminate the worst problem about televising NASCAR. To that point, the speed that was obvious to spectators in the grandstands just didn't come across on television. Fishman and Pearl were determined to "show speed." They did. Cars passing within a few feet of the low-placed cameras gave off that "zmp-zmp-zmp" sensation of shooting by on the screen that is so common on TV today. In coming years, further CBS innovations, such as the in-car camera, would revolutionize NASCAR coverage on television.

And so Bill France Jr. would maintain for the remainder of the 20th century that 1979, and the CBS telecast of the Daytona 500, was the watershed for NASCAR.

Richard Petty had been slumping—hadn't won a race in 1978, and in midseason had finally given up on Dodges and switched to Chevrolets—but now the King was the center of attention for another reason. His eighteen-year-old son, Kyle, had made his racing debut by winning the undercard ARCA 200 at Daytona. The kid not only won right out of the gate, but he turned out to be better in front of a minicam than even the old man. It appeared that the third Petty generation would go on winning and dazzling without missing a beat. That is how wrong first impressions can be. Kyle's entire career would amount to one long-running disappointment.

*T*here was one other turning point that February. It would go hand in glove with the television revolution. It came inside a blue-and-yellow Buick, unsponsored and therefore plainly painted. The car, Number 2, was owned by California construction magnate Rod Osterlund, who was rich enough to finance the racing effort himself.

The driver was a rookie who didn't behave like one, on or off the track. Both his demeanor and his moves in the draft during preliminary races were downright arrogant—cocky, without discernible reasons. He was unknown except for his surname—his late father had been a fairly well-known short-track driver in the Carolinas. And so at first, veteran NASCAR writers referred to the rookie in their conversations as "Ralph Earnhardt's kid."

At that point, Darrell Waltrip was the most daring and ruthless driver in NASCAR, by far. His DiGard team still couldn't put equipment under him that could be counted on to endure 500 miles of his all-out style, but in the 125-mile qualifying races at Daytona, he was murder—Darrell Waltrip was the Man.

That Thursday, in the second of the twin 125-milers, Waltrip led as the drafting freight train came off Turn 4 and headed for the flag. A. J. Foyt made a last-ditch, banzai run at Waltrip. Right with Foyt came this unsponsored blue car, Number 2, balls-out. Their charge didn't work, with Dick Brooks in the melee. Foyt did slip into second place behind Waltrip, with Brooks third, and the blue car fourth. But what a run it was, and what arrogance from the rookie, flying right up there with A. J. Foyt just like he *belonged* in such company.

When the blue car got to its garage stall, several media people were waiting. Inside the car, the helmet came off and out flowed a sea of long, sandy hair. There wasn't a drop of sweat in the hair as he climbed out. He glanced at the gaggle that had gathered around him with some surprise, and reacted with a cocky toss of the head. He had a long handlebar mustache that wiggled with its own sort of arrogance when he talked. His cobalt eyes were no less self-certain. The eyes, the brow, the mustache, and the smirk made him a dead ringer for pictures of the flamboyant Confederate cavalry general Jeb Stuart. The only difference was that Stuart wore a full beard. Otherwise, the two cocky countenances were so alike, it was eerie.

He glanced around the group and said, "How 'bout it, boys? Think I'm gonna make it?"

That was the first thing Dale Earnhardt ever said to the media at Daytona. He didn't wait for a question. "I thought I was goin' somewhere when I went with A.J. there at the end. Oh, well. Maybe I'll learn."

Waltrip was still the Man. But this guy Earnhardt surely acted like he was headed somewhere.

Maybe it wasn't cockiness. Maybe it was his way of showing sheer relief. He could do this, thank God; he could race with the big boys in the big time. He could *do* this.

After all those years of struggle. Dale Earnhardt was no kid when he arrived at Daytona. He was almost twenty-eight years old.

*H*e had dropped out of school in the ninth grade—"Couldn't hang, man, couldn't hang; failed a year and then quit," he would say, riding through his hometown of Kannapolis, North Carolina, in 1987, during a stretch when he was winning lots of races and leaving other drivers wrecked and steaming in his path, and arriving as the most controversial figure in NASCAR.

He had married first at age seventeen, begotten a son, Kerry, been divorced, and let his estranged wife and her new husband adopt his first son because "I couldn't afford to make the alimony and child support payments."

Still he raced. His own dad, Ralph Earnhardt, had done well on short tracks, even raced on superspeedways some, but he hadn't the material gifts for his son that Richard Petty had in store for Kyle. Ralph's legacy was driving style—entirely comfortable "sideways," on dirt, and therefore quite comfortable where others might panic when a car got "loose" on asphalt—and Dale absorbed the style by watching, watching, watching, as a helper at the short tracks.

And then in 1973, Ralph Earnhardt died of a heart attack. There went any little head start Dale might have gotten in racing. He was on his own. His second marriage produced a daughter, Kelly, and a son, Dale Jr. And for them and his second wife, Brenda, things got tough. Really tough.

By 1975, "I was borrowing five hundred dollars at a time on ninety-day notes from the bank, just to race," he would recall. "Maybe I should have gotten a regular job. It might have saved a family. Racing cost me my second marriage, because of the things I took away from my family. For our family cars, we drove old junk Chevelles—whatever you could buy for two hundred dollars." Some afternoons Brenda would stand in the doorway and cry as he backed out of the driveway in a pickup with his dirt car on a trailer. "I had it so damn tough that year. We didn't have money to buy groceries. We probably should have been on welfare. I signed on with the boilermakers' union and went out of town to work. It was Christmastime, and I was away from home, but I had to do something. Finally, we had groceries in the cabinet. I went back to racing.

"My wife wanted security. We didn't have it…and everybody I knew was saying, 'Boy, you better git you a regular job.'"

And so Earnhardt in NASCAR would heed no "crying," as he called it, from other drivers who felt victimized by his ruthless style.

"They ain't ever seen the kind of rough racing I've had to do in my life, just to survive."

On the hellhole dirt tracks, what your family ate the next week depended on where you finished. One night, when third place meant grocery money and fourth didn't, Dale was running fourth with veteran short-tracker Gene "Stick" Elliott third.

"Going into the last lap, I got right up on old Stick's back bumper and caught hold of him just right, and spun him around just as pretty as you'll ever see. After the race I was getting out of my car when somebody came running and told me one of his crewmen was coming with a pistol. So I ran out of the race track, jumped over the wall, and took off.

"The next Friday night at the drivers' meeting, here comes Stick with his boys. And I think, Oh, hell. Stick walks up and stands beside me. He folds his arms, grins at me, and says, 'You know, son, you just might make a driver yet.' "

*H*oward Augustus "Humpy" Wheeler, general manager of Charlotte Motor Speedway, had always been two things: a devout Catholic ever mindful of doing the right thing, and an absolutely driven promoter always looking for new ways to draw new fans.

Wheeler had been thinking for some time that NASCAR needed a black driver. There hadn't been one since Wendell Scott retired in 1973, and here was a large segment of the American public—which was to say, the American *market*—without a driver to identify with ethnically.

But there was a catch-22. Oval-track racing just wasn't a part of the African-American community's sports interests. So there were no young black drivers at the entry level. Since there were no black drivers to promote, there were no black stars to pique interest, and so, still no young black drivers at the entry level—it was an endless empty circle. Wheeler meant to break it.

Willy T. Ribbs, only twenty-three years old, was already doing well in Sports Car Club of America road racing. He was the son of a well-to-do plumbing supply business owner and sports car enthusiast from San Jose, California, Bunny Ribbs.

Handsome, polished, articulate, a one-line artist for the minicams—and one helluva road racer—Willy T. Ribbs would be transformed, Humpy Wheeler decided, into the first black star of NASCAR. Scott in his career had won only one NASCAR race—although he had participated in stock car racing since the pioneer days without overt ethnic barriers, Scott hadn't been given any breaks, either. For one thing, he never got sufficient financial backing from the outside corporate world. And because Scott was a struggling independent driver, there wasn't much time or reason to become a charismatic figure with the media.

Ribbs, Wheeler envisioned as an instantaneously charismatic driver.

Wheeler contacted Ribbs in San Jose, promised to get him a competitive ride for the World 600 of 1978, and the deal was on. Wheeler made a deal with Will Cronkrite, a former mechanical disciple of Smokey Yunick, to build a Ford Torino for Ribbs.

And the media blitz began. But then it all blew up in Humpy Wheeler's face.

Ribbs and Wheeler had, to put it mildly, a misunderstanding. Ribbs's misunderstanding of the way NASCAR worked was not ethnic. It was geographical. He was from the West Coast, where there was virtually no interest in NASCAR at the time, and perceptions were founded (a) in Tom Wolfe's old *Esquire* magazine piece about Junior Johnson; (b) in the film *The Last American Hero,* loosely based on Wolfe's story and starring Jeff Bridges and Valerie Perrine as a law-evading couple that made it into NASCAR; and (c) the *Dukes of Hazzard* television show, which melded racing with constant running from the local sheriff.

Humpy Wheeler's ongoing flair for showmanship was interpreted by Ribbs from a West Coast perspective. You run NASCAR, you have fun on the streets and roads.

And so it came to pass that, as *Charlotte Observer* motorsports writer Tom Higgins would recall, "I got a phone call at home at one o'clock in the morning. It was Willy. He said, 'Hey, Tom, I've got a great story for you.'

"I said, 'What's that, Willy?'

"He said, 'I'm in jail.'"

Ribbs, in a passenger car, allegedly had taken the Charlotte police on a merry chase, going the wrong way, on North Tryon Street, the city's main drag.

Humpy Wheeler wanted a black driver in order to tap the

black fan market, but he also wanted to do the right thing. But just beneath the surface, Wheeler was nervous. This was still the South and it was still 1978.

He summoned Ribbs to his home, and took the paternalistic approach he always took with any young driver. Ribbs didn't particularly like that. And Wheeler was trying to explain an issue that simply wasn't nearly as sensitive in Northern California as it was in North Carolina.

"I told him, 'Do you realize there could still be rednecks in that infield with deer rifles?'" Wheeler would recall. "He jumped up out of his chair, stood straight up, looked me in the eye and said, 'I don't *give* a shit!' I said, 'Well, that's it.'"

Ribbs had surrounded himself with more pre-race hoopla than even Wheeler had bargained for. And so the deal was off.

Meanwhile, Will Cronkrite had spent about $75,000 building and preparing the Ford Torino for Ribbs. Cronkrite had been out of racing for a while. He wasn't exactly Junior Johnson when it came to resources. He wanted to know just what he was supposed to do with the race car he'd taken a second mortgage on his home to build.

Wheeler was in a quandary. He and his top publicist, Joe Whitlock, conferred. What sort of a replacement driver could they provide for Cronkrite? It should be someone with some sort of name recognition.

Well, the late Ralph Earnhardt's name was still pretty big in the Carolinas. And Earnhardt's son had been doing pretty well on short tracks. Why not put him in the car?

Cronkrite agreed, and so Willy T. Ribbs was replaced in the World 600 by Dale Earnhardt. But come race day, Earnhardt's only role in the finish was to wreck with four laps to go. This bunched up the field under the caution flag and made for a decent shoot-out between Darrell Waltrip and Donnie Allison for the victory. Waltrip won.

Prior to 1978, Dale Earnhardt had run in four Winston Cup races here and there. He had essentially rented rides by scrounging enough money to help pay some struggling independent owner-driver's tire bill in exchange for the ride.

But after that World 600, Will Cronkrite still had the Torino. They might as well use it. He and Earnhardt ran three more races. They didn't even manage a Top Ten finish, but Earnhardt's wild style caught the eye of another crew chief, Roland Wlodyka.

Wlodyka had been brought south by Rod Osterlund from California. Dave Marcis was from Wisconsin. When Marcis signed on to drive for Osterlund, he and Wlodyka hit it off at first.

But late in '78, Marcis and Wlodyka had a falling out. Wlodyka, by then promoted to team manager, fired the crew chief Marcis had handpicked, Dewey Livengood.

Almost, it seemed, to spite Marcis, Wlodyka decided to add a second driver to the Osterlund team for the next-to-last race of the season, at Atlanta.

He decided to give Ralph Earnhardt's kid a shot.

Amid-race, coming out of the fourth turn at Atlanta, Marcis slammed his blue-and-yellow Chevrolet hard, broadside-to-broadside, into the blue-and-yellow Chevrolet of his "teammate." Nothing against Earnhardt, probably. Marcis mainly was making a statement to Wlodyka.

Earnhardt's car wiggled a bit, but he never cracked the throttle—never broke momentum. He drove back up beside Marcis and WHAM! He knocked the ever-lovin' crap out of Marcis, whose car wiggled considerably.

"Damn!" journalists were saying to one another in the press box. "Look at Earnhardt's kid!"

After that race, Marcis quit the team in a fury. Osterlund Racing needed a full-time driver.

Next stop for Dale Earnhardt was the Daytona 500 of 1979. With a full-time, competitive ride.

At last.

21

DARK SIDE

On the afternoon of Friday, February 16, 1979, in the quiet town of Madison, Florida, two hundred miles northwest of Daytona, a seventy-year-old woman stopped at a corner drugstore.

Mrs. Robbie Williams had three grown children, two daughters and a son, all of whom had graduated from Florida State University. Both daughters had married well and were living happily, affluently, in Atlanta. Robbie and her husband, Gordon, were semiretired, running their gift shop in Madison, entering the most tranquil days of their lives. So she thought.

Her son, Don, was leading a double life.

He was thirty-one years old. He was a traveling sales representative for a ball-bearing manufacturer. This his mother knew. He lived with his parents. He was a bachelor.

And for years he had been a race driver. Of this, his mother hadn't a clue. In 1979, the genteel South and the dirt-track crowd still did not mix. One was anathema to the other. On the live oak-lined streets of the better side of Madison, stock car racing was still equated with "sorry people." On the red clay tracks of south Georgia and north Florida, established society was seen as highfalutin, prudish, boring. Once at a track in the region I saw painted on the rear of a hotdog's car, bold enough for any trailing race driver—or any family who might be driving behind the car being transported on its trailer on a highway—to see it:

WAYCROSS, GA.
ADIOS, MOTHERFUCKER

Among the "dirt dobbers," as they were called, Don Williams had not even dared reveal that he had a college degree. At home, he had not dared mention that he traveled in these circles. His sisters and their children knew he raced dirt tracks, and once, on an outing with one sister's children to Daytona Beach, he had taken them inside the mammoth, deserted speedway and told them, "My life's ambition is to race here."

Some people around Madison knew he raced, "But we knew Miss Robbie didn't know it," said a family friend. "That's the way Don wanted it, and that's the way it stayed."

Until Miss Robbie stopped by the drugstore that Friday afternoon. "The girl behind the fountain said, 'Well, I heard Don made the race at Daytona,' " Robbie Williams would recall. "I said, 'What on earth are you talking about?' The girl realized she'd said the wrong thing. She said, 'Oh! I must have it mixed up.'

"I thought he'd gone down there to work—his sales territory covered all of Florida. And, I thought, he might go to the races as a spectator."

But she couldn't convince herself of that. Why would that girl have said such a thing? All night, Robbie Williams worried. Early Saturday morning, "I went out and got the Jacksonville paper. And there it was in the starting lineup: 'Don Williams.' "

* * *

*T*he 300-miler on Saturday at Daytona was for cars in what was then called the Late Model Sportsman division—now called Busch Grand National.

Before that week, Don Williams had never raced on any surface but dirt, nor on any track larger than a half-mile in circumference—which was one-fifth the size of Daytona International Speedway. In those days, there were no prerequisites for racing at Daytona, except a twenty-dollar fee for a NASCAR license, a routine physical exam, and a car that passed inspection.

Don Williams had bought a Sportsman car and brought some of his dirt-track friends as crewmen. And he was allowed to graduate from 85 miles an hour on short tracks to 185 miles an hour at Daytona, overnight, on his own, with no instruction. One of his crewmen would recall how, "after his first lap of practice, I asked him how it was. He said that as he was going down the straightaway, he didn't know how much to turn the steering wheel as he entered the banked turns, but that the car just went around like it was attached to the track. He said he was really surprised how it just came on around."

No veteran driver had told Don Williams anything. He just got in and drove. Learned on the fly, at 185 mph, how to go through the turns. Somehow he qualified for the race, on the tail end of a forty-car field.

On Saturday morning, Robbie Williams desperately phoned her son's motel room in Daytona Beach, to plead with him not to race. It was too late. He had left for the track at 6 A.M. and couldn't be reached.

*A*t 1 P.M., the Sportsman 300 started. James Colburn, owner of the dirt-track car Don Williams drove at home, was in the grandstands with about thirty other well-wishers who had come from Madison to see their friend fulfill his dream. Although Williams started at the back, Colburn could see through his binoculars that "Don was passing a car a lap."

But suddenly, far ahead of Don, up among the frontrunners, came the initial collisions of a massive crash. Shrapnel flew and fire billowed. Then a cloud of flame several stories high erupted, as Joe Frasson's Mercury was hit from behind and its fuel cell exploded. Far behind this primary melee, "All of a sudden there was smoke from Don's car," Colburn would recall, "so I know he hit his brakes—maybe a little too hard, out of inexperience." After that, the group from Madison lost sight of their friend's car due to the various obstructions in the infield between the grandstands and the backstretch.

In the press box, all focus was on the primary crash. It was reminiscent of those sickening Indy car infernos of the '60s. The driver who initially appeared to have no chance was Frasson. But somehow he crawled out of his car, ran out of the fire, and escaped with burns that were mostly minor.

CBS was using the Sportsman 300 to run a full dress rehearsal for the next day's landmark telecast. The press box monitors did not carry CBS sound, but did show all the live shots, and all of the tape as it was rewound and rerun in the production trucks downstairs.

CBS obviously had access to NASCAR's emergency crew channels, because the monitors kept showing a car that hadn't seemed to be involved in the worst part of the pileup.

And the graphic kept flashing:

09—Don Williams.
09—Don Williams.
09—Don Williams.

CBS had word that this guy, whoever he was, was badly injured. And in the trucks they kept rewinding the tape trying to see how he was involved in the crash. Each time, the rerun showed no involvement, and always ended with a camera panning back, far behind the primary crash and explosion, to a car that was just sitting there.

Mercifully, CBS wasn't carrying the race live.

At 1:13 P.M., the phone rang at the Williams home in Madison. Don's father, Gordon, answered. On the phone was a Baptist preacher the Methodist Williams family had never heard of, the Reverend Hal Marchman, chaplain of Daytona International Speedway.

At the same time, Dr. Thomas Scott, the duty neurosurgeon at Halifax Medical Center, less than a mile from the speedway, was paged to the emergency room to meet a severe trauma case coming in from the track. Initial examination revealed multiple fractures, and most seriously, bleeding from both ears, "suggestive of severe transverse fracture of the base of the skull," Dr. Scott would recall. "There was also a laceration on the front of the head with a fracture at the base, but not depressed."

"When Gordon hung up the phone," Robbie Williams would remember, "I could tell something was terribly wrong. I went to him. He said [and here her voice repeated a desperate, wailing tone], 'Ohhhhh! It's Don!' "

With a friend driving them, the elderly couple began the three-and-a-half-hour trip south, even though the preacher had told Gordon their son probably wouldn't live until they got there. In Atlanta, their daughters boarded flights to Daytona Beach. And the thirty friends left the grandstands and headed for Halifax Medical Center.

Hal Marchman had been the chaplain at Daytona International Speedway for eighteen years. And so at Halifax, through that Saturday night and into Daytona 500 Sunday, when Robbie Williams "wanted me to pray for Don just to live, I said, 'I can't do that, Robbie. You'll have to get somebody else to do that,' " Marchman would recall.

"She said, 'I will look after him the rest of my days if I can just have him alive.'

"I said, 'Be careful what you pray for, Robbie. You might get it.'

"She got it."

Don Williams was critically injured at the dawn of an era when death ceased to be a driver's worst fear.

"Once you get in there [a trauma unit] it's just difficult to die, with what we can do," another of his neurosurgeons at Halifax, Dr. Gilbert Tweed, would say years later, "until the vegetative function of the brain can take over."

The NASCAR medical insurance, which then had only a $15,000 cap, ran out after a day and a half of Don Williams's stay at Halifax. He lived on. NASCAR was not liable for any further medical costs—drivers were "independent contractors."

There was never a point where the doctors raised the issue of turning off life support. "I didn't see a point where we could have—without verging on manslaughter—terminated his existence," Scott would recall.

And the vegetative function of the brain set in. Even off life support, Don Williams lived on. And on.

Don," his mother said to him. "Don?"

He was lying in the same little hospital where he'd been born, in Madison.

His eyes were open. He looked as if he was about to speak.

He had been lying there for almost a year. It was February 1980. Two hundred miles to the south, engines thundered and seagulls squawked and crowds yahooed and country bands blared.

Here in this room in Madison, all was silent, save his mother saying, "Don?…Don, everything is all right. You were racing, down at Daytona. You were in an accident. You've got a little bump on your head, but everything is going to be all right."

She had been saying that, over and over, day in, day out, for nearly a year.

He lay there, staring, blinking occasionally. As if he were merely pouting about something. A nurse was removing a large condom, specially made to catch his urine. In each of his hands there was a rolled washcloth, to keep his fingernails from digging into his palms as his confused central nervous system ordered his hands to grip, grip, grip, as if in a critical moment on a steering wheel.

His father came into the room. Gordon Williams sat on the bedside and took his son's hands. Don Williams gripped his father's hands so tightly that they turned blue.

"Y-e-e-e-s," Gordon Williams said in baby talk to the thirty-two-year-old man. "He knows his dad-dy! Yes he does! He knows his dad-dy!"

A year. And there had been no contact from NASCAR or Daytona International Speedway, the family said. None. Not a call. Not a card. Not a letter.

The family did tell me off the record that they'd had a letter, and a check, from one NASCAR driver—Bobby Allison. They asked me not to print that at the time. And they wouldn't tell me the amount of the check. Bobby had asked in the letter that they not reveal this to anyone. Bobby Allison, for all his public walks against the wind, privately was a devout Catholic who didn't wear it on his sleeve, who believed the public needn't know about such things, that only God and those in need of help need know.

That Speedweek of 1980, in a 125-mile qualifying race, a

rookie from Paw Paw, Michigan, named Ricky Knotts was killed. Notified of this cataclysm to another mother, Robbie Williams wept on the phone.

"Those poor boys," she said. "Those poor, poor country boys, who don't know any better than to get out there and perform for that old devil."

She meant Big Bill France.

She hated Big Bill France.

*D*on," his mother said to him. "Don?"

She was eighty years old now.

Don Williams was forty-one now. He had grown mostly bald without realizing it. His father was one year dead, after a three-year struggle with cancer.

It was February 1989.

From an adjacent room in the nursing home, suddenly, came the almost overpowering odor of human excrement.

"Was it just ten years ago?" Robbie Williams asked. "It seems so much longer."

Still there had been no contact from NASCAR or the speedway, she said. "It would help," she said, "to know someone cares."

She asked if what she'd heard were true—that Big Bill France had Alzheimer's disease. She was told that the France family was keeping a lid on it, was very sensitive about it, and made their PR staff downright combative with the media about it, but that yes, it was true, and that Big Bill had been out of circulation for some time.

She sighed.

"I'm the kind of person who feels sorry for anybody who has trouble," she said. "But I can't help thinking, Well, Bill, you had it coming to you. Now isn't that ugly for a Christian woman?"

Since 1972, Bill France Jr. had been the official boss of

NASCAR, and in recent years the total boss of NASCAR. But an eighty-year-old woman in a little town with a comatose son who was by now on welfare had her own embodiment of the source of her family's trouble.

Independent contractors.

No unions.

No Federation of Professional Athletes.

No Professional Drivers Association.

No collective bargaining for insurance or other benefits.

Big Bill France.

Czar.

Law firms over the years had tried to convince the Williams family to sue.

"We're not that kind of people," Robbie Williams said.

She was asked if she still tried to explain to Don how he got this way.

"Not as much as we used to," she said wearily.

But in the course of the interview, Daytona was mentioned several times.

And then Don Williams's mouth dropped open, and there was a guttural, muted, "uhhh...uhhhnnn!"

Two hundred miles to the southeast the thunder was rising again, sending the seagulls fleeing again, and crowds yahooed, but here...

"Uhhh...uhhhnnn!"

"Don?" his mother said to him. "Do you remember what happened to you? Close your eyes if you remember, Don. Close your eyes tight."

He closed his eyes tightly, in a way that on a normal face might have been followed by the streaming of tears. But his tear ducts had long ago stopped functioning. His face contorted, especially his mouth.

"It almost seems like he's crying," the visitor said.

"He is crying," said his mother.

"He knows," said a nurse who'd been caring for him for

three years, Mrs. Rosa Mae James. She placed a hand on his forehead. "He knows."

His eyes had long been crossed, a complication of his brain stem injury. The visitor had been used to seeing that for years. This time there was something else in his eyes: emotional pain.

For years, with the coming of each Speedweek, Robbie Williams had said, "I wish they'd let me roll my son out in front of that crowd."

She was asked if she still felt that way now.

"Yes," she said. "Yes."

And now Don Williams raised his head, as if listening intently.

"Don, did Rosa raise your head up like that, or did you do it yourself?" his mother asked.

He had raised his head himself.

Two years he'd lain in the hospital where he was born, then seven years in his room at home, and then these recent months in a nursing home after his mother had been hospitalized for exhaustion and finally agreed to turn over his care to a professional institution.

He would not eat nursing home food nearly as readily as he would eat food prepared at home. He could tell the difference, those around him said.

"Don," the nurse would say as she put a spoon to his mouth, "these are mashed potatoes, from home."

And later, "This is apple pie, from home, Don."

And he ate it.

His old friends believed, as one put it, "Don doesn't know he's in this world."

His sisters in Atlanta believed it—rather, as his eldest sister, Wanda Corbett, put it, "I prefer to believe that my brother doesn't know. To picture him locked in a body, lying there, knowing, for ten years, is to picture a hell beyond belief."

* * *

*C*ould Don Williams know what had happened to him, and to those around him?

"I would be skeptical of it," said Dr. Scott, the elder of the two Halifax neurosurgeons who had attended him. "I can't be certain, but probably, even if he got a few words, it would just be fleeting."

But Dr. Tweed listened with knitted brow to a description of the sequence of Don Williams's apparent responses to Daytona-related conversation.

Based on the description, "he probably has some cognition," Dr. Tweed said. "He probably understands some amount."

He nodded understanding of fears that Don Williams might be trapped in his own body, trapped with the knowledge that his double life had ruined the lives of his aging parents.

Such conditions, Dr. Tweed said, are "what we call 'locked-in syndrome.'" It was dramatized by Edgar Allan Poe and later by Alfred Hitchcock...We see a number of those type things. It actually happens."

*D*on Williams died on May 21, 1989. There were no immediate news reports of it. One of his sisters phoned my wife in Atlanta so that she could relay word. I was in Charlotte, where NASCAR was running The Winston, an all-star race. The next day I connected back through Atlanta and down to Tallahassee—no one else remotely connected with racing was on either of the flights—and drove to Madison.

The only racing people at the funeral home were small-town, small-time racing people.

I'd gotten to know Don's sisters, Wanda Corbett and Sheryl Murray, and Sheryl's husband, Phil, fairly well over the years. Throughout the entire funeral home, not just the room where the body lay, the wall racks were full of flower arrangements, not from big-time racers, but from small-town genteel southerners and small-time dirt-trackers alike. Neither side was anathema to the other anymore; Don Williams had accomplished that. Wanda and I were walking among the flowers, glancing at the message cards.

I came across a simple arrangement of yellow and white chrysanthemums. The card read simply:

NASCAR

"Hey, Wanda," I whispered. She came over. Saw the card. She pulled it, crossed the room to her mother. Showed it to her.

"That," said Robbie Williams, and she wept hard at the sight of it, "is unbelievable."

Then she walked slowly down the hall to the room where her dead son lay. There she stroked the lifeless brow and kissed a cheek, spilling tears on his face.

"NASCAR finally remembered you, darling," she said. "NASCAR sent you a big, beautiful bunch of flowers."

They buried him on a Tuesday. The yellow and white flowers joined the mountain on his grave. I rode away in a van with Phil and Sheryl Murray and their kids.

"That's more than I expected NASCAR to do," said Sheryl. "I didn't expect them to do anything."

"What's NASCAR?" asked Michael, who was ten years old. Sheryl had been pregnant with him on the day Don was injured at Daytona.

In the driver's seat of the van, Phil breathed a sigh of thought-collection, a father preparing to explain so that a ten-year-old could understand:

"NASCAR is like the NFL, Michael," Phil said. "Except that they organize stock car racing."

"Why wouldn't you expect NASCAR to do anything, Mom?" asked Christopher, who was thirteen.

"Because for ten years they did nothing," Sheryl said.

"For ten years, not even a card or a letter," Phil said.

"Why?" Michael asked.

"NASCAR was afraid," said Phil, "that if they came, somebody was going to say, 'It's your fault.' They were afraid it might cost them money—that they might be sued. They were more concerned about it costing them money than about fulfilling their obligations to people."

"Why should NASCAR have done anything?" Michael asked.

"Think about your soccer team," Phil said.

"O.K."

"If someone got hurt on your soccer team, what would you do?"

"We'd get the first-aid kit."

"I mean, after that. After he went home."

"We'd call and ask how he was doing."

"NASCAR never asked, after the game, how Don was doing," Phil said. "Don was a member of the team, and they forgot him."

"Oh," Michael said.

22

THE FIGHT

Donnie Allison was a hard racer who believed that "no matter what anybody says, the object is to run the other guy into the ground." But he would say that as if it were somehow distasteful, that he wished there were a more pleasant, less ruthless way. He was not completely consumed with racing. Away from the tracks, Donnie was a more outgoing, regular guy than his brother Bobby. Donnie played golf. Donnie coached little league football—including Bobby's boys, Davey and Clifford. Donnie liked to hunt and fish. Donnie would have a beer with you.

Bobby raced. And raced. And flew his plane. And raced.

Neil Bonnett, the most fun-loving of the "Alabama Gang" of drivers around Hueytown, would stop by Donnie's house on midweek mornings and say, "Let's go play golf." And Donnie would grab his bag and go. And they would stop by Bobby's shop and invite him along. But Bobby always had his hands deep in some disassembled engine, or had a cutting torch, reworking some chassis he had redesigned.

Bobby kept grudges; let things eat on him. Donnie could let things go. In the fall of 1978, when Richard Petty was flagged the winner of the Dixie 500 at Atlanta, Donnie knew there had been a scoring error—that he actually had won. He drove into Victory Lane. After hours of controversy Donnie was declared the winner, and went through the winner's press conference, only to learn that the ruling had been changed and the win had been given back to Petty. Donnie knew that was wrong. But he let it go. He left the track in tears. Then in the middle of Petty's press conference, the ruling was changed again and Donnie was re-declared the winner. But Donnie had left. This was just the sort of thing that would have kept Bobby in the garage area, arguing with officials, until he won or hell froze over.

All morning before the 1979 Daytona 500, it drizzled. By the time CBS went on the air, the track was still damp. But NASCAR officials started the race under caution. After fifteen laps, the race went green.

On Lap 32, Bobby Allison, Donnie Allison, and Cale Yarborough all spun together off the backstretch.

"Bobby caused it," Donnie would remember. "Bobby hit me and knocked me into Cale. Yet Bobby blamed Cale for the wreck."

And *that*, Donnie Allison believes to this day, was the reason for the most notorious aftermath ever to a Daytona 500—The Fight.

On the Lap 32 incident, all three cars went into the muddy infield. Slick tires don't do well on mud and wet grass, and so all three drivers lost laps trying to drive out of the muck. Donnie lost one; Cale and Bobby each lost three.

Donnie considered the matter finished. He let it go.

Bobby didn't.

Donnie soon made up his lap, and even with considerable left-side body damage to his Oldsmobile, he retook the lead. Hardly remembered now is how dull most of the Daytona

500 was that day. Donnie Allison led and led and led and led, and the rookie Dale Earnhardt drafted right on Donnie's bumper most of the way. Earnhardt's Buick wasn't strong enough to pass, but he got himself mentioned constantly on CBS for most of the afternoon, by hanging on to second place.

Cale Yarborough may have been the best ever at making up laps. His philosophy of never giving an inch, no matter what—which caused the brush with David Pearson that cost Pearson the race in '75—was just part of his never-give-up nature.

With twenty laps to go, Yarborough was back on the lead lap and tucked in behind Donnie Allison. Together, they drafted away from the other contenders—A. J. Foyt, Richard Petty, and Darrell Waltrip, after Earnhardt had lost a lap pitting out of sequence.

As the laps clicked off the scoreboard, the obvious situation was, as Yarborough would say later, that "I had Donnie sitting right there where I wanted him." As Donnie in the candy apple red Hoss Ellington Oldsmobile and Cale in the blue, gold, and white Junior Johnson Olds circled relentlessly, it was clear that Cale was setting up the slingshot.

As the two took the white flag, no other contender was within half a lap of them. Out of Turn 2 and down the backstretch, Yarborough pulled out to pass.

Make no mistake about Donnie Allison. While he loved to golf and hunt and fish and work with kids, while he didn't hold grudges, while he accepted matters that were beyond his control, while racing wasn't his obsession every waking moment…when the white flag flew and he had a chance to win, he was as bent on victory as any driver who ever strapped in.

This moment, Donnie Allison knew, was as close as he had ever—or might ever—come to winning the Daytona 500. This day, somehow, he must not yield to Yarborough's slingshot.

BARNEY OLDFIELD, the first household name among American racing drivers, is remembered for his showdown against William K. Vanderbilt Jr. at the Winter Speed Carnival held in 1904. *(courtesy of International Motor Sports Hall of Fame Library, Talladega, Alabama)*

WILLIAM KISSAM "WILLIE K." VANDERBILT put Daytona on the map with a land speed record of 92.308 mph in 1904 and returned the following year with his Mercedes and his eyes set on another record. *(courtesy of International Motor Sports Hall of Fame Library, Talladega, Alabama)*

Twin brothers **FRANCIS AND FREELAN STANLEY** in one of the early passenger versions of their remarkable Stanley Steamer. *(courtesy of International Motor Sports Hall of Fame Library, Talladega, Alabama)*

FRED MARRIOTT set a world speed record of 127.660 in a Stanley Steamer at Ormond-Daytona in 1906. *(courtesy of International Motor Sports Hall of Fame Library, Talladega, Alabama)*

In 1927 **HENRY O'NEAL DE HANE SEGRAVE** thundered down the beach at 203.79 mph in his Mystery S. *(courtesy of International Motor Sports Hall of Fame Library, Talladega, Alabama)*

SIR MALCOLM CAMPBELL's Bluebird was a land speed record-chasing monster of the 1930s that became the singular symbol of Daytona's glorious pre-NASCAR history. *(Allsport)*

A young **BILL FRANCE** was a fair to middling race driver on the beach in the late 1930s and early '40s. What he was far better at was organizing and promoting races. *(courtesy of International Motor Sports Hall of Fame Library, Talladega, Alabama)*

FIREBALL ROBERTS, who acquired his nickname as a baseball pitcher, leads a modified race on the beach. *(courtesy of International Motor Sports Hall of Fame Library, Talladega, Alabama)*

THE SOUTH TURN at the old beach-road course often resembled a junkyard by race's end. *(courtesy of International Motor Sports Hall of Fame Library, Talladega, Alabama)*

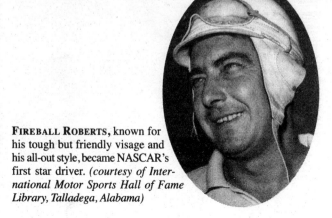

FIREBALL ROBERTS, known for his tough but friendly visage and his all-out style, became NASCAR's first star driver. *(courtesy of International Motor Sports Hall of Fame Library, Talladega, Alabama)*

BILL FRANCE became the czar of NASCAR in 1947. *(courtesy of International Motor Sports Hall of Fame Library, Talladega, Alabama)*

LEE PETTY is the patriarch of the four-generation Petty racing clan. He won the first Daytona 500 in 1959, after three days of protesting a photo finish with Johnny Beauchamp. *(courtesy of International Motor Sports Hall of Fame Library, Talladega, Alabama)*

Lee Petty

Breathtaking as he was as a racer, **JUNIOR JOHNSON** found NASCAR relatively boring compared to the moonshine running for which he was at least as famous. *(courtesy of International Motor Sports Hall of Fame Library, Talladega, Alabama)*

MARIO ANDRETTI brought an erratic driving style to the sport but nonetheless won the Daytona 500 in 1967. *(courtesy of International Motor Sports Hall of Fame Library, Talladega, Alabama)*

LeeRoy Yarbrough won the Daytona 500 in 1969, and later that year topped off his win in the Firecracker 400 at Daytona with a kiss from his wife, Gloria. *(AP/Wide World Photo)*

Nobody was tougher on the track or in the garage than **A. J. Foyt.** He won the Daytona 500 in 1972 and also won the Indianapolis 500 four times. *(courtesy of International Motor Sports Hall of Fame Library, Talladega, Alabama)*

BENNY PARSONS was the popular dark horse winner of the Daytona 500 in 1975. *(Allsport)*

DAVID PEARSON celebrates his win over Richard Petty in the 1976 Daytona 500 in what I still regard as the best NASCAR finish ever. *(AP/World Wide Photos)*

CALE YARBOROUGH *(r)* brawled with the Allison brothers after he and Donnie (with helmet in hand) wrecked while gunning for the win on the last lap of the 1979 Daytona 500. Brother Bobby drove up on the crash scene, and he and Cale went at it. *(AP/World Wide Photos)*

RICHARD PETTY, the King, won a record seven Daytona 500s and 200 NASCAR races overall. *(Allsport)*

DARRELL WALTRIP might have gone on to become the greatest NASCAR driver ever had it not been for a bad wreck in the 1983 Daytona 500 that took the edge off his all-out driving style. *(Allsport)*

CALE YARBOROUGH won more Daytona 500s (four) than any other driver other than Richard Petty. *(Allsport)*

DALE EARNHARDT won the Daytona 500 in 1998 on his twentieth try. He tragically died on the last lap of the Daytona 500 in 2001. *(Allsport)*

BILL ELLIOTT *(r)* won the Daytona 500 in 1985 and later went on to drive for Junior Johnson (l), who became a successful team owner after retiring from racing. *(Allsport)*

BOBBY AND DONNIE ALLISON have been regular fixtures at Daytona throughout their careers. *(Allsport)*

DALE JARRETT, the son of two-time NASCAR champion Ned Jarrett, won the Daytona 500 in 1993 and then went on to win the race two more times. *(Allsport)*

JEFF GORDON and his wife, Brooke, stand with the trophy after he turned in what many consider the best Daytona 500 driving performance ever, in 1999. *(Allsport)*

Yarborough zigged left, low on the track. Donnie zigged left to block. Yarborough dropped his left-side wheels onto the apron and drove up beside Donnie anyway.

Twice before, Cale Yarborough had won the Daytona 500. On paper, there was no way Yarborough should be as hungry—absolutely starving—as Donnie Allison for victory at this moment.

That is, if you didn't know Cale Yarborough—didn't understand his voraciousness behind the wheel of a car. To him at this moment, there were no other wins in his past, no fame, no wealth, there was only here and now.

"Cale and I are both greedy drivers—we both want it all," Darrell Waltrip had said just recently.

Donnie Allison was not a greedy driver. But he wanted his share. Now, he meant to keep it.

Cale kept coming on the inside, even as Donnie crowded him lower and lower on the track.

They bumped.

Once. This race is mine, and I'm going to take it, Cale said with his actions.

Twice. It is mine, and nobody is going to take it, Donnie said with his.

Thrice.

Thump. Thump. Thump.

Door-to-door they roared toward the third turn, with neither yielding a millimeter. By this point Yarborough's left wheels were in the infield grass, and his car was becoming uncontrollable. His car veered suddenly right, and the fourth hard thump of the encounter turned both Oldsmobiles hard right, locked in combat as they swerved, up across the banking of the third turn, into the retaining wall. Both cars hit hard, then drifted back down across the track into the infield. They were too badly damaged to continue.

By now, Foyt, Petty, and Waltrip were out of Turn 2, barreling down the backstretch. High above the start-finish line, in the control tower, NASCAR competition director Bill Gazaway flipped a toggle switch that set yellow caution lights blinking in all four turns of the speedway.

A. J. Foyt would have won a second Daytona 500 if it weren't for his magnificent eyesight and the fact that he was, most of the time, an Indy car driver. Indy's sanctioning body, the United States Auto Club, did not allow "racing back to caution"—that is, hauling ass back to the start-finish line, regardless of what was in your path, before slowing down for the orderly procession under caution.

In USAC, when the yellow lights came on in the corners, you slowed down immediately and maintained your position. In NASCAR, it was and is perfectly legal, after the caution lights come on, to continue racing, trying to gain position, until you get back to the start-finish line and actually see the caution flag itself being waved by the flagman—thus the term "racing back to caution." You must slow down and maintain your position only *after* you have passed the start-finish line the first time after the caution comes out. This was and is a controversial procedure because it is dangerous— especially if the path back to the start-finish line is impaired by wreckage.

As Foyt exited the second turn, he could see, far down the backstretch, the yellow light blinking in the third turn. And so his USAC-conditioned reflexes lifted his right foot off the throttle for a split second. By the time his less-used NASCAR reflexes kicked back in, Foyt saw Petty and Waltrip flash past him. They were NASCAR regulars, barreling ass, wreckage in the way or not.

All three got past the wreckage in Turn 3. Through Turn 4 Petty led, with Waltrip on his rear bumper. Out of 4 they came, Waltrip pulling out to make a bid, but Petty held him off at the checkered flag.

It was Richard Petty's sixth Daytona 500 win. And it broke a forty-five-race winless streak, the worst slump of his career to that point, that went back a year and a half to the Firecracker 400 of 1977. What a story—more than enough drama for CBS's maiden telecast. And CBS had held its audience, even through the middle stages when Donnie held the lead for so long, with Earnhardt hanging on to his bumper in the draft. Most of America was snowed in that day. From the middle of Georgia north, nationwide, CBS had a captive audience for Daytona. The race drew a 10.5 overall Nielsen rating, far beyond network expectations, and the rating in the final half hour soared to 13.5. What a day. What a finish.

Then The Fight broke out.

*C*ale and Donnie had gotten out of their cars and argued, but didn't fight. They had settled into a sort of dejected dialogue when Bobby drove up and stopped near them.

"It is partly true that Bobby stopped to see if I was O.K.," Donnie would recall. "But if you could open up Bobby's head and look inside, you'd see that what was really on his mind was the *first* wreck that day."

Bobby let the safety webbing down on the driver's-side window. He and Yarborough began arguing—Yarborough thought that on the white-flag lap, Bobby, running three laps behind, had intended to run interference for Donnie.

"As I was sitting in my car, strapped in, Cale came over and hit me in the face with his helmet," Bobby would recall. "I saw blood dripping down on my uniform. And I thought, If I don't take care of this *right now,* I'll be running from Cale Yarborough for the rest of my life."

"How Bobby got out of that car that fast, I'll never know," says Donnie. "But I knew what was going to happen. I'd seen that look on Bobby's face before."

This was the Bobby Allison who had taken out four drivers in one race in 1962.

"I kept yelling at them, 'We're on national television!'" Donnie remembered.

This was the Bobby Allison who had beat and banged with Richard Petty till their cars were often junk through a feud that lasted from '67 through '71.

"We're on national television!"

This was the Bobby Allison who called Cale Yarborough's car "the company car"—always implying that his old foe Junior Johnson was allowed to cheat freely by NASCAR officials—and would continue to give it that name into the '80s when Darrell Waltrip would drive for Junior.

Cale Yarborough had a temper that could cool as suddenly as it could ignite. He would in the future laugh off the incident of Turn 3 at Daytona as "a little misunderstanding."

"We're on national television!"

To Bobby Allison, this was another life crossroads.

"Bobby beat the shit out of him," Donnie would recall. "Hit him two or three good times right in the face. Cale tried to kick him, and Bobby grabbed his foot and turned him upside down."

The last picture shot at the scene by photographers before safety workers broke up the fight shows Yarborough's foot in Bobby's stomach, with Bobby grabbing the foot—and Donnie standing behind Bobby, wielding a helmet.

"I was actually just waving my helmet, saying to Cale, 'If you want to fight with a helmet, I've got a helmet!'" Donnie would recall.

That's the picture that made Donnie look so bad to the American public when it ran in newspapers the next day. And in magazines and books for weeks and months and years to come.

Cale Yarborough would go on to win two more Daytona 500s, in 1983 and '84, and twenty-four more races overall in his career. Bobby Allison would go on to win two more Daytona 500s, in 1982 and '88; a Winston Cup championship in '83; and thirty-three more races overall in his career.

Donnie Allison would never win the Daytona 500. Indeed, he would never win another race.

NASCAR officials at first put Donnie on probation and fined him $6,000. But upon hearing his appeal, they decided to fine all three of "the pugilists," as the media corps had come to call them, $6,000 each. All but $1,000 of each fine could be worked off with good behavior at the rate of $1,000 per race.

The next race scheduled after the '79 Daytona 500 was snowed out at Richmond. Two weeks after Daytona, ten laps into the race at Rockingham, Cale and Donnie crashed again. NASCAR ruled this one "a racing accident," and issued no penalties. But Richard Petty and Darrell Waltrip got caught up in the wreck, and both fanned the media flames.

"Somebody ought to drag Cale out of his car and whip his ass," Waltrip growled.

"If they keep this up," said Petty, "then *I'm* gonna start fightin'."

Then the next weekend the media descended on Richmond—not just the southern newspapers but *TIME* magazine, the *New York Daily News,* publications that almost never covered NASCAR—for the snow-postponed race, to see if there would be a Round Three of the "feud" between Cale and Donnie.

There was no third crash. The media people all went back to their cities—many likely disappointed—and forgot about the feud.

But Donnie Allison's career never recovered. Donnie Allison, who hadn't landed a blow at Daytona, singly paid the price for it all.

As that season went on, he would feel the entire Hoss Ellington team losing the spark, the intensity, around him.

They would begin partying too much on nights before races, and so on Sundays they would not be as sharp in the pits. Donnie would leave that team quietly, without complaining publicly, at the end of the 1979 season, and would never find another top-flight ride.

In 1981, Donnie would show up at Charlotte struggling with a half-ass car—the best he could get by then—and get hit so hard that he would suffer life-threatening head injuries and never be the same racer again. In the decades to come, he would accept his fate without complaint, would wind up with but ten career victories in the big time, but would always be grateful for what he did have, while his brother Bobby stormed on and on against the wind.

23

WORLDS APART

There was no telling how many thousands of miles Buddy Baker had put on his feet during Daytona 500 pole qualifying sessions alone. Baker was the greatest pacer in the history of NASCAR, maybe of any sport. No basketball coach who ever roamed a sidecourt could have paced as much as Baker, because Baker had more room to roam—the entire garage area—and he would cover every inch of it on a pole day. He loved winning the pole more than anybody else, and therefore was more intense—and tense—about it.

And so he didn't just pace, he went on what Australians would call walkabouts. He should have taken a knapsack. At six feet four, his long stride could cover a yard a step. He became notorious. Baker on parade. Everybody in the garage would wave to him as he passed by, and he would return a sheepish grin. He knew what everybody was thinking: Here he comes...there he goes...soon he'll be back around again...Sometimes we'd try to time his trips around the garages, to see if he got faster as the time neared for his qualifying run, or for some other driver to go out who had a chance to turn a better qualifying time than Baker had already clocked. But stopwatches were virtually useless on Baker's walkabouts, because he rarely took the same route through the garage area twice, and you never knew how many drivers, crewmen, and/or reporters he might stop to talk with for a few seconds on any given lap. The *Charlotte Observer* once asked him if they could outfit him with a pedometer, to determine exactly how much distance he did cover. He declined. The mileage might have been embarrassing.

Well, Baker wore out a pair of jogging shoes and won the pole for the 1980 Daytona 500. But the pole was nothing new for him in his nearly twenty years of trying to win this race. The question now was whether he could get as many miles on his car in the race as he had on his feet during qualifying.

Baker was driving, without question, the fastest car of its era, the "Gray Ghost," as the other drivers called it, because it had a silver-gray hood and nose that made it nearly impossible to see it coming in your mirrors. The rest of the car was black, and so the color scheme was à la Oakland Raiders. It was an Oldsmobile, owned by coal-mining wheeler-dealer Harry Ranier, who had made Waddell Wilson the highest-paid crew chief in the business. This was the same Waddell Wilson who had nursed Benny Parsons's one little engine to victory in 1975 at Daytona. But now, with excellent financing and resources, Wilson was turning out rockets. Inside the car, Buddy Baker's right foot had only one position, flat on the floor, and so here he would come, flying up on everybody else's bumpers during practice, and they wouldn't see him in their mirrors until he was *right there* in the Gray Ghost.

Baker had also won the pole for the '79 race, but no sooner had the green flag dropped than Wilson's superb engine was starved of electrical power and sputtered. Baker had switched to the backup ignition system that Winston Cup cars always carry on board, but that hadn't helped either, and so he'd parked the Gray Ghost after only twenty laps. Even more exasperating was that when they got the car back to the Ranier Racing compound in Charlotte the next day, the damn thing started right up and ran like a dream.

Then there was Baker himself. He was a purist, more akin to European and Indy drivers in his approach, in that to him, the definition of racing was to go faster than everybody else. Strategy and cat-and-mouse games bored him. Smokey Yunick, the sage old mechanical wizard who had fielded cars at both Indy and Daytona, always said it was a shame Buddy Baker was as big as he was, because he would have made an ideal Indy car or Formula One driver if he could have fit into the little cars.

And so when the 1980 Daytona 500 started, although it was clear that there were only two types of cars in the race—Baker's and all the rest—every lap was suspenseful, because you never knew as the Gray Ghost leapt through Turns 3 and 4 whether it was going to come flying down the frontstretch or down the pit road with problems.

When, at the end of Lap 200, the Gray Ghost sailed beneath the checkered and yellow flags, it seemed at first like a mirage. Buddy Baker had come so close, so many times before, that his actual winning seemed impossible.

Even though the race finished under caution, the last of five yellow flags that slowed the race for a total of fifteen laps, Baker recorded the highest average speed for a 500-mile race ever, anywhere, including Indianapolis—177.602 mph. He led 143 laps, giving up the lead only occasionally after his pit stops.

*I*t's a joke. It's not even fair."

John Bickford wasn't talking about Buddy Baker in Waddell Wilson's Oldsmobile in 1980. He was recalling Jeff Gordon in John Bickford's go-karts in 1980.

Bickford always speaks of that period in present tense.

"Jeff starts racing go-karts when he's nine years old. We show up at age nine with four serious racing years behind us, in quarter-midgets. Most kids race quarter-midgets twenty weekends a year, max. We raced quarter-midgets fifty-two weekends a year, somewhere in the United States. We had eight or nine cars. We practiced two or three times a week. We were the Roger Penske of quarter-midgets."

Having won every championship there was to win, and therefore team non grata at virtually every quarter-midget track in America, "We move on to go-karts; start in a rookie division. Now all the rookie kids' parents are saying, 'What the hell is this kid doing out here? He's lying about his age—he's not nine, he's just real little and he's probably twenty.'

"Nobody wants to race us. That's fine. We move up. We say, 'What if we run with the Juniors?' They say, 'That's fine.' O.K., for that class, we can take the restrictor out of the engine, and he kicks *everybody's* ass. It's embarrassing. These kids are thirteen to seventeen years old, and he's nine and killing 'em. So the parents said, 'You're too young. Get outta here.'

"So we go to Superstock Light. Now we're running with seventeen to unlimited age, and we're winning in that deal, too. So the competitors are going, 'There's no goddamn nine-year-old gonna run with us! You don't belong here! Get outta here!'

"Now what? We can go back to quarter-midgets, but I have this theory that you need to be a learner not a teacher when you're a kid. If you're better than the people you're racing with, then you're a teacher. You're only as good as the guys you race against. In order to run go-karts, we're now going to have to wait until he's like seventeen years old before he can get into a class where there are drivers he can really learn from."

Jeff Gordon had already developed instantaneous reflexes, skills, instinct, timing for setting up passes, timing for holding off challenges. Just to keep all that from atrophying, they returned to quarter-midgets. But there were no contests.

*F*riends since boyhood that Buddy Baker and Richard Petty had been, and racing teammates though they'd been at times, neither ever absorbed much of the other's driving style. Strategy was Petty's trademark as much as speed was Baker's.

"I've never claimed to be the best driver," Petty often said. "I'm a *racer.* There's a difference. "

To Petty, driving was a skill. Racing was an art—a comprehensive package of thought as much as deed—that could beat a better driver and a faster car with surprise tactics, developed on the run, as his beloved "circumstances" of a race unfolded.

And so Petty's last Daytona 500 win, in 1981, was in classic form.

His car was far from the fastest. But he snookered the frontrunners with his final pit stop, taking no tires and only a splash of gas in 7.8 seconds. That was half the final pit times of the faster Baker, Bobby Allison, and Dale Earnhardt, who all opted for full service on their last stops. That left Petty with enough cushion for a 3.5-second victory over second-place Allison.

"Allison had the best car," Petty would recall, deep in his retirement, "but we outflanked him on the last pit stop, just taking on gas. Then we ran good enough that he couldn't catch up. "

Petty didn't have David Pearson to outthink this time— the Silver Fox and the Wood Brothers had parted company in 1979, and Pearson languished in semiretirement, racing only occasionally, in a mediocre car. Clearly, the fun was gone for Pearson, and he had simply begun to fade away. Neil Bonnett had taken over the Wood Brothers ride, and though he put it up front in the early going of the '81 race, the clutch failed after 123 laps and the storied Number 21 was not around for the finish.

The King was drifting into twilight on the NASCAR tour overall. He rarely won much anymore. But "Petty" and "Daytona" remained synonymous.

Seven Daytona 500 victories. At the time, the record seemed unapproachable. Yarborough and Allison still had a few good years left, but not enough to equal Petty's mark.

"Seven Daytona 500s," Petty would repeat, nearly twenty years afterward, with the record still unapproached. "There were three or four where we flat outran everybody. There were three or four where we flat outran everybody and didn't win. There were two or three that we won with circumstances. Like the '79 situation [after the Yarborough– Donnie Allison wreck], and the '81 deal where we outflanked 'em.

"Looking back, if you luck into 'em like we did in '79, that was not as big a thrill as '81, when we did snooker 'em."

24

BUMPER BRILLIANCE

*I*t was either the most serendipitous Daytona 500 victory ever, or it was the slickest, most blatant, in-your-face, un-stoppable, unpunishable case of cheating ever in that race, if not in all the lore of NASCAR. It all depended on whom you believed—winner Bobby Allison, or virtually everybody else at Daytona that day in 1982.

Winston Cup cars were already far from stock by then, except that the bodywork still had to be pretty close to identical to the street version of a given model. For instance, the bumper placement had to be the same. The 1982 Buick Regal had a rear bumper that, when air flowed underneath the car on the race track, would catch air and form a pocket that slowed the car down. So the bumper acted as a sort of underside parachute. That was because this bumper extended a few inches lower than usual, and because the inside of the bumper, underneath the car, was a flat surface, perpendicular to the track. So, whoomp! It caught air like a parachute.

The Regal was otherwise an aerodynamically slick car, and so it was the model of choice for most top General Motors teams that year. During testing in December and January, teams had experimented with ways to overcome the problem of the rear bumper. Nobody seemed to come up with a satisfactory solution.

Until the race started.

On only the fourth lap, with the cars still tightly bunched in the lead drafting pack, Bobby Allison's rear bumper just happened to break completely off the car. It *flew* off—it looked like a long, slim kite rising over the fourth turn.

Supposedly, Cale Yarborough had bumped Allison from behind. The ever-accusatory Allison would later maintain that Yarborough had actually "hooked my rear bumper," and, rather than spinning Allison out, managed to tear his rear bumper off.

Well, it appeared to everybody who saw it that if Yarborough's car touched Allison's at all, it was no more than one of those normal little bumps that occur often when cars are running nose-to-tail in the draft. And Smokey Yunick, who was standing inside the fourth turn when the bumper came off, said he didn't believe Cale's car had touched Bobby's at all.

Anyway, off flew the bumper, and there wasn't a racer in the place who didn't know what this meant. Without that parachute on the back, Bobby Allison was gone. Checked out. Bye-bye. Barring bad luck or a blown engine, the only remaining question was whether he would lap the entire field on his way to victory. (But Bobby Allison wasn't one to flaunt an advantage—he would win by less than half a lap over second-place Cale Yarborough, whose Buick's rear bumper remained intact.)

Intentional or not, the breaking off of the bumper could have been dangerous. The bumper could have gone through a windshield—and Bobby's own brother Donnie was running only three or four cars back in the draft. Almost immediately, gossip spread up and down the pit road. One quickly emerging theory had it that perhaps Allison's DiGard team had meant for the bumper to come only partly off with the inevitable tap from behind, and then of course NASCAR officials would order Allison to pit to fix the dangling bumper, and of course the only solution would be to remove it entirely—and that even if Allison lost a lap during this procedure, the bumperless Buick would be so superior that he could make it up easily later on. But the thing had come completely off at full throttle, so Allison hadn't missed a beat.

Darrell Waltrip was one of the bumper-impeded drivers who ran his Buick to death trying to catch Allison, and after his engine blew with forty-nine laps, he said in an interview on the track's public-address system, "You've really got to hand it to Bobby. He's bringing it on home now." The implicit point was clear, and the race was that much of a lock, with fifty miles left to run.

*W*hen Gary Nelson was hired as NASCAR's top technical inspector in 1991—he would go on to become the smartest detective of cheating ever—NASCAR president Bill France Jr. was asked why Nelson, long considered one of the wiliest crew chiefs ever, had been hired as a de facto policeman.

"Well," said France, "when some of the big bankers got tired of being robbed in the 1930s, didn't they hire Willie Sutton as a consultant?"

If you still don't get France's point, think back to an old TV series entitled *It Takes a Thief*.

Well into Nelson's tenure as NASCAR's top cop, he was asked if indeed he hadn't pulled some of the slickest tricks ever, during his crew-chiefing days. He dropped his eyes and smiled sheepishly.

"Well," he said, "I never had to pay any fines."

Gary Nelson was Bobby Allison's crew chief for the Daytona 500 of 1982.

* * *

*A*llison and Nelson having issued all their denials and disclaimers during the winners' press conference, and all the newspaper writers having filed for the next morning, I got to the Boar's Head about nine o'clock that evening.

Never had I seen A. J. Foyt's crew so livid. They were cussing, slamming their beer glasses down on the bar, kicking the stools.

"You really think they dropped the bumper on purpose?" I asked.

"On *purpose?*" the hulking Texan Billy Woodruff hooted. He took a fresh dip of snuff, which he chased with a big swallow of beer, and growled, "Did you go down there and *look* at that bumper after it was off?"

"Well, no."

"Well, I did. All along the back of it, they'd attached it to the car with spot welds—looked like little old *turkey turds,* those welds were so tiny. So of *course* the thing popped off."

"Yeah, but Donnie was running just a few cars behind Bobby when the bumper came off," I said.

"Sh-i-i-i-t," said another of the big guys. "Listen: When *we* came down here to test over the winter [Foyt drove an Oldsmobile that year], we figured the way to go was to drop your *exhaust pipes.* And we did that a few times during testing. And you know why we didn't drop them today? Because we'd discovered in testing that there was too much chance of getting those exhaust pipes under our *own* rear wheels."

"So you tell us they didn't drop that bumper with them little turkey-turd welds on it?" another said. "Shit."

*I*t wasn't cheating, Allison maintains, to this day. Here is his version of the story:

"What *we* figured, based on testing, was that it actually helped if you *lowered* the bumper. So, I admit, we showed up at Daytona with the rear bumper a fraction of an inch lower than it was supposed to be.

"Well, Joe Gazaway [Bill Gazaway's brother, and sort of NASCAR's main street-cop enforcer at the time] spotted it. He said that bumper was illegal and that we had to move it. I said, 'O.K., Joe. If you know so much about where it's supposed to be, we'll take it off, and then I want *you* to hold it in place, precisely where you think it should be, while we weld it back on.' And so with Joe Gazaway, a NASCAR technical inspector, holding that bumper exactly where he wanted it, we welded it back. And so when that bumper came off, accidentally, it was because Joe Gazaway had made us move it."

Reminded of Billy Woodruff's charge of the "turkey turds," the spot welds, Allison maintained that "That was because the only welding machine we'd brought was a little portable wire welder."

Did Allison mean to claim that for a NASCAR-enforced modification, in that entire, sprawling, teeming garage area at Daytona, with all that equipment on hand, all they could find to do the job was a little wire welder?

He smiled. Shrugged. Plopped his hands on his thighs in a gesture of ending the discussion. "That's all we had."

*B*obby Allison might be telling nothing but the truth. But here's a hypothetical whole truth, based on circumstances, and on the craftiness of Bobby Allison—which bordered on genius. Think of it as a chess game, with Bobby Allison thinking several moves ahead.

First, Joe Gazaway was the NASCAR official Bobby Allison loved to hate, and, it sometimes appeared, the feeling was mutual. They'd had countless run-ins. So there was plenty of precedent for Allison to assume, going into Daytona, that they could have another run-in.

Second, it's hard to imagine the Buick Regal's rear bumper becoming less of an air-retarding parachute if it were placed even lower than regulation. Allison himself admits that was very curious, but maintains that it was so.

But what does a running back or a point guard do to fake off a defender? He starts in one direction, then goes the other.

At the bottom line, showing up at Daytona with a bumper that was too low, and then having Joe Gazaway spot it, and demanding that he personally hold the bumper in place, gave the DiGard team the perfect excuse for a hurry-up job that left the bumper flimsily attached.

And the flimsy attachment of that bumper was the key to winning the 1982 Daytona 500. Of that there is no doubt.

*T*he Boar's Head's last fortnight-long party was in February of 1983. The Howard Johnson's had a new manager, a devout Baptist woman who didn't believe in drinking, period. She felt the operation of such a sin pit as the Boar's Head wasn't worth the revenue it produced. We could all see the end coming.

Worst of all, one of the prime movers of the fun over the years, old Tony Foyt, A. J.'s father, was missing. Tony was dying, the crew guys said. It was cancer. He had maybe two months. He wouldn't even live to see another Indy 500.

If ever there was a tougher s.o.b. than Anthony Joseph Foyt Jr., it was Anthony Joseph Foyt Sr. Several years earlier the old man had felt an enormous pain in his chest, shrugged it off, kept on going. Months later, during a physical exam, doctors discovered old Tony had suffered a massive heart attack. The scar tissue was there to prove it. How he'd survived, let alone kept on trucking, they would never know. Tony was one of those guys who, after a while, you almost believed *couldn't* die.

In the 24 Hours of Daytona that year, A. J. Foyt and Darrell Waltrip teamed in a British Aston Martin prototype. It broke before midnight Saturday, and both drivers left the track. Through the wee hours of Sunday, two Frenchmen, Bob Wollek and Claude Ballot-Lena, co-drove a turbo Porsche 935 into the lead. The car's owner, Preston Henn, who had made a fortune in, of all things, flea markets in the Miami area, suddenly had a notion. Foyt was available to drive.

Henn awoke Foyt at 5 A.M. with a phone call. Would the winner of the 24 Hours of Le Mans be interested in co-driving what could be the winning car in the 24 Hours of Daytona?

Foyt said he would shower and head for the track, "and if your car's still in the race by the time I get there, I'll drive for you."

There was one condition: If the car won, Foyt wanted no share of the prize money. All he wanted was the trophy. Henn considered this odd—hell, didn't Foyt have enough trophies? But if that's what it would take, fine. Henn agreed.

By dawn, a drizzle turned into a steady downpour. Sports cars, using rain tires, could keep going through such a deluge, but driving was still precarious. Wollek and Ballot-Lena were masters in the wet. Foyt hadn't driven in the rain in many years.

Upon arriving at the track, Foyt was told that Wollek's latest two-hour stint was almost over, and was asked to get ready to climb into the car on the next pit stop. Foyt had never sat in a turbo Porsche 935 in his life.

When Wollek pitted, he was surprised to find Foyt waiting to take his place. Worse, as Foyt strapped in, he asked Wollek, "Hey, is this thing a four-speed or a five-speed [gearbox]?"

Wollek was immediately furious that Henn would go celebrity-hunting like that, especially when the big-name driver didn't even know the car. Turner Broadcasting was televising the race live, and just before 7 A.M., a pit reporter caught Wollek stomping, steaming, away from Henn's pit stall.

And Wollek spoke his mind on live national television: "All I know is that we [he and Ballot-Lena] have worked our asses off all night to get the car up front, and now in it they have put [he spat the name out slowly, syllable by syllable] Mis-ter A....J....Foyt. And I'm fucking pissed."

Wollek was a superb but snakebit endurance driver who almost perennially came heartbreakingly close to winning Le Mans. He was a big name in Europe. Here, at Daytona, he felt enormously insulted that Henn could think Bob Wollek needed any help from A. J. Foyt.

But out on the track, Foyt quickly made Preston Henn's decision look good even to Wollek. From behind the Porsche's whalelike tail there arose enormous roostertails of water, shooting several stories into the air, so that it looked not so much like a car as like a hydroplane racing boat skimming over water at full throttle. Foyt was flying through the wet. Hydroplaning at 235 miles an hour, downshifting—after he figured out the pattern—to 120 as he entered the infield road circuit, still hydroplaning, back out onto the banking, up to 235 again. For several consecutive laps, he broke and re-broke the course record for wet or dry conditions.

This was not only hair-raising, it was baffling. Foyt was forty-eight years old, with absolutely nothing left to prove as a driver. Yet he flashed through the deluge as if this was his one and only chance, ever, to prove himself.

They won the race. Foyt took the trophy, boarded his private jet, and flew home to Houston that night.

Back in the Boar's Head, his stock car crewmen explained why he'd gone home. He was taking the trophy to his father.

25

JAWS AND D.W.

Darrell Waltrip was hurtling headlong toward becoming the best there'd ever been in NASCAR. But then suddenly in the 1983 Daytona 500, he had to wake up Lee Roy.

For the occasion of Waltrip's final season of racing, 2000, his sponsor came up with a series of TV commercials called "The D.W. Stories." But they didn't let him tell his best one.

"We may have to wake up Lee Roy tomorrow," Waltrip would say on the eve of some race, usually at Daytona or Talladega, where he figured there was a big chance of a major pileup, in the late 1970s and early '80s, when he was the best, hands down.

And somebody would bite: "Wake up Lee Roy?"

"Yeah, man. You don't know about waking up Lee Roy? Well, there was this trucker, see, and he went for a job interview. The manager wanted to find out how good this guy was, so he gave him a little oral test.

"The manager asked him, 'What would you do if you were going eighty miles an hour on a five-mile downhill grade and your brakes went out?'

"He said, 'Well, I'd keep downshifting into lower gears to get the thing slowed down.'

"Manager said, 'Good. But what if your transmission broke and you couldn't downshift, and now you were going a hundred miles an hour?'

" 'Well, I guess I'd look for a runoff area.'

" 'Good. But what if you couldn't find a runoff area, and now you were doing a hundred and twenty, and up ahead you saw an eighteen-wheeler in the left lane, passing a Greyhound bus in the right lane?'

" 'Well, let me see...I reckon I'd look in the oncoming lanes, and if they were clear, I'd try to jump the median and go around the eighteen-wheeler and the Greyhound on the wrong side of the road.'

" 'But what if you looked, and in one oncoming lane there was a cattle truck, and in the other lane there was an auto-hauler with eight brand-new cars on board?'

" 'Now let me get this straight. My brakes are gone, my transmission's broke, there's no runoff area, I'm running a hunnerd and twenty miles an hour on a downgrade, and up ahead there's a Greyhound, an eighteen-wheeler, a cattle-hauler, and a fully loaded car-hauler. Is that right?'

" 'Correct.' "

"The ol' trucker kinda grins, and he says, 'Well, in that case, I reckon I'd wake up Lee Roy.' "

" 'Wake up *Lee Roy?*' the manager says. 'Who the hell is Lee Roy?' "

" 'Well,' says the trucker, 'Lee Roy, he's my swamper.' You know what a swamper is—he's the guy who rides in the jump seat and checks the tires and the chains and stuff.

"So the manager says, 'Why, what could your swamper do to help in a situation like that?'

" 'Well, nothin'.'

" 'Then why would you wake him up?'

" 'Well, because Lee Roy, he ain't ever *seen* a wreck *that* big before.' "

*I*n his youth, Darrell Waltrip would roll into some town on a race weekend and people would ask, "Are you with the show?" and he would grin and say:

"Nah. I *am* the show."

And he was.

How good was he? Put it this way: Until Daytona 1983, Dale Earnhardt was like a yapping puppy at Darrell Waltrip's heels, wanting to bite a piece of Waltrip bad, but not yet knowing how. And Waltrip would look over his shoulder and laugh.

The difference in the ruthlessness of Earnhardt and the ruthlessness of the pre-1983 Waltrip was subtlety. Balls-out, roughshod, slam-bang driving was nothing new when Darrell Waltrip came to NASCAR. But he was the first to disguise it—even make it pretty.

He was the first to go WFO with finesse and pizzazz and panache, and then walk coolly into cocktail parties with a certain dash and polish and sophistication and downright intelligence that there had never been before.

Where do you begin about D.W.? You begin before there was such a nickname as "D.W.," which is one he invented or at least encouraged for himself, after he wouldn't pull the trigger anymore. In the glory years he was Dirty Darrell or Daring Darrell, either loved or loathed by fans—mostly loathed. Courtesy of Cale Yarborough, Waltrip's longest-running moniker was Jaws, both for his Muhammad Ali–like mouth and for his knack for devouring other cars in his path, slamming or banging, whatever was necessary. Or he was, in garage-area parlance, "that goddamn Waltrip." But not D.W. His last decade in NASCAR was one long sad tale of a man who wouldn't quit long after it was time to go, who looked so silly putzing around Winston Cup tracks that there is now a whole generation of NASCAR fans who think of him only as a witty but washed-up senior statesman...a whole generation of fans with no idea...no idea at all...

You begin with the day he toppled four NASCAR icons in a single afternoon—Richard Petty, David Pearson, the Wood Brothers team, and storied old Darlington Raceway, called "The Lady in Black." After the storm called Waltrip blew through the Rebel 500 of 1979, none of those mystiques would ever be quite the same.

Pearson and the Wood Brothers were the first to crumble that day. With sixty-five laps to go, Pearson was "concentrating on beating Darrell out of the pits," he would say later. The Wood Brothers intended to change all four tires on Pearson's car. But when the jackman dropped the right side of the car—during a two-tire stop that would have been the signal for Pearson to go—Pearson popped the clutch and started to go.

"Whoa! Whoa! Whoa!" Leonard Wood shouted into his radio mike.

"Go! Go! Go!" was what Pearson thought he heard. And he was gone. But not far. All the lug nuts had already been removed from the left-side wheels, and as Pearson tore out of the pits, both came off. At the end of the pit road, the long-proud Number 21 Wood Brothers car belly-flopped and lay there like a beached whale. A caution period was necessitated for removal of the car. The incident was so humiliating that Pearson and the Woods fell out the following week, and split. Neither Pearson nor the Woods would ever again be the consistent winners they had been together.

Then it was the King and the Lady's turn to have their noses rubbed in Waltrip sacrilege.

You simply did not go into Turn 3 at Darlington two abreast in those days. You must not. Could not.

Screw that. Hadn't anybody heard? It was a new era.

Petty and Waltrip exchanged the lead four times on the final lap. Down the backstretch, Petty took the lead for what seemed to be for keeps—they were hurtling into Turn 3, and there was no more room for any more passing.

But Waltrip wouldn't back off. He ran the King down into Turn 3, side by side, wide open. All history at Darlington suggested that both cars would now skate wildly up the track and slam the wall. The old Lady in Black would slap you, the story went, for showing her even an inkling of disrespect.

At the last possible second came Waltrip's masterstroke. In Turn 3, he jammed on his brakes. The King ran on into the corner wide open, and sure enough his car skated high up the banking, and he had to back off. Waltrip, who had feinted high, now darted low, drove right on past the nonplussed Petty, and won.

Mystique? What mystique? Petty, Pearson, the Wood Brothers, and Darlington.

All with one shot.

Weeks later, one evening before a race at old Texas World Speedway, Waltrip and his wife, Stevie, were in a packed bar in College Station. Darrell was a life-of-the-party guy in those days, and when somebody mentioned the Pearson-Wood split, Waltrip burst out in song, to the tune of Kenny Rogers's hit "Lucille." At the top of his lungs, to mark the downfall of David Pearson, Waltrip sang, "You picked a fine time to leave me, loose wheels…"

*I*n 1981 Junior Johnson hired Darrell Waltrip as his driver, and they were no sooner out of the box together at Daytona than there was hell to pay.

On the last lap of the second 125-mile qualifier, Waltrip waited longer than was thought possible to make the final pass to win. Exiting Turn 4, he drove down under leader Benny Parsons. Parsons had the lane. Waltrip was by-god taking it. Parsons could either give him room or they'd slam broadside-to-broadside. Parsons gave way. That wasn't enough. Waltrip kept drifting high, nudging Parsons toward the outside wall. They both made it safely under the checkered flag, but Waltrip won.

Parsons was driving for Big Bud Moore that year. And a few minutes after that 125-miler, in the garage area, came the all-time ass-chewing I have ever heard a driver get from a car owner.

"Don't you *ever* let that sonofabitch push you around on the goddamn race track again!" Big Bud screamed at Parsons, spraying tobacco juice from his mouth in his rage.

Parsons, taken aback, said, "Bud, if I'd done anything else, I'd have torn up the race car."

"Don't you *worry* about the goddamn race car! We got plenty of race cars. And we'll *build* you some more race cars. We've got to break that dog from suckin' eggs!"

They didn't, though. And the next year, 1982, in another 125-miler, Dale Earnhardt and Neil Bonnett couldn't.

This was only for second place, but Waltrip was admittedly greedy. He wanted everything he could get. And so he left both Earnhardt and Bonnett's cars fishtailing toward the finish line—Bonnett almost completely sideways—after he slammed past them.

Afterward, another writer and I were walking along with Bonnett, who was seething, looking for Waltrip, through the garage area. Here came Earnhardt walking in the opposite direction, also looking for Waltrip.

"The last time I saw you," Bonnett said to Earnhardt, "you were wearing a big ol' green race car all over your ass."

They were converging on Waltrip's green Mountain Dew Buick as crewmen were pushing it through the garage. But Waltrip wasn't near it.

"That one look familiar?" said Earnhardt.

"Yep," said Bonnett. "I b'lieve that's the motherfucker right there."

The other writer asked Earnhardt, "What did Waltrip do—cut you off?"

"Cut me *off?*" Earnhardt howled. "Hell, he ran all over the side of my goddamn race car!"

But Waltrip could con his way out of anything. We found him over at his garage stall, sitting on a work bench, and he was giving us the usual "that's racin' " routine when, from about twenty yards away, here came Bonnett, making a bee-line toward Junior Johnson's garage stall, his eyes boring in on Waltrip.

"Y'all go on, now—here comes Neil and there's liable to be a ruckus," Waltrip said to the group of writers, the way a schoolteacher would say, "Run along, children." The hell he said. I wasn't going anywhere. Nobody played to the media quite as beautifully as Waltrip when he needed something—but when he deemed us in the way, he could be condescending and abrasive, and some of us just wouldn't take that one-way stuff off him. I stepped back just enough to let Bonnett pass. He was coming like a bull across a pasture at an intruder.

Bonnett's eyes were afire. I doubted he was even going to break stride before he threw the first punch.

But when Bonnett drew to within four or five paces of him, Waltrip threw up his hands as if bewildered, and there swept across his face the most innocent, compassionate look you can imagine.

"Neil!"—actually he said it as, "Neeeeeeel!" As in, My dear friend, I feel *so sorry* for you. "I looked in my mirror and saw you sideways. Neeeel, what *happened?*"

When his temper wasn't up, Neil Bonnett was the nicest and most polite guy in NASCAR. And somehow, in an instant, Waltrip defused his temper. As Bonnett slowed, he glanced at me and the fire had gone out of his eyes. Bonnett never liked media controversies. He was still breathing hard as he said to Waltrip, "What *happened* was, I nearly busted my ass." And then he went into such muffled tones that I couldn't hear. But it was a discussion. Not a fight.

Waltrip could do that to people.

Earnhardt he treated as a mere nuisance in those days. "With Earnhardt, every lap is a controlled crash," he once said. And then later, in touting his own plan for restructuring the Winston Cup points system, he added an afterthought: "And you ought to get at least five bonus points for takin' Earnhardt out."

The neon went out in Darrell Waltrip on February 20, 1983, on the sixty-third lap of the Daytona 500. He never would remember exactly what happened.

Journeyman driver Dick Brooks was running well enough to mingle with the leaders that day. He was ahead of Waltrip exiting Turn 4 onto the front stretch, but Waltrip was coming wide open, with a bead on Brooks. Suddenly there was a spin up ahead of them, and a caution came out. Brooks backed off radically, apparently trying to duck down the pit road.

Waltrip threw his car sideways to keep from rear-ending Brooks, and after that, Waltrip's Chevrolet was but a two-ton pinball. The car backed hard into the outside wall, bounced off, spun all the way across the track, slammed backward into the inside wall, came all the way across the track and hit the outside wall again, head-on.

This was one time when the legions of Waltrip haters in the stands didn't stand up and cheer when he wrecked. Clearly, this one was bad. The yellow Pepsi Chevrolet sat in the middle of the track, nothing moving in or around it. Waltrip was unconscious when the emergency crews got to him. He had a severe concussion.

The other events of the day—including Cale Yarborough's slingshot pass of Buddy Baker on the last lap for his third Daytona 500 win—were somehow anticlimactic. NASCAR's brightest and most controversial star lay in nearby Halifax Medical Center, and the usual crowd of more than 150,000 awaited word from the hospital. No matter how loudly NASCAR fans may boo a driver, they always want to see him back the next Sunday.

Indeed, Waltrip came out of the hospital to race at Richmond the next week. But his savvy car owner, Junior Johnson, noticed something was wrong. To this day, Waltrip does not remember driving in the Richmond race.

The following week at Rockingham, Waltrip realized he was beginning to wake up. I asked him if he remembered how hard he hit at Daytona. He didn't. I asked if he understood how close a call he'd had.

He sighed. Gave me a penetrating stare.

"Look," he said. "This ain't my first rodeo. I know you can get hurt in this business. I know you can get killed."

The only thing that saved his life, he figured, was that Junior Johnson had custom-built that car precisely to Waltrip's physical dimensions, so that the seat and the roll bars fit like a tailored suit.

Waltrip was never the same driver after the Daytona crash. Oh, he would always deny that it changed him. But Junior Johnson, who was a master of reading the psyches of his drivers, would always maintain that Waltrip never was the same.

"If it hadn't been for that wreck," Johnson would say fifteen years later, "Darrell would have had at least five more good seasons."

A good season, to Johnson, meant one with a double-digit wins total, accomplished by driving WFO, à la the young Junior Johnson himself. Waltrip had won a dozen races for Johnson in 1981, and another dozen in '82. In '83 he would win six.

His driving style began to change. Whereas before he would stick the nose of his car virtually anywhere, he now grew cautious. Conservative. Picked his spots carefully. Gave way where he used to run over people.

Earnhardt began to sense skittishness in Waltrip at Daytona, and began to probe the nerve. "Darrell doesn't like to run that fast anymore," he said.

By 1984, Waltrip would sit in the garage at Atlanta and say, matter-of-factly, "I want to win as many races as I can, going as slow as I can."

That was smart. But it was not Waltrip. It was a senior statesman called D.W. And the neon was gone.

26

"THE LAST ONE"

By 1984 it was sadly obvious that Richard Petty's reign was slipping rapidly toward emeritus status. There would be no more Daytona 500 victories, no more Winston Cup championships—seven would have to be his crowning number of each. His physical stamina was waning. Whenever you caught him with those sunglasses off, his eyes were tragically weary. And he grew thinner, not by design.

One other milestone remained reachable: two hundred career victories. At the end of the 1983 season he had 198.

But his team was falling woefully behind technologically. Young crew chiefs such as Gary Nelson were taking NASCAR high-tech, with methodical engineering rather than relying on seat-of-the-pants mechanical savvy. Waddell Wilson was pushing Daytona to the brink of becoming a test of clockwork machinery more than drivers.

Wilson engines had powered Cale Yarborough to victory in the last two Daytona 500s, in '83 and '84—this to go with his wins in '75 with Benny Parsons and '80 with Buddy Baker. In '83, Wilson's Pontiac had been so fast as to be over the edge of control—on pole day, Yarborough had turned the first 200-mph lap at Daytona, 200.503, only to have the car lift up off the pavement (the state of aerodynamic downforce at the time was not enough to stabilize Wilson's power) and roll over during his second qualifying lap. And so on race day his pass of Baker on the final lap was well anticipated, virtually inevitable. The '84 Daytona 500 had been déjà vu of '83, except that Darrell Waltrip replaced Baker as Yarborough's sitting duck on the last lap.

Petty Enterprises watched this high-tech surge go on, "but we said, 'Well, we've been winning for twenty years, so we just don't think we'll change,' " Petty would recall ruefully. "We had been the leaders. Before long we not only weren't leading anymore, we weren't even keeping up."

And in feeding the insatiable image—his life now consumed with promotional appearances—Richard himself had less and less time to give input into the preparation of the cars. He became more and more detached from his crew. By the fall of 1983 the team was so desperate to catch up that, without Richard's knowledge, they took a cheater engine to the Miller 500 at Charlotte. Richard had no idea that the engine was nearly 382 cubic inches, far over the legal 358.

He was thrilled to win the race and break another slump, then mortified during the post-race teardown and inspection. That Sunday night as the humiliating inspection continued with the allowed "cool-down" period—sometimes engines that measured too large immediately after a race would contract to legal size after several hours of cooling—Richard was strolling aimlessly, sadly through the dark garage when he saw feisty old Harry Hyde sitting in a passenger car. Harry was always good for a laugh, a pick-me-up. Richard walked over.

In the car with Hyde sat a young, wanna-be car owner named Rick Hendrick, discussing the possibilities of forming a team with Hyde.

"Harry said, 'Richard, don't worry about it. When that

thing cools off she'll check O.K.,' " Hendrick would recall. "Richard said, 'You could take that one to Alaska and she wouldn't check O.K. ' "

Officials let the win stand, but fined Petty a then-record $35,000. Then the deluge of mail hit Level Cross. Richard Petty could stand a lot. What he couldn't bear were the masses of commonfolk telling him how disappointed they were in him—that they never thought he'd cheat.

That was engine specialist Maurice Petty's last season as a mainstay figure in the Petty pits. Storied Petty Enterprises was coming apart. And so for the 1984 season, Richard Petty signed to do what he had never done before—drive for someone else. California lieutenant governor Mike Curb was a music-recording magnate, a Reaganite Republican, and a NASCAR fan. He would become the first boss Richard Petty ever had, other than Lee Petty in the late 1950s and early '60s.

Win 199 came at the ho-hum venue of Dover Downs International Speedway in Delaware, on May 20. The next week in the World 600 at Charlotte, Curb's Pontiac blew an engine and Petty wound up thirty-fourth; Riverside on June 3: Petty finished twenty-third; Pocono, June 10: Petty thirteenth; Michigan, June 17: Petty thirty-fourth.

Richard Petty was slumping again in the midsummer break. Next up, on the Fourth of July, was the Firecracker 400.

At Daytona.

Ronald Reagan was running for reelection as president. The Republican nomination was of course a lock, but he needed a launching pad for the '84 campaign against the probable Democratic nominee, Walter Mondale. A preemptive PR strike against the upcoming Democratic National Convention would be nice. And the Fourth of July would, of course, be an optimal date for Air Force One to land someplace special, someplace right down the gut of Middle America.

Such as Daytona.

Reagan gave the command to start engines via radio/telephone/public-address system hookup from Air Force One, en route. Out in the infield a temporary stage had been set up for a big political rally, featuring country singer Tammy Wynette, after the race.

Reagan was settled comfortably into a luxury box when the well-known Republican Richard Petty took the lead on the 128th of the 160 laps.

The political planets and stars all appeared to be aligning.

The one remaining problem was Cale Yarborough in Waddell Wilson's relentless, seemingly infallible Chevrolet. Cale stalked. Cale shadowed. His and Wilson's recent history on this track loomed—back-to-back wins in the last two Daytona 500s.

With just over three laps to go, a caution came out. Somebody named Doug Hevron had wrecked in the first turn, behind the leaders. Now the race would surely finish under caution—the wreckage couldn't be cleared in time for a restart. Were this the Indy 500, everybody would slow down and maintain position immediately, and Richard Petty would cruise to two hundred. But no, this was NASCAR, where they raced back to the caution, and so down the backstretch, Yarborough treated Lap 157 as the last, and pulled the slingshot. As against Pearson in the Daytona 500 of '76, Petty drove back under Yarborough through Turns 3 and 4, and side by side they came to the flag, to the president, to the milestone.

Petty made it by a foot.

Two hundred.

On the Fourth of July.

With the president watching.

At Daytona.

Richard Petty would never win another race.

At the end of the century I would ask him which of his two hundred wins was most memorable.

"The last one," he said. "That was pretty spectacular. And the more I look back on it, the more spectacular it gets."

*O*ut in California, that same summer of '84, another veteran racer was feeling finished, lost, burned out. "You get to be twelve years old, you're in quarter-midgets, you've been there eight years, you've won everything there is to win," Jeff Gordon would recall thinking. "What's the next step? There is none. You're done."

He had been banned from go-kart racing series for being too dominant. Above that, all racing was for adults only. Disheartened, feeling adrift, Jeff Gordon tried waterskiing that summer. Naaaaa. Then John Bickford read in a magazine about a kid in Florida who had started racing sprint cars at age thirteen.

Of all open-wheel racing in America, sprint cars on half-mile ovals were the wildest—and for many years had been the deadliest—form. The cult following was enormous, from upstate New York down to Florida out through Arizona and up the West Coast to the San Francisco Bay. The most notorious tracks were in the Midwest: the dirt hellholes at Eldora, Ohio; Terre Haute, Indiana; Knoxville, Iowa…the paved horror rides in Indiana—Winchester and Salem.

The baddest boys in this quintessentially badass world drove the World of Outlaws tour: grassroots American heroes Sammy Swindell and Doug Wolfgang and Mark Kinser and most of all his cousin, Steve Kinser, King of Outlaws, running thousand-pound cars with thousand-horsepower engines solely on dirt ovals, tearing sideways through the corners and slinging mud clods treetop high and over the catch fences and out of the ballpark, and trying to keep the cars from following the mud over the fences.

Deadlier still was the United States Auto Club sprint car series with its own cult figures, fearless flyers such as Tom Bigelow, Roger Rager, Rich Vogler...USAC rules prohibited the enormous "wings" on top of the cars that the World of Outlaws allowed. Those wings not only helped hold the cars down on the track aerodynamically, but in crashes they retarded the horrific rollovers that had killed so many sprint car drivers down through the decades.

But the World of Outlaws had a minimum age of sixteen for drivers, and in USAC the minimum was eighteen.

And then there was the All-Star sprint series. They did allow wings, and "they didn't have an age minimum," Jeff Gordon noticed. "Nobody had been fool enough to do it [race too young], so they didn't figure they needed a rule."

Burned out on quarter-midgets, banned from go-karts, too young for midgets.

"Why don't we just do a sprint car?" Bickford asked Jeff that summer of '84.

And the answer was instantaneous: "Sure!"

Midget cars would have been a less drastic next step, but their top series was controlled by USAC, with its age limit, so "Midgets were never an option—the only thing to do was go sprint car racing," Gordon would recall.

Bickford had experience building and maintaining sprint cars, and he had plenty of friends to help. So that part was easy. The tricky part would be to get Jeff Gordon to sit in a car that would be propelled by ten times the horsepower he was used to.

As they built the car, Bickford kept telling Jeff that the acceleration wouldn't feel that much different than in go-karts.

And Jeff believed.

Hey, the All-Star series rules limited engines to "only" about 650 horsepower.

That was more than Richard Petty had used to outsprint Cale Yarborough to a two hundredth NASCAR victory at Daytona that summer.

But Jeff Gordon, not quite thirteen years old, in Vallejo, California, still hadn't heard of Richard Petty or NASCAR or Daytona. Nor they of him.

That was more than Richard Petty had used to dominat
Or? Farnum, but it's two teams in one NASCAR Victory
Petrows this seasons

27

BOYS TO RAISE

In 1977, after Roger Penske and Bobby Allison split,
Penske decided to sell all his NASCAR equipment. He
found a buyer in one George Elliott of Dawsonville, Georgia.
George, from what some knowing Georgians said, was a
whole lot richer than you'd reckon from seeing him sitting
around his junkyard, or running his little Ford dealership.
George had three sons: Ernie, the eldest, then Dan, then Bill.

Growing up in Dawsonville, the thing for all boys to do
was race up and down Highway 9, the old Whiskey Trail, in
souped-up Chevys and Fords. That, or they would "oil
town." They would pour motor oil all over the town square,
which was within sight of Lloyd Seay's tombstone, and then
come tearing into town and slam on their brakes and turn
their cars sideways and see just how many 360-degree spins
they could do on the oil slick before they stopped or crashed
into something.

"Oh, they did love to oil town," Dan used to say wistfully.

Oiling town was relatively safe, but a lot of teenagers got
killed running Lloyd Seay's old routes on the highways.
George figured that if his boys were going to race anyway, he

would get them off the roads and into organized events on tracks. At least that was George's side of the story, till the day he died in 1998. Others would tell you that George Elliott was in fact determined to make at least one of his sons a star NASCAR driver. George had known Lloyd Seay and Roy Hall personally, and was a boyhood friend of NASCAR pioneer driver Gober Sosebee. George had grown up in an era when, during February, the whole town of Dawsonville emptied out and went to Daytona. George wanted to see that again.

Ernie tried short-tracking and said no thanks. Dan wouldn't do it. And so in some ways Bill, as the youngest, got stuck with the job. It is still uncertain whether Bill Elliott ever really wanted, deep inside, to be a driver in the first place.

The family went to Dixie Speedway, northwest of Atlanta, one night, and teenage Bill was the only son who hadn't tried racing, and George put him in a car for a few practice laps, and he did pretty good, and Ernie, standing there in the pits, said, "Daddy, there's your driver."

So they went short-tracking locally for a few seasons and weren't especially good at it—the real Georgia masters such as Jody Ridley and Billy McGinnis and Buck Simmons blew Bill's doors off with regularity.

But George had his eyes on the big time, and in 1976 sent Bill to NASCAR with an old Ford Torino to run eight races, six of which he did not finish. After George bought Penske's equipment in '77, the modus operandi was this: Ernie and Bill would run about ten NASCAR events per season, and George and Dan would remain at home to run the Ford dealership to finance the racing. They had no outside sponsorship to speak of.

It was truly a shoestring operation, and sometimes in the garages where twelve or fourteen crewmen might swarm each of the frontrunning cars, you'd see the two humble, red-headed Elliott boys over there, just the two of them, working alone. In 1979 Bill finally made a small splash—he finished a distant second to David Pearson, who was substituting for the injured rookie Dale Earnhardt, in the Southern 500 at Darlington.

God, what a touching, salt-of-the-earth character he seemed to be that day.

"Ma-an, I'm pra-oud!" he said, beaming. And when some fans came up and wanted to have their picture taken with him and gathered close around him, he flapped his arms in his sweaty uniform and grinned and said apologetically, "I know I must stink."

And, leaving the Elliott garage stall, Atlanta journalists were congratulating each other: If this wonderful ol' boy ever got to be a big winner, what an easy local story there would be, to cover regularly.

In 1983, Michigan industrialist Harry Melling bought out George Elliott's racing operation, allowed it to remain in the Dawsonville hideaway far from the Charlotte base of most of the NASCAR teams, and put Ernie in charge of the engine room and Bill in charge of the chassis department. Then, to a party the night before the Atlanta Journal 500 in 1983, a veteran publicist around NASCAR, Alexis Leras, brought three higher-up executives from the Coors breweries in Colorado. Alexis, New York–born and Westchester County–raised, was Harry Melling's point person for acquiring major sponsorship—she could talk the talk that the mountainfolk couldn't. She took me aside and told me they were completing a deal to sponsor Bill Elliott long-term. This, she said, was going to be major money—enough that Bill could become a big winner. The Elliotts deserved it. But the question was whether money alone could do it. Bill and Ernie still seemed relative babes in the woods. They were isolated from the big

NASCAR teams in every way: It was hard to lure experienced racing mechanics from the Charlotte hotbed to the remote outpost of Dawsonville, and at the race tracks the Elliotts didn't get much, if any, advice and help from other top Ford teams such as the Wood Brothers or Bud Moore. If it were even possible for the Elliotts to become consistent winners, it likely would take years—or so it seemed.

They completed the deal in Colorado on the way to California for the final race of the season, on the road course at Riverside. Coincidentally and astoundingly, Bill won the race. But pundits wrote off his first Winston Cup win to a little luck and to Bill's naturally developed road-racing skills from his youthful exploits on serpentine old Highway 9, the old Whiskey Trail—9 was even the number on the side of his Winston Cup car.

Ernie Elliott was far brighter, more world-wise, more cunning—and more vengeful—than any of us realized at the time. Dating back to the time of Raymond Parks, Roy Hall, and Lloyd Seay, metropolitan Atlanta still had an enormous racing techno-culture. In recent years the master mechanics had busied themselves building engines and cars for local short-track racers, but that in itself was a huge industry—on any given weekend other than in winter, no fewer than seven short tracks were up and running in the Atlanta area. Sometimes there were as many as nine.

With the big-buck backing, Ernie quietly assembled an armada of skill and talent that was unknown outside Georgia. He brought crack engine builders directly into the Dawsonville shop. Some came with mixed emotions—they went to work for the Elliotts because it was the only way they could test their skills at the NASCAR level and remain in Georgia. Ernie outsourced some of the work. Take, for example, those mysteriously effective cylinder heads that soon would leave the NASCAR masters—from Leonard Wood to Junior Johnson—bewildered, and give Ernie Elliott the image of a wizard. Those heads were in fact, Ernie would explain later, ported and polished by a short-track engine whiz named Kent Ford, in a shop on the northeast side of Atlanta.

Bill did an enormous amount of the chassis work himself. Although he hired staff for his department, he micromanaged, hands-on. This consumed most of his time—which would become a major problem for him later on.

In 1984 the Elliotts slipped quietly up on NASCAR's frontrunners. They scattered three victories—Michigan in June, then Charlotte and Rockingham in October. They sneaked up on the Atlanta media too. Their last two victories came in the middle of football season, so there just wasn't much attention paid to the Elliotts.

Then on Saturday, February 9, 1985, Bill Elliott won the pole at Daytona.

As it turned out, Dawsonville, Georgia, culture was hurtling toward collision not only with Atlanta, but with the whole mystique of Daytona.

Bill Elliott had been flung, in less than forty-four seconds—the time it took to complete his pole-winning qualifying lap at 205.114 miles per hour—from Dawsonville, Georgia, population about 550 and largely unchanged since the time of Lloyd Seay, onto center stage of American midwinter sports.

And he was overwhelmed. Bewildered.

He felt drawn and quartered by the speedway staff, who were relentlessly pulling him to this or that "official" appearance, and by Alexis Leras representing the multimillion-dollar interests of Coors and Harry Melling, and by the media whose numbers swelled around him with each passing day, each passing hour, of Daytona 500 week.

On the second afternoon, he sat down with several journalists for nearly an hour. He was pleasant again. He talked openly about boyhood and Highway 9, and how, growing up near the moonshine culture of Dawson County, you learned to leave the bootleggers alone and they would leave you alone. It was wonderful stuff—yet told now with tension in his voice and eyes.

The ol' boy who had been so proud to finish second at Darlington, years ago, was gone.

In his place sat perhaps the must reluctant sudden star in any form of sport or entertainment. Anywhere. Ever.

Ninety miles up Interstate 95, in Jacksonville, Jeffrey Michael Gordon, age thirteen, was going through an ordeal of his own.

*Y*ou lied to me. You told me this was gonna be a lot like go-karts and quarter-midgets. And I'm telling you this is *nothing* like go-karts and quarter-midgets."

Jeff Gordon stood, helmet in hand, near tears, confronting his stepfather in the pits of a mudhole half-mile dirt track on the other side of the continent from home. He had just been rocketed into a realm he had never imagined.

Towing cross-country from California to Florida—where Jeff would be "legal" in adult racing for the first time, running with the All-Star sprint car series—John Bickford had assured him that the change wouldn't be drastic.

And now, just minutes earlier on this February day in 1985, Jeff had climbed behind the wheel of a sprint car for the first time. And suddenly he had felt "650 horsepower underneath my foot," he would recall. "And I had control of it—no, I didn't. At that point, I had no control of it."

And he had smacked the wall.

He was unhurt physically, but his confidence was devastated. And here they were, standing amidst a swarming, hardass, balls-out world of which Bickford had never even hinted. Every short track within a hundred miles of Daytona International Speedway runs races every night during the frenzy of Speedweeks, tapping into the mass migration of race fans. The All-Star sprints would start in Jacksonville and work their way down through Florida. And on every highway in the state there were trucks and trailers hauling modifieds, supermodifieds, late models, sprinters, more kinds of race cars than Jeff Gordon had any idea existed.

There was even word the great Steve Kinser was towing down from Indiana to plunder the big purses at any and all sorts of sprint races up and down the state of Florida. How would a thirteen-year-old kid like to race against Steve Kinser? How would a Little Leaguer like to find himself suddenly playing second base in the American League in 1914 and see Ty Cobb prancing and snorting at first base, getting ready to steal second like a freight train?

Bickford coaxed. Bickford cajoled. Bickford coached. Jeff Gordon climbed back into the monstrous bucking package of 650 wild horses and began to ride them, feathering the throttle, getting the feel, little by little sensing some control. He raced. He didn't win, but he raced with the badasses.

And then later that week the traveling show pulled out for Tampa, where, "When he was thirteen," Bickford would recall, "he raced Steve Kinser."

Sitting behind 650 horsepower was the only place Bill Elliott found peace in February of '85. Ernie and the Georgia wizards had given him more power than anyone else, and Bill was fearless at high speed. Compared to the zoo that had engulfed him all week, the Daytona 500 was almost serene.

The first sign of sea change was when Cale Yarborough, gunning for a third straight Daytona 500 win, blew the engine out of Waddell Wilson's Thunderbird, just trying to keep Elliott in sight. The Thunderbird that year had such aerodynamic advantages over General Motors cars that even Wilson and Yarborough had switched to Ford. So the real mechanical duel came down to engines, between Wilson the Daytona maestro and the upstart, unknown, almost unknowable Ernie Elliott. It wasn't even close. It was Ernie by a knockout.

Then other engines died of the exertion of the frantic chase of the red Number 9 Coors Thunderbird: Bobby Allison's. Dale Earnhardt's. A. J. Foyt's. Richard Petty's. Benny Parsons's.

But the isolated Georgia boys mustn't show their whole hand. NASCAR officials were watching. They liked to keep competition even. If one car got too dominant, they might change the technical rules in midseason to level the playing field—they might take away some spoiler height here, or a specific cylinder head configuration there.

Bill won by less than one second over Lake Speed. How could the journeyman Speed have finished second? Because the Elliotts had run the serious competition into the ground.

Just as parity had seemed to set in in NASCAR, the Elliotts blew it right out the window. Suddenly the big-time Ford team owners and crew chiefs, who had snubbed the Georgia boys before, began to cozy up to Ernie. So did Ford's international racing director, Michael Kranefuss, and his factory engineers. C'mon, Ern, ol' pal, let your Ford brethren in on some of the secrets.

Nossir. None of the big guns had given the Elliotts the time of day through the hard years. Now he was on top, and he wasn't telling anybody anything.

The Elliotts won at Atlanta; won at Darlington; and then at Talladega in May, they had to show just how strong their hand really was. Bill won the pole for the Winston 500 at a then-record 209.398 mph. But on the forty-eighth of the 188 laps, smiles and vengeful grins broke out along the pit road. The red Thunderbird came in smoking. So much for the upstart loners. They'd blown an engine.

Or had they? Ernie went under the hood, found a loose oil-line fitting, tightened it. The engine was undamaged.

Bill roared away again, but he had lost two laps in the pits. Way out front were the archenemy Ford cousins: Yarborough in Waddell Wilson's Thunderbird, and Kyle Petty, now driving for the Wood Brothers.

And then began the most astoundingly powerful comeback in the history of NASCAR. There had been nothing like it before. There has been nothing like it again, to this day.

Making up laps with the help of caution flags is one thing. Because NASCAR allows "racing back to caution," a driver who is a lap down need only nose out the leader at the start-finish line, at the completion of the first lap on which the caution first flies, in order to regain a lap. Then, as the cars proceed slowly behind the pace car, the driver recovering from the deficit can circle all the way around and bunch up behind the leaders.

But there were no more cautions at Talladega that day. That was the scary part. That was the day one of the Atlanta TV sportscasters dubbed Elliott—without the slightest exaggeration at that point—"Awesome Bill from Dawsonville."

At 200 miles an hour, under the green flag all the way, Bill Elliott simply hunted down Kyle Petty and Cale Yarborough and blew by them. Three times. Twice to unlap himself, the third time to take back the lead with forty-three laps to go. And then he simply drove away from them.

It amounted to an earthquake in stock car racing. All the technological savvy learned through all the decades in the Carolinas and Virginia was futile on that day, and the epicenter of the industry had shifted back to Lloyd Seay's Georgia mountain town in a single afternoon.

After forty-four years, Dawsonville was the pinnacle again.

And George Elliott stood on the fringes of his dream, looking in. Slowly, surely, George Elliott, who had spent a million dollars getting his boys off the old Whiskey Trail and onto superspeedways, was being shuffled aside.

"George," Harry Melling would say, "is officially unofficial."

George got to wear a team uniform at the races. That was about it.

With the Daytona 500 and Winston 500 wins under his belt, Bill became the first driver ever eligible to win the Winston Million bonus, offered to any driver who could win three of four designated races—the Daytona 500, Winston 500, Coca-Cola 600 (formerly the World 600) at Charlotte, and the Southern 500 at Darlington.

For Memorial Day weekend, the Elliotts went to Charlotte with a chance to complete a sweep of the first three Winston Million races, and leave the Southern 500 irrelevant. In the garage stall next to them, the legendary Junior Johnson and his flamboyant driver, Darrell Waltrip, turned up the psychological blowtorches.

"If them boys was slippin' around, gettin' by with somethin' [cheating], I wouldn't be sayin' a word except more power to 'em," Johnson said. "But that damn car of theirs is legal. That's what pisses me off."

He was lobbying for a rules change that would help out his and other Chevrolet teams. But NASCAR was handcuffed. None of the other Fords were nearly as dominant as the Elliotts' car. If NASCAR singled out the sudden folk heroes from the Blue Ridge Mountains, it would be a PR disaster.

The media drove the Elliotts bonkers that week. And Charlotte ringmaster Humpy Wheeler had a staff assigned specifically to Bill to drag the poor guy from one ring of Humpy's usual circus to another. It was all getting to Bill; it was getting to Ernie. Three or four of the top Atlanta television stations had sent satellite trucks and pushy camera crews. Dawsonville lay only sixty miles north of Atlanta, but in those days was still blessedly isolated, still Mayberry. But now Atlanta had reached out and snatched the Dawsonville boys as its own, which is to say that Hollywood had come to Mayberry, breathing down the Elliotts' collars and looking over their shoulders at every turn, and the Elliotts were by no means prepared for it. Even media-comfortable racers such as the Pettys didn't have the kind of burden that was crushing the Elliotts. No driver in NASCAR at the time had remotely as big a "hometown" media following as Bill Elliott.

Bill's first wife, Martha, was a genuine and down-to-earth person. Nothing seemed to get to her. As the TV mobs swarmed the garage, I saw Martha sitting alone at the back of the team's truck.

"Will a million dollars change things even more?" I asked her.

"What million dollars?" she said.

"Why, the Winston Million."

"If Bill wins it, we'll get sixty thousand dollars, and we'll still live in Granny Reece's basement," Martha said. I knew they lived with Bill's maternal grandmother, "Miss Audie" Reece, but I was fishing for any plans they might have to build a new house.

"Harry Melling will get fifty percent of it," Martha explained. "Then Ernie and the crew get bonuses. Bill's share is ten percent. After taxes on a hundred thousand, I figure we'll get to keep sixty thousand."

It was a helluva story and I wrote it—which didn't exactly send Martha and me to the top of the Christmas card lists of Harry Melling, Winston, Coors, or NASCAR.

God, no wonder Bill Elliott had a horrific time dealing with all this. This whole thing about the Huck Finn lookalike from the Georgia mountains finally reaping the fruits of his labor was a tractor-trailer load of bullshit.

One night that week, at a catfish house on Lake Norman,

Bill took a sip of beer and looked across the table at me with a discernible pleading, bordering on despair, in his eyes.

"See, all I ever wanted to do was race," he said. "I never knew it would be like this."

He didn't win the Winston Million at Charlotte. A tiny metal spur on an improperly polished wheel cut a brake line on the Thunderbird, and the brakes went out. Repairs in the pits cost him twenty-one laps.

So his ordeal remained relentless through the summer. By Darlington on Labor Day weekend, he was not only trying again for the Winston Million, but he was locked in a close duel for the Winston Cup championship with, for him, the worst possible opponent: Darrell Waltrip in Junior Johnson's car.

Two South Carolina state troopers were posted in the Elliotts' garage stall at Darlington to keep away, by force if necessary, the media. This was unprecedented, and the track people said it wasn't their idea but the Elliotts'. Further, Bill sent out word that he was too busy working on the chassis of the car to be interviewed.

Waltrip seized on the situation and played it like a violin. His car was parked nose-to-nose with Elliott's. As twenty or so reporters stood as near as the troopers would let us to the Number 9 car, Waltrip grabbed a shop rag and began wiping the windshield of his Number 11 Chevrolet. And he launched into a satirical impression of Bill Elliott.

"Y'all better leave me alone!" Waltrip hollered at the reporters, in a mock whimpering tone. "I'm just so busy workin' on my car, and y'all are gonna *drive me crazy!*"

The writers flocked to Waltrip and he held court in a loud voice, so the Elliotts could hear his satire. At one point I saw a red head appear from behind the Number 9 car. Two blue eyes were wide as saucers. Then they disappeared.

Bill eventually held a press conference, but in the process of telling the truth, he spoke in platitudes. "It's the combination," he would say of the supposed secrets that were taking him toward an eleven-win season. And that was true: There was no single gimmick with pistons or rods or heads or aerodynamics. There was no secret. There was simply optimal preparation of every part of the car. And as usual, when asked to predict anything, Bill would say, quite truthfully, "It's hard to say." But that didn't come across colorfully on television or in print.

That night, Winston threw a big party at a country club, in "honor" of Winston Million hopeful Bill Elliott. Darrell Waltrip showed up early. Bill arrived late. Waltrip and I were standing over by a wall, just talking. (Bear in mind here that NASCAR drivers often referred to one another not by name, but by car number. Instead of "Earnhardt," they might say "Three." Instead of "that damn Waltrip," they might say, "that damn Eleven.") Waltrip, dapper, totally comfortable amidst the tinkling of ice cubes, glanced over at the clearly uncomfortable Elliott making his bashful entrance.

"That's just what you media fuckers need, Hinton," Waltrip said.

"What do you mean?"

"A few more nerds like that Nine that just walked in."

"Aw, hell, Darrell. He's trying. He'll be all right."

"Now tell me the truth, Hinton. How many times did he say, 'It's ha-a-a-r-d to say' out there today?"

"Oh, about a hundred and fifty."

"See? Just what y'all need. *That'll* make y'all appreciate me."

For the Southern 500, Waddell Wilson gave Cale Yarborough every ounce of power possible to keep Bill Elliott from winning the Winston Million. But with forty-four laps remaining of the 367, and Yarborough leading, a cloud of smoke suddenly engulfed the front straightaway and the pits. Out of the cloud roared the red Thunderbird, in the lead. The smoke was from the failing power steering in Yarborough's

T-Bird. Yarborough was tough and strong, but Darlington was a treacherous track to navigate. Having to muscle his car around was just enough of a handicap to Yarborough that Elliott won the race by half a second.

After the race, Waddell Wilson was so exasperated that he just stood there waving a towel around his head for several minutes. He and Yarborough weren't eligible for the million-dollar bonus. And the whole thing was good publicity for NASCAR. So, really, was Waddell *that* disappointed that he hadn't been able to *prevent* Elliott from winning the bonus?

"Why, hell yeah!" Wilson said, incredulously, still whirling the towel around his head.

It wasn't just the bonus. It was the whole damn season of Elliott domination that had started with the upstart Georgia boys snapping Waddell Wilson's winning streak in the Daytona 500.

"It's—it's *flus-ter-atin'*," Waddell said, coining a word, still whirling the towel around his head, somehow stuck in this motion of despair.

In Victory Lane the Winston PR people showered "Million-Dollar Bill" with play money for the photographers. How fitting. What a crock.

But Bill posed grinning for the pictures as if the money were all his. George Elliott got to pose with the team in the official Victory Lane picture of the Winston Million celebration. That was about it.

Jeff Gordon had just turned fourteen. "And when he was fourteen," Bickford would recall, "he *really* raced Steve Kinser. Oh, Kinser won the race. But they swapped the lead several times. Jeff weighed ninety-seven pounds at the time. After the race Kinser walks by, looks over at the kid, looks at Lee Osborne [an Indiana mechanic who was helping Bickford], never says a word to Jeff, just looks at Lee and says, 'That kid's gonna be a good one.' "

Back in California it was hard to get the dirt tracks to waive their age minimum. Besides, the best sprint car racers and tracks were in the Midwest. John Bickford's mantra remained, "You're only as good as the guys you're racing with," and here's how deeply he meant it: He and Carol sold their house in Vallejo, sold their machine-shop business that specialized in equipment for the handicapped, sold everything. And they moved to Indiana so that Jeff could race against the best. They didn't buy the best house they could afford—they saved their money to pour into his racing effort—but settled into a small one in Pittsboro, Indiana, eighteen miles west of Indianapolis Motor Speedway. John started a sprint car parts business, and most of that income went into Jeff's racing.

That drive from California to Indiana in 1985 symbolized the sacrificing of John and Carol Bickford's whole lives to the nurturing of the prodigy.

28

HIGH ROLLING

Rick Hendrick grew up turning wrenches on his daddy's tractors on their farm outside South Hill, Virginia. Things mechanical fascinated him. But business enthralled him. In 1976, when he was twenty-six years old, he borrowed $50,000 and bought a car dealership in Dentsville, South Carolina. A decade later, on Daytona 500 week of 1986, Rick Hendrick was *the* young baron of automobile retailers, on his way to acquiring more dealerships than anyone else in the country.

He had started a NASCAR team in 1984 with Harry Hyde's help, and hired the moody upstate New Yorker Geoff Bodine as driver. Now, though, Hendrick had just gone and done precisely what everyone in NASCAR told him he shouldn't—he had expanded the team to a two-car, two-driver operation. To the surprise of no one, Hyde and Bodine, both strong-willed, both a tad eccentric, didn't get along. So what had Rick Hendrick done? He'd thrown two even greater individualists into the stew: crew chief Gary Nelson, and the wild-driving, wilder-living Tim Richmond. For the '86 season Hendrick put Nelson in charge of Bodine's wing of the team, and Hyde in charge of Richmond's unit. (The Hyde-Richmond pairing would be the basis for the Harry Hogge–Cole Trickle [Robert Duval–Tom Cruise] relationship in the 1991 film *Days of Thunder.* Such a mover and shaker was Hendrick that it was he who germinated that film, by inviting Cruise to take a test drive in a Hendrick race car and selling the young actor on the idea of a movie about NASCAR.)

That Thursday of Daytona 500 week, Hendrick's public relations entourage organized a glitzy brunch at Indigo Lakes golf club, a couple of miles from the speedway, so that Rick could explain his plunge into a two-car team. Not even the sage and savvy Junior Johnson had been able to make a two-car team work well, not even with Darrell Waltrip and Neil Bonnett as teammates, in the past couple of years. And that team's shortcomings had cemented conventional wisdom that here in the intense '80s, you just couldn't fragment your efforts like that. If Junior couldn't, nobody could—especially a newcomer like Hendrick.

Things were sort of helter-skelter in the parking lot as the brunch broke up and everybody hurried back to the speedway for the qualifying races. I asked Rick if he wanted to ride back with me. He said sure and hopped in. That was Rick Hendrick: He was comfortable around everyone he knew, and everyone he knew was comfortable around him. A mile from the speedway, we hit gridlocked traffic. Hendrick was in no hurry—both Bodine and Richmond were in the second 125-miler—so there we sat with half an hour to burn.

"What about Fishel?" I asked Hendrick. He knew what I meant. Herb Fishel was Chevrolet's director of racing, and held most of the control over how much factory support a given team would get. Junior Johnson, who was such a politician that with a different background he could have been a U.S. senator at least, made sure the lion's share of factory support came to him. And Richard Childress's up-and-coming team, with Dale Earnhardt as driver, was rapidly gaining favor with Fishel. So could new kid Hendrick expect to get the factory support he needed for a two-car operation?

Hendrick smiled. "You know who Roger Smith is?"

"Well, yeah." Roger Smith was chairman of General Motors at the time, and was Fishel's boss's boss.

"Night before last, I had dinner with Roger Smith in Las Vegas."

"Oh. So you'll get what you need?"

"I think so," Hendrick said. He gazed out the window at the milling crowds pouring toward the grandstands. "Now all I have to do is sit on Tim Richmond."

"You mean make him behave? Oh, no, please don't. He's one of the most colorful guys who's ever come along in this stuff."

"That's the trouble," Hendrick said.

"No it's not! He'll get you fantastic media exposure with all his escapades."

"It's not me," Hendrick said. "It's P and G."

Procter & Gamble, the huge household products conglomerate based in Cincinnati, was as straitlaced in its image-consciousness as corporations came. One of its brands was Folger's coffee. And Folger's was the primary sponsor on the Number 25 Hendrick Motorsports cars that Hyde maintained and Richmond drove. (Hyde and Richmond would appear in the original TV commercial featuring the jingle, "The best part of wakin' up is Folger's in your cup." And I would laugh every time I saw and heard that commercial, because for Tim Richmond, there was *no* good part of waking up, hungover and screwed-out as he usually was. For example, one morning in Atlanta he woke up and realized that not only had he pissed away about a thousand bucks on Dom Perignon at one sitting, but that the little honey he'd dropped off from his limo in the wee hours had gathered up not only her bra and panties from the backseat but also his

$10,000 Rolex while he lay snockered. Folger's in his cup didn't do a helluva lot for his mood that morning.)

"You gotta let Richmond be Richmond," I said to Hendrick.

"No way. Gotta sit on him."

*W*hen Richard Childress was five years old, his father died. Richard's mother couldn't even afford to pay for his lunch at school—to earn it, he swept the floors of the cafeteria after the other kids had finished lunch and gone out to play. He sold Cokes and popcorn at the stock car races at Bowman Gray Stadium, the local quarter-mile track in his native Winston-Salem, North Carolina, and watched Junior Johnson and Curtis Turner and Joe Weatherly race. By his high school years, Richard Childress decided he wasn't going to be poor anymore, that he would do whatever it took.

He went into "the liquor business"—Winston-Salem euphemism for the moonshine industry. But he was never a tripper—those were the fancy-pants glory guys, in his mind. "I was on the hard end of the business," he once told me. "The really dangerous end."

Teenage Richard Childress worked at an all-night gas station in Winston-Salem. But he wasn't there to pump gas. The hotshot trippers would roll in with their liquor-laden Olds 88s, leave them parked behind the gas station, and walk away—go and visit their girlfriends in town, or whatever. Richard Childress would then get into the moonshine cars and drive slowly into the black neighborhoods, stopping to make the actual deliveries to the "drink houses." They were not licensed bars. They were private homes where customers came in and sat at the kitchen tables and paid fifty cents for jelly glasses full of moonshine poured out of quart jars. The deliveries in the wee hours were agonizingly slow. He would go inside one house, deliver a case, collect the money, come out, drive on—the car itself was a giveaway if lawmen were near, with its big throaty motor, its loud rumble even at 20 miles an hour through the neighborhoods. He would go inside the next house, deliver another case or two, and so on…and with the hard drinking of the bad whiskey going on inside, there was no telling when a fight would break out.

But it was worth it. "Nobody at school could understand how I, of all people, could afford to drive a brand-new '59 Chevrolet."

One morning just before dawn, he entered a house carrying two cases. He heard violent arguing inside. Before he could drop the cases and run, "One guy came up with a sawed-off shotgun and wasted another guy," he would recall. The morning he saw the blood and guts spatter all over that drink-house kitchen wall was "the day I stepped out of the liquor business."

By 1969 he was a struggling independent NASCAR driver, running a Camaro in the sideshow Grand American series. When Richard Petty and the Professional Drivers Association rolled out of Talladega to boycott the inaugural race of 1969—this out of concern that tires would not perform safely on the gigantic, 2.66-mile, 33-degree-banked track—Big Bill France asked Richard Childress if he would help fill out the field for that first makeshift Talladega 500. Childress was game—hell, as hard as he'd come up, he wasn't afraid of anything, certainly not the wrath of some drivers' union. He ran the race. The France family would never forget.

He moved up into the Grand National—later to be called Winston Cup—division, but he was still a struggling independent. He was different, though—he had a style about him, a touch of class, and yet he was still something of a wildass from the hard-knocks days. Once at a big party in Winston-Salem, he was in the bathroom taking a leak when some guy came up behind him and—Childress thought—brushed a bug off his shoulder. But Childress noticed something flying out the left side of his neck. It was blood from a severed artery. The guy, sort of a crazy, had reached around and cut Childress's throat with a hawkbill knife.

Childress would have died on the spot if a doctor hadn't been present at the party. The doctor pinched off the artery and was helping Childress out to a car to take him to a hospital when Childress spotted the guy who'd cut his throat. He broke away from the doctor's grasp and beat the ever-lovin' shit out of the guy—beat him until Childress passed out from blood loss.

In 1979 I traveled with him for seventeen days on the NASCAR tour, with a few detours—from Texas down into Mexico out to Riverside back through Las Vegas up to Michigan. He had little money; he drove his own truck, an old gasoline-powered Chevrolet C-300 at a time when every other team had big diesel rigs that kept blowing by us on the highways in the wee hours. Then he would get to the tracks and work on the car himself with little help, and then drive in the races. While some poor-mouthing independent drivers were inclined to skim sponsorship money and take their wives to Europe or buy cattle for their farms, Childress was plowing every cent of his meager sponsorship and his meager winnings back into that racing team. Someday, he said, he was going to have enough money to make his race cars better, and then get out of them and put a younger driver in. And he was going to make it as a team owner.

More than anything he was a gambler—literally and figuratively. "You're gamblin' with your life every mornin' when you get out of bed," was his mantra. The evening we left Las Vegas, we were supposed to meet at a certain craps table in the casino at Circus Circus. When I got there he was $5,000 down. "Gimme a few more minutes," he said. "Then we'll go." In those days I didn't think he could afford to lose five thousand, but it was none of my business, so I went over and played the dollar slots for half an hour and came back. He was five thousand ahead. He was ready to go.

That night we were coming down a mountain toward Hoover Dam when I felt the brakes begin to slip on that old truck, and on the trailer carrying the shitbox race car behind. Childress took a breath and sort of glanced at me and kept on driving, kept on pumping gently at the brake pedal.

"You know," he said, "I hear all sorts of incredible stories about this dam. Heard there was a foxy woman that came out here one night, had lost everything she had, all her money, all her jewelry, everything but her fur coat. Heard she came out here in that fur coat and walked out to the dam and the fur coat fell open and she was naked underneath. Then she just jumped right off. Did a swan dive. Killed herself. I hear lots of people have gone off this dam after they've lost everything in Vegas."

The brakes kept slipping—sort of brief, groaning sounds—and Richard Childress kept talking.

When we got to the bottom he rolled into the parking lot of the dam and downshifted. The brakes were so hot they were almost gone.

"God-a-*mighty!*" he said. "I didn't want to say nothin' back up the mountain there. But I didn't think we were gonna make it down here."

"I was sort of wondering myself," I said. "Was it that close?"

"Damn close." He sighed. He laughed. He shrugged. "But hey: You're gamblin' with your life every mornin' when you get out of bed."

*I*n midseason 1981, Dale Earnhardt's benefactor, Rod Osterlund, sold his race team out from under Earnhardt, to J. D. Stacey, a man Earnhardt could not stand. Earnhardt wanted off the team in the worst way. And he had a major sponsor-ship from Wrangler jeans to take with him.

Junior Johnson heard that Earnhardt wanted out. Junior had major connections with Winston. And Junior thought the world of Richard Childress. At Talladega that August, there were secret meetings, brokered by Johnson and the Winston people, at the end of which Richard Childress announced he was retiring as a driver, hiring Dale Earnhardt, and bringing in the Wrangler sponsorship.

Earnhardt finished out the season for Childress, who thought he'd struck gold with that Wrangler deal. But Earn-hardt was so rough on equipment, and wrecked so many cars, that when Childress sat down to balance his books at the end of the season, he found himself $75,000 in the hole. Rather than blame Earnhardt, Childress told him, "This team's just not ready for a driver of your caliber. Give us a couple of years to build. Then maybe we can get back together."

Childress managed to get a fair-to-middlin' sponsorship from Winston-Salem–based Piedmont Airlines, and hired a fair-to-middlin' driver, Ricky Rudd. Earnhardt went off to drive for Big Bud Moore in '82 and '83, won a few races, and tore a lot of Big Bud's Fords to pieces.

At the end of the '83 season, Earnhardt signed to drive again for Childress. On a hotel balcony at Riverside, Big Bud looked Childress in the eye and gave him the best advice he could about Earnhardt:

"Boy, he'll break you."

But what the hell: You're gamblin' with your life every mornin' when you get out of bed.

In '84, Childress wound up in the hole again. They blew engines everywhere; couldn't buy a finish. Childress told Earnhardt he was free to go to a better team. "I ain't goin' nowhere," Earnhardt said. "We've got a deal."

In '85, hardly noticed amidst the Elliotts' eleven-win onslaught, Childress and Earnhardt slowly put their act together. They won four races.

By the season-opening Daytona 500 of 1986, there were two teams to beat: Hendrick Motorsports featuring Geoff Bodine and Tim Richmond, and Richard Childress Racing featuring Dale Earnhardt.

NASCAR racing is an endless game of technological leapfrog. A team that is winning consistently is reluctant to change what it's doing technologically. A team that isn't winning consistently has nothing to lose, and so is willing to experiment. So nothing ever stands still. In 1985 the Elliotts had leapt over the Waddell Wilson–Cale Yarborough tandem, and even the Junior Johnson–Darrell Waltrip team (though Waltrip won the points championship, he won only three races—and even he admitted that for Bill Elliott to win eleven races but not the Winston Cup amounted to a travesty of the points system). In 1986 it was the Elliotts' turn to be leapt over. Hendrick and Childress leapt.

Earnhardt couldn't have had more opposite feelings toward two drivers than he did toward teammates Richmond and Bodine. Richmond was Earnhardt's big buddy. They didn't party together as much as they once had—Earnhardt had in 1982 married his third wife, Teresa Houston, and she had reined him in, big-time—but they were still pals around the garage area. Bodine, Earnhardt fairly despised. Earnhardt didn't even try to rationalize it—"I just don't like the little motherfucker."

And so, had it been Earnhardt and Richmond dueling in the waning laps of the '86 Daytona 500, they might have wrecked each other and then climbed out laughing about who had landed on top of whom—as they'd done once, at Pocono. But Richmond, after leading in the middle stages of the race, had fallen twelve laps back with mechanical troubles.

Geoff Bodine was and is a strange little character—witness his latter-day demand in the twilight of his career to be called "Geoffrey"—who in conversations and interviews almost never put periods in his sentences, only maybe an occasional comma or pause, and sort of talked on and on like this, sort of like Casey Stengel, and went on about how he and his wife, Kathy, and the boys would do such and such…So it's hard to recall a specific quote from Geoff Bodine from either the buildup to, or the aftermath of, the '86 Daytona 500, but all you really need to know is this:

Geoff Bodine took no shit whatsoever off Dale Earnhardt on the race track. Maybe in the garage, but never on the race track. Ever.

And that is really why Earnhardt hated Bodine.

Geoff Bodine came from hardass racing himself, in the East where the track announcers called the modified drivers "the men who live by the grace of God and eight hundred horsepower," and once he got to NASCAR, there simply wasn't a thing Dale Earnhardt could do to scare him. Earnhardt would slam, and Bodine would slam back. Earnhardt might win the wreck du jour, but Bodine would come out slamming in the next race.

And so when the '86 Daytona 500 came down to Bodine and Earnhardt, everbody got ready for a finish that surely would go down right alongside the Petty-Pearson wreck of '76 and the Allison-Yarborough fight of '79.

It was just as well that Bill Elliott had been caught up in a wreck earlier in the race and was limping around on the apron, out of contention. Fearless as Elliott was at speed, he was quite skittish about this beatin'-and-bangin' business. And now in the waning laps, Bodine led, with Earnhardt so thoroughly stuck to his rear bumper that you could see and hear and smell it coming—there was about to be hell to pay;

somebody had better wake up Lee Roy, because Lee Roy, he ain't never seen a wreck as big as was fixin' to happen.

Earnhardt was hard on gas mileage—on and off the throttle; on and off the throttle. He could run out of fuel at any second. But in the Childress pits, all was calm. Should they stop? Hey: You're gamblin' with your life every mornin' when you get out of bed.

With three laps to go, Childress turned his head to the side, ever so slightly, and listened in his headset. Then in the calmest of voices, he said:

"He's out of gas."

The blue-and-yellow Monte Carlo SS sailed into the pits on sheer momentum and took on fuel, but wouldn't restart. The hood went up, and Childress reached underneath and sprayed ether from an aerosol can into the carburetor. That was an efficient, but very dangerous, way to get an engine to start.

Earnhardt popped the clutch and smoke billowed from the tires as he tore out of the pits, and then within two or three seconds, from off down the pit road, came an enormous KA-BLOOM, like a bomb going off. The injection of ether had caused the engine to blow.

And at that moment began the mystique—that Dale Earnhardt could win anything in NASCAR except the showcase event, the Daytona 500. It was a story that would continue for another dozen years.

Bodine then cruised to an eleven-second margin of victory over second-place Terry Labonte. But through the rest of that season, Bodine won only one more race. By contrast, Richmond, who finished a terrible twentieth in the Daytona 500, went on to win seven other races—including an uncanny summer streak of six wins in ten events. The Bodine-Nelson side and the Richmond-Hyde side polarized. Each side complained to Hendrick that the other was getting better equipment. The multicar team became a nightmare. Hendrick would cajole them into a team meeting at the shop and it wouldn't be ten seconds before Hyde was on Bodine's case again.

Richmond won the season finale at Riverside, and Earnhardt won the Winston Cup points championship. In Victory Lane, Richmond grabbed the hand of his buddy and raised their arms aloft together, like two tag-team wrestlers flaunting victory. Then Earnhardt went home to North Carolina. Richmond stayed over for a party with the Hollywood crowd that lasted a couple of weeks. He'd begun running with them while dating Mary Frann, an older but very well-preserved woman, co-star and sweater girl of the *Newhart* television sitcom.

Richmond partied too long, too hard. By Christmas he was back home in Ohio, in the Cleveland Clinic, diagnosed with double pneumonia. He almost died—even that first time.

*R*ichmond sent out word in January of '87 that he wasn't going to show for the Daytona 500. In February, the gossip started in the garage area. Double pneumonia? How weird. How could the aftereffects of pneumonia keep him down for so long that he was going to sit out nearly the first half of the season? And Richmond was, after all, such a wildass...

Oh, well. Out of sight, out of mind—that's how NASCAR racing dealt with absenteeism. The more immediate concern at Daytona was speed, so high that drivers were losing their sense of control. Ernie Elliott had brought another missile to Daytona, and Bill drove it onto the pole at 210.364 mph. The aerodynamic design of his Thunderbird allowed him to keep to the ragged edge of control. General Motors drivers felt themselves going over the edge. Even Junior Johnson had appealed for a rules change to slow down the cars. NASCAR took a wait-see attitude.

Earnhardt had his own ideas about how to even the competition with Elliott's Thunderbird. "There's only one way to lead a lap on him," Earnhardt said. "*Move* him. *Scare* him. Mess with his head."

And so with eighteen laps to go in the '87 Daytona 500, "Earnhardt drove up and hit me for no reason at all," Elliott would complain.

"I scared the hell out of ol' Bill," Earnhardt would boast. "That little boy will never forget that little deal. I didn't hit him. I just got up there and got the air off his spoiler and got his ol' car loose."

Earnhardt took the lead, but a few laps later his pit stop for a final splash of fuel took ten seconds, to six for Elliott's final splash. Gary Nelson elected to go with no final splash of fuel for Bodine, who stayed out, inherited the lead after the others had pitted, and gambled that he could make it to the finish on fumes. But with three laps to go the yellow-and-white Hendrick Chevrolet sputtered and slowed. Bodine was out of gas at precisely the stage his archrival, Earnhardt, had run out the year before.

And so Bill Elliott swept to his second Daytona 500 victory in three years.

"I drove the wheels off that bitch today, Hinton," Earnhardt said gleefully inside Childress's hauler after the race. I couldn't understand why he was so thrilled—he'd wound up fifth—until he asked, "Pea Brain [one of his milder names for Bodine] ran out of gas, didn't he?" I confirmed it, and he gave a little pump of the fist that said, Yes!

Earnhardt would go on to his best season ever, winning eleven races and another Winston Cup. Still no Daytona 500 victory, but no big deal, then—"Gotta happen sometime!" he would say, and shrug it off.

* * *

*T*he '87 Daytona 500 was the last one in the 20th century with 200-mph-plus qualifying and race speeds. That May at Talladega, Bill Elliott would set the all-time stock car qualifying record that stands today, 212.809 mph. And early in the race, the Winston 500, Bobby Allison's Buick would spin, become airborne, and very nearly sail into the packed grandstands. The car tore down a hundred-yard section of the catch fence along the frontstretch. If two huge steel cables that ran behind the fence to reinforce it hadn't held the car and kept it out of the packed grandstands, there could have been a disaster far worse than auto racing's worst on record—when Pierre Levegh's Mercedes flew into the crowd at Le Mans in 1955, killing more than eighty people on the spot and ultimately resulting in more than 130 deaths. But because the cables held at Talladega, there were no fatalities and few serious injuries.

Rookie Davey Allison won the race, having pressed on even after seeing his father's terrible crash in his mirrors. How could Davey keep racing under the circumstances? It was just the Allison way. "I'd seen how my dad handled the situation at Charlotte in '81 when Donnie was hurt so badly," Davey said after the race. Bobby, knowing there was nothing he could do for Donnie, had gone on to win that day at Charlotte.

But after Bobby's car almost went into the stands at Talladega, NASCAR took drastic measures to bring speeds under 200 and hold them there. Henceforth, at both Talladega and Daytona, carburetor restrictor plates were mandated—reducing air flow through the carburetors stifled the power, from about 650 horsepower at the time down to about 400. But at all other tracks, the cars remained at full power.

Tim Richmond returned to racing at Pocono in June of 1987, and won. The next week at Riverside, he won again. It was a storybook comeback. But now Richmond had put himself under the microscopes of his peers. He competed in six more races that season, but each weekend he seemed more sluggish and fatigued. At first the other drivers figured it was just his hangovers. But it got worse. The others grew suspicious, and then fearful. They held private meetings with NASCAR officials.

Dr. Jerry Punch, a trauma specialist turned broadcaster, kept his own terrible fear to himself during those last few races Richmond ran. Punch was afraid that on any lap, Richmond might simply loosen his safety harness, drive head-on into a retaining wall at 180 miles an hour, and go out in a blaze of glory. What others had begun to suspect, Jerry Punch knew. He adhered to the code of secrecy between physician and patient, even though Richmond had sought only an understanding ear and counsel when he'd told Punch the truth. Tim Richmond had AIDS.

29

THE END OF THE PARTY

Without so much as turning a wheel on the track, Tim Richmond was the star of Daytona 500 week, 1988, by a landslide. That annoyed the hell out of Bobby Allison, and at the end of the week, he fixed it. Until then, the imminent race was but a backdrop to the media circus surrounding Richmond—and to the urgent, nervous, private conversations of huddled groups all over the garage area, all day, every day.

Richmond had formally quit Hendrick Motorsports, and NASCAR racing, in August of 1987, vaguely citing health reasons. And a lot of people had sighed relief. Richmond was well liked, but he was just too much trouble. Not only was undercurrent speculation rampant that he had AIDS—people talked in code, e.g., "I don't want what he's got," Darrell Waltrip said—but his boozing was gaining notoriety in public places, and he was rumored to be a drug user.

Good guy, but good riddance—that was the undercurrent consensus.

And then in January of '88, Richmond changed his mind. He wanted to come back. And a lot of people, privately, gasped. Richmond was eligible for the Busch Clash, a bonus race held one week before the Daytona 500. He no longer had a ride with Hendrick, but under the rules of the Clash, it was the driver, not the car, who was eligible. Richmond made a preliminary deal to use a car normally driven by independent Ken Ragan. Not a very good car. Strange plan.

NASCAR, perhaps motivated by Richmond's carousing of recent years, had instituted a drug test as a prerequisite for driving at Daytona. It was a simple urinalysis, the same as the jock sport leagues were already using. But those leagues had already had drug scandals; NASCAR hadn't.

So Tim Richmond came to Daytona and peed in the cup, and the sample was sent to Dr. Forest Tennant, then the drug-testing guru for all sports leagues, in Los Angeles.

"Tennant called back, and said, 'I've found something,' " an inside source would tell me later. "At that point he wasn't sure what."

NASCAR seemed so anxious to rid itself of the general Richmond nuisance that it jumped the gun. It announced that Richmond had failed his drug test and had therefore been banned from the Busch Clash. That nixed the deal for Ragan's car, and Richmond missed the race.

Then Tennant's lab called back. Specific analysis of the substances he'd found showed nothing more than the basic ingredients of the over-the-counter medications Sudafed and Advil—no illegal substances.

NASCAR had screwed up. Big-time. NASCAR had left the impression that an illegal substance had been found, and that that was the reason Richmond had been barred from the Busch Clash. Now it was recanting. The confusion, coupled with the widespread suspicions about AIDS, made it anybody's guess as to what was really going on.

Richmond sat holed up in his suite at the Daytona Beach Hilton, seething, pondering. Tim Richmond had been a spoiled kid in a well-to-do family, and was still something of a mama's boy who wasn't used to being told no. While watching a network morning news show on television, he saw Barry Slotnik, the high-profile New York criminal lawyer, being interviewed about his defense of "Subway Shooter" Bernhard Goetz. Richmond had a brainstorm. He was going to sue NASCAR's ass, and he was going to hire Barry Slotnik to do it.

This was a classic case of Tim Richmond overkill in glitz—Slotnik was a criminal lawyer, but Richmond wanted him for a civil case charging defamation of character. But Richmond got on the phone and agreed to pay the retainer up front, and Barry Slotnik flew to Daytona Beach.

With word that Slotnik was on his way, a most bizarre web of intrigue began. My first indication was this: An official from within International Speedway Corporation, parent company of Daytona International Speedway, eased up to me in the media center and said he needed to talk to me privately. We went outside. He handed me a slip of paper. Printed on it were the name and phone number of a physician. "She works at the Cleveland Clinic," he said. "You know, where Richmond was originally hospitalized with pneumonia. You didn't hear this from me. If you say you did, I'll call you a liar. But if you call this number, you might find out some things. I'm telling you this in strictest confidence, only because you're a helluva reporter, and maybe this will help you get to the bottom of this."

All afternoon, I noticed other reporters in other hushed, one-on-one conversations with other officials. Something was obviously afoot, but we'd have to figure that out later. You followed your leads, and then decided whether you had anything to write. I made the phone call to the Cleveland Clinic. A male nurse answered the doctor's line. On a hunch, I feigned an effeminate voice, and asked to speak to the doctor. I wanted to give the impression that I was someone who feared having contracted AIDS, and hopefully garner some sympathy. I was told that the doctor was out until the following Tuesday, after the Presidents' Day holiday.

"Can you tell me if she treats AIDS cases?" I asked.

"Her practice involves communicable diseases," I was told.

"Does that include AIDS?"

I tried to sound pitiful and frightened. The nurse wasn't buying.

"It includes communicable diseases. Anything else?"

"No. Thank you."

You learn after a while when to hold 'em and when to fold 'em—when you should stay after a story and try to scoop everybody else, and when you might as well admit you're up a blind alley and aren't going to get any story at all unless you exchange a little information. Back at the hotel that evening, several writers gathered at one guy's room to have a beer before going out to dinner.

"Anybody getting any leaks on Richmond?" somebody asked.

"I'm a helluva reporter, so I got a phone number in Fort Lauderdale," one said.

"Me too, but mine's in Cleveland," I said.

"Makes three of us who are goddamn good reporters. Here's my slip of paper."

"Four. Do I hear five?"

"They think I'll do the right thing."

"Then you ain't shit. Where we going for dinner?"

"Wait a minute. We need to sort this out. We're pretty damn sure Richmond's got AIDS."

"And we can't prove it."

"So we can't write it."

"Right."

"They're fuckin' with us, guys."

"Course they are."

"Who?"

"NASCAR, the speedway, all of 'em. They're trying to get us in between them and Richmond and Slotnik."

"Course they are. Why shouldn't they?"

"What do we do?"

"Nothing. We can't. Privacy laws. These docs couldn't tell us the truth if they wanted to."

"Then why are we getting these leaks?"

"Fishing. Grasping at straws. Hoping one of us will hit."

"Wait a minute. Why are they fuckin' with us about the AIDS stuff when their big problem is the drug test?"

"Maybe it was never anything like cocaine or opiates they thought they'd found anyway. Maybe that was all a front. Maybe Tennant found something else entirely."

"Like what?"

"Like AZT."

"Can they detect AZT in a drug test?"

"Dunno. I can make a call—"

"Then why wouldn't they just say they found AZT?"

"Couldn't. Privacy laws. Saying you found an AIDS treatment drug would be the same as saying Richmond had AIDS."

"Why would they ban him from the race if they thought he had AIDS?"

"Well, say Richmond gets in a wreck. Say he gets cut, he's bleeding. Those safety workers reach in there and one of 'em gets AIDS later on. Then *they've* got a lawsuit, because they weren't warned."

"Just tell the safety workers to wear gloves [not a common practice among emergency workers in those days]."

"Yeah, right. You tell your safety workers to wear gloves, and then everybody knows something's up."

"Anybody gonna stake out the Hilton again tonight?"

"Hell, no! I know every pattern in every Oriental rug in

that lobby by heart. I'm sick of that place. Richmond ain't gonna come out of that room."

"I've called his suite about fifty times. I don't think he's in there anyway. He's probably somewhere else and using the suite as a decoy. Every time I've called, his PR woman has answered and said he couldn't come to the phone."

"We're just spinning our wheels, guys. Fuck it. Let's go eat."

*B*arry Slotnik and Tim Richmond called a press conference at the Hilton for the next morning. On the dais with them were two of Slotnik's junior partners. One acted as sort of a herald for Slotnik, announcing him with a brief biography in which the big gun was always referred to as "Barry Ivan Slotnik." The other was Bettina Schein, who has since gone on to become one of the top criminal lawyers in New York.

When Tim Richmond walked in, he stopped to shake hands with every writer he knew, and gave out little slaps on the back. This seemed calculated, so that everybody could get a close-up look at him. He looked healthy—if anything, he was a little overweight. We were somewhat surprised that he wasn't emaciated—the stereotype of an AIDS patient in those early years of knowledge of the disease.

Barry Ivan Slotnik could say "besmirched" better than anybody. He said it maybe a dozen times, and he never got his tongue twisted. Ms. Bettina Schein, Barry Ivan Slotnik announced, would handle the specifics of the case, and she went through yet another statement in high legalese. Tim Richmond made a statement but didn't take questions.

Bottom line: He was going to sue NASCAR—but we'd known that. Otherwise, the press conference was largely a waste, except that in sizing up Barry Ivan Slotnik and Bettina Schein, you had to figure that for once, NASCAR's high-rolling law firms, which were scattered from Daytona Beach to Washington, were going to have some serious competition.

As the press conference was breaking up, I noticed an official of the speedway mingling with the media. I'd always thought of this particular guy as Vice President of Intrigue. He was the best at dropping one-line innuendo. He seemed to be saying something short and sweet to everybody. Out in the lobby it was my turn. He strolled up to me and said, "Morning."

"Morning. Slotnik's no slouch," I said. "This might be a tough one for NASCAR."

"Oh, you don't think that guy's serious, do you?" He didn't refer to Slotnik as Slotnik, because Slotnik was too much in the news at the time. To brush him off as "that guy" was a subtle dismissal of concern.

"Sounded serious to me," I said.

"Oh, that guy just wanted to spend a free weekend in Daytona with his girlfriend—that's all."

"If those lawyers wanted to take a weekend off," I said, "they look to me like they could afford to go to a lot nicer places than Daytona Beach."

This of course pissed him off, and he moved on to someone else.

A lot of us were livid when we found out CBS was going to be allowed into Richmond's suite at the Hilton to tape an interview that would air during the Daytona 500. But Ken Squier, who conducted the interview, indicated to me that nothing earth-shattering was going to come out of it. And sure enough, when the tape aired, it was pretty namby-pamby—nothing about drugs, AIDS, or even lawsuits.

Later, Rick Hendrick gave me a phone number in south Florida. I called. Richmond answered. After a few seconds of greetings and small talk, I asked him if he had AIDS. He gave me a nondenial denial.

"Thank God I never had anything like that," he said. "What I had was bad enough."

*T*im Richmond's suit against NASCAR never got to trial. It was settled out of court, and the case was sealed. What I was told later was, "It's pretty hard to prove you're not a drug user when there's someone sitting right there giving a deposition that you provided him with cocaine."

Richmond died in August of 1989. Shortly thereafter, his physicians and family announced that he had indeed died of complications of AIDS, and that he'd gotten the disease heterosexually.

And then the undercurrent of fear swept through the garage areas on the NASCAR tour. The traveling show had for decades been, to some, an ongoing, sexually free party, both in the hotels and, sometimes, even inside the tracks. It was not unheard of for track doctors in the infield emergency centers to dispense shots of penicillin to drivers or crewmen who thought they might have gotten "a little dose" from some groupie or town girl. But gonorrhea was one thing. AIDS was quite another. There had been a lot of denial through the initial reports that AIDS might be transmitted heterosexually. But now came confirmation, with someone they knew. And someone who'd been, shall we say, in the loop of the partying. There was a lot of, "If Richmond slept with girl A, and then she slept with guy B, and then B slept with girl C, and then she slept with me—oh, shit!"

Dr. Jerry Punch became the go-to guy for the worried. In all, he sent more than ninety people for AIDS testing, he later told me. One former race queen would go public with the acknowledgment that she contracted AIDS from Richmond. Otherwise, the disease didn't surface anymore within the traveling show for the remainder of the century.

30

THE NATURE OF
THE OCCUPATION

*B*obby Allison was up to the gills with talking about Tim
Richmond. In case anybody hadn't noticed, Allison reminded people, there was a race to be run here. By Wednesday of Daytona 500 week, 1988, he introduced me to his car,
just to make sure I knew what it was: "This is a new 1988
Buick Century," he said in a soft, even, subtle, surly, sarcas-
tic tone. "It's painted gold. It has 'Miller' painted on the
side—that's my sponsor. Also on the side, you'll note that the
number 22 is painted. We feel we have an excellent race car
here—one capable of winning the Daytona 500. If you'd like
to talk about any of that, I've got some time right now. If you
want to talk about someone who isn't even in this race, and
has no bearing on this race, I'm very busy right now."

Within the framework of NASCAR, Bobby Allison could
be candid, iconoclastic, even disruptive, and he was always
up for a good controversy. Outside racing, Bobby Allison
was a good Catholic who behaved himself by the teachings
of the church, and had raised his sons, Davey and the
younger Clifford, to do the same. He wasn't interested in
someone else's off-track activities.

Davey Allison was coming off rookie of the year honors in 1987 in Winston Cup racing. There was no nepotism involved. Davey drove for Robert Yates, whom he had encouraged to buy the team from Harry Ranier. Yates was a brilliant engine builder who'd worked his way through several teams and finally become an independent engine supplier. By late '87, Ranier owed Yates so much money for engines that Yates was able to purchase the team for relatively little cash. That still required bank loans, but young Allison encouraged Yates, saying it wasn't much of a risk because they surely would do well together. Davey and Robert were in this together, on their own, with no help from Bobby Allison whatsoever. Indeed, Davey had come all the way up through the ranks on his own.

"When he first told me he wanted to go racing," Bobby recalled, "I said, 'There's the shop. There's all the tools. Go to work.'"

"And that," said Judy Allison, Bobby's wife, "was a sore point between Bobby and Davey for some time."

Kyle Petty, with all of Richard's help, had flopped—mainly he just never had been hungry enough to focus totally on racing. Davey came into Winston Cup laser-focused, and never turned the burners down.

Davey had a lot of his father in him—he could be headstrong, defiant, surly, fully candid—tempered with some of his uncle Donnie's warmer, easier-going nature. Donnie gave Davey his first good race car, a Camaro, to run on the outlaw short tracks of the South.

"I had told his daddy, 'Why don't you give that boy a car he can go race with?'" Donnie would recall. "Bobby said, 'He'll do all right.' And that was it. That boy was at a stage where he needed help. And for whatever reason, he didn't get it. Davey came and got my car on a Tuesday afternoon. He won in it that Friday night."

Clifford, the youngest, was the charmer, the con artist.

"When they were little boys," Bobby would say, "Clifford could be guilty and talk himself out of a whipping. Davey could be innocent and talk himself into one. I was always enterprising, willing to work for everything, and that's how Davey was. Clifford felt like, why should he work when he could trick Davey into doing the work for him?"

And yet Clifford by 1988 was subjected to Bobby Allison's university of hard knocks, and was towing a short-track car around the country, learning on his own.

And here in the garages of Daytona International Speedway, Bobby and Davey Allison were situated precisely as Bobby thought they should be: not as teammates but as rivals. Competitors, who would do all they could to beat each other.

Davey qualified on the front row, beside pole-sitter Ken Schrader. Bobby qualified third. When the race started, Bobby blew by his son and led the first lap. Darrell Waltrip, now driving for a three-car Hendrick Motorsports team that included Schrader and Geoff Bodine, charged up to lead the second lap. Most of the race would be a duel between Waltrip and Bobby Allison.

Waltrip was the subject of one of Allison's favorite grudges—and Bobby Allison had a whole portfolio of grudges. Waltrip never could quite figure out the animosity, except that perhaps it was rooted in the years when Waltrip drove for Junior Johnson, "the one man Bobby hated worse than he hated me." And that went back to the Allison-Johnson split of 1971.

*M*idway through the 500, one of Allison's other classic grudge objects, Richard Petty, became the first victim of the worst drawback of the newly introduced restrictor plates. With power stifled, drivers couldn't get much "throttle response." That is, they couldn't accelerate suddenly when they needed to. They'd described it this way: "Think of when you get into a rental car that's choked down with all that emission-control equipment, and drive out to an expressway, and get on an entrance ramp. There's a lot of traffic on the expressway and you need to accelerate rapidly to merge into the traffic. You stomp the accelerator to the floor and wohhhnk! Almost nothing happens. The car just chugs along. It just won't accelerate like you need it to. That's what it's like with restrictor plates."

Richard Petty had complained that you couldn't get away from slower cars, whose drivers might be making unwise moves, when you needed to. Sure enough, on Lap 104, Petty couldn't escape a rub with the car of Phil Barkdoll, an occasional NASCAR driver from Arizona. Petty spun, and the onrushing A. J. Foyt couldn't avoid nailing him. The rear of Petty's car went airborne. It clipped the retaining wall and the catch fence and went into a violent, rapid series of tumbles— ten to twelve flips by most counts—disintegrating as it went. The carcass of the car came to rest upside down in front of the main grandstands. Brett Bodine, Geoff's younger brother, couldn't avoid hitting Petty again, and this time, what was left of Petty's car went into a terrible, whirling spin, upside down, like some horrific pinwheel. The initial, naked-eye view made me think Bodine had hit Petty right on the driver's-side door—the notoriously deadly "T-bone" effect. There seemed to be no way anyone could have survived a hit like that last one, with so much of the car already torn away. But when CBS rerolled the tape, it was clear that Bodine had hit Petty slightly forward of the door. That could make all the difference in the world. And it did.

Petty escaped with a sprained ankle and Bodine wasn't injured. Petty's wife, Lynda, was badly shaken by the awful-looking crash. She had been pleading with him to retire, and he had told her he wasn't going to quit as long as he was still having fun. "In the infield emergency center, I was lying on a stretcher and looked up," Petty would recall, "and I saw Lynda standing there. She had tears in her eyes. She said, 'Well! Are we still having *fun?*' "

*L*ate in the race, Waltrip's engine began to misfire and he fell back. Bobby Allison took the lead with seventeen laps to go, and had no more grudge duels to fight for that day. But he did have one more big rival to deal with: He looked in his mirror and saw his son, coming fast.

Davey came on WFO, but out of Turn 4 on the final lap, the old man stood on the gas and shook the kid by two car lengths at the checkered flag.

No other father and son had ever finished one-two in the Daytona 500. Statisticians pored over the records, and found, in all of NASCAR racing history, only one other such finish—by Lee and Richard Petty at a little track in Pennsylvania in 1960.

Judy Allison, asked whether she'd been pulling for her husband or her son, said, "Bobby. He's the one who pays my bills."

And Davey called it the happiest day of his life, better even than if he had won himself, because, "He's always been my hero."

Bobby said it was indescribable to "look back and see somebody coming that you think is the best driver coming up, and the best young man in racing, and know it's your son."

It was a feeling Bobby Allison would savor for 124 days. Then he would know it no more. And he would never win another race.

*W*ith the last words Darrell Waltrip ever heard Bobby Allison utter as a driver, "he called me an asshole," Waltrip would remember.

Pocono Raceway, near Long Pond, Pennsylvania, Sunday morning, June 19, 1988. One of reigning Daytona 500 champion Bobby Allison's favorite grudges had flared up again. Waltrip and Allison had wrecked each other the previous Sunday at Riverside (to this day, each man still blames the other for that crash). To exacerbate Allison's foul mood, he had trouble qualifying at Pocono and would start a lousy twenty-eighth.

The last thing Bobby Allison would ever remember of June 19, 1988, was "Drivers' meeting." After the officials briefed the competitors, "They asked if there were any questions. I raised my hand. I said, 'What are you supposed to do if some asshole spins you out?' Michael Waltrip spoke up. He said, 'I'm not the asshole. I'm just his brother.' "

"Before the race started," Darrell Waltrip would recall, "some of the guys who worked on the 22 car came up to me. They said, '*Please* watch out for Bobby. He's had a terrible week, and he's *crazy.* He says he's gonna wreck you, and he's gonna wreck you big.' Bobby had qualified poorly and was starting toward the back of the field. I was starting up near the front. On the parade lap, I radioed my guys and said, 'Let me know if Bobby gets anywhere near me. I gotta keep an eye on him today.'

"We took the green flag, made the first lap at speed, and"—Waltrip's eyes would mist when he told this part—"there he was. Sitting there. Wrecked."

Allison's last radio transmission to his crew was, "I've got a tire going down."

But as the air leaked out of the tire, Allison kept going. Was he gunning for Waltrip? Could he have been looking for Waltrip? Waiting for Waltrip to come back around? Allison would not remember, but would maintain that it just wasn't his style: "Never in my career did I allow myself to carry a problem from one track to another. If I didn't take care of the situation then and there, to have waited until the next race to retaliate...would have been wrong."

Whatever the case, on the second straightaway of the odd, triangular Pocono track, the Buick began to fishtail. Then, a hundred yards or so short of what drivers call the "Tunnel Turn," the Buick turned completely sideways and stopped, crossways in the middle of the track.

The onrushing car of Jocko Maggiacomo hit the Buick dead solid on the driver's-side door at maybe 180 miles an hour. Watching it live, with the naked eye, it appeared that Bobby Allison's Buick jumped—didn't slide, jumped—sideways for maybe fifty yards. Such was the enormity of the impact.

It was one of those crashes where *you knew*. Immediately. A sickened silence fell over the press box.

Inside the car, Bobby Allison was dying. He slumped in the seat, with brain injuries and a shattered left leg. Death *had* him for a moment, until a paramedic could climb into the car and perform the tracheotomy that gave him a thread to hang by.

Lap after lap, slowly, under caution, Davey Allison drove by and saw his father slumped and still. And then the car was empty. And then the helicopter lifted out of the infield, flew over the circling cars, and away. Davey pressed on. Again: the Allison way: "I had watched how he handled it with Donnie in '81," Davey would say again.

Davey finished fifth, climbed out of his car, and rushed to find several of the Allison family and entourage discombobulated. "All right, everybody hold it just a damn minute!" he ordered.

And from that moment, Davey Allison was the head of the family. He took charge. And not until the neurosurgeon made him conscious of his father's status that night did his legs come out from under him, nor did he fall straight down onto the floor and sit there thinking, What am I gonna do? What am I gonna do? (this he would tell me later), and even after that he arose and took charge again.

The first miracle, as the Allison family—and the doctors—saw it, was that Bobby Allison lived through that night. The next day, at Lehigh Valley Medical Center in Allentown, Pennsylvania, Davey took charge of a media briefing. Most of the reporters then left town. I stayed. Donnie was there, and he took me up to a small waiting room adjacent to the room where Bobby lay in a coma. Eddie Allison, Bobby's older brother who had been a mechanic with him in the early years in NASCAR, came in and sat with Donnie and me in the waiting room. Davey was in and out, organizing things, and then he left—he had a race to run in Michigan that weekend. Through it all, I sat in silent amazement at how composed the Allison men were, how they simply *accepted* this.

Just outside the waiting room, Eddie Gossage, the PR guy for Bobby's team, was taking calls from all over the country. All were sympathetic, of course, but by Monday afternoon there were some calls applying for the ride in Bobby's Number 22 Miller Buick. That is the hard reality of big-time motor racing—even in the depths of tragedy, there are always struggling drivers out there, grasping for some break, somehow, some way…and besides, due to sponsorship contracts, a team usually continues to field a car even when its driver is down or dead. The Miller car would indeed return without Bobby. The business of racing goes on, regardless.

I remembered sitting in Bobby's office on the second floor of the old shop in Hueytown one day in 1978, and asking him about the risk of injury or death. He pointed to a picture on the wall. It was of an old modified car, rolling in a cloud of flame down the backstretch of some dirt track.

"See that?" he'd said. "That's me on fire." He'd shrugged. "It's just an occupational hazard."

31

"DON'T LIE TO ME!"

*T*he apparition came to Daytona International Speedway on the afternoon of February 10, 1989. Moving oh, so slowly. And all around, people fell silent and still.

Bobby Allison.

Risen from the all but dead.

Every shuffled step was obviously painful. Every word was strained and slurred.

But triumphant. After the days with little chance of living. The weeks in a coma. The months in fog. The agonizing rehabilitation. The beginning again at home.

"Bobby went all the way back to being a baby," Judy would recall. "He had to be retaught everything: going to the bathroom, brushing his teeth, taking a bath, getting dressed, everything."

But he was alive. And he was walking. And he was back at Daytona. And no one who saw him was less than amazed.

Clifford Allison was entered in the Automobile Racing Club of America race that weekend. Having served his time on the bullrings, he still had two more steps to the big time:

First ARCA, then the Busch Series, before Winston Cup. Davey was entered in the February 19 Daytona 500.

"I...am...very...glad," Bobby Allison said slowly, with terrible difficulty, slurring every word, "that...both... Davey...and...Clifford...are...out there...racing...because... there...is...a lot...more...good...out there...than...bad."

*D*avey Allison wanted more than anything to win that Daytona 500 for his hero, to try to make up somehow for the one from the year before, the one-two finish that his hero could no longer remember. And Davey and Robert Yates had a capable car. But on only the twenty-third lap, Davey's Thunderbird was bumped by Geoff Bodine's Chevrolet, then spun, then slid down the infield grass off the backstretch and rolled over. Even in a crumpled car, Davey pressed on, finished the race, then climbed out and went after Bodine in the garage area afterward. The scuffle was broken up, but Davey still seethed, for he felt Geoff Bodine had taken away from the Allison family far more than just a Daytona 500.

But oh, he was his father's son: Keep going no matter what, and then take care of business then and there.

Late in the race, as usual, Dale Earnhardt had the strongest car on the track. But his flaw showed again: on and off the gas pedal, on and off, on and off. His aggressive style was simply murder on fuel mileage. And so near the end, he and Ken Schrader, who'd stuck with him in a drafting tandem so strong that they seemed for a while to be the final duelists, had to pit for gas with eleven laps to go.

And it left victory to a man too old, too wise, too cautious to drive anything but smoothly, conservatively.

*H*e won on fumes and prayers. He won on desperate whiffs of draft from other cars, saving precious ounces of gasoline.

He won on the radioed shrieks of advice from, and the body English of, his pit crew. He won by willing his fuel-pressure needle to wiggle a bit off rock bottom of the gauge.

But Darrell Waltrip did win the Daytona 500 of 1989, at last, on his seventeenth try.

"Oh! Thank God!" he screamed as he climbed from one of Rick Hendrick's Chevrolets. "I've won the Daytona 500!" He grabbed a TV reporter, shook him by the shoulders, making sure the guy understood: *"I've won the Daytona 500!"*

Then his eyes went wider: "This *is* the Daytona 500, isn't it? Don't lie to me! I'm not dreaming, am I?"

By staying on the track while Earnhardt and Schrader pitted stronger cars than his, Waltrip built a cushion they couldn't overcome when they roared back out to give chase. But he hadn't believed in the waning laps that he had enough fuel to finish.

"Several times I told them [his crew] on the radio, 'It's gone! It's out!' And they'd say, 'Shake it! Shake it!' " (By jerking a car around on the banking, drivers could sometimes cause the last little bit of fuel in the tank to slosh into the fuel intake.) "I'd move the car around, and it would suck up another ounce or two. With two laps to go, the fuel pressure dropped. But it came back up! *The fuel pressure came back up!"*

Out in the garage, Earnhardt, who'd finished third, grumbled, "I didn't think Waltrip would make it. I'd like to see that gas tank." Illegal fuel cells, larger than the NASCAR limit of twenty-two gallons, had been discovered in some cars over the years.

But, "our car will be checked thoroughly [by NASCAR inspectors] and I can give you my word nothing bogus is going on," said Waltrip.

By sunset, inspectors did clear the car, and Waltrip had indeed gotten his blessed first Daytona 500 win. But it was won by a forty-two-year-old man who now called himself

D.W., going as slow as he could, and not by the fiery, smashing, dashing Jaws of yore. And so it was, if you had known and seen the original Waltrip, a bit sad.

Now, though, he would at least no longer be hounded every February with questions as to why he could win everything there was to win in NASCAR except the Daytona 500.

That misery would now belong to only one man: Dale Earnhardt.

The night before the 1989 Indianapolis 500, Jeff Gordon and John Bickford showed up at Indianapolis Raceway Park, a five-eighths-mile oval a couple of miles west of the big Speedway, with a brand-new, USAC-legal car. It was their first USAC race, and Jeff, seventeen, hadn't raced on a paved track since his quarter-midget days—for four years now he'd been digging dirt with the All-Stars and the Outlaws. But he rolled onto the paved oval at IRP, won the pole, set a new track record, and won the race. "A few weeks later," he would recall, "I graduated from high school."

He had won three track championships in the Midwest before he was old enough to get an Indiana driver's license. Then when he turned sixteen, both the state of Indiana and the notorious World of Outlaws recognized him as a legal driver. And so finally, staid old USAC made an exception from its minimum age of eighteen, and let him race.

And out of the box, USAC got a shot of John Bickford's way of racing, right in the face. Since the early years in quarter-midgets, the modus operandi had been precisely the same: "When we got to a track, our first goal was to sit on the pole, with a track record if we could. Then we wanted to lead every lap and win the race."

Along the way there had been times "when I saw the school activities and all the other kids wearing their jerseys and playing football and basketball and going to the games, that I wished I was out there," Jeff would remember. "There was something inside me saying maybe I had missed out on some of those things."

John and Carol wanted Jeff to go to college as soon as his racing success began to taper off. But it didn't taper off. Even after all the activities of high school graduation day, he and John hurried down to Bloomington, Indiana, for a World of Outlaws race. Jeff jumped into his dirt sprinter and qualified second to Doug Wolfgang, then finished fourth to Steve Kinser in the race.

And so for Jeff, "That night, I pretty much knew what I was going to be doing."

All of his experience was in open-wheel cars. And so it was up that path that John's exploration went. Bickford "practically got down on my knees, begging" Indy car teams and their subsidiary Indy Lights teams, to have a look at Jeff.

"They said, 'Sure. Bring money. Show us the money and we'll show you the seat,' " Jeff would recall. Ability to bring in big sponsorships was the foremost concern with Indy car teams; talent was second. "We didn't have the money."

32

THE DAYTONA 499

Some superb race cars had soared along the banking and/or scurried over the road course at Daytona International Speedway through the decades: prototypes such as the Ford GT40 that won the first 24 Hours of Daytona in 1966 with Ken Miles and Lloyd Ruby aboard; Pedro Rodriguez's "longtail" Porsche 917 of '70 and '71; the Ferrari 312P of Mario Andretti and Jacky Ickx in '72; Richard Petty's dominant hemi-engine Plymouth of '64; Junior Johnson's Ford missile, guided by LeeRoy Yarbrough in '69.

But the sublimest race car, in its class, that ever touched tires to pavement at Daytona was a Chevrolet Lumina, painted black, numbered 3, wrought by Richard Childress and driven by Dale Earnhardt in the 1990 Daytona 500.

It was a 3,400-pound ballerina. It stalked like a panther, struck like a water moccasin. No slot car has ever hugged a track more perfectly than this one did, in any groove where Earnhardt chose to put it, anytime. Its engine was the most advanced to that point in dealing with the stifling restrictor plates—Childress had spent more than $400,000 on research and development of such subtleties as minute changes in valve angles.

Earnhardt and that car were nearer to being one—a single entity—than any other car and driver I've ever seen at Daytona.

It didn't win the pole—Childress and Earnhardt weren't interested in showing their hand too soon. But it won its 125-mile qualifying race on Thursday, and then on Friday and Saturday in practice, it was refined to perfection.

Late Saturday afternoon, for the last half of Happy Hour—the final practice before the race—I went up top, to the press box, to time some top contenders. I never even started my stopwatch. There was no need.

Through the turns, Earnhardt was driving right down at the bottom of the race track, the same perfect line on every lap, and the car's grace and grip were so superb that it made you wonder if Childress hadn't come up with some sort of "ground effects" aerodynamics like the systems that made Indy cars and sports cars literally suction themselves down to the track.

The reason pari-mutuel wagering would never work on motor racing is, of course, that there are too many mechanical variables. Dominance can't be counted on. Even so, when Chip Williams, then NASCAR's chief publicist—and a man who was always up for a friendly wager on anything—walked by, I couldn't resist.

"Tell you what," I said. "You see that black Three car down there?"

"I think I know the one you have in mind," he deadpanned.

"I'll take that car tomorrow, and I'll give you the rest of the field."

"Now don't get carried away," he said. "I know what you mean, but he could cut a tire or something."

"I don't care. That's the best car I've ever seen, for the job it was built to do. I'll take Three, you get the rest of the field. Twenty bucks."

"Done."

Derrike Cope, of Spanaway, Washington—a former baseball catcher who took to racing after he shredded a knee in a home-plate collision with a runner—was such an obscure driver that the Seattle CBS affiliate didn't even carry the Daytona 500 live that day. There just wasn't enough local interest in NASCAR, the program director assumed.

But Buddy Parrott, Cope's crew chief, was one of the truly remarkable coaches of drivers. On the radio, he could literally talk a young driver up through the field. And so he kept coaching and coaxing Cope up among the frontrunners.

But Cope was hardly noticed. Most eyes were on the dominant black Number 3, which led at Earnhardt's will. It was relentless. That it would lead "only" 155 of the 200 laps was due mainly to Childress's reluctance to rub it in on the competition.

When a caution came out with eight laps to go, Parrott ordered his pupil to stay out on the track and inherit the lead after the frontrunners pitted. That, Parrott knew, was Cope's only chance. As the field prepared to go green again, with Cope in the lead, I saw Chip Williams grinning at me from about forty feet away. Not only did he have a chance to win the bet, but part of Chip's job was trying to get publicity for NASCAR's younger, lesser-known drivers. He'd been trying to get me to do a Derrike Cope story all month, and I'd said no way—hell, Derrike Cope had never even won a race.

When the green flag flew for the final time with five laps to go, Earnhardt shot past Cope with the greatest of ease. Seconds later I heard, "Here, dammit!" from over my shoulder and saw a twenty-dollar bill float down on the desk in front of me. "I usually don't pay off till they finish, but you've even got *me* convinced he's a lock."

All that remained was to click off the laps. Four...three...two... one.

Into the third turn of the final lap the black Lumina sailed. One more mile to go.

One lousy mile.

And then the Lumina wiggled, lurched high toward the wall, and slowed.

Cope, Terry Labonte, and Bill Elliott shot past—thump-thump-thump.

Earnhardt "did an incredible job of keeping his car off the wall," Cope would say later. Earnhardt had had one or two seconds' warning. He knew he'd run over a piece of metal coming out of the second turn—race cars vibrate so much at high speed that parts can literally shake loose, and something had come off another car. Going down the backstretch, he'd felt his right rear tire going down. And so when the tire blew in the third turn, it wasn't a total surprise to him.

I sat back in my chair in amazement, and when I did, I felt somebody standing right behind me. I turned and looked. It was Chip, grinning, with his hand out.

Richard Childress would say later that the loss cost the team nearly half a million dollars, counting prize money and lost promotional and endorsement fees. Throw in the R&D on the car, and it was nearly a million-dollar loss for them.

From that day forward, Dale Earnhardt would develop a sad mantra of his own:

"It's not the Daytona 499."

The sight of the great black Lumina being pushed back to the garage in defeat, sad as it was, was not the saddest sight at Daytona that February.

Through the garage area one day had cruised, very slowly, a big Pontiac Bonneville, the type that Big Bill France used to drive when he patrolled the speedway as the man in charge. But in this car, Big Bill sat on the passenger's side in the front seat. Someone else was driving. A couple of VIPs were in the back. It was a rare glimpse of Big Bill by this point. The France family was very protective, very sensitive, very secretive about his condition. But we all knew he had Alzheimer's. Inside the big Bonneville with the windows rolled up, Big Bill seemed to be speaking little.

A friend of the France family who worked at the Daytona Beach newspaper nodded when told of the sighting. He said that certain, understanding VIPs would occasionally take such tours with Big Bill.

And on these tours, he would say to them, "I built this place." Then moments later: "I built this place, you know." And then again. "I built this place…"

"Wallace told me to make sure all these sonsabitches are legal…"

"I built this place…"

*B*y 1990, John Bickford was at a loss again, much as he had been when Jeff Gordon was thrown out of go-kart racing for being too good, too young. Jeff was well on his way to winning the USAC midget-car season championship. *"You're only as good as the guys you race against."* Now the Indy car people wanted money John didn't have. They were getting feelers from Formula 3000 teams in Europe, but that was a "Bring money" proposition too. Where was the next step up?

Well, what about this full-bodied racing down South? It seemed to be growing. Bickford began to investigate. He wasn't sure much would come of it. The only full-bodied cars Jeff had ever driven were passenger cars. The transition might be considerable. Hmmm. Any instruction available? Well, it seemed there was this Buck Baker Racing School, down in some place called Rockingham, North Carolina.

"But we couldn't afford that, either," Bickford would recall. He pondered. Jeff Gordon had become a popular figure on ESPN's *Thursday Night Thunder* sprint car shows. His age made him a sought-after interview, and got him lots of mention during races.

Bickford got on the phone to North Carolina. "I called Buck Baker and asked him what if, in lieu of our paying the fees for Jeff to go through his school, we could get ESPN to come shoot a documentary. The subject would be this young open-wheel driver trying to make the transition to NASCAR. The documentary would follow him step-by-step through the Buck Baker Racing School. Buck thought it was a good idea. It would be good publicity for him. He said we could work something out." Then Bickford worked the deal with ESPN.

When it was time to head south, logistics turned out to be awkward. Jeff, still eighteen, was too young to rent a car. Someone had to go with him. John had to stay in Indiana to run the parts business. Carol could go, but to keep the hardened stock car guys from snickering when Jeff's mother came along, she would stay at the hotel each day.

On the first morning at Rockingham, Jeff climbed into a type of vehicle he hadn't really imagined. "It was different than anything I was used to," he would say later. "It was so big and heavy. It felt very fast, but very smooth. I loved it. The sprint cars were so rough. This car just glided over bumps."

After a few laps, "I said, 'This is what I want to do. This is it.'"

At lunchtime that first day, John Bickford answered the phone in Indiana. It was Carol. She said Jeff had something important to tell him. She put Jeff on.

"Jeff said to me, 'This is what I'm going to do for the rest of my life.' I said, 'Jeff, you've been there four hours! You already know *this is what you want to do for the rest of your life?*'

"He said, 'This is it.'"

33

BLACKJACK AND OTHER GAMES OF CHANCE

*B*ill France Jr. walked in wearing that owl-eyed look that said he was rattled or pissed or both, and it was aimed toward the corner of the bar where Richard Childress was standing. This was in the hospitality suite of the Goodyear Tower inside the garage area. It was lunchtime, Monday, February 11, 1991. France headed immediately in Childress's direction, and a look flashed across Childress's face that acknowledged he was about to catch hell about something.

"Hello, Mr. Childress," France said, and shook hands, and the owl eyes got about the size of teacups.

As president of NASCAR, Bill France Jr. didn't show favoritism, but privately, he thought the world of Richard Childress—had once, according to an insider, put his arm around Childress at a dinner table and said, "This man is my hero. You know why? Because he started with nothing." France usually addressed Childress as "R.C.," or "Richard," and the

"Mr. Childress" was a giveaway that Childress was going to catch it about something.

"How you doin', Bill?" Childress asked warily.

"I *was* doing O.K.," France said.

"Was?" Childress repeated.

"Until your man threw me in the grease yesterday," France said—his way of saying, in the frying pan. He thrust a thumb back toward the garage area. "Now every Ford team owner in there is on my ass."

France just looked at Childress. The previous day, Dale Earnhardt had not only won the Busch Clash, he had rubbed the competition's noses in it. The Clash that year was divided into two segments of ten laps each. The starting order of the first segment was determined by draw. Then after the first segment was run, the finishing order was reversed to make up the starting order for the second segment. Earnhardt had started sixth in the first segment, but shot into first place in a single lap and won going away. In the second segment, he had started fourteenth, and rocketed back to the front in only a lap and a half and run away again. He was flaunting it. He was showing off.

And now the Ford teams were howling for a rules change. They didn't need more rear spoiler, or more front air dam, but Earnhardt's little exhibition had given the Ford owners, and the media, an excuse to question France hard about the situation.

"But Bill," a bystander at the bar said. "It looked like Earnhardt was just that much better at working the air [using the draft] than anybody else."

"Shit," France said, never taking the owl eyes off Childress. "A guy passes that many cars a lap, that's horsepower."

He turned on his heel and left.

Childress cringed.

Just how the hell was he supposed to tell Dale Earnhardt to cool it—not make it so obvious?

*E*rnie Irvan had set out from Salinas, California, in a pickup truck, towing a bare-bars roll cage and chassis he had built himself, in 1982, bound vaguely for North Carolina. He had three hundred dollars in his pocket, which wasn't enough to cross the country, "so I stopped in Las Vegas and won about four hundred more playing blackjack," he would recall.

He made it to Charlotte, began working odd jobs, and began building—piece by piece with a few dollars at a time—a body onto his homemade chassis. For an engine, further fortune took him to a builder named Keith Dorton, the same benefactor who'd once extended credit to a struggling dirt-tracker named Dale Earnhardt.

"Keith told me about the times when Earnhardt wouldn't have food but had to have an engine," Irvan would recall. "Keith would let him have one and not worry about it—Dale could pay him in six months, or whenever."

Irvan worked on his race car at night, worked the odd jobs during the day, ran local dirt tracks on Saturday nights, and spent Sundays in a rented mobile home watching Winston Cup races on a borrowed black-and-white TV set.

Earnhardt hadn't forgotten his own hard times, and had a habit of cruising the shops, scattered around the northern and western perimeters of Charlotte, where the struggling drivers worked. In 1987 Irvan assembled a Winston Cup car of sorts out of borrowed parts, and Earnhardt gave him $3,000, and Irvan scraped all that together and rolled the dice in the fall 500-miler at Charlotte. He finished eighth—enough to impress small-budget team owner D. K. Ulrich—and began driving Ulrich's car farther toward the front than it had been before.

By 1990, Irvan had caught the eye of Larry McClure,

principal of the Morgan-McClure team, and won a Winston
Cup race, at Bristol. But Larry McClure believed in rolling
the dice for the big ones—most of his team's testing efforts
were concentrated on Daytona.

All of this is to tell you what a go-for-broke guy Ernie
Irvan was with five laps left in the 1991 Daytona 500 when,
on a restart after a caution, he drove right past Dale Earnhardt
and into the lead.

The consensus of Irvan's peers at the time was that he was
at least as reckless as he was good—they'd already begun to
call him "Swervin' Irvan," because of the risks to which he
so often subjected himself and anyone else who happened to
be near him on the track when he broke taboos. For example,
although "two wide" racing—that is, two cars abreast—was
perfectly all right, "three wide" was a different matter. The
gentlemen's agreement was that you shouldn't run up on a
pair of cars and drive between them, inside them, or outside
them to make it three wide, especially in the turns, unless
there were urgent circumstances—such as a major contender
who'd lost ground by some fluke, struggling back toward the
front in the waning laps of a race, to reenter contention for
the win. Ernie Irvan at times seemed to make it three wide
just for the hell of it.

Other than being wary of Irvan when they were near
him, the established stars somehow didn't seem to take him
seriously. Rarely indeed do you ever detect snobbery
among NASCAR drivers. Nearly all of them started out on
Saturday-night short tracks. But in Irvan's case, there was a
sort of tacit attitude that he was one guy who maybe should
have stayed on the bullrings for a lifetime—that he didn't
belong here.

Whatever their reasons, after Irvan took the lead in the
waning laps of the Daytona 500, Dale Earnhardt and Davey
Allison, who was running third, became more concerned
with each other than with the upstart in the yellow car that

was hurtling into the distance ahead of them. After second place was decided between them, then the victor of that duel could and would easily draw a bead on Irvan—or so it seemed.

Exiting Turn 2 and entering the backstretch, Allison made what would have been a clean pass on the outside, but Earnhardt stayed alongside until the rear end of his car slid and nailed Allison. The contact sent Allison's car crashing, and Earnhardt's car spinning.

Their momentary, side-by-side preoccupation with each other, in and of itself, likely would have allowed Irvan to get away to win anyway, even if they hadn't wrecked. As it was, Earnhardt and Allison brought out the final caution under which the race would finish, allowing Irvan time to cruise and let the shocker sink in a bit.

Allison was furious. "The Intimidator. Yeah. Right," he said wryly of Earnhardt afterward, indicating there might be a whole season spent in payback, à la Bobby Allison and Richard Petty of yore. But it was now the '90s and payback was no longer acceptable, so in ensuing weeks Davey's sponsors would get to him and cool his vengeful mood.

After his Daytona 500 win, Irvan's "swervin'" would draw even more vehement criticism from competitors—their way of admitting they now took him seriously without admitting respect. At Talladega that May, he would initiate a twenty-car crash that would leave Kyle Petty with a compound leg fracture and bring the criticism to a boil.

"I knew it was going to come crashing down on me sooner or later," Irvan would recall regarding his early wild style. "You've got to be accepted in this sport. If you're not, you're going to get shuffled out."

And so that July, in a drivers' meeting before the second Talladega race of '91, Irvan stood up and made a gesture previously unheard of in Winston Cup: He openly apologized to the other drivers. He promised to earn their respect. He was wrecked in the race later that day—perhaps a final reminder from his peers—and after that, he became one of NASCAR's leading advocates of careful driving.

He would never win the Daytona 500 again. After suffering life-threatening head and lung injuries in a crash during practice at Michigan in 1994, he would earn enormous respect from his fellow drivers for overcoming what doctors at first rated as a ten percent chance of even surviving the injuries—let alone coming back to drive. He was racing again by late 1995, but after two more head injuries in crashes, his doctors would advise him to stop pushing the odds. He would retire in 1999.

But he'd had his enormous moment in '91, when he alone had been sure he was as good as anybody else—good enough to win the Daytona 500.

John Bickford had worked a deal for Jeff Gordon to drive a few Busch Series races late in 1990 for Hugh Connerty, an owner who'd happened to see Jeff at the Buck Baker school. It was a shoestring effort, with a car that wasn't capable of winning, but Jeff's driving was enough to catch the eye of engineer Lee Morse, the top talent scout for Ford's Special Vehicle Operations arm.

Michael Kranefuss, Ford's director of SVO—which is to say, Ford's director of international racing, from NASCAR to Formula One—was a talent-monger. He believed in finding drivers while they were very young, providing opportunities for them, and thereby winning their career-long loyalties to Ford.

Morse followed Gordon to the USAC open-wheel races to have a further look. No doubt about it. In stock cars or open wheels, the kid was spectacular. If Ford could sign him, he had potential to go up in any direction—NASCAR, Indy cars, even Formula One.

Morse reported back to Kranefuss that they really should try to do something with this Jeff Gordon.

Kranefuss at the time was much more obsessed with another kid named Gordon—Morse had found Robby Gordon of Orange, California (no relation to Jeff), in off-road racing. Top Ford team owner Jack Roush ran what he called his "Gong Show" every year at Sebring, Florida, to try out unknown drivers. There, Robby Gordon had made an astoundingly quick transition to sports car racing. He too had three-pronged potential—NASCAR, Indy cars, Formula One—but Kranefuss had hopes of making Robby Gordon America's first winning Formula One driver since Mario Andretti.

But, sure, they'd find a little something for this other Gordon, this, uh, *Jeff* Gordon.

They paired Jeff Gordon with Bill Davis Racing for selected Busch Series races in Fords. And in 1991, even while winning USAC's Silver Crown series championship—this one for "big cars," larger than sprinters—Jeff Gordon moonlighted his way to Busch Series rookie of the year honors.

But Jeff simply had no mechanical knowledge of full-bodied cars. He could not tell mechanics specifically what the car needed in order to perform better.

What he needed was a crew chief who could both understand what he was saying, and teach him what to look for. Specifically, he needed a former driver who also had vast mechanical knowledge.

*B*y the fall of 1991, a thirty-three-year-old modified driver from Hazlet, New Jersey, was coming to terms with himself. He had crashed hard on a short track at Flemington that summer, and suffered a brain-stem bruise that left his depth perception—crucial to any race driver—impaired.

Ray Evernham accepted that he had to quit. The crash

hadn't scared him into it—"When you wreck that bad, you don't remember anything about it," he would say. But as a driver, "I couldn't meet my own expectations, and that frustrated the hell out of me."

He had aspired not to NASCAR but to the Indianapolis 500. In high school he had ignored the admonitions of a science teacher that he was wasting his time on racing. "I was seventeen and building my first race car, and the only thing slowing me down was school." At eighteen he'd turned down a college art scholarship.

At twenty-six, to learn more about race cars, he had taken a job as a chassis specialist with the International Race of Champions series, partly owned by Indy car magnate Roger Penske. What impressed the star drivers in the IROC series—from Dale Earnhardt to Danny Sullivan—was that Ray Evernham, chassis mechanic, could translate what they were saying as drivers about how the cars were behaving into technological adjustments.

And now, even as he faced the end of his driving career, his obsession remained, full force. All he could do now was apply all that mechanical knowledge...somewhere. After Christmas of 1991, he went south to work for the Wisconsin-born mechanical engineer turned NASCAR driver, Alan Kulwicki. The job would last six weeks before the two high and headstrong intellects clashed.

34

"WHEN I...
SAW THAT BOY
WAS DEAD..."

During Daytona 500 week of 1992, Ray Evernham
quit. On the spot. He couldn't take Alan Kulwicki
anymore.

"He was a genius," Evernham would maintain later.
"There's no question. It's not a matter of people just feeling
like he was a genius. The man *was* a genius. But his
personality paid for that. He was very impatient, very
straightforward, very cut-to-the-bone."

There is no tact, no warmth, to physics or calculus. Solutions to equations carry no apologies; they are not open to
discussion or debate. They are absolute. Final.

Alan Kulwicki, engineer, thought in equations. When
asked a question—be it by a crewman, a fellow driver, a journalist, a fan—he would calculate. He would compute the solution, bring it to the simplest terms, and then translate the
mathematical answer back into spoken English.

The solution might well be, "No."

No discussion. No debate. No apology. No encouragement that perhaps the problem could be worked in another way in search of a more satisfactory answer.

"No."

Once, a newspaper photographer asked him to pose with his hand on his chin and a finger alongside his jaw, to illustrate a thinker.

"No."

Not, "Well, don't you think such a picture would look contrived?"

Not, "I don't care to be known as an intellectual; it's hard enough to blend in as just another driver as it is."

Not, "I hope you can understand my position. It would just be uncomfortable for me."

Not, "Sorry. Maybe we could try something else."

No explanation, no apology. Final. Absolute.

Similarly, all information in Alan Kulwicki's head was given out strictly on a need-to-know basis.

Therefore, whatever it was that drove him, he kept to himself. Only he need know.

It is not exactly true that he never smiled. It was that he had his own peculiar way of smiling—in his eyes. There, you might see amusement or fascination or satisfaction or keen understanding or, rarely, confusion or bewilderment. But always in the eyes.

He was a bachelor. The handful of people who felt they knew him well considered him quite a ladies' man. He never flaunted that. Some wondered how a man so sparse with words and so apparently void of mirth could attract so many women. The only possible answer is that the women were intrigued by the absolute absence of any line of bullshit.

He was his own crew chief, even during races. Whatever was done in the pits, he directed from the cockpit. At 200 mph he would calculate the necessary chassis changes and tire combinations, and order them before he pitted.

He had to be the boss. The absolute dictator. In 1991, he

was offered the top ride with the Junior Johnson team. He turned it down to remain head of his own struggling independent team. Nobody in such a position had ever turned down Junior Johnson before. The rap on him in NASCAR changed from that of the dour, eccentric engineer who carried a briefcase around the pits and garages to that of, at the essence, just a damn screwball.

And yet in 1992, even after Evernham had quit, Kulwicki beat not only the Junior Johnson team, with Bill Elliott as Johnson's top driver, but the powerful Robert Yates team for which Davey Allison drove.

"He beat them for the Winston Cup on a tenth of the money they had," Evernham would recall. "And those people should be embarrassed by that to this day. He was a smart guy. We just couldn't get along."

Smarting from one Kulwicki admonition too many, Ray Evernham was taking a hike right out of the garage area at Daytona International Speedway, and right out of NASCAR, when Lee Morse and Preston Miller, another Ford engineer, stopped him. Kulwicki was a Ford driver, and Morse and Miller worked directly, day to day, with all the crew chiefs on all the Ford teams. It hadn't taken Morse and Miller long to see just how good Ray Evernham was.

The engineers suggested that perhaps Ford could find Evernham another assignment. What they had in mind wasn't Winston Cup—not yet. But in 1990, Evernham had worked briefly with Jeff Gordon—given him some help with chassis setups on a Pontiac. Now Gordon was in the Ford stable, and he had mentioned that he'd like to work with Evernham again. So, the engineers asked, would Evernham be interested in taking on the project of nurturing the prodigy?

Evernham thought back to a brief stint with Gordon, and remembered that "From the first day we ever worked together, boom! We hit it off. We had fun, we did good, he was what I wanted, and I was what he wanted."

So: Work with Gordon full-time? Sure. Why not?

"Bill Davis didn't want me," Evernham would recall. "But Ford paid my salary to go and work for Bill Davis, because Jeff wanted me there so bad."

*F*ord's attentions quickly shifted back to the present, because Davey Allison won the '92 Daytona 500 in Robert Yates's Thunderbird, and finally had the big one to dedicate to his hero. Davey won it mightily, dominating the second half of the race after he'd navigated masterfully through a fourteen-car storm of wreckage on the ninety-second lap—and Dale Earnhardt hadn't. For once, Earnhardt was knocked out quickly enough that his albatross and his late-lap mischief didn't ruin Davey's day at Daytona.

Still this was the second-best day in racing for Davey—"not as special," he said, "as finishing second to my dad."

Yet it was Clifford who soaked up Bobby Allison's attention. Bobby was behaving differently toward Clifford's climb through the ranks than he had toward Davey's. Perhaps Bobby, since his devastating injury, was trying to give Clifford what he hadn't given Davey. Or perhaps Clifford still simply charmed him more.

Or perhaps, as Judy Allison would assess it, "Bobby was living through Clifford."

Whatever the case, from the time Bobby Allison could walk again in 1989 he nurtured Clifford's rise through the Busch Series—just one step from the big leagues, Winston Cup racing—"and Clifford was stimulating me *so* much," Bobby would confirm.

Davey Allison suffered rib and shoulder injuries at Bristol in April, and drove hurt the very next week to win at North Wilkesboro. At Pocono on July 19, he was hit from behind by Darrell Waltrip and took the most horrific tumble of his career, the Yates Thunderbird disintegrating as it rolled over and over through the infield, tearing up dirt like mortar rounds exploding in the grass, and then onto an Armco guardrail, still tumbling, crushing the barrier as it went. Davey was taken by helicopter to the same trauma unit, at Lehigh Valley Medical Center in Allentown, where his hero had gone in 1988. It turned out that his skull wasn't fractured as initially feared, but his right arm, wrist, and collarbone were broken. Waltrip maintained that Davey had cut down in front of him; Bobby Allison saw Davey as the victim, opened a new chapter in his grudge against Waltrip. The next weekend, with a black eye and wearing multiple casts, Davey was back in the car at Talladega. Davey was tough; Davey could take it; Davey was a success; Davey was, oh, yes, his father's son.

Clifford was the charmer. On Thursday, August 13, 1992, the Allisons arrived at Michigan International Speedway to begin practice for Saturday's Busch race, and Sunday's Winston Cup race. Clifford was twenty-seven years old. The Busch cars went onto the track first.

"Clifford had just turned a really fast lap in that practice session," Bobby would recall. "He came into the garage, and his crew made some minor adjustments. As he backed out of the garage to go back out on the track, he looked at me and he grinned and said, 'We're gonna get 'em, Dad.' His last words to me were, 'We're gonna *get* 'em, Dad.'

"He went back out. Then suddenly his crew chief threw down his radio headset and said, 'He crashed.'

"I said, 'Is he O.K.?'

"The crew chief put the headset back on and said, 'Clifford? Are you O.K.? Clifford? Can you hear me?…Clifford?…Clifford?'

"I started walking. All the safety vehicles came tearing down the pit road the wrong way—very unusual. Out on the track I saw Bobby Labonte stop his car, get out, and look into

Clifford's car. Then Labonte stepped back, climbed into his car, and drove away.

"I kept walking. A NASCAR official came up and said, 'Bobby, they don't want you out there.'

"I said, 'That's my son. I'm going.'

"He said, 'I'll walk with you.'

"And I walked up to that car…

"I've been hurting since 1988. I'm hurting right now, sitting here, talking to you.

"But when I walked up to that car, as close as from me to you, and saw that boy was dead—*knew* that boy was dead—there began a pain I had never known before, never imagined.

"And it kept hurting. Kept hurting. Kept hurting…"

And never went away, the echo of the whisper said.

"He had a wound on his face that never even bled—that's how fast his heart stopped."

Davey Allison took charge again.

"After that, Davey became really attentive to me. He would always say, 'Come on, Dad, go with me in my plane.' Or, 'Come on, Dad, let's go get a bite to eat.'"

On Saturday, March 14, 1992, Rick Hendrick was climbing the stairs to a luxury skybox high above Atlanta Motor Speedway. A Busch race was going on, but Hendrick wasn't very interested—his cars were entered in the Winston Cup race the next day. He was just cruising the VIP lounges, visiting.

But on his way up the stairs, directly above Turn 1, "I caught this white car out of the corner of my eye. As it went into the corner, I could see that it was extremely loose. I said, 'Man, that guy's gonna wreck!' Earnhardt and Harry Gant were leading, and this white car was right up on them. I told the people with me, 'You just can't drive a car that loose.'"

"Loose" means oversteering—means a car is set up to turn so sharply left that the rear end wants to slide out to the right. The loose condition gets a car through corners faster than any other setup. But except in the hands of masters, "loose" handling is dangerous—it throws a car sideways, tends to make it spin out. Few drivers are comfortable "loose."

"Well, I got up into the suite and kept watching, and this guy in the white car went on to win the race," Hendrick would remember. "I asked people who that was. Somebody said, 'That's that Gordon kid.'"

Back in Charlotte, Hendrick phoned ESPN and asked to borrow tapes of the Gordon kid's races. He was more than convinced. He was amazed. He put the general manager of Hendrick Motorsports, Jimmy Johnson, on the case. Hendrick, whose team ran Chevrolets, figured Gordon was probably tied up every which way with contracts, with either Bill Davis Racing or Ford, or both. Johnson did some checking. Gordon was under no contracts—none!

Hendrick said simply, "Call him. Right now."

What they needed now was a face-to-face meeting with the kid. Talent was vital, but so were personality and looks in a sport now driven by huge sponsorship fees from image-conscious corporations.

Hendrick feared finding an arrogant, difficult prodigy. "What I found was a mature young guy who was kind of humble—a little bashful. A sponsor's dream. I was almost in a daze. Jeff had it all. It was just scary. He was good-looking, and I couldn't believe how well he handled himself at age twenty—and he was going to be *that good.*"

*F*ord people would claim Hendrick blindsided them, and that Gordon sneaked out on them. Jimmy Johnson would maintain that "Ford was aware of our interest in Jeff. That's a fact."

At any rate, Ford team owner Jack Roush "called me and wanted to hire Jeff," John Bickford would recall. "I told Jack that was a huge compliment. I explained that this was a package—Ray Evernham and Jeff Gordon. Jack explained to me that his drivers did not select crew chiefs. I told Jack that I appreciated the call and to have a really great day, and I hung up.

"Jack called back and said, 'Why did you hang up on me?' I told him the conversation had been completed, and I didn't want to waste his time. I said, 'You've made the decision that you're not going to allow the driver to pick the crew chief. The crew chief for Jeff Gordon in Winston Cup racing will be Ray Evernham. It's not an option. It's not a negotiable point. That's the way it will be.' "

"Then at one point, Jackie Stewart called," Jeff would remember. Stewart, the three-time world Formula One champion, and a longtime Ford associate, "talked to me about going to Europe to do some Formula 3000 racing." That was one step away from Formula One, the world's elite and glamorous Grand Prix tour.

And Ford provided Cosworth engines for several top Indy car teams. Now the world was pounding on John Bickford's door, begging for Jeff Gordon.

"John Bickford is a smart, smart racer," Hendrick would say in looking back at the key to the deal. "On identifying what it takes to win, John is as smart as anybody I've ever talked to. He knew what he wanted for Jeff. He looked at our equipment. He already knew our program pretty well from the outside. Money wasn't as important as the commitment you make to your program. John wanted an opportunity for Jeff to grow into.

"Then at one point, Jeff said, 'What's the chance of Ray Evernham coming aboard?' " Hendrick would recall.

"Jimmy Johnson said, 'Fine. If that's what you want, we'll hire him.'"

But in making the best possible deal for Jeff Gordon, John Bickford had just dealt himself out of a job—and, in large part, out of what had been his life.

*I*n the summer of '92, Ray Evernham's wife, Mary, stayed in New Jersey with their year-old son, Raymond John—called "Ray J." because it rhymed with "A.J.," as in Foyt—while Ray waded into the launch of the new arm of Hendrick Motorsports. Before Ray had even signed up for Hendrick company insurance, he got a devastating call from Mary: Ray J. had been diagnosed with leukemia.

Rick Hendrick immediately stepped in, telling Ray everything would be taken care of, including all medical bills for Ray J.'s treatments at New York's Memorial Sloan-Kettering Cancer Center, widely considered the best such treatment facility in the world. Ray could go home when he wished, but meanwhile he could know that everything that could be done for Ray J. was being done.

A man like Hendrick deserved a winner. And Evernham "thought to myself, The only way we're going to excel is to think at a different level than everybody else."

He would not think like a traditional crew chief. He would treat NASCAR racing at the same level as the National Football League or the National Basketball Association. Nothing would be left to chance. Nothing.

He began hiring mechanics, and began devouring books on management and winning. Vince Lombardi was buried in the same cemetery as Ray's grandfather in Red Bank, New Jersey. Ray had visited there often as a kid, had heard the stories that Lombardi had turned the Green Bay Packers from one of the worst teams in the NFL into a dynasty. Now he began to study just *how* Lombardi had done it.

In his new building, Evernham put up a big, Lombardi-esque sign on the most prominent wall. It was a checklist, with boxes to be marked off by each item as the months and years wore on. It read:

FROM NOBODY TO UPSTART
FROM UPSTART TO CONTENDER
FROM CONTENDER TO WINNER
FROM WINNER TO CHAMPION
FROM CHAMPION TO DYNASTY

As Major League Baseball teams sometimes bring up minor leaguers for a look-see in late season, Winston Cup teams sometimes bring up rookies-to-be for a race or two in the fall. And so Rick Hendrick sent Jeff Gordon and Ray Evernham and their fledgling crew to Atlanta for the season-ending Hooter's 500 on November 15, 1992.

They were hardly noticed. This was Richard Petty's final race, and 165,000 fans turned out mainly to bid the King good-bye. Plus, there was a five-way horse race—including Richard's son, Kyle—for that year's Winston Cup championship. Davey Allison, Bill Elliott (now driving for Junior Johnson), and Alan Kulwicki were the real contenders. Fifty-four-year-old Harry Gant also had a mathematical chance.

Richard Petty was caught up in a crash on the ninety-fifth lap, and as his Pontiac spun into the infield it burst into flames. Emergency workers came quickly, but Petty, sensing them mainly gawking at the King's last moment as a driver, and seeing no fire extinguishers in their hands, bellowed into his radio mike, "Tell 'em to get the fuckin' fire extinguishers over here!" Later he would laugh and wonder if they weren't mainly interested in autographs.

"This was not," Petty said at the end, "the kind of blaze of glory I wanted to go out in. But I've been doing this for thirty-five years, and I'm still walking and talking."

In the rush to fill the void left by the retirement of the King, two primary candidates seemed to emerge from that final race of '92. One was Davey Allison, who came into the race leading the Winston Cup points but was knocked out of the title when Ernie Irvan spun and collected him seventy-three laps from the finish. The other was Alan Kulwicki, who won the Winston Cup by finishing second in the race.

The kid who crashed at the halfway point in the weird-looking, rainbow-colored car? Well, he'd won three Busch races that season. But up here in the big leagues, he was somewhere between a nobody and an upstart.

Next stop, Daytona.

35

"WHO IS THIS GUY?"

I was wowed before I ever met her," Jeff Gordon would say of Brooke Sealey, one of the new models hired for "Miss Winston" ceremonial duties in the 1993 NASCAR season. Ty Norris, Winston's chief publicist on the tour, was Brooke's boss, and Jeff's friend. There was a strict if unwritten rule that Winston models mustn't date drivers, and part of Norris's job was to enforce that rule. But in this case he couldn't resist—he not only made a secret exception, he played matchmaker. Before the season started, Norris began showing Jeff pictures of Brooke, and telling him they ought to get together.

They met briefly during a couple of preseason autograph sessions in North Carolina, "but we never really talked," Jeff would recall. He thought it was just the hustle and bustle of the public appearances.

But Brooke, two years older, was skeptical. "I was like, 'Who *is* this guy? Ty was trying to arrange for us to meet, because he thought our personalities matched perfectly. But I was thinking the whole time that Jeff was probably this arrogant kid coming into the sport thinking he could rule the tracks, and could make a couple of phone calls and get me to go out with him.

"I didn't know anything about racing before I became a Miss Winston." And so they didn't have much to talk about. "Then we went to Daytona."

Jeff Gordon had been on Daytona International Speedway for two brief winter test sessions, but that was no preparation for running in traffic, in the draft.

But when his 125-mile qualifying race started, he shot straight to the front pack and tucked in right behind Bill Elliott, as if he belonged there.

One flaw you watch for in rookies at Daytona is skittishness at 190 mph-plus. Few of them have ever driven that fast in traffic before. The late Butch Lindley, a superb short-track driver, came to Daytona in the 1970s and, upon completing his first fast practice laps, climbed out and said with a stunned look on his face, "You don't ever back off over there." He meant the backstretch. And he never was comfortable at Daytona.

Clearly, Jeff Gordon was totally comfortable. There was not the slightest unnecessary wiggle of the rainbow-colored Number 24. On the radio, Ray Evernham was telling the twenty-one-year-old driver, "Take it easy...take it easy..."

He *was* taking it oh, so easy when, on the twenty-second of the fifty laps, he breezed past Elliott and took the lead.

In the media center, many were waiting for the kid to make a mistake. Young drivers usually suffered lapses in concentration after a few laps. Not only that, but this guy had little experience in full-bodied cars, and virtually no experience at Daytona, with restrictor plates. The bobble had to come sometime.

But it didn't.

He drove into Victory Lane, where, he knew, Brooke Sealey would be waiting to present the trophy to the winner.

When he climbed out of his car, "*Then* we had something to talk about," he would remember, chuckling.

He winked.

She winked.

"It was like sparks, right from the start," as Brooke would put it.

And there were sparks in the grandstands, the media center, the press box…this guy was phenomenal: smooth as Darrell Waltrip in his youth, self-certain as Dale Earnhardt at his prime. And this guy was twenty-one—the youngest driver ever to win a race at Daytona.

But he was cool only in the race car.

"Back in the garage after the race, he came up to me and his little voice was just shaking," Brooke would recall. "He was trying to talk to me, telling me we were around the same age, that no one else in racing was our age."

Earnhardt won the second 125-miler and, during his interview, was rattling off a list of his top competition for Sunday's 500. His old rival Geoff Bodine would be a threat, and so would Bill Elliott and Davey Allison, and, as an afterthought, "uh, the Gordon boy."

This was no boy. This was a man with sixteen years of hard racing, and winning, behind him.

For eight seasons, Dale Jarrett had struggled, in and out of Winston Cup racing. Being a second-generation NASCAR driver didn't do him much good. His father, Ned, had won championships in 1961 and '65, back when they didn't mean much, back before the "modern era" began in 1972 with full-fledged Winston sponsorship of the series. After retiring in 1966, Ned had concentrated on the family lumber business, and knocked around NASCAR in part-time jobs, mainly for fun. He'd been a PR rep for Busch Beer and a sometime radio announcer, and promoted races at little Hickory Speedway near his hometown of Newton, North Carolina. When CBS took over Daytona 500 telecasts, Ned became the primary color analyst. But he'd been gone from active driving for so long that "Jarrett" didn't carry nearly the electricity of "Petty" or "Allison."

Out of high school, Dale Jarrett was a scratch golfer, and Ned and wife Martha encouraged their son to work toward the Professional Golfers' Association Tour. Ned's primary concern was that "I didn't want to see him have to make the sacrifices I knew he'd have to make in the racing business."

Still, Dale turned down a golf scholarship to the University of South Carolina and set out on a path of sacrifice that not even Ned had imagined. Through the mid-'80s he ran Saturday-night short tracks, mostly Hickory, and found a ride for a Winston Cup race here or there. In '87 he went into Winston Cup full-time—and into full-time disappointment. By 1990, winless in Winston Cup, he had gone back to the Busch Series. Then that April, after Neil Bonnett suffered a brain injury and amnesia at Darlington, the Wood Brothers needed a substitute driver for the remainder of that season, and called Dale Jarrett. The Wood team wasn't nearly what it had been, but in '91 Jarrett won a race for them at Michigan. So he had at least a little résumé when National Football League coach Joe Gibbs, a longtime racing enthusiast, started a Winston Cup team in '92. Gibbs hired Dale's brother-in-law, Jimmy Makar, as crew chief, and Makar recommended Jarrett as driver. But the new team wiped out two brand-new cars at Daytona right out of the box, and went winless that first season.

Daytona is a realm that sometimes smiles on the downtrodden, sometimes awards a glorious moment. Daytona had a track record of benevolent fortune that ran from Tiny Lund to Derrike Cope to Ernie Irvan.

Dale Jarrett's moment began with two laps to go in the 1993 Daytona 500. He had led briefly on two occasions earlier in the race, but mostly he rode, biding his time, while Dale Earnhardt dominated as usual, this time with "the Gordon boy" tucked in on Earnhardt's bumper, dogging him relentlessly.

With every pit stop, Jimmy Makar had gotten Joe Gibbs's Chevrolet working better and better. As the laps waned, Dale Jarrett knew the hand he held. When two furled flags went up, held vertically parallel to signal two laps remaining, Jarrett played the hand. He passed Gordon and drew a bead on Earnhardt.

Ned Jarrett wasn't supposed to be—and wasn't prepared to be—a play-by-play man. That was Ken Squier's job. But in the control truck, CBS producer Bob Stenner had an impulse. He said into his microphone, "Take it, Ned."

And Ned's reflex reaction was to coach more than announce. "Come on, get up under him and get him loose," he said to Dale, who of course couldn't hear him. But Dale did precisely what Ned had suggested. Coming to the white flag, Dale Jarrett discombobulated Earnhardt with one of Earnhardt's own tricks. Through Turns 3 and 4, Jarrett ran up on the left rear of Earnhardt's bumper, which had the effect of taking air off Earnhardt's rear spoiler and making the notorious black Number 3 skate up the track. Then Jarrett pulled alongside, and Geoff Bodine—never intimidated by the Intimidator—chose to go with Jarrett rather than Earnhardt. Going through Turns 1 and 2 on the final lap, Bodine drove in behind Jarrett and gave him an aerodynamic "push" past Earnhardt in the draft.

"And Dale Jarrett is gonna *win* the Daytona Five *Hundred!*" Ned said gleefully to the CBS audience.

*I*n January of 1992, Joe Gibbs had won his third Super Bowl as coach of the Washington Redskins, immediately announced his retirement from football, and added that he was going to start a NASCAR team. Born in North Carolina, son of a deputy sheriff who'd regaled him with stories of chasing moonshiners, Gibbs had grown up in California playing football and drag racing. His life could have gone either way, but, "my first job offer was coaching football." And so he had taken a considerable detour from his true love of things mechanical and fast.

As Gibbs made the transition, I was the only *Sports Illustrated* writer versed in both the NFL and NASCAR, and so I drew the assignment of a massive piece on Gibbs that was scheduled to run in the swimsuit issue in February of '92. I knew Gibbs shied away from media coverage, so I phoned an old friend, Redskin publicist Charlie Dayton, to see if he would help convince Gibbs to cooperate. When Charlie told Gibbs the story would be largely NASCAR-oriented, that was fine with Gibbs. But then Charlie called back and said Gibbs wanted to know if the story would involve football.

"Well, it would be pretty hard to catch a coach retiring right off a Super Bowl win and *not* mention it," I said. "But look, Charlie. It'll be mostly looking ahead to his career in NASCAR. And hey: This is scheduled for the swimsuit issue."

The last part was for the benefit of Charlie and the Redskin publicity department. The swimsuit issue is read—well, at least looked at—by more than a hundred million people, worldwide.

Then I got a phone call at home.

"Ed. Joe. Look, I just can't do this."

First, he said, allowing himself to be singled out for such a major magazine story would go against everything he'd ever preached to his players about not trying to stand out as individuals.

But mainly there was this swimsuit issue thing. Joe Gibbs is a born-again Christian, who, though he doesn't wear it on his sleeve, practices his religion every minute of his life. He just didn't want a story about him in an issue that was sold essentially on sexuality.

After we hung up, I decided to fly to Washington for one last appeal, face-to-face. Gibbs was finishing up his business at the Redskins complex near Vienna, Virginia, and was in his office when I came in from Dulles Airport. He was most cordial, and we talked for a few minutes, and then he picked up a copy of *Sport* magazine off a table. Several smaller magazines were doing copycat swimsuit issues in those days, and *Sport* was one.

He opened up *Sport*. On facing pages, there was on the left a picture of an enormous, silicon-pumped, oiled, tanned pair of boobs hanging out of a string bikini top, and on the right a big picture of Gibbs's face. Apparently he hadn't known the story was going to appear that way. As you closed the magazine it appeared that Gibbs's face was being buried right in the cleavage of said enormous, oiled, tanned etc.

"Look at that," he said. "I don't need that."

"Joe, *Sports Illustrated* wouldn't do it that way. I think you know that."

He sighed and said, "I can't stop you guys from doing a story, but I just don't feel that I can cooperate."

I went out and phoned New York. The assigning editor agreed with me that we wouldn't force the story if Gibbs didn't want to be interviewed for it. I went back to Gibbs's office and told him, "We're not going to do a story you don't want to do. We've called it off."

He was astounded, relieved, deeply grateful. "I can't tell you how much I appreciate your understanding," he said.

Well, on February 14, 1993, after Dale Jarrett had made the Daytona 500 Joe Gibbs's first Winston Cup win, and after Gibbs and practically the entire Jarrett family had been interviewed ad infinitum, I spotted Gibbs sitting on a stool in the back of the press box, getting ready to leave.

I couldn't resist. I walked over and said, "Hey, Joe. You
ow which issue this news story just happens to fall into?"

He looked up. At first he winced, then he grinned:
"Swimsuit?"

"You got it. I can call off a feature story, but if you go
ound winning the Daytona 500, there's not a thing I can do
r you."

He laughed. "But just remember," he said, "this story isn't
out me—it's about Dale Jarrett."

Same old Joe.

"Yeah," I said, "but you're still pretty good at drafting tal-
t nobody else could spot."

At Daytona, Brooke had told Jeff, "Well, call me when we
t back" to Charlotte, where, as it turned out, they lived only
out five minutes apart.

"I wanted to take her to lunch. She stood me up the first
y, though. I called her the Monday morning after the Day-
na 500. I was ready to go. She said, 'No, wait till tomor-
w.'"

But they began to date on the road, on Winston Cup race
eekends, and Ty Norris helped them keep the secret.

"In restaurants I would literally have to run into the
chen and hide when other racing people would show up,"
ooke would recall. "And then they'd ask Jeff, 'Why are
u here by yourself?' One time we were about to get on a
ane and Jeff saw Darrell Waltrip's team boarding the same
ght, so I had to go change my ticket and take a three-hour-
er flight. When we had weekends off, we'd go to Las
gas, because nobody there would recognize Jeff or me."
hat was a far cry from the NASCAR-crazy Las Vegas of
day, where even the presence of one of Jeff Gordon's show
rs at a hotel draws equal billing on the huge marquees with
rs such as Chris Rock.)

The NASCAR traveling crowd is a gossipy lot, so the garages and hotel lobbies buzzed all that season of '93 about the handsome young driver who should have been a magnet for women but never seemed to have a date.

"Reporters and everybody kept asking me, 'Don't you have a girlfriend?' " Jeff would recall. "Earnhardt asked if I was gay."

The mouths also wondered why Brooke Sealey didn't have a boyfriend and didn't bring dates to social functions. The gossips just never linked the two juiciest items of the season.

By autumn, Jeff would proclaim himself "a master at sneaking in and out of hotels."

The big sting on the gossips came at the NASCAR awards banquet in New York that December. Jeff was being honored as rookie of the year, but brought John and Carol Bickford, and his peers and the media were nonplussed, asking him, "Couldn't you even get a date for the *banquet?* " But that was Brooke's last official function as Miss Winston. She was giving up the modeling job. As the banquet broke up, Jeff and Brooke walked out arm in arm, revealed their romance, and left the gossips standing there gaping.

At Daytona in February of '94, the shy Jeff Gordon would reserve an entire room of a French restaurant in Ormond Beach. Brooke would be baffled when they were seated, all alone, looking around her at the empty room, when Jeff silently handed her the enormous diamond ring.

She accepted.

*B*efore the plane went down on April 1, 1993, outside Bristol, Tennessee, Ray Evernham and Alan Kulwicki had talked things out, made their peace, become friends again. Evernham was especially glad of that after Kulwicki was gone.

As reigning Winston Cup champion, Kulwicki had made

stop for a promotional autograph session in Knoxville the day before practice was to begin for the April 4 Food City 500 at Bristol. Routinely, he and three others got on a private plane owned by his sponsor, Hooter's restaurants, for the quick hop over to Tri-Cities Airport near Bristol. Just before final approach, the plane crashed. There were no survivors.

But in Ray Evernham, Kulwicki would live on "as a benchmark. Alan actually brought out the best in me. I wanted to prove to him that I was good enough and smart enough to do it. Alan was able to cut through all the bull, boom! Get the job done. Here's the race, it doesn't matter about the fluff and buff and chrome and the parade. Alan cut through all that stuff.

"Alan showed all of us that we didn't have to conform to be successful. When we first came down South, you almost had to be a stereotype to be successful. Alan gave us all the confidence that we didn't have to be that. Business changes. Life changes. Management changes. When something grows as fast as Winston Cup racing, it becomes more and more like any other big sports league. You've got to change your style of management—I don't care if you're from North Carolina, New Jersey, or Alaska."

Evernham questioned everything—Why did the mechanics who worked on the cars in the garage have to be the "guys who go over the wall," the ones who handled the pit stops on Sundays? Pit crews in their synchronized moves had long been compared to football offensive linemen firing off the snap of the ball. O.K., so instead of asking mechanics to be athletes one day a week, Evernham went out and hired athletes. Now he literally had former football players firing over the pit wall in synch. They needed a coach. Evernham hired Andy Papathanasieu, a former Stanford University offensive lineman with a master's degree in organizational behavior. "Andy Papa" taped each Sunday's pit stops, and analyzed the tape like football film during the week. A mock pit stall was built in the Hendrick Motorsports complex, and pit stop practice was held several afternoons a week. Andy Papa refined virtually every movement of a pit stop. For example, tire changers had long held on to the air hoses to their wrenches as they moved, and cleared the hoses out of the way with a whiplike snapping motion. Still, occasionally, they tripped on the hoses. Andy Papa taught them just to let the hoses drag flat on the ground. And there was no more tripping. As for the mechanics, they'd still do better if they were fit, so Evernham got Hendrick to build an elaborate gym and began requiring regular workouts of all staff.

Evernham the head coach needed "coordinators." As his "offensive coordinator," he hired engineer Brian Whitesell away from the Mack truck manufacturing company. Whitesell was put in charge of the offensive nature of the cars—aerodynamic slickness, proper weight distribution in the chassis for optimal steering...Ed Guzzo had come out of the service department of a Ford dealership in New Jersey to become Evernham's hundred-percent-dependable detail man on modified cars. So Evernham made Guzzo his "defensive coordinator," to make the cars as failsafe as possible—simply, "to make sure nothing falls off during a race."

All this was to be done at the Hendrick complex before "loading day," which on a typical Winston Cup race week was a Wednesday. Two meticulously prepared cars—a race car and a backup—plus spare engines, plus tools, plus spare parts, plus gear and clothing for crewmen, all were loaded according to checklists.

Thursday was shipping day. The transporter would roll out, headed for the track, be it in New Hampshire or California. Thursday night, Evernham and his mechanics would fly to the race city on one of Hendrick's private planes.

Friday morning the primary race car should roll off the truck set up pretty close to what the particular track required. Gordon would climb in and practice, and if the car was off,

en there was a Plan B set of charts and records and check-
ts, for an immediate audible on the car's entire setup. If
at still wasn't quite right, there was an elaborate Plan C.
othing would be left to chance.

Sunday morning on another private plane, the "Sunday
ew," the athletes, would fly in. Their sole concern, all their
aining, all of Andy Papa's choreography, was to produce
e fastest pit stops in NASCAR.

Before Evernham's arrival in NASCAR, twenty seconds
as considered an excellent pit stop for four tires and a full
ad of gas. When he was finished honing the procedure, a
ew had better get four tires and gas done in sixteen seconds
their driver would come out of the pits way behind the
aders.

It was nothing short of revolution.

 I get killed in a race car," Davey Allison had said to me,
lmly, thoughtfully, in 1991, "I'm gonna die with a smile on
y face."

Davey died with no expression on his face, in a coma, in
Birmingham, Alabama, hospital, early on the morning of
ly 13, 1993—eleven months to the day after his brother
as killed in Michigan.

The Alabama Gang amounted to the Allisons' extended
mily of racers—especially Neil Bonnett and Charles "Red"
rmer. And so when David Bonnett, Neil's son, scheduled
s first test drive in a Busch car for Talladega on July 12, the
hole gang wanted to be there in support of the youngster.

The Bonnetts would drive the sixty miles from Hueytown,
ross Birmingham, to the speedway. But Davey had a new
y. Robert Yates, his car owner, had begged him not to buy
at helicopter. Pleaded. Like Bobby, Davey was an expert
lot of fixed-wing aircraft. But choppers were different—
ore tricky to fly.

But a sixty-mile trip across Birmingham was precisely the sort of short hop for which Davey had bought the helicopter. He could land it right in the infield. So he was going—even though he had only about sixty-five hours in helicopters, and only ten hours' flying time in the new, sophisticated Hughes 369-HS he'd bought only a month earlier.

Tough old Red Farmer was still fearless at age sixty-one. He hopped right in with Davey, and off they flew.

They made it to within one foot of touching down safely in the parking lot of the garage area in the infield at Talladega, according to witnesses. Then the helicopter began oscillating and suddenly rose about twenty-five feet into the air. It spun counterclockwise, rolled, and crashed, its tail rotor striking a fence on the way down.

Farmer would recall that just before what he'd expected to be an easy touchdown, the helicopter "just shot up in the air." What happened next, "you can't describe unless you've been in a race car that is flipping, turning over. You get disoriented. I could see the sun, I could see the ground, I could see the sky, I could see the dirt and asphalt, and everything was spinning and the helicopter was just going crazy and Davey was fighting the controls.

"I braced myself. I put my left hand against the console and my right hand against the window. I guess natural instinct from driving race cars tells you to always brace yourself when you figure something's going to happen.

"Davey was still fighting the controls and couldn't brace himself. When it went down on the left side, he probably hit his head against the side of the helicopter. Then it flipped over and spun a couple of times and landed on my side.

"I hollered, 'Davey! We gotta get out of here before it catches on fire!' I knew it was full of fuel and the motor was still running, wide open. I've been in situations where friends of mine have turned over in race cars, and if they're hanging upside down, you don't pull the safety belts, because if you do, they crash down, and sometimes that hurts them worse than hanging there. And with one arm [the other was broken in the crash] I couldn't undo the seat belt and hold Davey up at the same time.

"I knew we were at the track, where there would be help coming. The windshield was busted out, and I kicked more of the glass away and tried to wiggle out. I got about halfway out, and Neil [Bonnett] was there. He dragged me fifteen or twenty feet away from the helicopter, and I said, 'Neil! Go get Davey! He's unconscious. He's got to get out before it catches on fire.'

"So Neil ran back to the helicopter, and I lay there for a few minutes, and someone said, 'We've got Davey out, and we're gonna get you to the hospital.'

"They took us to the infield hospital to wait for the helicopters [from Birmingham's Carraway Medical Center], and that's about all." Red Farmer's recollections would give way to sobbing.

"I didn't see Davey anymore."

*T*he day before, "I rode home with Davey from the New Hampshire race in his Cheyenne airplane," Bobby would recall. "I sat in the copilot seat. We talked about all kinds of things. Some old things. Some current things. His outlook. His ambitions.

"The next morning I had a physical therapy session and then went to my office, in the old shop, down the hill there from the house. I was on the phone. Another line rang. Donnie Johnson [Bobby's brother-in-law and former business manager] answered it. He listened, and he looked at me and said, 'Hang up the phone.' He had never said such a thing to me before. I looked at him. He said, '*Hang up the phone. And get that other line.*'

"The other line said Davey's helicopter had crashed at

Talladega. I went to the house and told Judy we had to go. We got to the hospital in Birmingham before the rescue helicopter got there with Davey. They were gathering doctors. There was one they had a lot of confidence in for head injuries. They worked on Davey for about three hours. Then they said we'd have to wait and see.

"I went and found a room by myself. I waited there for an incredibly long night."

Just after dawn, just as my commercial flight was touching down at Birmingham airport, Davey Allison died. I heard the news within seconds after I turned on the rental-car radio. The voices on all the news stations were somber, speaking of nothing else. Birmingham was in shock and grief, much as it had been a decade earlier when Bear Bryant had died.

I'd gotten the call from New York the previous evening, booked the earliest morning flight from Atlanta to Birmingham, and then telephoned Father Dale Grubba at his church in Princeton, Wisconsin. Father Grubba was a longtime friend of the Allison family who had been through every tragedy with them. He was also flying in the next morning, and was booked into an airport hotel. We agreed to meet there for breakfast.

But upon hearing the news on the radio, I drove straight to Carraway Medical Center. There was a mob scene of news camera crews. Then security and police officers began to move the camera crews back. Bobby and Judy were brought out quickly, hustled into a van, and taken away.

I went back to the airport hotel to meet Father Grubba.

He sat staring at his breakfast for a long time, wondering, sometimes aloud, what he would say to the Allisons *this* time. Only three months earlier he had said the funeral Mass for Alan Kulwicki in Milwaukee.

As a waitress cleared our table, she said, "Excuse me, Father, but I just wanted you to know…Everybody's asking, Why? Why? Why?"

He did not attempt to answer. He only muttered:

"Yeah."

As she left, he pondered. "One of the worst things a priest or a counselor can do is try to come up with an easy answer," he said. "Something like, 'God needed him more than we did' is a terrible answer for the family. Sometimes people are blessed with a certain simplicity in their faith. I think the Allisons have this very simple, deep faith that is not the faith of maybe a priest or someone who has studied religion."

Then he decided what he would do: "Be present and listen. A lot of times people talk through things and resolve them within themselves."

He got up to leave. "Are you going over?" he asked, meaning the Allison family compound in Hueytown.

"Well, I don't know if the media—"

"Come with me," he said.

The police had the compound cordoned off, to keep away curiosity seekers. But Father Grubba's face and collar were familiar, so they let us pass. We parked across the lane from Bobby and Judy's house, beside the home of Bobby's mother, Kitty, who was eighty-six years old. We sat in the rental car for a few minutes and Father Grubba spoke of Rose Kennedy. As a seminary student in 1963, Father Grubba had participated in John F. Kennedy's funeral.

"Those of us who lived through that era said the same thing: How many more of these does the lady have to endure? She too was that epitome of tough Irish Catholicism." And as he spoke, up walked Kitty Allison, to the car.

"How much more can Bobby and Judy take, Father?" she asked. "God give them strength."

"They've got people like you, though, who are examples of strength," he said.

"I just hope I can be enough for them, that's all," she said.

"You have to go on and accept it. You can't ask why. Someday we might know. You've got to say, like Davey said, 'When my time comes, I'm gonna go,' and he was very philosophical about that, right along."

She heaved a sigh. "Have you seen them yet, Father?" she asked, meaning Bobby and Judy.

"Just going in now, Mom," he said. "How are they doing?"

"It's terrible hard, Father."

*I*rish, Catholic, southern, whatever the sort of instinctive tradition, the women all seemed to have gathered up at the big house, and the men were all down in Bobby's offices at the old shop at the bottom of the hill.

We went to the shop first. The room was jammed with racing men. Bobby was standing in the middle, and Father Grubba headed straight for him. I stayed near the door, talking with Hoss Ellington, who'd been Donnie Allison's car owner in the notorious Daytona 500 of '79.

"I know I'm a walking miracle," Bobby Allison said to the priest. "Honestly, I asked for a miracle again when we were in the hospital with Davey. I didn't get the miracle. But it doesn't mean I won't ask for another miracle again sometime."

After a while Bobby came over to me. Father Grubba had brought me here, and at heart I was here as someone who'd known the Allisons for nearly twenty years, but by task at hand, I was media. As such, I wasn't sure I was welcome.

Bobby put his arms around me and we hugged, very tight—two men whose jobs had clashed numerous times, had had our ups and downs and disputes, and some laughs—and we stood there weeping as hard as two men can weep.

His head was buried in my shoulder and he sobbed, "It

hurts," then screamed: "Ohhhh, it hurts! All the joy…all the success…now all the heartache."

After the requiem I walked out of the church, St. Aloysius in Bessemer, with Mario Andretti.

"Why?" said Mario. "It is beyond my comprehension. If ever there was goodness in anyone, it is in that family. The whole family. They are the example of goodness."

Far across the parking lot, standing alone, smoking a cigarette, stood Bill France Jr., the president of NASCAR. Not a very religious man, he had left before Communion. He had taken his jacket off. It hung over his shoulder.

Big Bill France had died in June of 1992, two months after Annie B. He was eighty-two years old and long out of touch with the NASCAR mainstream, so Bill Jr. had understood why few active racers had come to the funeral.

"But you know," Bill France Jr. said, standing there in the parking lot at St. Aloysius, "Bobby and Davey came. Best I recall, Davey was the only active driver there."

He lit another cigarette and exhaled. "Bobby and Judy had to work hard for everything they had," he said, "and it seemed like early '88 was the best they'd ever had it. Since then, they haven't had a break."

36

CASUALTIES
OF WAR

*N*eil Bonnett went lightly, easily, politely, and most of all cheerfully through life. He could put a punch line on any situation. After he suffered the brain stem injury at Darlington in April of 1990 that left him with amnesia, and left the Wood Brothers ride open to Dale Jarrett, Bonnett came to Talladega that May to announce he'd decided to sit out of racing, at least for a while.

"When you have to be told who your wife is, and who your kids are, that gets your attention," he said. I asked if he had talked with Bobby Allison about all this, and I got some dirty looks from other writers who thought that even asking about a conversation between two close friends with memory-damaging head injuries was brutal. But I had walked into Bonnett's punch line. "Sure have," he said. "Matterafact, I went over to Bobby's house just the other day to get some advice. And I'm tellin' you, between Bobby trying to think of what he wanted to say, and me trying to remember what he'd just said, we had a helluva time." The room exploded with laughter.

The amnesia went away eventually, but the doctors still

said Neil should stay out of race cars. He'd taken so many hard shots that his head and body were fragile. The months turned into years, and the nicest guy in NASCAR grew restless. He had long considered racing an addiction. He had told the teenage Davey Allison, "You don't want to get involved with these damned old race cars." Once in, Bonnett believed, you never got out.

His best hunting and fishing buddy, Dale Earnhardt, understood the craving and talked it over with Richard Childress. They began putting Bonnett in their cars for test sessions, and in 1993, Childress put Bonnett into two races in "research and development" cars.

In the months after Bonnett had scrambled into the helicopter wreckage to pull Red Farmer free and then gone back for Davey Allison, he yearned more and more to get back into racing. He knew that Childress and Earnhardt didn't need distractions in their effort to break Earnhardt's winlessness in the Daytona 500. And so for the '94 race, Bonnett got a ride with a smaller, independent team.

On February 11, 1994, during a practice session at Daytona International Speedway, Bonnett's car dropped slightly onto the apron in Turns 3 and 4, then suddenly, inexplicably, turned sharp right and shot head-on into the outside retaining wall.

Neil Bonnett was dead in the car.

No television cameras had been taping the practice session, so it was never clear what actually happened. That same week, rookie Rodney Orr was killed in a crash in Turn 2. All Bonnett and Orr appeared to have in common was that they were on Hoosier tires. And so questions naturally arose about the tires.

*B*efore NASCAR and Goodyear reached an agreement in 1997 whereby Goodyear would be the exclusive tire supplier for Winston Cup racing, there used to arise, from time to time, "tire wars." Whenever there were two or more tire manufacturers involved in NASCAR, the competition always got scary. Literally week to week, the tire companies would try to one-up each other. To go faster, a tire usually needed to be softer, to grip the track better through the corners. And softer meant more fragile, which of course meant more dangerous.

There had been the Firestone-Goodyear war in the 1960s before Firestone pulled out due to the Talladega debacle. Then Goodyear had dominated in peace until 1988, when little Hoosier Tire Company of Lakeville, Indiana, run by a colorful and enigmatic man named Bob Newton, entered the fray. Hoosier was a longtime supplier of tires for Saturday-night short tracks, and at first most racers doubted that Newton could go toe-to-toe with mighty Goodyear in Winston Cup. But Hoosier came on strong, beat Goodyear occasionally, and it got to the point that on a given weekend at a given track, racers didn't know which tire was going to be faster until the race actually started. It was a mess. You could hardly walk through the pits, because so many tires were mounted and ready. It wasn't uncommon for a team to start a race with a dozen sets—say, eight Goodyear and four Hoosier—or forty-eight tires stacked in the pits.

By April of 1989, the coolest, most cheerful driver in NASCAR stood in the garage area at North Wilkesboro, North Carolina, and looked around him. He was atypically nervous—very jittery. His voice trembled as he talked. Two or three other drivers walked past, limping on legs broken in crashes caused by tire failures in the previous twelve months. And across the garage stood Buddy Baker, who during the '88 season had been saved by nick-of-time brain surgery to relieve a hematoma—a blood pool on the brain—suffered in a tire-related crash.

"I'm afraid it's going to take somebody getting killed to

end this thing," the usually cool driver said. He glanced all around and added, "You just wonder which one of us it's going to be."

He asked for anonymity should his remarks be used in a story at the time. It doesn't matter now. His name was Neil Bonnett.

Goodyear had introduced a racing radial tire for the Daytona 500 in February of '89. Radials, though common for passenger cars, were new to NASCAR, which had always run on old-fashioned "bias-ply" tires, which were more forgiving. Goodyear claimed introduction of the radials was solely a matter of technological advancement. But Hoosier didn't make radials and wasn't big enough to retool anytime soon, so it could effectively be forced out of NASCAR if the radials worked at Daytona.

They didn't. On the first day of practice, a right front radial blew on Dale Earnhardt's car on the backstretch. The steel belt in the tire came loose and ripped off the right front fender. Earnhardt did a masterful job of avoiding a serious crash. Still, Goodyear wouldn't withdraw the radials. Later that afternoon, a radial disintegrated on Bill Elliott's car and he hit the wall hard in Turn 3, suffering a broken arm. That night, several eighteen-wheelers backed up to the Goodyear building in the garage area, unloaded a supply of traditional bias-ply tires, and took the radials away.

But Goodyear came back with different radials at the other tracks that spring. By Talladega in May of '89, Newton knew he was whipped, and Hoosier withdrew from NASCAR. Every driver breathed a little easier.

But by 1994, Hoosier was making radials, and setting up deals to give teams free tires at Daytona. Low-budget teams, including Bonnett's and Orr's, jumped at the chance. And in January testing, "the Hoosier was a good half-second [per lap] quicker," said Darrell Waltrip, who also went with Hoosiers—he had started his own team and was looking both to save money and to break out of a slump. "But when we came back here for the race, we slowed down three-tenths from what we'd tested. One of the problems I ran into as I went into the Hoosier deal was that we'd go do tire tests, get a tire we were happy with, and then he [Newton] wouldn't bring them back."

Whether Hoosier brought different tires to Daytona in February than in January of '94, "I don't know for sure," Waltrip said. "It just wasn't as fast."

After the deaths of Bonnett and Orr, Hoosier withdrew from the Daytona 500 that year. "I don't think it's ever been established that there was anything wrong with the tires," Bill France Jr. would recall. "But the drivers got spooked."

Waltrip didn't believe there were tire failures per se. "Anytime you've got a tire that's fast, and built the way that tire was built, there's always a chance of an inexperienced driver not being able to handle that kind of tire. Those were narrower tires, which made them faster."

In theory, when a tire has a narrower tread width, or "footprint," as racers call it, it goes faster down the straightaways because there's less rubber in contact with pavement to cause friction. The downside is that the narrower tire also gets less grip, and behaves in trickier ways, through turns.

"If the car got loose, it might get out of control," Waltrip said. "But it wasn't because the tires were built wrong. It was just the design of the tire."

Orr was inexperienced, and Bonnett was rusty.

After withdrawing from the '94 Daytona 500, Hoosier returned for the other races that season, and the weekly one-upsmanship raged again, with more sporadic tire failures.

Ernie Irvan was on Goodyears when the right front tire failed during a practice session at Michigan that August, sending his Thunderbird slamming broadside against the concrete wall. (Reports, at the time, of a nearly head-on hit were erroneous.) Irvan's skull was "cracked like an

;gshell," one of his doctors would tell me later. At the auma center, Irvan was given a ten percent chance to live rough the night. In addition to his head injuries, he also suf-red massive internal injuries, including collapsed lungs.

"We could just *bet* this was going to happen," said his car wner, Robert Yates, who by now was devastated. Yates had red Irvan to replace Davey Allison. Now this.

By that point, the height of the '94 tire competition, both oodyear and Hoosier had managed to augment tread width bit of a misnomer in that the tires were of course slicks) to even inches, on wheels that were only nine and a half ches wide. That meant the tires would grip for flat-out cor-ring. The extreme side stress of turning so fast on tires too ide for their wheels could, Yates feared, "jerk the tire right f the rim."

Leo Mehl, Goodyear's director of racing at the time, dn't believe Irvan's tire failure was related to the tire war. ut Mehl did concede that "from a safety standpoint, the ly tire we never quite explained [that year] was Ernie's e."

Irvan recovered almost miraculously—within two months was not only up and around again, but bouncy, chipper, xious to climb back into a race car. And the next year, he ould.

But Neil Bonnett was gone. And after 1994, there would no more tire wars for the remainder of the century.

37

"YOU BETTER GO—
HE'S COMIN' "

Sterling Marlin came into the 1995 Daytona 500 with only one career Winston Cup win—the 1994 Daytona 500.

And he left with two career wins.

In '94 he had outsprinted Ernie Irvan, Terry Labonte, and Jeff Gordon to the finish, keeping his cool by "telling myself it was just like a thirty-lap Saturday-night feature at Nashville."

Sterling pronounces it "Nayshful," as many natives do. He grew up in the suburb of Columbia, Tennessee, working on race cars with his father, the inimitable independent NASCAR driver Clifton "Coo Coo" Marlin. Sterling had started out running weekend races on the five-eighths-mile oval in the Nashville fairgrounds, and in the late '70s had eased into Winston Cup with a race here and there in his father's cars.

He'd gone full-time to the big time in '84, and remained winless coming into that Daytona 500 of '94. But hey, he just envisioned himself at Nayshful and pulled the trigger. And as reigning Daytona 500 champion through the '94 season,

terling Marlin didn't change a whit. What a pity that the
rm "good ol' boy" has been so misused and overused—if
ou use it in its very best connotation, Sterling is about the
est ol' boy still running in NASCAR.

That sincerely country-boy, no-frills persona of his left
nlight on the memory of a Daytona 500 that had started
adly due to the deaths of the beloved veteran Neil Bonnett
nd rookie Rodney Orr during practice sessions the previous
eek.

Sterling's popularity surged through '94—it was as if old-
ne NASCAR fans, feeling deluged by the new wave, had
een waiting for him, one of their own, to win.

But here is a microcosm of the way popularity goes for
terling:

Most racers employ full-time drivers for those luxury
notor coaches in which they live at the tracks on race week-
nds. Sterling, however, loves to drive his own coach when-
ver possible—especially to Talladega, which is only a short
in from Nashville.

So one Sunday night in '94, the Daytona 500 champion
as driving his motor coach in heavy, creeping traffic, com-
g out of Talladega Superspeedway after a race.

"The guy in the car in front of me wouldn't move on up
the traffic—he kept leaving big gaps in front of him," Ster-
ng would recall. "So I started really crowding him, getting
ght up on his bumper. He wouldn't move on, and I'd crowd
im, and this went on for a little while and finally he sticks
1 arm out the window and starts flippin' me off.

"Then he pulls over to let me by, and I wheel on around,
nd he's *really* givin' me the finger. And as I go around, I can
∙e that he's got a Number 4 Kodak [Sterling's ride at the
me] pennant on his radio antenna, and he's got 'Go, Ster-
ng!' all over the sides of his car and the windows [in wash-
ɔle paint].

"I waved as I passed, but when I got ahead of him he was

still givin' me the finger. Guess he never realized he was flippin' off his favorite driver. "

*T*o understand Sterling, you must first understand Coo Coo. Although the older Marlin originally got his nickname in a far more innocent way than you might suppose—as a toddler he hadn't been able to pronounce "Clifton," and it came out "Coo Coo" to his parents and siblings—it stuck because the NASCAR boys thought it fit.

Coo Coo Marlin drove Winston Cup for sixteen years without a win, and didn't care a helluva lot. He made his living farming and he raced for fun, and fun he had. Coo Coo was of that generation of drivers who could still be seen out carousing in the honky-tonks on race weekends.

One night in the '70s, Coo Coo and the hilarious car owner Hoss Ellington—who was then fielding cars for A. J. Foyt—were thrown in jail in Anniston, Alabama, which was everybody's motel town for Talladega races. Coo Coo's wife, Eula Faye, who until her death of cancer was the absolute darling female stand-up comic of many a NASCAR cocktail party, was hauled in with them. She was soon let go, but the two men had to spend the night in the slammer.

Next day at the track, Hoss commenced telling the story of their ordeal.

"We'uz in my brand-new Lincoln, cruisin' down that main drag of Anniston, what you call it, that Quintard Boulevard. Me and Coo Coo had been drinkin', y'know, Eula Faye was sober, so she was drivin' my new Lincoln. She was *chauffeurin'* us.

"Well, Eula Faye was speedin' a little bit, so the cops pulled us over. Eula Fae says to me and Coo Coo, 'Now you boys keep yo' mouths shut; don't cause no trouble, an' let me talk to this man.'

"But Eula Faye don't know how to operate the power

indows on my new Lincoln, and she fumbles around with
e control buttons tryin' to let that window down, and
amned if she don't hit the button for the seat adjustment,
d so here's the cops lookin' in the window an' Eula Faye's
ttin' in there goin' *up and down, up and down, up and
wn,* and she can't get the seat to stop, and she can't get that
indow down.

"So now the cops figure Eula Faye's drunk too. Finally
e gets the seat stopped and she opens the door and gets out.

"But now Eula Faye starts talkin' that ol' Tennessee talk
hers, and these cops can't understand a word she's sayin,'
d now they sho' *'nuf* figure Eula Faye is drunk.

"So they take us all down to jail. Now we get down there
d they see that Eula Faye is sober after all, and they let her
. But me and Coo Coo? Uh-uh, buddy. They throwed us in
il.

"Now I get in there and I think, Well, I might as well get
yself some sleep. So I lay down, roll over, get comfortable,
d in the next cell there's this drunk a-hollerin',
)HHHH!…OHHHH!' for about half the night. I keep hol-
rin' for him to shut up, and finally he does. Now I go to
eep.

"Before long I wake up hearin' this beatin' and poundin'
pise. I look around and there's Coo Coo, down on the floor
f our cell. He's got his cowboy boot off and he's got a tin
il cup, and he's just hammerin' on that tin cup, beatin' it all
pieces.

"I say, 'Coo Coo, what in the hell are you doin'? Knock
ff that racket and go to sleep.'

"He says, 'Shhhhh!' He whispers, 'Be quiet, Hoss. I'm
akin' us a key. I'm gonna bust us outta this place.' "

Before Coo Coo finished his improvisation so they could
ake good their escape, Eula Faye spoiled the fun by return-
g with the bail money.

*   *   *

*T*he point is, the Marlin boys are unperturbable.

Take the night Sterling backed the motor coach into an eighteen-wheeler.

"I'd pulled into this truck stop to get something to eat. I brought a hamburger back to the coach, got in, started it up, put it in reverse, got ready to back out. Then I noticed there were pickles on my hamburger. I hate pickles. So I was sittin' there with my foot on the brake, gettin' the pickles off. I didn't realize my foot was easin' up off the brake, or that the coach was rollin'—until I heard a crunch at the back.

"I got out to go see what I'd backed into—figured it was a fence or a post. When I got around back there was this eighteen-wheeler sittin' there, up against the back of my motor coach. The driver was gettin' out, and he looked pretty hot.

"I figured I'd better go on around and face him. So I walked up to him and said, 'Hey. How you doin'?'

"He looked at me for a second. Looked at me real hard. Then he said, 'Are you Sterling Marlin?' I nodded. Sort of grinned, y'know. He said, 'Well I'll be—Sterling Marlin!' He grinned and stuck out his hand.

"We shook hands and went on. Nothin' else was said."

Everything goes easy, with the Marlins.

And so with one simulated Nayshful sprint to a Daytona 500 win under his belt, and with his Morgan-McClure Chevrolet getting faster with each practice session at Daytona in '95, Sterling Marlin felt not a bit more pressure the second time around.

After Happy Hour on Saturday afternoon, he plopped down at the back of the truck, shrugged, and said, "Well. The o' hotrod's runnin' pretty good."

It was the fastest thing out there.

Of all Dale Earnhardt's magnificent failures in the Daytona 500, his onslaught in the waning laps in '95 was the only one that truly qualifies as great. Had he been chasing down anybody but Sterling Marlin, Earnhardt likely would have won.

As the tenth and final caution period of the day ended with eleven laps to go, Marlin was leading with Earnhardt running a seemingly hopeless fourteenth. But Earnhardt had dived into the pits during the caution and loaded his guns—four new tires and a full tank of gas.

Marlin, seeing this, nonchalantly said into his radio mike: "Well, what you wanna do?"

His crew chief of the time was a diminutive, whole other piece of work named Tony Glover, who spoke in a similar drawl and was similarly unperturbable. Here was the Daytona 500, theirs to lose, and they were talking in the tones of two guys sitting on a back porch, whittling and chewing and chitchatting.

"We-e-lllll," Glover droned. "Let's just stay out."

"Aaarrright."

They would take no tires, no gas. Let Earnhardt come to them.

And godamighty, here he came. A storm. Blowing with all the vengeance of seventeen years of what would have been heartbreak if Earnhardt had been the type ever to admit his heart was broken.

Only in bad racing movies had there ever been a charge like Earnhardt mounted. He made up a dozen positions in eight laps. The black Monte Carlo was part of him, and he darted, he plunged, he slithered, he passed—with a little drafting help down the straightaways from, of all people, Jeff Gordon, who had lost a lap on a bad pit stop and was running twenty-second, but was now racing strong again.

With three laps remaining Earnhardt moved into second place, and 175,000 people stood in unison and roared at what surely seemed was about to conclude as the greatest late charge to victory in the history of the Daytona 500.

As thunder rained down from the grandstands in front of the pits, Tony Glover drawled softly into his radio mike:

"You better go—he's comin'."

Sterling Marlin went—worn-out tires and all. Just another Saturday-night sprint at Nayshful.

Earnhardt could run right up to Marlin through the corners, but Marlin would simply pull back out front down the straightaways.

Earnhardt fell short again, this time by .61 of a second.

How had he fallen short? Earnhardt shrugged and growled, "This is the Daytona 500. I ain't *supposed* to win the damn thing."

"Maybe after I retire, he can win it," Sterling Marlin cracked.

He had won it on the straightaways. So maybe the secret lay in the engine, which on Marlin's car that year made a sort of banshee-wailing sound, almost like Indy and Formula One cars—*wheeee-ow!* Was it a matter of horsepower? Or was the sound caused by a newly streamlined design of exhaust pipes that might have given Marlin an aerodynamic edge?

"Y'all might not need to know," Runt Pittman, Marlin's engine builder, told reporters. "It seemed to work pretty good, though. Yep. It seemed to work pretty good."

Going into the '95 season, Dale Jarrett had taken an enormous gamble by jumping from the secure but so-so team of Joe Gibbs to the ultra-powerful, star-crossed Thunderbirds of Robert Yates Racing. With Ernie Irvan out indefinitely with the Michigan injuries of '94 but intent on coming back, Jarrett took the Yates ride with the understanding that the job might last only a few weeks.

"And I knew when I went there that I'd be in a no-win situation," Jarrett would remember. Davey Allison had won fifteen races in the black Number 28 cars in the four years prior to his death. Irvan had won five times for Yates in his one-year stint before his life-threatening injuries.

"If I go there and win races, hey, you're supposed to, because that car wins," Jarrett said. "If I go there and don't win, then Dale Jarrett can't drive."

Then why would he walk into such a situation? "To learn to work with a team that I thought was championship-caliber—to find out what it was like to race up front week in and week out. I thought I could learn enough there to be able to start my own team, which I had aspirations of doing at the time."

Out of the box with Yates, Jarrett won the pole for the Daytona 500. But while Marlin and Earnhardt were warring for the win, the mighty Yates Thunderbird ran fifth. Robert Yates was a patient man. Larry McReynolds, the crew chief, was a different story.

McReynolds and Davey Allison, friends since Catholic youth groups back in Birmingham in the '70s, had made each other stars. McReynolds, as media-friendly as he was brilliant on chassis setups, had become the highest-profile crew chief in NASCAR by the time of Allison's death. Then Irvan had come in and agreed to the same setups McReynolds had used for Allison, and McReynolds looked even better.

So Jarrett should be willing to be plugged into the winning formula—right?

But there were subtle technical changes for '95. Cars had been lightened by one hundred pounds. And Chevrolet introduced an aerodynamically superior new Monte Carlo body style that set the Ford teams scrambling to catch up.

So when Jarrett didn't win...and didn't win...and didn't win..."Larry and I had our differences through the first part of the season. He felt like I should be able to drive the car the way it was—it had won in the past. And I didn't feel like they were paying attention to what I was asking for in the car."

By Charlotte in May, Jarrett told his wife, Kelley, he

wasn't sure how much longer he'd be driving the 28 car. He met with McReynolds and Yates and they tried to sort things out. Still, they won only one race all season, at Pocono in July. To media and fans, Larry McReynolds seemed virtually infallible as a crew chief, and so the problem must be the driver.

"And a lot of bad things," Jarrett remembers, "were said and written—basically that Dale Jarrett couldn't drive a lick."

But when Irvan returned in the fall of '95, Yates received lucrative offers from Ford to provide sponsorship for a second team car. Ford wanted to snatch Earnhardt away from Chevrolet—perhaps a payback for Chevy's theft, as Ford saw it, of Jeff Gordon three years earlier. But Yates was something of an aesthetic traditionalist who believed that Dale Earnhardt belonged with Richard Childress and Chevrolet, and that such a major shift toward all-out free agency would make NASCAR racing look as bad as baseball and football to fans. There would be no more sense of loyalty. And so Yates was relieved when negotiations with Earnhardt fell through.

Yates wanted to keep Dale Jarrett, but feared he was the only one in the process who felt that way.

"Then one afternoon, Larry McReynolds came into my office and said, 'Robert, I've been thinking. If you're going to do that second team, the driver ought to be Dale Jarrett.' I sat back in my chair. I heaved a huge sigh of relief. I said, '*Thank you.* I've been waiting to hear you say that.' "

For Jarrett and the new branch of the team, the Number 88 car, Yates decided to go outside the team, to find someone who hadn't even been a crew chief before but was ready to move up.

"Crew chiefs can be like NFL or NBA coaches who keep getting fired and hired, kind of circling until they find the right place," Jarrett believed. "But we decided that instead of bringing in a veteran crew chief with all his habits, good and bad, we'd start with someone fresh."

Yates and Jarrett chose Todd Parrott, son of the savvy veteran crew chief Buddy Parrott. Todd had been Rusty Wallace's ace chassis man for several years, but hadn't bossed a team yet.

"Todd didn't come in with ideas about what he'd been doing for years and years and years," Jarrett would recall. "Todd was willing to listen, and talk with me. He came in and said, 'I've got some notes on what we learned with Rusty. We'll use those when we think it's appropriate. Otherwise, Dale and I are gonna discuss the setups, everywhere we go.'"

They went first to Daytona.

38

NO PROZAC—YET

Dale Jarrett, who "couldn't drive a lick" for Larry McReynolds, won the 1996 Daytona 500 for Todd Parrott in their very first time out of the box together. Parrott had listened to Jarrett, had understood where Jarrett wanted the car to feel loose, where he wanted it to feel tight, and had responded with intricate combinations of spring weights and shock absorber stiffness.

But Richard Childress's crew had long listened closely to Dale Earnhardt, and so his Monte Carlo handled just as well as Jarrett's Thunderbird.

"What Earnhardt didn't have," Jarrett said afterward, "was a Robert Yates engine." Twice now in last-lap duels in the Daytona 500, Jarrett had beaten Earnhardt.

"I'm no better than Dale Earnhardt," Jarrett said. "But I had a better car than Dale Earnhardt."

At first Earnhardt tried to be cool about it. "Well, that's the Daytona 500," he said while still parked in his car in the garage area. "Finished second again. No problem."

But as he climbed out and was pressed for details, he clearly had a big problem. "We couldn't do nothin'! The damn Fords were too strong! Could you not see that? Jarrett pulled us by himself. We couldn't draft up to him."

Then Earnhardt stomped off. He had now lost three of the last four Daytona 500s by a total of less than a second, .89 to be exact—to Jarrett in '93 by .16, to Marlin in '95 by .61 and to Jarrett again in '96 by .12.

Earnhardt was now oh-for-eighteen in the Daytona 500, even though he was the winningest driver in the history of Daytona International Speedway. He'd won the summer Firecracker 400 (later the Pepsi 400) twice. And he'd won twenty-six various preliminary events of Speedweeks over the years—125-mile qualifiers, Busch Clashes, Saturday 300-milers.

This time, Jeff Gordon hadn't even gotten close enough to get his heart broken. He'd been bumped from behind and crashed into the wall on only the tenth lap. But already, "the Gordon boy" was feeling a Daytona 500 monkey of his own, even at only oh-for-four. "I was beginning to wonder if I wasn't getting started toward the same sort of situation Earnhardt was in," he would admit.

*I*n April of 1996, as John Bickford and I sat in his office, he answered a question for me by picking up his telephone.

"I think this thing still works," he said, and listened for a dial tone. "Yes, it still works."

The question had been, "How much contact do you have with Jeff nowadays?"

Jeff Gordon was now in the hands of Ray Evernham, Rick Hendrick, Brooke Sealey Gordon, and an agent/business manager named Bob Brannon.

John Bickford, who had given his life to making Jeff Gordon the best young race driver alive, was now the odd man out. He was adrift—working as publisher of *Racing for Kids* magazine, which was a subsidiary of a company jointly owned by Dale Earnhardt and Jeff Gordon.

How did it feel to be separated from Jeff's racing effort now that it was peaking?

"Well," Bickford said, "I haven't attempted suicide yet. I haven't been in a psychiatric hospital yet. I haven't gone on Prozac yet. Other than that…"

His voice trailed off. It was hard on him. Very hard. Here was this man of enormous energy, a living, whirring super-computer of ideas, one of the brightest organizational minds for racing in the country if not the world—I'd always thought of John Bickford as Roger Penske without the megabucks—selling advertising for a kids' magazine.

And how was Carol?

So devastated, Bickford said, that "she won't even talk to you about it." (Many times over the following months I would try to call Carol at home, and not once would the phone be answered.)

I had begun to suspect a problem a year earlier upon leaving Jeff's house on Lake Norman, north of Charlotte, with a *Sports Illustrated* photographer. In the rental car, the photographer had told me he'd asked Jeff to pose with John and Carol for a picture to go with the story I was working on. But, the photographer said, Jeff had refused—"He said he needs to be his own man now." Strange. Mario and Aldo Andretti a few years earlier, in their fifties, had been delighted to pose with their mother for *SI*. And God only knew how happy A. J. Foyt would have been to pose with his dear mama if she were still alive.

Darrell Waltrip had given me his theory—that the crustier drivers, especially Dale Earnhardt and Rusty Wallace, had tormented Gordon so much with teasing about being a "baby" that Gordon was now hypersensitive about seeming dependent on his parents in any way.

But after the day Bickford checked his phone to see if it

still worked, the next race was at North Wilkesboro, North
Carolina. I needed to talk to Jeff about Bickford, and I didn't
need any interference or spin-doctoring from his legion of
public relations people, handlers, business managers, whatever. So I waited until I saw him walking across the garage
area at Wilkesboro by himself (you'd never catch him walking anywhere alone at a track nowadays—he wears a constant swarm of minicam crews and autograph hounds around
him everywhere he moves) and I approached him.

"It's—it's tough," he said. "I'm always trying to figure
out more ways to get John involved. But from the racing
standpoint, even in the Busch Grand National days, he
hasn't been involved with the day-to-day running of the cars.
But he and Mom felt fairly active in it because they were at
more races.

"Then it got down to where they were driving my motor
home, doing my business, doing my schedule, making a lot
of decisions that I just wanted to be making on my own—not
because they were doing it wrong; they were doing a great
job.

"I definitely wish they could still be involved more, because they're the ones who got me here." And here his voice
cracked: "I mean, I *love* 'em. I thank God for 'em. For what
they did...

"We've offered...like when the Hendrick truck program
came about, we were like, 'John, do you want to run the truck
program?' And he's like, 'No, I don't.' "

The Supertruck racing program was for upstart drivers,
not Jeff.

"And John still wants to be involved with things that I'm
involved with."

Which of course was understandable. You give your life
to something, you want to see it through, be a part of the success. I felt for John Bickford, probably because I had known
George Elliott so well as he'd languished on the sidelines a

decade earlier, cut adrift from Bill and Ernie's success after years of self-sacrifice to get them started. I told Bickford about George, and how George had poured a million of his dollars into his boys' racing, only to become officially unofficial. Bickford smiled knowingly at the "officially unofficial" part. But other than that, it didn't help.

*B*y 1996, Rick Hendrick had made Hendrick Motorsports the most sophisticated and high-tech motor racing organization in the United States. The complex, a few miles west of Charlotte Motor Speedway, consisted of five sprawling buildings on fifty-five acres. No Indy car complex could compare—they worked on more sophisticated cars per se, but Hendrick used far more sophisticated equipment and constructed virtually every piece of its own cars. Indeed, only two motor racing technical facilities in the world could compare to the Hendrick operation—Williams Grand Prix Engineering Ltd., hidden in the English countryside near the village of Didcot, Oxfordshire, and McLaren Cars Ltd., at Woking, Surrey, south of London.

Hendrick outsourced only two items—tubular steel for building chassis, and basic engine blocks. Hendrick cars were built from the ground up. Even the engine blocks, obtained from General Motors, went through a sophisticated finishing process at the complex. Cylinder heads were fashioned and finished by machinery driven by a million-dollar computer that Hendrick engineers had converted from its original purpose, which was manufacturing artificial human joints for surgical implant. Pistons were milled by robotic machines imported from Germany for $150,000 each. Every part was examined by magnafluxing, a sort of X-ray system for metal, before and after races.

In one building, Randy Dorton supervised the massive engine department. In another building, Eddie Dickerson as in charge of construction of all team cars, each built to e precise specifications of each driver and crew chief. The tire blueprint of each car was recorded in computers so at, if a particularly fast car were demolished, it could be re-oduced to within one one-thousandth of an inch of the erall dimensions. That building also housed the offices of ary Eaker, once the top aerodynamicist for General Mo-rs—until Rick Hendrick hired him away.

Each team occupied a building of its own, and on any ven day you could walk into any of the three and get the nsation you were in a house of mirrors. There on the shop oor would sit not one, not four or five, but a dozen copies Terry Labonte's red-and-yellow Kellogg's Number 5, or ff Gordon's rainbow Dupont Number 24, or Ken hrader's (Ricky Craven's by 1997) red-and-white Bud-eiser Number 25. Identical as the cars might appear to the ked eye, they were all different, built with their weight stom-distributed, and their bodies placed precisely on the assis. This one might be tailored for the short track at Mar-isville, Virginia; that one for the road course at Sonoma, alifornia; those three for intermediate-size tracks such as harlotte or Atlanta; these two for the mammoth super-eedways at Talladega and Daytona.

Ray Evernham ran the 24 team and oversaw development the weaker 25 team. Savvy Gary DeHart was the man in arge of Labonte's team.

They didn't always see eye-to-eye. "There are two ways doing things around here," DeHart once said, sitting in his fice. "There's the New Jersey way, and the North Carolina ay." Specifically, he said, "I'm not going to have my guys it here running wind sprints around the building at ten clock at night, after they've put in more than a full day's ork."

Over at the 24 building, and in the gym, Evernham ran

things like...well...Vince Lombardi. All was intensity. All the time.

DeHart was a thoroughbred, North Carolina-steeped, NASCAR traditionalist. He hired the best people possible and then refused to put any more pressure on them than they already put on themselves.

In '95, the New Jersey way worked—Gordon and Evernham won the Winston Cup.

In '96, the North Carolina way worked—Labonte and DeHart won the Winston Cup.

It all worked.

Like clockwork.

And like the Hendrick Automotive Group—which by the autumn of '96 included eighty-nine retail automobile dealerships nationwide, and generated $2.2 billion annually in revenues. Combined, Hendrick Motorsports and Hendrick AG had more than five thousand employees. That meant Hendrick could offer far better salaries and benefit packages than other teams. Not many years earlier, the average NASCAR mechanic had been paid by handwritten check, without even taxes or Social Security withheld, and no insurance. Now Hendrick was raising the bar for the industry—mechanics had medical and life insurance, retirement plans, profit sharing.

Rick Hendrick, nice guy, had it all. And would give it away to anyone in need. That, insiders would tell me, was where the trouble started. Hendrick's retail empire included eighteen Honda dealerships. I was told that after a top executive at American Honda was fired, he pleaded for help from Hendrick to keep from losing his home, and Hendrick gave it. Who knows? All that's certain is that in the fall of '96, the roof fell in on nice guy Rick Hendrick.

A bribery scandal had been brewing for a couple of years regarding dealers trying to keep steady inventories of the very popular Honda automobiles during the early '90s, when

emand was outstripping supply. Several U.S. Attorneys in
ne eastern states were working on the investigation. Some of
nem, it was felt by Rick Hendrick's supporters, were grand-
tanding. It was felt that the prosecutors wanted to go after
Iendrick because of his high profile, as both the largest
Ionda dealer in the country and a racing magnate.

So Hendrick had been anticipating that some problems
night arise in his life. What he hadn't anticipated was what
is doctors told him in November of '96—that he had
hronic myelogenous leukemia—a particularly difficult form
f the deadly disease to treat.

Then in December, two days before he was to step onto
ne stage at the Waldorf-Astoria's grand ballroom in New
fork to accept his team's second consecutive Winston Cup
ophy, the federal indictments were announced. The timing
f that announcement was what had Hendrick's friends in the
merican motor racing community growling that the prose-
utors were grandstanding.

If convicted on all thirteen counts of the indictment, Hen-
rick could have faced up to 210 years in prison. Which was
lackly absurd, considering that he might not live another
ear.

39

BY A KNOCKOUT

Never had Ray Evernham been closer to his boss.
Evernham was Rick Hendrick's most understanding
cheerleader, believing that Hendrick could survive leukemia,
"because I live with a little miracle every day." Ray J.'s treatments were bringing him nearer and nearer to full remission
at age six. But Hendrick's adult form of leukemia was more
complicated—a marrow transplant was the only consistently
effective method of treatment, and no matching donor could
be found. The outlook on interferon and other chemotherapy
was long and bleak.

In February, Evernham and DeHart supervised the loading and dispatching of three eighteen-wheelers bearing six
race cars, dozens of engines, and thousands of spare parts,
south toward Daytona. Just before flying out himself, Evernham phoned Hendrick and asked if there was anything else
he could do.

"You can finish one-two-three in the Daytona 500," Hendrick said—chuckling, of course.

Not since the mightiest Porsche factory team ever assembled finished *ein-zwei-drei* with prototype 956s in the 24

Hours of Le Mans in 1982 had a single team swept the top three spots in a major automobile race. Such a feat had never been accomplished—and probably never would be—in bam-bang NASCAR. At Le Mans, the manta ray–shaped Porsches had simply stretched out and run away, out all on their own, single file, through the night and into day. In the hellish traffic of Daytona, with positions shuffling several times a lap in the draft, and multicar crashes possible at any given second, well, a sweep was sheer fantasy.

On Thursday, before the start of the 125-mile qualifying races, came a formal, all-star outpouring of support for Rick Hendrick. Roger Penske, Joe Gibbs, Bill France Jr., and even Hendrick Motorsports's archrival, Dale Earnhardt, all held a joint press conference. Formally, the purpose was to appeal for support for a bone marrow transplant network Hendrick was initiating—he had even turned his illness into charitable work. Tacitly, the gathering was a major display of moral support for Hendrick in his legal troubles as well.

But once the race started, Earnhardt's only concern was his own oh-for-eighteen agenda. The Gordon boy and the mission for Rick Hendrick notwithstanding, Earnhardt was bent on getting this thing done and over. Whatever it took.

And that would lead, late in the 1997 Daytona 500, to the most profound confrontation since Richard Petty and David Pearson in 1976. For supremacy among NASCAR drivers, for a few seconds, it would be the grizzled badass Intimidator versus Wonder Boy. Nose-to-nose. Door-to-door. To be determined by a knockout.

With eleven laps to go, Bill Elliott led, with Earnhardt second and Gordon third. First, Gordon and Earnhardt had to fight it out for the privilege of running up on Elliott and pressuring him.

Going into Turn 1, Gordon charged low and got underneath Earnhardt. Side by side they flew into Turn 2. Earnhardt, on the outside, wouldn't yield an inch. But Gordon had a plan. Earlier, he had noticed Earnhardt's car "pushing up"—skating high—as he exited Turn 2 and entered the backstretch. Gordon knew that if he hung beside Earnhardt, then Earnhardt would come out of Turn 2 looking at nothing but white concrete retaining wall on the outside, and—if prudent—would back off and let Gordon take second place.

But as they flew out of the second turn, Dale Earnhardt was, by God, Dale Earnhardt, and now for half a second here he was face-to-face with solid concrete at 190 miles an hour, and that wall could just kiss his ass, 'cause he was coming anyway, wasn't about to let that right foot twitch, let alone lift.

Masterfully as usual, Earnhardt managed to hit the wall with only a glancing blow and bounce off, and slam Gordon's car broadside-to-broadside.

Gordon's Number 24 wiggled, but that was all—a twitch-twitch of the steering wheel by Gordon and he was straight again, and gone. Earnhardt hadn't the lightning touch to snatch the black Number 3 back straight before the onrushing Dale Jarrett nailed him, turned him sideways, and right behind Jarrett came Ernie Irvan, unavoidably plowing under Earnhardt and turning him over, sending the fierce black 3 car tumbling down the backstretch.

Gordon saw it in his mirror. On Gordon's radio channel there was a moaning cry, a sort of whimpered "Ohhh-hohhh" of concern for Earnhardt, just before the channel went dead.

There should have been a boxing announcer present that day to announce, essentially, NASCAR's own "New…heavyweight CHAM-pion of the WORLD…JEFF…GOR-RRRRDON!"

Because that is what happened. Whatever the Gordon haters and the Earnhardt worshippers might ever say, that is what happened in a total of maybe six seconds, between Turn 1 and the backstretch, on the 190th lap of the Daytona 500 on February 16, 1997. Many in the Earnhardt cult will tell you to this day that Gordon hit Earnhardt and knocked him into the wall. That simply wasn't so. Earnhardt bounced off the wall and into Gordon.

Dale Earnhardt was, beyond doubt, one of the four or five best NASCAR drivers ever. And he was *the* best of his era. But now his era was over, tumbling down the backstretch at Daytona, crumpling.

Earnhardt for nearly three years—since Gordon's first Winston Cup victory at Charlotte in May of 1994—had teased and publicly mocked Gordon, propagated the torturous nickname Wonder Boy, and, who knows, perhaps even played a part in taunting Gordon away from attachments to John and Carol Bickford.

And out of Turn 2, Earnhardt had driven up against the wall in a contest of testicular size, for a man-to-boy showdown, and it had turned out man-to-man.

And Earnhardt had lost. By a knockout.

Oh, he made a grandiose show of saving face. Sitting in the ambulance, he saw that when his car was righted by the wreckers, none of its four tires was flat, and so he leapt from the ambulance and climbed back in and drove the crumpled black Number 3 slowly around the apron to finish the race.

Rarely does a NASCAR driver take blame for a wreck upon himself. It's nearly always the other guy's fault. Even following that standard procedure, all Earnhardt could bring himself to complain about was that "Gordon got a little impatient," and even that was ludicrous from the man who for so many seasons had run over, under, around, and through opponents, anytime he chose. No one howls like a bully with a bloody nose. To Earnhardt's credit, he didn't howl very loudly after Jeff Gordon kicked his ass—fairly, squarely, straight up, nose-to-nose.

Under the ensuing caution, Gordon switched to radio frequencies that linked him with his teammates, Terry Labonte and Ricky Craven.

Except for Elliott, who was still leading, Earnhardt's crash had taken out the only other non-Hendrick contenders for the win, Jarrett and Irvan. And so as Gordon cruised behind Elliott under the caution caused by Earnhardt, he looked in his mirror and there magically appeared, up close and cozy behind Gordon, the cars of Labonte and Craven.

"I'm sitting there on the restart, and I've got Bill Elliott in front of me and my two teammates behind me," Gordon would say after the race. "That was a sign. A good sign.

"I switched to Terry's channel and I told him, 'Terry, it would be pretty neat if we could get these three Hendrick cars by Elliott.' Terry said, 'Yeah. That'd be neat. I'll be with you.'

"I turned to Ricky's channel and said, 'Terry's going with me. Who are you going with?' Ricky said, 'I'm going with you.'"

This wasn't Bill Elliott's first rodeo. "With three Hendrick cars behind you, you ain't got a chance," he said afterward. "I was dead meat, and I knew it. It was just a matter of when and where."

The *when* was the 194th lap. The *where* was Turn 1.

Elliott was still ahead, but Gordon was being shoved along by enormous blasts of pushed air from his teammates, lined up behind him. Labonte and Craven pushed Gordon aerodynamically to just enough momentum that he could rocket down to the inside of Elliott, and then Labonte and Craven peeled off like a pair of fighter pilots and went high on the banking to distract Elliott in the other direction.

"I had a ton of momentum from Terry and Ricky," Gordon said. "Bill knew I was going low. But I kept going lower and lower to see just how low he wanted to go to block me. Hey: I would have gone down by the people cooking out in the infield if that's what it took. I was going by, no matter what."

As Labonte and Craven veered right, "Bill didn't know who to block—them or me," Gordon said.

All three Hendrick pilots blew by Elliott on both sides, and that was that—especially when another multicar pileup on Lap 196 caused the race to conclude under caution, allowing the Hendrick cars to parade one-two-three, in formation, nose-to-tail, just as the Porsches had paraded at Le Mans.

When the race was over, they got Rick Hendrick on the phone.

"Hey, boss?" Ray Evernham said. "You said all we had to do was finish one-two-three in the Daytona 500. What's my next job?"

Said a clearly weakened Hendrick, "You're going to have to run the dealerships."

40

DON'T CRY OUT LOUD

*T*wenty times Dale Earnhardt had tried. Nineteen times he'd failed, often astoundingly, sometimes magnificently. And so it was an old man who climbed out of Earnhardt's car in Victory Lane on Sunday, February 15, 1998, fifty years to the day after the first NASCAR race on the sands of Daytona Beach. The cobalt eyes were weary. The hard face was ashen, suddenly lined with wrinkles beyond his forty-six years.

"How 'bout it, boys? Think I'm gonna make it?" a rakish young man had said on a balmy winter morning in 1979.

Now it was as if all the sorrow of those nineteen losses had deluged him at once. As he'd driven down the pit road to Victory Lane, virtually every member of every team had lined up to slap hands with him as he drove by. It was the most monumental salute in the history of American motor racing—not even when A. J. Foyt won the Indy 500 for a then-unprecedented fourth time, in 1977, had there been such an emotional outpouring for a winner as he brought his car in.

"So, who's gonna win the race, Earnhardt?"

"Me—I ain't got enough sense to lose."

Earnhardt drove into the infield grass in front of the pit road, and across the enormous painted word "Daytona," he did the most artistic "doughnuts" ever by a victor—he spun and whirled his car until the tires gouged out of the grass a gigantic "3" in earthen colors.

And then in Victory Lane all the heartbreak came in one last crashing wave, then ebbed, and an overwhelming relief flowed. Not only had the most overdue victory in NASCAR's fifty-year history finally arrived, but Earnhardt had broken a personal fifty-nine-race losing streak on the Winston Cup tour overall.

"I've got this fear, see, that one day me and ol' Waltrip are gonna be sittin' on a front porch, old, retired, rockin' in chairs, and I say, 'Darrell, you know, I won seven Winston Cup championships—same as Richard Petty. Now Darrell, I don't b'lieve you won but three, did you?'

"And he says, 'Naw, Earnhardt, I didn't win but three championships. But I did win the Daytona 500 once. I don't b'lieve you ever won the Daytona 500, did you, Earnhardt?'

"And I have to say, 'Naw, I reckon I didn't.' "

By early evening Earnhardt was in his prime again, the color was back and the wrinkles were gone, the eyes no longer weary. On his way up to the press box for the winner's interview he had coveted for so long, some fan handed him a little stuffed monkey. He tucked it down the back of the collar of his driving uniform, and proceeded upward.

When he arrived he stomped, with an attention-demanding thud, onto the interview podium.

"I'm here," he crowed. "And I've finally got that goddamn *monkey* off my back!"

And he flung the stuffed animal into the crowd of reporters.

The little toy monkey, once white, was dingy and worn. But Earnhardt, the ninth-grade dropout from the Mill Hill town of Kannapolis, North Carolina, was youthful and cocky—*relieved*—again. He could still do this. Thank God, he could still do this. He announced, rather than predicted, that this would be the springboard to his unprecedented eighth Winston Cup championship, which would be won that year. (That of course was overexuberance, for it didn't happen.)

He had won $1,059,105—at the time the richest winner's share in the history of NASCAR. But that was so beside the point on this day that he cracked, "What's the extra five dollars for?"

*T*he record books show that Jeff Gordon's engine failed with three laps to go and he wound up sixteenth in the 1998 Daytona 500. The truth is that Gordon had the race won, and then lost it, à la Earnhardt all those years. Gordon started twenty-ninth, but gained ground at a lightning pace from the start, snatched the lead from Earnhardt on Lap 59, and proceeded to "check out," as racers say when a driver goes up front and drives away—has the field covered. By the halfway point, Gordon was so dominant that he appeared to be a lock.

But just after Lap 120—not even Gordon was sure of the moment—he hit a chunk of rubber from a tire off the car of Dale Jarrett. That damaged the air dam below the nose of Gordon's car just enough to throw off the handling and force him to strain the engine the rest of the way.

Other than that, Gordon probably would have won his second straight Daytona 500, and Dale Earnhardt would have been oh-for-twenty.

But hey: Earnhardt had lost several Daytona 500s by such nuances—pieces of metal on the track, slight miscalculations on fuel, and once his albatross had even shrunk itself to the size of a seagull and flown into his path on the backstretch, damaging his bodywork and ruining his day.

Now it was Gordon's turn to feel how fleeting dominance can be.

On Lap 123, Earnhardt blew past the slowing Gordon and into the lead. One more time, the black Number 3 was the strongest car on Daytona International Speedway. But Earnhardt had been there so many times before. This time, at last, "It all played into my hands in the last few laps," Earnhardt said afterward.

With twenty-seven laps to go, Penske-Kranefuss Ford teammates Jeremy Mayfield and Rusty Wallace were hooked up and preparing to draft past Earnhardt when John Andretti and Robert Pressley crashed together, bringing out a caution. All the leaders pitted under the yellow, and Earnhardt got back onto the track first. I remembered hearing Gordon's plaintive radio transmission earlier in the day during a round of pit stops: "Damn! If that Three ain't speedin' off the pit road, I don't know what is!" For safety, NASCAR now required speed limits on the pit road, usually about 55 mph, and officials used radar guns to enforce it. But pit road speed checks had become very similar to ball-and-strike calls in baseball. Could NASCAR—on this twentieth try by Earnhardt, on this fiftieth anniversary of the first NASCAR race—be giving Earnhardt a little bit larger strike zone to pitch? Perhaps. But it was a judgment call, and not blatant massaging of the situation.

The previous year, Earnhardt had balked at the notion of adding a teammate, Californian Mike Skinner. Earnhardt was an old-schooler who, despite the success of Hendrick Motorsports and Roush Racing's multicar teams, still didn't believe in fragmenting the effort. But Richard Childress had forced the issue and hired Skinner. Earnhardt had groused about it through '97, but now, suddenly, when the caution period ended with twenty-three laps left, Earnhardt was glad to have a teammate. Skinner tucked in on Earnhardt's bumper and gave him an aerodynamic catapult out front, away from the pack of pursuers—Mayfield, Wallace, Bobby Labonte, and the struggling Gordon—just as the race went green again.

From there, for once, Earnhardt was able to keep the late-lap battles in his mirror. "People say, 'Did you hear things in the car [imagined rattles or other precursors of mechanical failures]? Did you wonder who was going to pass you? I wasn't thinking about what could happen. I was thinking about what I was doing and what I had to do. I was working to keep the race car up front. I was working to do that until somebody turned me over or I got to the finish line, one of the two. I got to the finish line without anybody turning me over."

Just behind him in the waning laps, Gordon and Wallace rubbed broadside...Mayfield tapped Earnhardt from behind...Gordon's engine blew with three laps to go...Bobby Labonte drove high around Mayfield into second place...Labonte was coming fast, as Earnhardt had stalked the leaders so often...and then Labonte's onslaught was aborted by a final caution with a lap and a half to go. John Andretti was entangled in another wreck, this time with Jimmy Spencer and Lake Speed.

"I saw it in my mirror," Earnhardt said of the final wreck, "and I knew when I saw the white flag and the yellow displayed together that I was going to win the race if nothing happened to my car (such as a shredded tire as in the Daytona 499 of 1990) before I got back to the start-finish line."

When it was over, Earnhardt at first admitted to "crying a little bit" when he knew the race was won. Then he grunted, groused, recanted: "I don't think I really cried. My eyes watered up a little bit."

Mustn't cry, old man. Old quintessential badass.

*F*requency 467.0625 was, by now, the most listened-to radio channel in NASCAR. The Jeff Gordon–Ray Evernham show was eavesdropped upon by every good crew chief, every time the Number 24 turned a wheel on a track, and, during races, by tens of thousands of fans on their scanners. Even the Gordon haters. Especially the Gordon haters.

Competitors were doing intelligence work, trying to get a step ahead, or at least keep up with, the strategies of the most efficient team on the tour. Some teams had individuals assigned to do nothing but monitor frequency 467.0625. Gordon haters were listening for rays of hope—signs of trouble.

Silence on the channel was terrifying—if Gordon wasn't complaining, the car usually was working perfectly.

But they all got a kick out of Gordon's complaining, grousing, even whining to Evernham on the radio. He became notorious for it.

"I can't see a thing!" he whined at Atlanta in the spring of '98, after the crew removed a plastic, peel-off windshield coating sheet. Each sheet was meant to take the sandblasting and oil-smearing that goes on during a race, and then be peeled off, leaving the driver with a clear view. But this one didn't work—it left a residue of glue that left Gordon flying virtually blind.

"The right rear's getting ready to go!" he might howl. Or, "I'm big-time loose!"

And Evernham was constantly coaching, calming, cajoling—and occasionally becoming exasperated, as when Gordon kept harping on an overheating problem on his way to winning the '98 Pepsi 400 at Daytona: "Ten-four, bud. We'll fix it next stop. Now think about what *you* are doing."

What rival crew chiefs relished most was learning that Gordon had lots of complaints but few, if any, solutions.

"I'm not sure Jeff gives Ray a lot of good feedback," said Larry McReynolds, then Dale Earnhardt's crew chief. "Jeff just tells him what the car is doing. I've never, in all the times I've monitored them, heard Jeff say, specifically, 'You need a heavier right front,' or 'We need this,' or 'We need that.' Jeff will just say the car's tight or loose."

Inside Dale Jarrett's hauler one rainy afternoon, crew chief Todd Parrott pondered.

"I think Jeff Gordon's a great race car driver—probably the best in this garage area right now," he said. "But I think without Ray, Jeff's probably just a Top Ten driver."

To be sure, Evernham was the most meticulous, and yet aggressive, crew chief NASCAR had ever known.

"He don't half-ass anything," said Parrott. "He pays attention to every detail of that race car."

More and more, the most pervasive hypothetical question in NASCAR was becoming, How well would Jeff Gordon do without Ray Evernham?

But the sage Waddell Wilson, by now past his prime as a crew chief, would observe that Evernham had another vital ingredient going for him: "A driver who's fearless and has a ton of talent."

Bobby Allison, still as astute an observer as you'd find in the garage, believed Gordon's whining on the radio was faked, to throw off the competition.

"I think," said Allison, "he sits on the side of the bed at night and goes, 'Wa, wa, wa, this car's too loose!...How does that sound, Brooke?...Wa, wa, wa, this car's pushing big-time! How does that sound, Brooke?'"

"No, it's real," said John Bickford, who knew perhaps better than anyone. "Jeff has had a temper since he was a little kid. He used to get into fights. There are times when he just needs to be calmed down."

Channel 467.0625 was, media people were learning, the only place where you could hear Gordon saying anything remotely controversial or even undiplomatic.

"You'll never maneuver Jeff into a controversial answer to a question," Bickford told me. "He can process a gigabyte of information a second. I trained him that way. While he was

ming up through racing, we'd watch Winston Cup races on
evision. If a driver was angry and blurted something con-
oversial on TV, I'd say, 'Now you wait and see. He's going
be in trouble next week for that.' And Jeff would follow
hat happened afterward."

Media people grew more and more annoyed. The public
ght *think* it wants diplomacy and tact, but it really wants
ndor from sports figures—indeed, colorful candor, with
me rough edges, as when Earnhardt got "that goddamn
onkey off my back!" And so reporters are, above all, inter-
ted in the true feelings of sports figures.

Great driver, cooperative with the media, but too artful a
dger on controversial incidents, such as his last-lap slam-
ng match with Jeff Burton in the 1997 Southern 500 at
rlington—that was Gordon's rap with the media. While
rton admitted up front that "To be honest with you, I tried
knock the shit out of him," Gordon namby-pambied
ough the winners' interview, maintaining that he'd just
en focused on winning the race and the Winston Million
nus that happened to go with it.

He was becoming too good to be true, and the media
uldn't crack him, and that probably exacerbated the public
noyance with Wonder Boy.

He seemed, said one observer, like "A little robot with a
percomputer inside."

41

THE BEST THERE'S
EVER BEEN

After 134 laps, Jeff Gordon keyed his radio and spoke matter-of-factly into the microphone. "We've got no friends out here," he said.

"Yeah," Ray Evernham replied. "But you knew that."

No friends? That was a masterpiece of understatement, from a twenty-seven-year-old man who had just driven a 335-mile masterpiece just to defend himself, to stay in the 1999 Daytona 500 to this point.

No friends? Jeff Gordon had forty *enemies* out there. As for his own teammates, Terry Labonte had been caught up in an early crash, and Wally Dallenbach was running too poorly to get close enough to Gordon to help. Gordon was being tag-teamed by other teams, and gangs of teams. He had been shoved, squeezed, blocked, buffeted, gang-passed, and left hanging out of the drafting lines.

For a decade now at Daytona, due to the combination of draft and power-stifling restrictor plates that kept cars tightly bunched, it had been considered virtually impossible to get to the front alone. You had to have help—those enormous aero-

ynamic pushes and pulls from lines of cars behind and in
ont.

This time, Gordon not only had gotten no help, but he had
een relentlessly attacked from all sides, sometimes at the
te of several times a lap. Several cars would line up behind
m as if they were going to "push" him past somebody.
hen they'd suddenly peel off, fall in behind the guy Gordon
as trying to pass, and leave Gordon hung out by himself so
at he would drop back eight or ten positions at a time in the
afting lines. Blatantly, on this day, it was Everybody versus
ff Gordon.

When you have emerged as a typhoon upon the NASCAR
cords; when you have won more races (forty-three) by age
venty-seven than Richard Petty had by age twenty-eight
orty); when you have won the Winston Cup in three of the
st four seasons; and when you are coming off a year in
hich you tied Petty's modern-era record of thirteen wins in
single season...well...you come to Daytona to open the '99
ason and you step into a storm of mass jealousy.

You know those old thirties movies where a gang of
reet-tough kids would form a big circle around one little kid
ho had offended them and start shoving him and punching
m back and forth within the circle? That was what was hap-
ning to Jeff Gordon. Except that the fists weighed 3,400
unds each, and were flying at 190 miles an hour—and yet
ey couldn't hurt him.

Many legions of fans have chosen to despise Gordon.
ey think he's too successful, too rich, too young. They
ink he has always had it too easy—they never saw him
eping in the back of the truck as John Bickford drove the
ernight hauls from Pennsylvania out to Iowa or from Indi-
a down to Florida. They resent his Tom Cruise looks—
en you sit in the grandstands you can see why the men boo

him thunderously: It is because their wives and girlfriends are all swooning over Gordon, crying, "Ohhhh, baaaaaay-beeeee!" during driver introductions, and the men resent the hell out of it, so they boo. He does not fit the rough-hewn mold of the classic NASCAR driver; he does not butcher the English language. One key racing figure at General Motors has a pretty solid theory about why Jeff Gordon is booed so much: Despite NASCAR's spread in popularity into the youth of mainstream America, those people can't get tickets to races. The majority of tickets are held by people whose average age is fortyish, and who have been renewing their tickets at the same tracks for many years. Fans often live vicariously through drivers, and identify closest with the older ones. "They can't identify with Jeff or fantasize about being him," says the GM guy, "because they're already way older than he is."

Former National Basketball Association star Charles Barkley, a self-proclaimed "dedicated Jeff Gordon fan," once expressed his exasperation with the Gordon haters: "We live in a very warped society. We're always talking about how we want athletes who are role models—who are never in trouble, and are the best at what they do. And now we've got one, and we treat him like crap. It's absurd. People are just nuts."

*A*lready it was the loneliest drive ever witnessed at Daytona. And so far, it was the best.

Sixty-six laps, or 165 miles, to go—and the worst, by far, was yet to come. And so was the best. By far.

As the laps ticked down on the towering pylon scoreboards, the jostling, the bumping, the hanging out of Jeff Gordon continued without mercy. Then, during a caution with twenty-five laps to go, word came from his crew that someone wanted to be his friend:

"Dale wants to work with you."

Earnhardt.

"I'll help him all the way up to second place," Gordon
plied. "Tell him I'd *love* to work with him."

Earnhardt?

The head-honcho bully of them all? The very symbol of
ti-Gordonism?

Earnhardt.

Yeah. Right, Wonder Boy.

When the caution period ended, Gordon was all set to
ok up with Earnhardt, but then he looked around and won-
red where that big bad black car went.

"They dropped the green flag and he took off," Gordon
ould say later. "I got stuck back there with some other guys,
d I had to make some moves I wasn't really thrilled about.
was having to go between cars and make it three wide, with
e in the middle. I saw Earnhardt getting out of there, and I
dn't want him to get away."

Finally, with fifteen laps to go, Gordon caught up to Earn-
rdt and settled in on his bumper. They were running third
d fourth. Rusty Wallace was leading, with his teammate,
remy Mayfield, running second.

Earnhardt and Gordon, drafting together, forced their way
front of Mayfield and drew a bead on Wallace. Earnhardt's
ammate, Mike Skinner, was sneaking up from behind to try
catapult Earnhardt out front, just as he'd done in '98.

And at that point, there began the most hair-raising,
mbfounding series of moves ever in the Daytona 500. Be-
use the moves were so magnificent, they didn't cause a
ash, and therefore would create nothing like the sensations
Richard Petty and David Pearson in '76, or Cale Yarbor-
gh and Donnie Allison in '79. But they were better than
ything done on those landmark days.

The developing pattern appeared to be that Gordon would
llow Earnhardt past Wallace, that Skinner would also blow
Wallace in the fray—and, if you were thinking out the

chess game three or four moves ahead, Skinner would then gang up with Earnhardt against Gordon.

But instead of following, Gordon suddenly darted inside Earnhardt. With that move, he instantaneously dropped himself in front of Skinner—and thereby stole the aerodynamic push from Skinner that was supposed to go to Earnhardt! So Gordon powered in front of Earnhardt with a push from Earnhardt's own teammate.

With that same charge, Gordon shot down alongside Wallace, going for the lead. But dead ahead of Gordon as he swept low, onto the apron, limped the slower, lapped car of Ricky Rudd.

"Rusty was doing everything he should," Gordon would say afterward. "He ran me down low. There's a lot of apron there, and I utilized as much of it as I could. Then I got down there and saw Ricky Rudd running real slow, and I thought, Oh, Ricky! I hope you see me coming, because I'm coming *real* fast. It felt like I was coming up on him at a thousand miles an hour, and I was getting ready to hold on tight. I was going to have to get on my brakes real hard, or—I don't know what else could have happened.

"Just a split second before I got to Ricky, he moved over a little bit."

And Gordon had an inkling of a gap in which to pop back up in front of Wallace.

But no sooner had Gordon edged ahead than here came Skinner, far to the outside, on the other side of Wallace. Now it was Gordon and Skinner side by side for the lead, with Earnhardt rushing up to interfere.

But Gordon dropped down in front of Earnhardt and this time stole the push from Earnhardt that was reserved for Skinner. Twice now in two blinks of an eye, Earnhardt and Skinner had tried to gang up on Gordon, and twice now he had used them against each other. It was the unintended push from Earnhardt that put Gordon in the lead for keeps.

Gordon's moves had come and gone before the naked eye like the jagged path of lightning across the sky. Zig-zag-zig.

That sort of move, almost right up the rear of Rudd's car to get past Wallace, in my mind at that moment, would have even been attempted by only one other driver on the planet: Michael Schumacher of Formula One. After thinking about it a while, the difference dawned on me: Schumacher wouldn't have made it. He would have crashed.

Having watched Schumacher, and the late Ayrton Senna, and the late Ronnie Peterson, and the late Jochen Rindt, and the great *Le Professeur,* Alain Prost, and Dale Earnhardt, and David Pearson, and A. J. Foyt, and Cale Yarborough, and Darrell Waltrip, and whole lineages of Pettys, Allisons, Andrettis, and Unsers, it occurred to me at that moment on February 14, 1999, that Jeffrey Michael Gordon just might be the best racing driver, in any type of car, anywhere, that I had ever seen.

With eight laps left, Earnhardt tucked in on Gordon's bumper and they took off to duel it out. What was brewing was a rematch of the '97 toe-to-toe fight for the heavyweight championship of NASCAR. But it didn't happen. Earnhardt never even got a fender alongside Gordon. He followed helplessly the rest of the way.

"I was looking for some help from the Thirty-one [Skinner] or the Twenty-eight [Kenny Irwin]," Earnhardt said afterward. "But they got to racing each other."

There was no one to push Earnhardt past Gordon—but even if there had been, Gordon likely would have found a way to steal that aerodynamic shove too.

And so in the final analysis, Earnhardt admitted, "I got beat."

"I felt about the loneliest out there today that I have ever felt," Gordon said when it was over. "There were times when they [packs of drafting cars] were right behind me and I thought, Oh, yeah, they're going to give me a push right on by whoever I was trying to pass. Then *pheeooo!* They'd just go away. They'd push me enough to help me get side by side with a car, and then they'd make sure I was left out there by myself.

"But you know what? I don't expect any different. I really don't."

The loneliness, he said, felt "almost like an honor."

42

EBB

Rick Hendrick had been able to visit his team in the garage area during Daytona 500 week of 1999, but, weak from his treatments, he'd gone home to North Carolina to watch the race on television. He had plea-bargained with the federal prosecutors, pleading guilty to one of the long list of what his friends felt were trumped-up charges, and received a sentence of one year of home confinement, which had now been completed.

"They say problems build character," Hendrick said in the garage at Daytona. "I ought to have a lot of character right now. There were days when I thought I was going to die any minute. I'm not out of the woods yet, but I'm a long way toward being well."

Three years after his awful December of 1996, near Christmastime in 1999, Rick Hendrick's doctors would declare him in full remission from leukemia.

But first, Hendrick must endure another ordeal: the breakup of the magnificent "24 team," as they were called in tones of awe throughout NASCAR.

Ray Evernham was ambitious to run his own team—

totally. By September of 1999, according to sources deep inside Hendrick Motorsports, Rick Hendrick had mapped a plan whereby Evernham would become vice president of the company, with authority over all three units—Jeff Gordon's, Terry Labonte's, and, for 2000, Jerry Nadeau's.

It wasn't enough.

The lightning bolt came from far beyond left field—it came all the way from Stuttgart, Germany, from the descendent company of the car manufacturers that had first dominated on the beach at Ormond-Daytona, back at the previous turn of a century.

Daimler-Benz had merged with Chrysler Corporation in 1998 to form DaimlerChrysler. The automotive giant was already well represented in Formula One, but that didn't impact the U.S. market much. DaimlerChrysler was heading for NASCAR, under the brand Richard Petty had made synonymous with racing in the 1970s, Dodge.

To head the effort, targeted for debut in the Daytona 500 of 2001, DaimlerChrysler wanted the best NASCAR man alive: Ray Evernham.

Insiders said Hendrick, when he got the news, was as angry as they'd ever seen him. Evernham was in the first year of a seven-year contract that bound him to Hendrick through 2006. But the good guy in Hendrick—some believed too nice a guy for his own good—came out as usual, and he and Evernham negotiated an end to the contract, and hugged when they parted.

Now the hypothetical question roared to the fore of reality:

How would Jeff Gordon do without Ray Evernham?

Gordon responded by winning the first two races out of the box without Evernham—at Martinsville Speedway in Virginia, and at Lowe's Motor Speedway near Charlotte—with engineer Brian Whitesell, Evernham's former "offensive coordinator," as interim crew chief. But there would be no more wins as the 24 team continued to fragment in the coming months.

Hendrick moved quickly to sign over a piece of the company to Gordon as part of a lifetime contract. But then, at season's end, five Sunday "over-the-wall" crewmen from Evernham's celebrated Rainbow Warriors jumped as a group to Robert Yates Racing, to pit Dale Jarrett's cars in 2000.

Replacing the pit crewmen wouldn't be much of a problem—Andy Papathanasieu was still at Hendrick, and could recruit five new athletes, train them, drill them, choreograph their every move.

Replacing Evernham—there lay the monumental problem. During the off-season, Whitesell was promoted to team manager, and Gordon handpicked crew chief Robbie Loomis away from car owner Richard Petty and his driver, John Andretti.

But for the long term, Petty Enterprises secretly stood to be compensated for the loss of Loomis. It would get the expertise of Ray Evernham.

Quietly, behind the scenes, Richard Petty, who had left Dodge in 1978, negotiated a reunion for 2001. Petty Enterprises had plummeted from dominance for the past two decades, but had a precious commodity to offer:

Teenager Adam Petty, Richard's grandson, was showing flashes of potential as the next great Petty driver. Adam would be the first fourth-generation driver ever in major motor racing. Around NASCAR, it was said that the genes had skipped a generation—from champions Lee and Richard Petty, past Kyle (who had never been as intense or focused as the rest of the bloodline, and had only eight Winston Cup wins to show for twenty years of driving), to Adam.

Kyle had loved music, motorcycles, and girls more than

race cars as a teenager. "Adam is focused," Richard Petty said.

On an autumn afternoon in 1998, as Richard and Adam Petty walked on Richard's lawn at Level Cross, talking intently, their lanky frames almost joined at the hip, Kyle Petty watched them through a kitchen window, then turned to his mother, Lynda, and said, "Richard Petty's finally got the son he never had."

Kyle said it with no bitterness whatsoever toward his son—indeed, he and Adam were, Kyle would say often, "best friends."

"Everybody knows," said Adam, "that my dad is just a big old kid in a man's body."

It was becoming more and more apparent that Kyle's place in the history of Petty Enterprises was as nurturer of Adam.

Adam won his first superspeedway race, a 100-miler at Lowe's Motor Speedway in October of '98, with some moves that frightened all family members present—blazing past other cars where there appeared to be insufficient room between them and the concrete retaining wall, or lapped traffic. But he was on his way. He was eighteen.

Late in 1999, the enormous package began to take shape: Evernham would lead the research and development, would field a two-car team of his own, and would share all technology with a three-car Petty Enterprises team that in 2001 would include Adam and Kyle Petty, and John Andretti. Evernham's team would be backed to the tune of a reported $20 million a year by Dodge; Petty Enterprises Dodges would be at least as well-funded with outside sponsorships, mainly with U.S. Sprint (for Adam) and General Mills (for Andretti). The stakes got so high that Richard Petty's long-time sponsor, STP, couldn't—or wouldn't—keep up with the bidding.

Kyle's career had largely been ruined in the bud by a rush

to the big time—he'd gone into Winston Cup too young, he felt, at age nineteen. He would not subject Adam to such pressure—Adam would be brought along slowly, methodically, through the Busch Series.

The new dawn of the Petty dynasty was scheduled, signed, and sealed to break in the Daytona 500 of 2001.

*N*ASCAR 2000" was the corporate marketing label given to the fifty-third year of NASCAR racing. It was a hard season.

At the beginning of the year, Bill France Jr. revealed that he had cancer, but would add only that it was "treatable," and wouldn't reveal the exact nature of the disease. Rumors were rampant that France, a heavy smoker for most of his life, might have lung cancer and that it was being kept hush-hush due to the long-running Winston sponsorship of NASCAR's top series. More reliable sources, close to him, indicated that the cancer had at least begun in his prostate—where it might have spread, they didn't know. France was just that secretive about personal matters—always had been.

What was clear was that Billy France was regularly undergoing treatment, and was more and more conspicuously absent from races. His son, third-generation Brian France, a senior vice president of NASCAR, was more concerned with the marketing and communications end of the business than day-to-day direction of the competition. For the first time ever, a France was not clearly and solely at the helm of NASCAR.

Vice president and chief operating officer Mike Helton, savvy, level-headed, rational, up through the ranks—but without France blood to give him unquestioned authority among the racers—was now in charge. He faced an unenviable year.

Dale Jarrett became only the fourth driver to win three or

more Daytona 500s, joining Richard Petty, Cale Yarborough, and Bobby Allison. But Jarrett was the victor in the dullest 500 in thirty-five years. There were only nine lead changes, the fewest since the seven of 1965, when Fred Lorenzen had led the Ford parade during the boycott by Chrysler Corporation over the hemi engine.

Ford and Chevrolet produced new racing body styles for 2000, and at Daytona the Ford Taurus design proved vastly superior, aerodynamically, to the new Chevrolet Monte Carlo. To exacerbate the disparity, NASCAR had stopped teams from using their own custom-made shock absorbers for the Daytona 500, and began doling out its own uniform shocks. They were too springy in front. They allowed air, rushing underneath the cars at high speed, to lift up the front ends, making the cars hard to turn. The effect was especially profound on the Monte Carlos. NASCAR would change the rule after only one race, but not before Jarrett led a Ford sweep of the first five positions.

Dale Earnhardt and Jeff Gordon, in their fitful new Monte Carlos, were blatantly absent as factors in the race. Neither led a single lap. Earnhardt struggled to a twenty-first-place finish, Gordon to a miserable thirty-fourth. In a foreshadowing of the long haul to come without the meticulous Evernham supervising preparation of the cars, Gordon's Chevy developed an oil leak early in the race and dropped five laps behind, hopelessly out of contention, in the pits.

Life without Evernham would be so hard that Gordon would not win a race in 2000 until the DieHard 500 at Talladega on April 16. And at last the boos would subside a bit, as even the Gordon haters took pity on the driver whose talent was buried under the ills of the misbegotten Monte Carlo and the recurring glitches in the car's preparation and setup in Evernham's absence.

Dale Earnhardt Jr. would emerge as the charismatic prodigy of Winston Cup. But within days after "Little E" got his second victory, at Richmond on May 6, to become the first multiple winner of the season, NASCAR suffered what seemed its blackest blow of modern times, but would turn out to be only the beginning of a dark sequence of tragedies.

It was on May 12, the Friday of Mother's Day weekend, on what had started as a routine practice lap for a Busch race, that Adam Petty crashed into the concrete retaining wall in the third turn at New Hampshire International Speedway, at perhaps 150 miles per hour.

And at that moment, everything the Petty dynasty had planned "for the next twenty years," said Richard Petty, "just evaporated."

Adam was dead at age nineteen. "At first," said Richard Petty, "I thought, He got killed in a race car. And he was in a race car because of me." But, watching local Greensboro, North Carolina, television news the night before Adam's memorial service, the King learned that two teenagers had drowned in a nearby lake, and two men had been killed in a private-plane crash in the area. "And I said, 'O.K.'"

Young people died tragically in all sorts of ways, he decided—and the King had always been fatalistic. Adam's time had happened to come in a race car.

Adam's younger brother, Austin, eighteen, had no interest in racing. Kyle, brokenhearted, would struggle to continue to race, too old now, at age forty, to ever hope to become the second King.

Fifty-one years the Pettys had raced, without a driving fatality in the family. Their fortunes had seemed the opposite of the Allisons', until April of 2000, when patriarch Lee Petty died of complications from a stomach aneurysm. And then in May the Petty dynasty collapsed for the ages.

Just eight weeks later, almost to the hour, on July 7, in almost the same spot in the same turn at New Hampshire, Kenny Irwin, who'd been Winston Cup rookie of the year in 1998, crashed and died.

Mike Helton, as the vice president now in charge of NASCAR—indeed, at season's end he would be named president, succeeding Billy France—turned his attention and concern to search for ways to prevent further fatalities. Had the throttles hung on the cars of Adam Petty and Kenny Irwin—the accelerator pedals stuck to the floor, the cars barreling into the wall at unrelenting speed? Perhaps. NASCAR mandated engine kill switches on the steering wheel, within reach of the driver's thumb, in addition to the "on-off" toggle on the dashboard that was hard to reach instantaneously in an emergency.

There is an old superstition in NASCAR, all the way up to Bill France Jr. himself, that bad things happen in threes. The third tragedy of 2000 was Tony Roper, thirty-five, a little-known driver in NASCAR's Craftsman Truck Series. During a night race at Texas Motor Speedway on October 14, Roper's truck slammed the wall head-on, and he was gravely injured. He died the following day of massive head and neck injuries. Media coverage was not nearly as heavy as it had been for Adam Petty and Kenny Irwin. But it was a third fatality in a pattern, and so there began rumblings of media scrutiny of NASCAR safety in general.

Somehow, some way, with Mike Helton in charge, NASCAR must regroup and come again, as it had so many times before. Perhaps the tide would flow, flood again in 2001, with the outset of a dramatic new television package, six years for $2.7 billion from Fox, NBC, and Turner. Promotion of NASCAR would be wider, more intensive than ever before, and might send the sport surging again to yet uncharted levels.

Surely things would look brighter next year. Surely this season's outbreak of death was a bottoming-out of NASCAR's spike of bad luck. Surely this was but an ebb tide, which, as on the timeless shores of Daytona Beach, would be followed inevitably by the flow.

But flood tide would be an awful deluge.

43

FADE TO BLACK

February 17, 2001. Daytona 500 eve. Dale Earnhardt's last one. Nobody knew that, even sensed it. Except maybe Dale Earnhardt.

A business meeting was going on inside Earnhardt's million-dollar motor coach, inside the high-fenced and heavily guarded drivers-owners compound which, right in the middle of the teeming, jam-packed infield of Daytona International Speedway, might just be the most private and peaceful place for miles in any direction in a city and county paralyzed by the gridlock of an imminent Daytona 500.

At such times, at this point in his life, nobody—nobody—saw Dale Earnhardt unless he wanted them to. Only a handful of people could see him without an appointment. Anywhere. Anytime. Elvis himself was hardly more reclusive at the end. Earnhardt wasn't ill or drugged like Elvis—just sick of the throngs, the legions, who grappled and clung, sought to sap the life from him, make their own banal lives of quiet desperation somehow brighter by living vicariously through him. He was sick of the media, their faces, their voices, their questions. He had long been sick of all of that.

And so he had led the NASCAR drivers' movement into seclusion. No figures in all of sports are more reclusive nowadays than NASCAR drivers, especially on the eve of a race. Their "accessibility" to fans, and to the overwhelming majority of media, is a myth. It is a throwback notion to the primes of Richard Petty and David Pearson, who would hang out in motel parking lots with their fans, back when there weren't nearly so many of them, nearly so aggressive, clinging, desperate, stifling, smothering.

There are some wise insiders who are concerned about that motor coach compound, that nomadic village that recurs at every stop on a Winston Cup tour now forty weekends long, the longest season in sports. They wonder if it is a fully healthy place for its tiny population, terribly removed from reality as it is. Square foot for square foot it is the richest community on earth. Hardly anyone who lives there isn't a millionaire. It is Monaco adrift, Beverly Hills on wheels. Children grow up inside—the moving compound even has its own child-care center, fitness facility, sports-injury treatment unit, parsonage.

NASCAR has come to this, and Earnhardt brought it here. Led it. To the big money. Enormous money. And the obsessive seclusion of the very rich.

Earnhardt, by Daytona 500 eve, 2001, was worth maybe half a billion dollars and coming up fast on NASCAR chairman Bill France Jr., whom *Forbes* magazine reckoned to be worth a flat billion (but the knowing feel fairly sure that figure is quite low). If you counted everything—merchandising, endorsements, sponsorships, salary, bonus money, prize money, appearance money—then $100 million a year was not a far-fetched estimate of the gross revenues of Dale Earnhardt Inc. Then there were his vast investments outside racing. The numbers were known only to Earnhardt, his wife, Teresa, and the Internal Revenue Service. He no longer bothered with Wall Street brokerage houses. He had purchased

his own seat on the New York Stock Exchange. He had acquired a minor league baseball team, which he named the
Kannapolis Intimidators, for fun. Had he wanted to enter the
business of professional stick-and-ball sports seriously, it is
likely that Dale Earnhardt could have written George Stein-
brenner a check to purchase the New York Yankees, or Jerry
Jones a check to purchase the Dallas Cowboys, for cash.

His seventy-two-foot yacht, *Sunday Money,* was docked
at Daytona Beach Marina, over on the Halifax River, brought
up from its home port in the Bahamas for occasions when
Earnhardt might feel like being spirited to its decks to have a
banana split, made by the crew. He'd called it *Sunday Money*
because that's how he'd paid for it in cash—with some of his
race winnings, pocket change in a realm where peripheral income had long since shot past prize money.

He might be driven secretively over to Beach Street by
car. Mostly he slipped in and out of tracks aboard his helicopter. Then away on his Learjet to wherever his little
leather-bound schedule book told him he was supposed to be
at any given hour of any given day.

Sometimes in midweek he would jet from the little airport
near his farm in North Carolina to Daytona Beach, just for an
hour or two, to visit Bill France Jr. Billy France had grown
weary of fighting the cancer, his younger brother, Jim, would
indicate later, until Earnhardt would fly in on those afternoons and kid him, razz him, dare him, pump him up, and
then jet away.

"I credit Dale Earnhardt," Jimmy France would whisper
to me, off on the fringes of the most awful press conference
ever held at Daytona International Speedway, on February
19, 2001, "with saving my brother's life."

This would be the last trip to Daytona for *Sunday Money.*
A new boat, twice **as long**, 150 feet, was under custom construction at the Hatteras yards in North Carolina.

Earnhardt would soon be fifty years old. Deep down he

was still a big old kid who liked banana splits a lot more than margaritas or daiquiris. He would still have a little Jack Daniel's "ever' now and then." But that was rare now, twenty years and a million light-years from the Daytona 500 eve of 1981 when he'd sat slumped in a booth in the packed Boar's Head Lounge drinking Jack Daniel's and jeenjale wide fucking open in front of the public and blurted, "I ain't got enough sense to lose," and then left so hurt when we laughed at him.

Few deemed Earnhardt dumb now, here, at the head of his empire.

Five or six people were in the meeting in the motor coach. Terry Labonte was the only other driver. Labonte was the latest—and, as it would turn out, the last—man Dale Earnhardt wrecked in order to win a race, at Bristol, Tennessee, in 1999.

But Labonte could not bring himself to hate Earnhardt, only to remain in awe—not of Earnhardt the driver, who did indeed piss off Labonte more or less chronically, but of Earnhardt the man.

Their recent elk-hunting trip to New Mexico, for instance.

No sooner had they helicoptered out of Atlanta Motor Speedway and hopped aboard Earnhardt's Lear and taken off than Earnhardt was on the airphone, snapping orders to the outfitters out West. Then he made business deals on the phone until finally, somewhere over Texas, he fell suddenly and soundly asleep.

One of the pilots came back to the cabin to ask Earnhardt something.

"Y'all please don't wake him up," Labonte said. "He's about to wear me out back here." Just listening to Earnhardt was draining on the easygoing Labonte. So Earnhardt slept on—for more than twenty minutes. Then he popped awake again and was back on the phone.

More business. Then the outfitters in New Mexico again. Did they have the Chevy Suburban packed and ready to go at the airport? Was the engine running? The Lear would land in minutes.

Off the Lear, into the Suburban, away into the mountains, up to a base camp that had been so thoroughly prepared that the sleeping bags were laid neatly open. Three hours' sleep— a lot for Earnhardt—and up before dawn, onto the horses, higher into the mountains until the trail ran out.

Now on foot, higher, higher, Earnhardt moving as fast as if he were hurrying through a garage area fleeing autograph seekers, the long legs pumping tirelessly, the short-legged Labonte huffing, puffing, laden with heavy backpack and rifle, falling farther and farther behind.

Earnhardt turned back for Labonte. Took Labonte's rifle and threw it over his own shoulder. That made two Earnhardt was carrying, plus his own backpack.

Up into the rocks, Earnhardt never breaking stride, Labonte falling back again, Earnhardt turning back again, this time to take Labonte's backpack.

Earnhardt the pack mule. Still faster by far up the rocks than Labonte.

Finally Earnhardt said: "Look."

Across a valley, on another ridge, lay two bull elk. Nearly half a mile away. Some eyesight, that Earnhardt. Still.

Earnhardt, softly: "Shoot one."

Terry Labonte is a helluva shot with a rifle. He grew up hunting on the sprawling ranches in the South Texas scrub-lands where property is measured not in the hundreds of acres but the hundreds of square miles. A three-hundred-yard shot was nothing to him. But six hundred? Seven hundred?

Labonte lay down on the ground and rested the rifle on his backpack, carefully focusing his scope.

Earnhardt, impatiently: "Shoot him!"

Labonte took a deep breath, let out half of it, eased his right forefinger onto the trigger, squeezed with practiced smoothness.

Through their scopes, they saw a spot of dust fly up, a few feet from one of the bulls, which were so far away they were not at all perturbed by the rifle report. They just looked, curiously but lazily, over to where the dirt had kicked up.

Earnhardt: "Shoot again!"

Labonte worked the bolt action, went through the same methodical process.

In the distance, another little puff of dust from the ground.

Earnhardt: "Again!"

Labonte grew intense. This was it: the third and final round in the rifle.

This time, one of the bulls rolled over, dead.

Now the other bull came fully alert, stood up, sniffed, glanced around, ready to run. Two or three more seconds and he would be gone.

Earnhardt, standing to watch Labonte's last shot, instantaneously threw his rifle to his shoulder for what appeared to be a potshot at best, and in a split second pulled the trigger.

Across the valley the standing bull, poised to bolt, dropped in his tracks.

Earnhardt said nothing. Slung his rifle over his shoulder, grabbed his backpack, headed immediately back down the mountain. Labonte followed, stepping precariously down through the rocks in the wake of Earnhardt's march. The guides would go across the valley and butcher the bulls, then pack the meat back down the mountain, ice it, and ship it by air to North Carolina. Earnhardt always ate what he shot. Always. Hundreds of millions of dollars, yachts, Lears, helicopters—none of this had sapped the primal instincts of one who must hunt daily to survive.

Business-savvy as he'd become, perhaps the essence of Earnhardt's appeal to the masses lay not in his mind as a whole, but deep at the center, in what some psychiatrists call the "old brain" and some neurosurgeons the "medial forebrain bundle." There lie the ancient instincts of prehistoric man, the conflicting urges to flee or fight, that have not yet evolved out of any human.

In some, when the urge to flee prevails, it may manifest itself as substance abuse, even addiction. In the old brain also lie the pleasure centers that can be stimulated biochemically to enhance the sense of well-being—to ease the urge to flee. These humans often are perceived by societies as "the weak."

In others, the urge to fight prevails. Danger can stimulate the buildup of neurotransmitter molecules between nerve endings in the old brain, and a sense of pleasure ensues. From this phenomenon stem societal perceptions of some humans as "the strong."

And so the hackneyed nickname the Intimidator, far from a promotional label attached by the masses to endorsements and T-shirts and caps and jackets and bumper stickers, might have been true in the most ancient anthropological, fundamentally scientific of ways.

On the track and off, Earnhardt was by instinct the hunter, the predator, and in his fellow humans all around him, there arose some instinct to stay on his good side or become his prey. There were indications that even his fans vaguely feared him. Atlanta Motor Speedway president Ed Clark once held a reception for Earnhardt, and noticed how the admirers, after skittishly obtaining his autograph, would move away, so that Earnhardt wound up on one side of the room and all the fans on the other, "as if," said Clark, "they were afraid he was going to punch them or something."

Earnhardt always seemed fine, almost serene, in danger or in confrontation.

It was in what would be, to other mortals, the usually placid times, that his demons emerged.

"I'm in the dying business," a clergyman both Earnhardt and I knew well once told me. "I see all kinds. Earnhardt has bigger hangups about death than anybody I've ever known."

Earnhardt had a certain mini-notoriety among insiders for his undulant death phobia. It was common knowledge that he absolutely, positively would not go to funerals.

In November of 1994, near the end of fifteen years when I could kid him—kid him hard, like he kidded everybody—without permanent damage, he was lying on a sofa in his agent's office, grousing on about how everybody wanted a piece of him, and now if you knew him you could sense the demon rising and now he burst out, "I don't even have time for family life, man!" The tone was desperate—a shriek. Suddenly he popped up from the sofa. "Come in here." Into an outer office teeming with scurrying secretaries he marched, went straight to a filing cabinet, snatched a thick file, turned, and handed me a letter. "Look at the kind of stuff I get."

We walked back into the inner office, he trying to shrug the demon and I reading the letter. Sure enough…

The letter was from the new widow of some common man somewhere, requesting that Earnhardt come and drive the hearse bearing her husband's body from the church to the grave. It had been the man's dying request. So would Earn-hardt…please?

He sat there wide-eyed, staring, waiting for a response. His sense of humor was largely a "bust your balls" attitude toward everybody else. And now I couldn't resist. He was going to get one right back in his face. First I had to rub my mouth to keep from snickering.

"Well?" I deadpanned. "Did you do it?"

Never, before or since, have I heard the word "shit" howled out into so many syllables. It was a siren wail, part anger, part terror, part pain.

"She-e-e-e-e-e-e-e-ITTT-NO!"

Then he muttered something very low, hard to understand. Later, many times, I replayed it on the tape recorder. As near as I could tell, he had said of the hearse:

"I'll be in one of them bitches soon enough."

It might have been precisely the placidity of the eye of the gathering storm of humanity, the plush motor home deep in the guarded compound, that conjured the demon on Daytona 500 eve, 2001.

It was a light business meeting. Mainly fun. It was to work out a promotional campaign to sell little toy die-cast cars—which may sound trivial unless you have watched the sales numbers soar on Home Shopping Network or QVC and realize the fortunes to be made in little replicas of race cars, especially Earnhardt's. (There were times when Earnhardt sold his "official, limited-edition merchandise" at rates approaching a million dollars an hour on the television shopping channels.)

If you've ever wondered why, in recent years, various drivers would run selected races with "special paint schemes" on their cars, the major underlying motive was always financial: to sell toy cars to collectors. At the beginning of a season, for Earnhardt's latest-model Chevrolet, in his traditional black with its GM Goodwrench logos, sales of the die-cast replicas would be hot. Collectors and fans just had to have the latest model. But once the demand was supplied, then what? It had been Earnhardt, in the mid-1990s, who'd come up with the idea of *creating* new demand, time and again throughout the season. Say that at Charlotte, instead of the black Goodwrench Number 3, he ran an orange Wheaties Number 3. That created yet another collectible toy that the multitudes just *had to have*, or else their collections—and indeed their total loyalty to "Our Hero Dale," as they referred to him en masse in many an e-mail and letter to many a sportswriter or broadcaster—might be seen as lacking. At $29.95 or even $9.95 or even $5.95 per toy, multiplied by millions, you can imagine...

This latest scheme had to do with the mythical "Iron Man" title in NASCAR. It was for consecutive starts without missing a race, injured or otherwise, in Winston Cup. It was about to pass—it seemed—from Labonte to Earnhardt.

They had been rookies together in 1979, and Earnhardt, by far the wilder of the two, had crashed at Pocono Raceway in Pennsylvania and broken his collarbone so badly that he had to sit out several races that summer. Labonte hadn't missed a one, from the beginning of '79 through midseason of 2000.

Labonte had driven in pain through many a race on his way to becoming the Lou Gehrig of NASCAR, with 655 straight starts. But at the Pepsi 400, Daytona's summer night race, in 2000, Labonte had crashed and suffered a blow to the head that caused him nagging inner-ear problems and therefore dizziness, a very real threat to control of a car at high speed. And so he withdrew from the Brickyard 400 at Indianapolis in August, and then sat out the road race at Watkins Glen, New York, the next week. He was back in the seat after that. But his Iron Man streak was forever frozen at 655. Earnhardt, driving hurt through the years even more often than Labonte and in even more pain—broken legs, cracked sternum, whatever, what the hell—had not missed a race since the broken collarbone had put him in a too-confining torso cast in '79.

The 2001 schedule forecast that Earnhardt would tie Labonte's record at Martinsville, Virginia, on April 8, then seize the Iron Man title with his 656th consecutive start at Talladega on April 22.

Earnhardt could easily have seized all the profits from the toy cars too. It was conventional wisdom in NASCAR's mushrooming marketing swirl that Earnhardt could sell anything he wanted, anytime. All by himself.

"But Dale said he wasn't going to do it at all unless we did it together," Labonte would recall.

That was Earnhardt in a microcosm.

He was not the type to say: Terry, I'm sorry I wrecked you

at Bristol and not only kept you from winning but risked getting you hurt, bad, just so I could win.

His image was too hard and harsh for him to say: Terry, thank you for never coming after me for payback, somewhere else, for that rotten thing I did to you. Or any of the rotten things I ever did to you.

He was not a man who could bring himself to say: Terry, I couldn't have done what you always did—let it go, swallow my pride, swallow the vengeance.

What he could say was: I'm not going to hog this pot all by myself. Let's go make some more money—together.

That was the best Dale Earnhardt could do, and that was enough if you knew him well enough, because deep down he meant all the other things too—the tacit message of remorse, gratitude, friendship, admiration, was boundless.

And what a tidal wave of toy sales they schemed to create, in that late-afternoon meeting of February 17, in the motor coach.

"Texas was going to be my last race as Iron Man," Labonte said, meaning the Harrah's 500 at his home-state track, Texas Motor Speedway, on April 1. "So I was going to run an Iron Man car [special paint scheme, and therefore another new line of collectible toy cars] there. At Martinsville we were both going to run Iron Man cars [two new lines of merchandise]. Then Dale was going to run one at Talladega [likely the biggest seller by far among the new die-cast cars]."

Legal pads and calculators were out, and the managers and agents were taking notes, when, out of the blue, but very matter-of-factly, Earnhardt said:

"That's if I make it that far."

There was a second or two of surprised silence. Then somebody said, "Yeah, right," and somebody else chuckled, and the nervous laughter spread through four or five people.

Earnhardt didn't laugh.

Was he deadpanning a joke? The others passed it off as such, and the moment passed, without their considering that if you knew Earnhardt, really knew him, you knew he never considered such a line funny:

"That's if I make it that far."

By the next sundown, at the blackest hour in the history of the Daytona 500, those words would return as a thunderclap to Terry Labonte's mind.

As the weeks and months passed in the bleak aftermath of the 2001 Daytona 500, many a story of premonitions would emerge. A preacher would claim that Earnhardt grasped his hand harder, longer than usual during a pre-race prayer. Television viewers would claim that Dale and Teresa, embracing just before he climbed into the car to start the race, suddenly developed strange looks on their faces.

The widow of J. D. McDuffie, the journeyman NASCAR driver killed at Watkins Glen in 1991, would tell her son, in front of the TV set, at the moment she saw the black Number 3 hit the wall, "Dale's dead."

"Maybe not, Mama," Jeff McDuffie said, knowing his mother had been phobic about crashes ever since she sat at home and watched her husband's fatal crash on television nearly a decade earlier.

"Dale's dead," she said, and then silently got ready for evening church services in Sanford, North Carolina, without watching further. Later, she would in no way be surprised at what the preacher told the congregation.

Such intuitions snowball in remembrance, become more pronounced in the retelling. But the enormity of one sentence has neither grown nor receded in Terry Labonte's mind.

"Everybody sort of laughed," Labonte said of the late afternoon of February 17.

"Then," he said of the same time of day on February 18, his jaw still dropping, his mouth still gaping, his eyes still misting, months later. "Man. I thought of it. And I could not believe it."

*E*very driver in this garage *knew* what was going to happen," Jeff Burton would say, the week after the Daytona 500.

They didn't know who or how many. But, "I can't tell you how many times I told [wife] Kim, even before we got to Daytona, 'There *will* be a big wreck.' "

There was a reason they knew. It was almost a mathematical equation. It had a name: the "aero package." It was a group of small but significant changes to the bodywork of the cars, mandated late in 2000 by NASCAR officials only for Daytona and Talladega, intended to make the racing closer, and the passing more frequent, at the two giant tracks.

Since 1988, when NASCAR had ordered power-sapping carburetor restrictor plates at Daytona and Talladega to keep the speeds below 200 miles per hour, the drivers had openly loathed "plate racing." It gave them little or no "throttle response"—that is, when they floored their accelerator pedals, the cars didn't jump in obedience to the command for power, as they did on all the other tracks, the "unrestricted" ones.

Nobody loathed plate racing more than Dale Earnhardt. From 1988 to 2001 he had said, many hundreds if not thousands of times, "This ain't racing." You couldn't pass when or where you wanted to. You were at the mercy of the turbulence created by the cars all around you. You had to use them, work them, hoping you could get from them the aerodynamic "pushes" and "pulls" that helped you make a pass. The racing at Daytona and Talladega appeared close, not because the drivers were driving that way, but because they simply could not escape one another. They were shackled together due to lack of power.

Detroit kept coming with sleeker and sleeker body designs, which had the effect of making plate racing duller and duller. Rather than plowing huge holes in the air as the boxy cars of the Petty-Pearson heyday had done, the cars now sliced through surgically, almost like the prototype sports cars of Europe. The effect, at Daytona and Talladega, was inescapable one-by-one racing.

The 2000 Daytona 500 had been the dullest in thirty-five years, with only nine lead changes. Then the Pepsi 400 at Daytona in July of 2000 had produced only ten lead changes, and after that race, Earnhardt had said simply but profoundly, "We're not racing. We're just existing on the track together."

Then Earnhardt had issued his final commonsense appeal in the form of a question no one would answer publicly. "What's wrong," he asked, "with going 200 miles an hour? They do it in CART and the IRL, and in drag racing."

The answer, many knowing observers felt—but NASCAR would never admit—was that 200 was the danger line where the risk of cars going airborne increased. Airborne cars might go into the grandstands and kill spectators. That was the last thing NASCAR wanted.

Earnhardt's much-publicized remarks after the 2000 Pepsi 400 had helped spur NASCAR officials to act—which had been his intent. But Earnhardt had meant to make things better, not worse. NASCAR officials simply would not give up the restrictor-plate concept. They set about making the racing better with plates, and their testing and development yielded the "aero package."

The aero package included two key elements: the "wicker"—a thin strip of metal to be mounted across the front of the roofs of the cars—and the increase of the rear spoiler angle from forty-five to seventy-five degrees. The effect was to "dirty" the cars aerodynamically—make them artificially less sleek than the intent of the Detroit designs. That would slow them down, and cause them to knock huge holes in the air, as of yore. And that in turn would increase the push-pull effects of the draft, even bring back the "slingshot" effect in which the wash of the air would catapult one car past another.

The first race with the aero package was the Winston 500 at Talladega in October of 2000. Earnhardt won it, of course. Nobody ever was, or perhaps ever will be, better at restrictor-plate racing, even with tricked-up aerodynamics. Nobody was better at "working the air." Legend had grown that Earnhardt could even *see* the air as it swirled and streamed. What he really could do was feel it and hear it. That was one reason that, in an era when nearly every other driver wore enclosed "full-face" helmets, Earnhardt still wore an open-face helmet, cut back even more drastically at the jaw, near the ears, than most. He literally could hear the air roiling when another car would rush up beside him.

At Talladega he had won by passing eighteen other cars in the final four laps. He should have been proud, exhilarated—indeed, the cocky Earnhardt of his youth. Instead, he had said after winning, "I hate restrictor plate races. All of 'em. None of 'em are good."

NASCAR had tantalized the drivers at first with the new aero package. Because it would slow down the cars so radically, the teams were given larger restrictor plates—one inch in diameter, rather than the old seven-eighths inch. This increased air flow into the carburetor, revived some power, and gave them back some blessed throttle response. They loved it. They could maneuver again. But in the first practice sessions at Talladega, speeds had soared back to 198 mph, dangerously close to 200, and so on the eve of the race, NASCAR officials had handed out new, smaller mandatory plates, fifteen-sixteenths of an inch. The new throttle response all but vanished. Yet the "aero package" kept the highly enhanced drafting effects in place. A trailing car would "suck up" to a leading one at a horrific closing rate, so drivers literally had to jam on the brakes to keep from rear-ending one another.

Now they had the worst of all possible worlds. Earnhardt knew that. And so there was pride but no joy in his win.

The Talladega race had gone off without a major crash. But 2.66-mile Talladega was roomier, more forgiving, than 2.5-mile Daytona. So Earnhardt and all the other drivers had left Talladega in October knowing that come February, where they would be running too close, with too little control and too little margin for error, there would be hell to pay.

After the 125-mile qualifying races on Thursday, February 15, 2001, Earnhardt remarked that "the cars seem a little more out of control than usual." For them to be any worse than Earnhardt had noted at Daytona in recent years meant they were downright scary. And so as he spoke, his tone connoted no anger—just a sort of frightened resignation.

And there were other growing concerns that, combined with the aero package, left the forty-third Daytona 500 looming as perhaps the most frightening to drivers of any since the first one in 1959. Back then, the fear was of the unknown track itself. Now the fear was of known, or suspected, elements.

In a five-month stretch of 2000, NASCAR drivers Adam Petty, Kenny Irwin, and Tony Roper had all died of the same essential cause—violent movement of their heads, which had been restrained inadequately in crashes. Autopsies on Petty and Irwin had determined that they died specifically of a terrible syndrome called basilar skull fracture. No autopsy had been performed on Roper, but attending physicians described some symptoms consistent with basilar skull fracture.

Soon after Irwin's death on July 7, an undercurrent movement had begun among Ford Motor Company and General Motors racing engineers to persuade all NASCAR drivers to begin wearing a revolutionary head-restraint device called the HANS, an acronym for "head and neck support." Nearly twenty years of testing and development had scientifically proven the HANS to prevent the violent thrusts of the head that cause basilar skull fracture. But NASCAR drivers are notoriously slow to change, and early on, only two drivers began wearing the device—Brett Bodine, and Kyle Petty, Adam's father.

Sitting in the predawn traffic crawling toward Daytona International Speedway on 500 morning, February 18, I pondered the possibility that somebody was going to die that afternoon. Nobody had ever been killed in the Daytona 500. Drivers had died in qualifying races, practice runs, preliminary races for lesser classes of cars. But never in the Daytona 500 itself. With no fatalities and no rainouts in its history, the race was reputed among the savvy to have led a somewhat charmed, perhaps blessed, existence that stemmed from some vague alchemy of the good luck and the wisdom of Big Bill France himself. Today, I thought, this very possibly could change.

This was in no way prescience nor prophecy, nor even premonition. It was a tense, sad, largely frustrated calculation of current circumstances and scientific facts. I had spent the previous seven months reporting and writing a massive series of stories on safety standards and practices in motor racing worldwide, but particularly in NASCAR—which, though America's richest and most popular form of motor sport, was also significantly behind other forms, especially Formula One and Indy cars, when it came to scientific advancement of driver safety.

There'd been hundreds of hours of interviews with numerous engineers, physicians, and research scientists who were experts in racing injuries, but especially with three. Dr. John Melvin, a renowned professor of biomechanical engineering, had begun studying the causes of racing injury and death at the University of Michigan in 1971, continued through a thirteen-year stint at General Motors, and now, at

Wayne State University's bioengineering center in Detroit, had become the world's leading authority on basilar skull fracture as it occurs in racing. Dr. Steve Olvey, medical director of Championship Auto Racing Teams Inc., and an associate professor of neurosurgical intensive care at the University of Miami medical school, had developed more firsthand knowledge of basilar skull fracture in racing than any other M.D. on the planet. Dr. Robert Hubbard, professor of biomechanical engineering at Michigan State University, had taught in both the engineering and medical schools there, and was the inventor and developer of the HANS device.

Early on in the reporting process, during the fall of 2000, the essence of the NASCAR situation became apparent.

Inertia is the physical tendency of a mass to continue in motion at a sustained rate unless interrupted by another force. As the cars stopped so terribly suddenly on impact with concrete walls, inertia kept the driver's body moving at the same velocity as before the sudden stop, until it was restrained by the safety harness. Then the body stopped. But there was no harness to restrain the head, at ten to twelve pounds, the heaviest part of the human body, so it continued to move at a sustained velocity under inertial forces.

John Melvin's most recent research had shown that this violent forward thrust of the head caused enormous G-loading on the head and neck. Contrary to what most pathologists and trauma specialists still believe, the head does not have to strike anything, such as a roll bar inside the car, for basilar skull fracture to result. The horrific forces are essentially trying to shoot the brain right through the top of the skull, or tear the head right off the body. But the top and sides of the skull are strong. So are the neck muscles and vertebral column, which act as the only tethers for the forward-thrusting head.

The weakest part of the skull is the lower rear area, the "base," which is irregular and thin. During the tremendous pulling force of the head away from the body, when something has to give, the base does. A crack occurs around the foramen magnum, a hole in the base of the skull through which the medulla oblongata, or brain stem, passes and narrows to become the spinal cord. Nearby run vital blood vessels, including the interior carotid arteries.

Basilar skull fracture in and of itself would not be fatal, nor even a particularly serious injury. But as the crack runs through the area like a tiny earthquake, it cuts the vital arteries, causes massive axonal, or nerve, trauma to the areas of the brain stem that control breathing and heart rate, and can snap the spinal cord. It is hard to imagine more massive or devastating damage occurring more rapidly—usually in less than one-tenth of a second—at any other part of the human body.

So essentially, the rigid car stops—WHAM! The body continues forward by inertia until the safety harness stops it—OOMP! Now the head is virtually a cannonball fired forward with tremendous force, trying to separate itself from the body. It pulls itself apart at the base of the skull, causing immediate, catastrophic bleeding and brain stem trauma. The driver dies three ways, almost instantaneously: He bleeds to death, his heart stops, and his breathing stops.

Steve Olvey was the only physician in the world who both understood the racing version of the basilar skull fracture syndrome fully, and had seen it up close at race tracks. He had attended CART rookie Gonzalo Rodriguez on the site of the youngster's fatal crash at Monterey, California, in 1999. Rodriguez's car had hit a concrete wall padded with a tire barrier head-on, then flipped rear-end first over the wall. Rodriguez's basilar skull fracture had been so severe that "he bled out before he even hit the ground," Olvey said. "Most of his blood volume was on the wall and the sign he flipped over." That meant a complete blood loss in a matter of one or two seconds. And *that* is just how cataclysmic an injury basilar skull fracture is.

The immediate answer, the first line of defense, was the HANS, whose nylon tether straps attach at one end to the helmet, and at the other to a carbon-fiber collar that fits over the driver's shoulders. The HANS is essentially a safety harness for the head. When a crash occurs, the HANS stops the head at the same rate the harness stops the body. Because the HANS tethers take the force, the base of the skull doesn't have to. Voilà! The head is not driven by inertia to separate itself from the body. And the driver walks away from the crash. CART's safety procedures were so technologically advanced that it took only eight days following the death of Rodriguez for CART doctors and engineers to develop and run a computer model that showed mathematically that wearing a HANS device would have saved Rodriguez's life. NASCAR had no such procedures or computerized database, and so as the months dragged on after the deaths of Adam Petty and Kenny Irwin of basilar skull fracture, nothing was done to significantly reduce the danger to NASCAR drivers.

There were other ways to ease the horrific forward launch of the head. Softening the cars and/or the walls they hit would slow down the stopping process. Late in 2000, there had arisen an outcry for energy-dissipating "soft walls" to replace, or at least to pad, the unforgiving concrete. The loudest calls had come from Jeff Gordon, Rusty Wallace, and Dale Jarrett.

Dale Earnhardt had publicly scoffed at the outcry of his peers, saying drivers who didn't want to face the danger like men should stay home, and "tie a kerosene rag around your ankles so the ants won't crawl up and eat your candy ass."

At a press conference at Indianapolis, on the eve of the 2000 Brickyard 400, I had asked him if he'd tried, or planned to try, a HANS.

"I got no idea what it is," he had said, a bewildering answer in that GM engineers had been privately showing their drivers a very graphic videotape of crash dummies' head movement in sled tests with and without the HANS. "If it's a proven piece and becomes part of our racing, I'll do whatever NASCAR wants to do."

By then he had softened a bit on the notion of soft walls. Track owners complained that soft walls might fragment on impact, causing lengthy delays in races—annoying the crowds and television audiences—while cleanup crews removed the debris.

As part of his answer to my question at the Indy press conference, Earnhardt had looked me in the eye and said something that, as it turned out, would be reported in the national media time and again throughout the following year, after the next Daytona 500:

"I'd rather wait fifteen or twenty minutes for them to clean up that mess," he said of fragmenting soft walls, "than for them to clean *me* off the wall."

He had continued: "I've hit the wall hard in my time. Hard at Daytona, in the 1980s, when I blew an engine. But with my safety harness and my helmet, the things I wear, I've not broken my neck." His tone had crept toward braggadocio for all the seat-of-the-pants safety provisions he'd made for himself through the years, because they looked good by common sense, such as sitting lower in the car than any other driver. "I've not pulled my brain stem apart. And I'm comfortable with what I have."

NASCAR had done nothing, at least nothing proactive, about the HANS. CART had already mandated the HANS for its drivers on oval tracks in 2001. NASCAR refused to mandate the HANS, and by Daytona Speedweeks of 2001, NASCAR president Mike Helton had finally gotten around to using a word as strong as "recommend."

My series of stories on racing safety began to run nationally on the morning of February 11, 2001—the Sunday of the

Bud Shootout bonus race, the kickoff to the weeklong frenzy of racing that would conclude with the following Sunday's Daytona 500.

How was the series received at Daytona? Largely with silence. NASCAR officials either didn't agree there was a crisis, or chose not to comment on it. Some of the drivers were looking over the stories privately, in their motor coaches, but most remained somewhat in denial over the Petty, Irwin, and Roper deaths. And most remained resistant to the idea of wearing the HANS.

On Valentine's Day, the eve of the 125-mile qualifying races, I conducted an informal poll of drivers as to who would wear the HANS in the Daytona 500. Only seven drivers in the field of forty-three would wear it, and Earnhardt was the staunchest holdout. He was so anti-HANS that he had referred to it, to David Poole of the *Charlotte Observer,* as "that damn noose." I encountered Ken Schrader walking hurriedly through the garage area and began asking him about the device, and he kept shaking his head at every question until I asked, simply and firmly, "Why?" He stopped. Pondered. Shook his head again and said, "I'm just comfortable with my stuff." Surely he echoed Earnhardt's attitude. Ever since Kenny Schrader had arrived in Winston Cup, Earnhardt had been his guru on most matters, including safety.

For all of Dale Earnhardt's stage machismo, his public loathing of candy-asses, his resistance to scientific safety innovation versus good ol', down-home, seat-of-the-pants common sense, there was one thing he was not: a damn fool.

Whether or not he told himself the HANS was a noose that would hang him rather than save his life, he clearly had been pondering the problem of basilar skull fracture. He had even propagated the scientifically absurd—though it made sense to him and his listeners—idea that full-face helmets were the cause. The bottom of the face of the helmet, the part that covered the chin, he reckoned, wedged against the chest in violent crashes so that it acted as a fulcrum on which the head rotated forward to, in his parlance, "pull the brain stem apart."

Because he understood restrictor-plate racing better than anyone else, he also fathomed the dangers of the aero package more profoundly than anyone else.

All of the circumstances, plus his demon, the death phobia, were somewhere in Dale Earnhardt's mind when he said to Terry Labonte and the others in the meeting that projected the Iron Man string of consecutive starts, "That's if I make it that far."

*T*housands of fans, and a lot of journalists, make a practice of using scanners to monitor radio transmissions between drivers and their pit crews during races. Some of these running dialogues are more entertaining than others—Rusty Wallace at the wheel, and Roger Penske spotting for him, were renowned for their running chatter. Terry Labonte, taciturn outside his car, could be profusely profane on the radio in the heat of a race. Dale Earnhardt and Richard Childress were, historically, boring to listen to. They spoke little, and when they did, it was usually all business. You had to be patient indeed to find some gems—an example coming at Darlington in the 1980s when Earnhardt radioed, "Tight in the middle," meaning the car was understeering through Turns 1 and 2. Several laps passed. "Tight in the middle." Several more laps. "Tight in the middle." Finally the black Number 3 slid into the concrete wall in Turn 1, and Earnhardt radioed stoically, "I just knocked the goddamn wall down."

And so, amidst all the intensity of NASCAR's showcase race, on February 18, 2001, few in the media bothered to eavesdrop much on Earnhardt. According to some fans who tuned in, the reporters missed an aberrant stream of profane fretting over the claustrophobic craziness of the artificially close racing and the fitfully behaving cars with the aero package. Some fans claimed to hear Earnhardt howl at one point, "What are they trying to do? Kill us all?"

Yet as always, there was never a twitch or wiggle of the notorious black Monte Carlo, at any moment during the day, that indicated any fear whatsoever in its driver. As always, Earnhardt was—as even history professor Wanda Ellen Wakefield of the State University of New York at Brockport would put it later in an academic paper—"driving his ass off."

Earnhardt in Childress's car, and all three of his protégés in Dale Earnhardt Inc. cars—Dale Earnhardt Jr., Steve Park, and Michael Waltrip—led the race at one time or other. With twenty-five laps remaining, Park was caught up in the big wreck Jeff Burton and the others had anticipated. Tony Stewart, running third, was bumped from behind on the backstretch by Robby Gordon, and that detonated a nineteen-car melee. Stewart's car slammed nearly head-on into the wall (John Melvin would later suspect that Stewart's forward-surging head hit his steering wheel, his full-face helmet saving him from severe facial injury and the impact with the wheel stopping his head from firing far enough forward to cause basilar skull fracture). Then Stewart's Pontiac went tumbling, landing at last on top of the Pontiac of his teammate, Bobby Labonte. Some drivers would later opine that when the third-running car (Stewart's) lands on top of the twenty-fourth-place car (Labonte's) in a wreck, you know the racing is entirely too close for comfort.

Typically, Dale Earnhardt escaped the mess cleanly because it happened behind him. So did Dale Jr. and Michael Waltrip. From that point, those three appeared ready to determine the victory among themselves, the only other threat being from Sterling Marlin in a Dodge.

But with seventeen laps remaining, the elder Earnhardt

seized the lead from Marlin and was clearly in command of the race. One lap later, the black car handed the lead to Michael Waltrip, and an amazing strategy began to unfold. Earnhardt looked to be escorting Waltrip to the finish line. Even Darrell Waltrip, just retired as a driver and now serving as a Fox television commentator in the booth, remarked that it seemed "the Earnhardts are doing everything they can to help my brother win this race."

Michael Waltrip, who held on to win the race, was the classic underdog, having gone winless since he arrived in Winston Cup in 1985, deep in the shadow of his flamboyant older brother's eighty-four-win, three-championship career. But late in 2000, Dale Earnhardt had slapped the struggling younger Waltrip on the shoulder and handed him the dream break of a lifetime. Earnhardt the business tycoon had secured a huge sponsorship from the NAPA auto parts company to field a third Dale Earnhardt Inc. car. He'd asked Michael Waltrip to drive it.

And now, clearly, Earnhardt was doing everything he could to bring that dream home to the driver who'd long been lightly referred to as "Mikey." At the very least, Earnhardt was going to send his son and Mikey out front to duel it out between themselves, while he flew escort to make sure nobody else got near them.

With three laps left, and Marlin's Dodge coming so hard that it appeared to be the fastest car on the track at that point, Earnhardt, running third, dropped low on the apron, almost into the grass, in the dogleg at the start-finish line, to block Marlin's charge.

On the final lap, through Turns 3 and 4, Marlin made one last surge, one last gasp at the lead. He dropped low on the track.

But there are of course no rules for the last lap of the Daytona 500. It's every driver for himself. Now into the fray, straight up the middle of the track, roared Rusty Wallace's

Ford Taurus. As Marlin charged below Earnhardt, Wallace ran right up to the rear of the black Number 3.

Wallace's car, as drivers say, "got the air off the back" of Earnhardt's car. That is, it changed the airstream so that it skipped over Earnhardt's rear spoiler, drastically reducing the aerodynamic downforce so crucial to sure steering. The black Number 3's rear end wiggled, left and right, left and right, over the edge of control for virtually any driver other than Earnhardt.

Earnhardt at that split second appeared to make a judgment call. He hadn't the reflexes of the Earnhardt of old, but he was still plenty gifted enough to straighten the fishtailing car and continue straight.

But no, hell no, he was Dale by God Earnhardt, and he was going to drop down low and block Sterling Marlin one more time. He was going to make a move that would have required a stable car at best, and he was going to do it in a car that was almost out of control.

The black car dropped to the apron in Turn 4, right in front of the onrushing Dodge of Marlin. Whether Marlin's car clipped Earnhardt's—as many fanatic Earnhardt worshippers would claim, as some of them phoned and e-mailed death threats to Marlin in ensuing days and weeks—was irrelevant. Dale Earnhardt got into big trouble when, and because, the left rear tire of the ominous black Chevy dropped off the banking onto the "flat," the paved surface of the apron.

For reasons yet unexplained by drivers, engineers, or physicists, when your left-side tires drop onto the flat at Daytona or Talladega, at speed, there's only one place you're going: hard right, straight up toward the outside retaining wall.

Fifteen years ago, perhaps, the uncanny reflexes and the amazing instantaneous savvy of Dale Earnhardt might have gotten him out of even this virtually impossible situation. But this was Earnhardt nearing fifty, Earnhardt in the twilight of his greatness.

Still, he almost made it to a relatively safe angle of impact. As the car yawed hard right, it appeared to be rotating around so that it would hit either head-on, or on its left front. Such a hit might have driven Earnhardt's face straight into the steering wheel. It might have blackened his eyes and broken some teeth, but it might also have stopped the cannonball forward surge of his head before it went so far, so fast, as to tear apart the base of his skull, cut the nearby arteries, devastate the brain stem.

"I've not pulled my brain stem apart."

But in the last-lap free-for-all, up rushed Kenny Schrader on the outside, just as Earnhardt's car reached the wall. Schrader's car slammed into Earnhardt's right front fender, interrupting the rotation of the black Number 3 just enough that it hit at the deadliest possible angle for modern-day NASCAR cars, the right front, "1 o'clock" angle.

By the best scientific estimates, Earnhardt's head apparently shot forward and slightly right, just missing the life-saving steering wheel on its outward arc. Then, as his head rotated downward, the underside of his chin apparently caught the steering wheel.

In a later evaluation of the evidence, Dr. Barry Myers of Duke University, who is both a Ph.D. in biomechanical engineering and an M.D. specializing in head and neck trauma from automobile crashes, determined that the violent forward thrust of Earnhardt's head could have provided enough "inertial head loading" to cause the fatal injuries. And the impact of the underside of the chin probably had enough force to kill him.

Which specific event actually killed Earnhardt didn't matter. Either could have. Probably both did. And at the bottom line, Dale Earnhardt died of basilar skull fracture caused by the violent movement of his head. The chin impact had occurred as a function of the head-whip.

NASCAR officials would, five days later, announce they had found a broken lap belt in Earnhardt's car. Enormous controversy would erupt that has not settled to this day. Tommy Propst, one of the first emergency medical technicians to reach Earnhardt, would later state that he unfastened Earnhardt's safety harness, and that he did not believe the belt was broken at that point. Speculation would abound as to whether the belt broke, or was somehow cut or torn later, in all the confusion. NASCAR would launch a lengthy, secretive investigation.

But it would all be so much ground clutter on the radar screen of truth: At worst, the lap belt separation had occurred under "high G-loading," meaning the highest point of stress, according to most experts, from John Melvin to Barry Myers. That meant the mechanism of fatal injury, the head thrust, occurred, *and then* the lap belt broke, tore, or separated, or whatever. The belt separation, by the laws of physics, simply *did not matter* in the outcome.

Did Earnhardt ever know what hit him? Did his life flash before him? Was there a split-second thought of the HANS? Of terror?

No way.

The fatal injury occurred, Barry Myers later calculated, in less than an eyeblink—less than one-tenth of a second. Earnhardt may have known he was headed toward the wall, felt the impact of Schrader's car from the right, and then...oblivion.

Countless times since that afternoon, I've been asked by other media people, both in formal interviews and casual conversation, how it felt "to know you'd predicted just such a thing," or "to know you'd called it beforehand," or "to be prescient" with the stories that had run the week before.

It felt no way at all. It felt numb. Empty. It felt like autopilot—the mechanism that has always kicked in, for many an auto racing writer and, I suspect, many a war correspondent. Old friends die suddenly and there is no time for shock or grief or even a shudder. There is only the awful truth and the merciless deadline for telling it. Simplistic as it sounds, you do what you have to do.

It would be hours—perhaps three; hard to recollect—after the crash before Mike Helton would step up to a microphone and make what he acknowledged was the most difficult announcement of his life: "We've lost Dale Earnhardt."

But the knowing, the savvy, knew within minutes after the crash. There are signs you look and listen for, if you have done this long enough. You watch the replay on the television monitors, and you think, Bad angle. Very bad angle. Meaning the angle of impact. You see another driver, this time Kenny Schrader, walk hurriedly up to the wrecked car to check on his friend, and you can tell by his gestures, frantic, desperate, terribly shaken, pleading for the emergency workers to hurry. I would never need to be told what Kenny Schrader saw at that moment. I knew what basilar skull fracture's devastation looked like: blood gushing, not from any open wounds, but from the mouth, ears, nose…Few injuries, even in war, are more awful to behold than what Kenny Schrader saw.

You study the causes and effects of basilar skull fracture with the world's leading experts, for months on end, and then you see the angle of impact again on the replay, and then you listen as the silence rises like thunder on a press box PA system, where by now they should be saying he is out of the car, conscious and alert, talking with safety workers…and you know. Yes, this is another head-whip basilar skull fracture death in NASCAR, entirely predictable, a mathematical equation.

But it is entirely separate from the passing of a person you have known so well, for so long.

C'mon, Hinton, get your ass in. Let's go ride around...

Hinton, you a prick—you know that?...

Cute lil' ol' girl, ain't she, Hinton? I think I might just marry her. What do you think?...

Hinton, go get us some more Jack Daniel's. And get some more jeenjale.

Hinton, why don't you shut up?...

T'resa, Hinton's stayin' for supper...

How's that young 'un of yours doin'?...

How's Snow doin'?...

Wake up, Hinton. Let's go huntin'...

You folks know Ed Hinton? He's more family than press, but I let him come around with a notebook once in a while...

Yeah, well, you WROTE it, though, didn't you, you mother-FUCKER!

Hinton, you still take a drink ever' now and then?

Yeah, Earnhardt, every now and then. How about you?

Yeah, ever' now and then...

Hinton, no matter how screwed up your and my relationship gets, Snow will always be a friend of mine. You tell her that when you get home...

Earnhardt, how much money is enough?

Ain't countin' it by dollars, Hinton... Just countin' how it gives me a chance to race. Crank on that steerin' wheel. C-r-a-a-n-k on that steerin' wheel. It's still the one, Hinton. Still the one...

Earnhardt, what did you think in that crash? Was that an "oh, shit" crash?

Lemme tell you somethin', Hinton. You crash like that, you don't say "Oh, shit," you don't say "Oh, God," you don't say, "Honey, I love you," and your life doesn't flash before

*you. You just do this [flinch, scrunch, squint] until you hit.
Then you open your eyes and look around for the ambulance...*

Earnhardt, do you realize just how big a deal you've become? Do you understand that?

All I know is, it's unbelievable, Hinton. UNNN-bee-lievable.

Gone.

In an eyeblink.

And you know it, know what he looks like inside that car, already dead, the blood cascading down the uniform and turning it solid scarlet. When you know this both personally and academically, the only way you can go is numb.

Then you watch the movements of the emergency workers and doctors around the car, and you see that they cease to be frantic and become somehow slow and deliberate and resigned. Somewhere on a tier above yours in the press box, you hear someone say, "They're cutting him out of the car," and that's it—final. You know the car was not damaged in such a way as to hamper his removal—that the only reason they're cutting him out is that the driver himself must be, at the very least, unconscious. You watch the replay one more time. Then you see the workers cover up the car with a tarpaulin. That is to keep the photographers from taking sensational pictures of a vehicle in which something terrible has just occurred.

You neither retch nor weep, largely because there is no time for either. You pick up the phone and, in a muffled voice, start alerting editors up and down the line, coast-to-coast, that the layout of every newspaper, the plan of every newscast, in America is about to be turned upside down, inside out. The biggest, gravest news story off this continent, to the world, tonight and tomorrow morning, will come not from Washington nor Manhattan nor L.A., but from Daytona.

Dale Earnhardt is dead.

Elvis.

Princess Diana.

Earnhardt.

It is not John nor Bobby Kennedy, nor Martin Luther King. It will not fray the very fabric of American existence. But it will devastate American fantasy, the vicarious living of every common man and woman who needed to get a life, and did, through Earnhardt. He was—in reality or not— what so many whipped-down, debt-ridden, job-despising, poorly educated, desperate people had longed so hard, so long, to be.

"All I know is, it's unbelievable, Hinton. UNNN-bee-lievable."

He was the ordinary man, risen by extraordinary guts and resolve to extraordinary heights. If he could do it, maybe they could—well, at least there abided the possibility they could—someday do it. He was, for the masses, quite simply but profoundly:

Hope.

And now he was gone, confirming the awfulest certainty of the commonfolk—that no one gets out of here alive. As with Elvis, there could be no closure at the grassroots. The sociological mourning will pass down through generations, into larger and larger legend.

From this, the most cataclysmic single event in the history of Daytona, would spring, paradoxically, even more national, and international, interest in NASCAR. Youth, so drawn to "extreme sports," would send the television ratings soaring, twenty percent higher across the board in 2001 than in 2000. By this measure, NASCAR would be second only to the National Football League in popularity.

Was it a symptom of societal sickness? Confirmation that people do indeed watch motor races to see people get killed? Perhaps. But few people would ever admit that, and so no public opinion poll, no matter how scientific, could ever fathom the meaning.

More likely it was rooted in Ernest Hemingway's old certainty of human attraction—good, bad, or inherently tragic—to endeavors that cause humans to live gloriously at the high risk of dying suddenly, and that beside such sports, all the rest are games.

Such is the controversial mystique that keeps the place in the human spirit, called Daytona, roaring relentlessly into its second century.

EPILOGUE

Still, each February, during the lulls that grow fewer and fewer from the frenzy at Daytona International Speedway, the best way to absorb Daytona is to walk the beach, looking only rarely at the ever-changing jumble of hotels and high-rise condominiums, gazing mostly straight ahead and seaward at what never changes, the green surf rolling onto the trillions of quartz crystals brought by the rains and rivers of the ages down from the granite mountains of Georgia and the Carolinas to form the natural birthing bed of speed...where William J. Morgan and Ransom Olds and Alexander Winton walked...where Willie K. Vanderbilt and Barney Oldfield raced, rich man versus common man...where Hemery threw his fiery tantrums...on Major Sir Henry O'Neal de Hane Segrave's "veritable marvel of nature"...on the World's Most Famous Beach...where Frank Lockhart's Stutz Black Hawk came screaming out of the mist and flung him to his death...where Malcolm Campbell's Bluebird thundered "solely for the honor of Sir Malcolm and the Union Jack," as the great Henry McLemore wrote...where a lanky mechanic from Washington, D.C., named Bill France came puttering along in his Hupmobile with his little family, wife Annie and toddler Billy, with their belongings on a little trailer hitched to the car...where Lloyd Seay and Roy Hall ripped up sand and slung it skyward in Raymond Parks's refitted whiskey-running cars...where Red Byron and the three Flock brothers and Fireball Roberts and Junior Johnson and Little Joe Weatherly and Curtis Turner drove NASCAR from its infancy to adolescence and then sent it inland to Daytona International Speedway... where the beach police stopped a smartass one night in 1979 for stunt-driving in a four-wheel-drive truck, up and down the dunes that rose between the beach and Highway A1A, and looked with a flashlight at the unknown face and asked, "Where'd you learn how to drive, boy?" and heard, "Oh, North C'lina, I guess," and read on the North Carolina driver's license the unknown name Dale Earnhardt...the surf where kids named Davey Allison and Dale Jarrett and Kyle Petty played, and later Adam Petty played, and where his kids would have played...walk down to where a long-standing sign that rises from the sand reads:

WELCOME TO DAYTONA BEACH
SPEED LIMIT 10 MPH

INDEX